Diversity Education for Social Justice: Mastering Teaching Skills

Dorothy Van Soest, DSW
> Dean, School of Social Work
> University of Washington

Betty Garcia, PhD
> Professor, Department of Social Work Education
> California State University, Fresno

D0059169

Council on Social Work Education
Alexandria, Virginia

Cover photos copyright © by *The Washington Post* and reprinted with permission of
the District of Columbia Public Library.

Library of Congress Cataloging-in-Publication Data

Van Soest, Dorothy.
  Diversity education for social justice: mastering teaching skills/Dorothy Van
Soest, Betty Garcia.
      p. cm.
Includes bibliographical references and index.
  ISBN 0-87293-099-8
  1. Social work education—United States. 2. Multicultural
education—United States. 3. Social justice—Study and teaching—United States.
I. Garcia, Betty, 1943- II. Council on Social Work Education. III. Title.
  HV11.7.V36 2003
  361.3'071'073—dc21
                          2003001801

Council on Social Work Education
1725 Duke Street, Suite 500
Alexandria, VA 22314-3457
www.cswe.org

Printed in the United States of America

Contents

Part Three—Teaching Methodologies

Preface

The changing demographics in the United States that reflect a growing social diversity have resulted in heightened awareness of the need to develop culturally competent social workers and other human services professionals. The intensification of dialogue in the classroom, by the inclusion of complexity introduced by all cultures and their interaction, is a challenge both to faculty and to students. A significant challenge accompanying this change is the growing presence of individuals with multiple social identities that cannot be simply categorized as bicultural. These dynamics have direct implications for how the dynamics with which faculty engage have changed. The implications for teaching in multicultural classrooms are vast and preparation for effective teaching methodologies has become essential. Increasingly, traditional concepts about working with classroom dynamics and maintaining control need to be balanced with knowledge about student learning styles, knowledge regarding experiential learning processes, and utilization of activities that are not limited to lectures.

This book is primarily aimed at helping social work educators to develop culturally competent practitioners who have a commitment to promoting social and economic justice for diverse individuals and populations. It is based on our conviction that, for services to be provided in a culturally competent way, social workers must understand the causes, dynamics, and consequences of oppression on the life experiences of diverse populations. Further, they must understand and become skilled in using social change strategies to overcome oppressive conditions. Unlike most cultural diversity and multicultural education books, the perspective of this book is not about culture or cultural differences, which is sometimes referred to as the anthropological approach. Rather the focus is on learning and change processes and strategies related to teaching about difference.

This book is not about developing cultural competence as usually conceived but as we conceive it. We propose that cultural competence is a mindset characterized by inquiry rather than by assumptions that one knows a culture different from one's own. It is also characterized by process and interpersonal skills that facilitate engagement with different others. We take an antiracist stance that sees culturally competent practice as a proactive stance in dealing with oppression. Also, we approach diversity as a concept that is embodied in all individuals, in that it highlights the uniqueness and richness of all individuals' heritage and social identity. Such a perspective suggests taking responsibility for being informed about one's own biases about other cultures (Anderson & Goolishian, 1992; Shapiro, 1995).

Based on our years of teaching cultural diversity and social justice courses and workshops and conducting research, this book provides experience- and research-based information about teaching and learning processes and teaching strategies. Betty Garcia's approach to teaching sees learning in social work education as involving personal development as well as intellectual growth. As a professor of practice theory she sees her role as one of finding a balance with several aims. One aim involves challenging student curiosity and critical thinking through the presentation of content and probing students to explore the issues and their own perspectives on those issues. This process involves students becoming familiarized with the interaction between their individual experience and sociopolitical influences in their lives, such as the family, culture, and dominant society. Betty's goal is to create a classroom environment that fosters dialogue and creative exchange between herself and the class, as well as among the students. Because students come into social work programs with a wide range of diverse experiences, she believes it is essential to build a learning community that supports students using their experiences to guide their learning. This requires that students learn from one another as well as from Betty modeling the utilization of her personal and professional experience as a foundation for ongoing professional development.

Dorothy Van Soest's educational philosophy is grounded in the concept of emancipatory learning, i.e., learning that "frees people from personal, institutional, or environmental forces that prevent them from envisioning new directions, from gaining control of their lives, their society, and their world" (Apps, 1985, p. 151). She believes that there is a parallel process between emancipatory learning and social work empowerment practice with clients. In other words, the helping process is also aimed at freeing clients from personal, institutional, or environmental forces that prevent them from envisioning new directions, from gaining control of their lives, their society, and their world. Grounded in the concept of emancipatory learning, Dorothy's educational philosophy related to preparation for professional social work practice includes five key principles:

1. Educating for critical awareness is liberating education.

2. Education presumes change, not a static notion of reality.

3. Education promotes critical thinking.

4. Education aims to achieve political clarity, which is the ability to break free from distorting perspectives imposed by oppressive groups so that we can see the inequitable and hierarchical relationships in society clearly and fully.

5. Education is a political and value-laden activity in that learners tend to expand their awareness of self and environment, their range of wants and interests, their sense of justice, their need to participate in decision-making activities, their ability to think critically and reason rationally, their ability to create alternative courses of actions, and ultimately their power or control over the forces and factors that affect them.

While this book is based on our experience as social work educators and researchers, we believe it will also be beneficial for educators in other helping professions who are concerned with promoting social change as well as providing individual services. It aims to serve as a guide for educators, both in formal academic and continuing education settings, as they navigate the new and potentially explosive terrain of cultural diversity, which is inevitably coupled with societal oppression.

Education that integrates cultural diversity and social justice is both a process and a goal. Ultimately, the goal is to prepare social workers and other helping professionals to transform oppressive and unjust systems into non-oppressive and just alternatives (Gil, 1998). The educational processes for achieving this goal must be consistent with the desired outcome. In other words, teaching methods and interactions must reflect a parallel process that models empowerment. This suggests that teaching methodologies and student–faculty and student–student relationships need to be non-oppressive and just. To help students deal with difficult material and to foster a willingness to engage in the necessary risk taking that this learning requires, the educational process itself needs to be characterized by a safe classroom environment where students feel respected. There needs to be a sense of equality, active listening, dialogue, shared problem solving and decision making, affirmation and support of students, encouragement of critical thinking, and faculty modeling of non-oppressive concepts.

This book attempts to provide educators of social workers and other help-ing professionals with an understanding of what professors and students bring to the learning situation and what the learning process involves. It is intended to be an aid for diversity courses but it will be helpful as a guide to managing diversity discussions as they arise in other courses where the primary focus is not diversity. The book also provides strategies and tools to help with this admittedly daunting and transformative task. The Introduction delineates the assumptions upon which the book is based and describes the contents of the book's three parts: theoretical framework and context, teaching and learning processes, and teaching methodologies.

Dorothy Van Soest
Betty Garcia

REFERENCES

Anderson, H., & Goolishian, H. (1992). The client is the expert: A not-know-ing approach to theory. In S. McNamee & K. Gergen (Eds.), *Therapy as a social construction* (pp. 25–39). Newbury Park, CA: Sage.

Apps, J. W. (1985). *Improving practice in continuing education: Modern approaches for understanding the field and determining priorities.* San Francisco: Jossey-Bass.

Gil, D. (1998). *Confronting injustice and oppression: Concepts and strategies for social workers.* New York: Columbia University Press.

Shapiro, V. (1995). *Subjugated knowledge and the working alliance: The narra-tives of Russian Jewish immigrants. Session: Psychotherapy in Practice, 1*(4), 9–22.

Introduction

> Understanding injustice and oppression and their sources—domina-
> tion and exploitation—tends to be fraught with multidimensional
> existential dilemmas and emotional stress, for it implies the need for
> people to make significant changes in their ways of life, work, and
> patterns of social relations. It means therefore exchanging the "bliss
> of ignorance" for the burden of holistic social knowledge along with
> difficult new choices, conflicts, and fears. (Gil, 1998, p. 130)

Considerable attention has been paid during the past decade to the increasingly diverse appearance of the United States. Much of the attention has focused on the significant increase in non-White populations and projections
of increasing numbers of "minority majority" cities, regions, and states. There
seem to be two prevailing responses to this reality. First, dominant White
America clearly shows signs of being threatened, as evidenced by increased
use of institutional and individual violence to maintain dominance and oppression over people of color. Some examples are widespread anti-immigrant
and anti-affirmative action sentiment and political action, growing numbers
of hate crimes, and a proliferation of White hate groups and on-campus accusations of balkanization of student bodies. The intensity of the anti-immigrant sentiment has even spilled over to include immigrants with European
backgrounds.

A second predominant response is an attempt to successfully prepare for
a significantly more diverse workplace. This response is characterized by a
proliferation of education and training efforts aimed at cultural awareness
and multicultural competence in the workplace. For social work and other
helping professions, this translates into a focus on preparing professionals to
effectively serve clients from diverse cultures. The notion of cultural competence has become the center of this response, which is defined by Cross, Bazron,
Dennis, and Isaacs (1989) as a "set of congruent behaviors, attitudes, and policies that come together in a system, agency, or among professionals and en-

able that system, agency, or those professionals to work effectively in cross-cultural situations" (p. 13).

While the two predominant responses to changing demographics represent a stance of either resistance or one of working together to strengthen the economy, we propose a third response. The fundamental premise of this book is that the current focus on learning about other cultures and diverse populations is not sufficient for successful multicultural interaction. We maintain that, in order to be truly culturally competent, it is necessary to understand the context in which that interaction takes place, that is the meaning of diverse cultures and difference. The experience of difference means both culture as a source of strength (i.e., capacity to overcome life circumstances and mobilize social movements) and group membership as a basis of inequity, injustice, and oppression. The threat many people feel in the face of an increasingly diverse U.S. society is related to fear of losing their position of dominance and privilege over those who are assigned a subordinate status primarily because they are perceived as "different."

Thus, while successfully navigating the new multicultural terrain indeed requires an understanding and appreciation of diverse cultures, it also requires an equal understanding of the sources and dynamics of injustice and oppression that are inextricably connected with cultural difference. While social workers in particular have professional responsibilities to provide culturally competent services, they have historical mandates to challenge social injustice and to promote social and economic justice. These mandates are expressed in the National Association of Social Workers' *Code of Ethics* (NASW, 1996), the *International Declaration of Ethical Principles of Social Work* of the International Federation of Social Workers (IFSW, 1994), and the *Educational Policy and Accreditation Standards* of the Council on Social Work Education (CSWE, 2001).

The approach of this book about developing cultural competence includes the following definitions and perspectives:

- We define cultural competence as a mindset of critical inquiry; openness to other's experiences; the goal of eliminating oppressive conditions; and skill in micro and macro practice, the use of micro skills as a tool for advocacy for social change.

- Our framework is based on the theoretical framework that racism is central to understanding all oppressions. We see diversity as including all types of diversity. We use the term race as a socially constructed category that is linked to relations of power related to institutional practice and socioeconomics, processes of struggle, and as a construct whose meaning changes over time. We take an antiracist stance that undergirds anti-oppression work as an essential part of cultural competence.

- What we mean by multiculturalism is inclusiveness of all heritages and life experiences within the context of the dynamics of oppression related to race, ethnicity, language, culture, gender, sexual orientation, physical and mental ability, religion, and class. The following quote from Audre Lorde (1983) captures this perspective:

As a Black, lesbian, feminist, socialist, poet, mother of two including one boy and a member of an interracial couple, I usually find myself part of some group in which the majority defines me as deviant, difficult, inferior, or just plain "wrong." From my membership in all of these groups I have learned that oppression and the intolerance of differences comes in all shapes and sizes and colors and sexualities; and that among those of us who share the goals of liberation and a workable future for our children, there can be no hierarchies of oppression. (p. 14)

This book is based on the fundamental assumption that social justice curriculum content is an integral part of cultural diversity curriculum. It is further based on the assumption that such cultural diversity teaching and learning processes aimed at promoting social justice will do the following:

- Focus on power and privilege related to social identity and the meaning of difference, the resulting impact on personal growth and development, and access to services and opportunities that are essential for creating a full and rewarding life.
- Insist that diversity issues include everyone in the equation: both those who benefit from oppression and those who are marginalized.
- Emphasize self-awareness of the practitioners, particularly in regard to the effects of their biases on their interaction with others, and awareness of and willingness to work with the consequences of those effects on such interactions.
- Promote development of a spirit of inquiry that is characterized by curiosity and motivation to learn about others whose lives are different from one's own and the strengths utilized by those individuals and groups.

- Focus on the development and use of a perspective that recognizes the formative role of institutional and organizational policies and practices both in creating fundamental change and imposing obstacles.

- Emphasize understanding the historical context and intergenerational dynamics when dealing with diversity issues as opposed to the usual ahistorical perspective that denies, minimizes, and makes invisible the richness and struggles of people.

- Advance the view that social identity influences knowledge development and ways of knowing and the need to include those historically marginalized in the construction of knowledge.

- Utilize advocacy as a means to create change.

What all of this adds up to is a tremendous challenge for social work educators. It is a challenge that we believe is unlike any others that we face in preparing students for professional practice. In short, while diversity and social justice curriculum are often held up as wonderful educational objectives, it is important to acknowledge that genuine diversity, i.e., diversity aimed at the goal of social justice for all diverse groups in society, is extremely difficult to achieve. We must be in the struggle for the long haul and not look for simplistic solutions that only deal with surface issues instead of addressing the role of power and dominance.

What is ultimately called for is a major transformation at the level of a paradigmatic shift in our way of thinking about difference that disengages difference from domination and power. This shift represents learning in the service of advocacy and social change.

This book is divided into three parts. Part One establishes the context for integrating cultural diversity and social justice content into the curriculum and provides educators of social workers and other helping professionals with an understanding of the dynamics of injustice and oppression as connected with diversity of culture, ethnicity, gender, sexual orientation, class, disability, religion, and other social identities. Chapter One provides the theoretical foundation and educational framework. Chapters Two and Three define key concepts, present the dynamics of oppression, and discuss societal and educational issues related to multiculturalism. Chapter Four conceptualizes change processes within a socialization framework. Chapter Five presents processes that can facilitate transformative change resulting in advocacy for social justice.

Part Two provides information about what both professors and students bring to the learning situation and what occurs in the change process for these two groups. Chapter Six is devoted to what students bring to the learning situation and what happens to them. Chapter Seven focuses on what professors bring to the classroom and what happens to them in teaching and learning about cultural diversity and social justice. Chapter Eight discusses the interactional dynamics both in and out of the classroom. Part Two concludes with a dialogue among three professors about teaching and learning about cultural diversity and societal oppression in Chapter Nine.

Part Three is a practical section on teaching methodologies that provides curricula content, concrete methods, strategies, and processes for meeting the considerable challenges. Some organizing concepts and methods for teaching oppression content are presented in Chapter Ten. Chapter Eleven presents critical incidents from actual classroom situations and presents strategies for transforming such critical incidents into teachable moments. Chapter Twelve includes the description of a concrete teaching model that takes into account developmental issues with the class as well as the individual student. Chapters Thirteen, Fourteen, and Fifteen describe specific teaching methodologies: joint journaling, an interactive website forum, and the use of literary resources. Chapter Sixteen is devoted to providing teaching resources that readers can adapt to their specific educational settings.

REFERENCES

Council on Social Work Education. (2001). *Educational policy and accreditation standards.* Alexandria, VA: Author.

Cross, T. L., Bazron, B. J., Dennis, K. W., & Isaacs, M. R. (1989). *Towards a culturally competent system of care.* Washington, DC: Georgetown University Child Development Center.

Gil, D. (1998). *Confronting injustice and oppression: Concepts and strategies for social workers.* New York: Columbia University Press.

International Federation of Social Workers. (1994). *International declaration of ethical principles of social work.* Oslo, Norway: Author.

Lorde, A. (1983). There is no hierarchy of oppressions. *International Books for Children,* Bulletin 14.

National Association of Social Workers. (1996). *Code of ethics.* Washington, DC: Author.

Educating for Cultural Competence: It's About More Than Appreciating Diversity, It's About Eliminating Oppression and Promoting Social Justice

INTRODUCTION TO PART ONE

Part One elaborates on three fundamental premises upon which this book is based: (1) that culturally competent social work practice requires an understanding and appreciation of diverse cultures along with an equal understanding of the sources and dynamics of injustice and oppression that are inextricably linked with difference; (2) that the ultimate goal of diversity education for social justice is to prepare professional social workers to transform oppressive systems into just and nonoppressive alternatives (Gil, 1998); and (3) that it is essential that social work educators understand learning and change processes in order to help students move from information and ideas to beliefs about injustice and ultimately to actions for social justice.

The first three chapters in Part One establish a rationale and context for integrating cultural diversity and social justice content into the curriculum. Chapter One begins by examining three persistent obstacles—issues of privilege, lack of a coherent educational framework, and current social and political realities—that create substantial barriers to the development of an effective diversity-for-social-justice curriculum. The greater part of the chapter provides four essential components of a coherent educational framework aimed at overcoming the barriers, including the centrality of race and racism, the role of socioeconomic class, the complex interaction of multiple social identities, and transformative learning processes. Chapter Two further elaborates the educational framework by discussing key concepts and issues, structural and interpersonal dynamics, five diverse social justice perspectives, and the role of critical analysis. Chapter Three provides a more in-depth examination of the obstacle to curriculum change posed by the current social and political reality of living in a troubled and polarized country and world. Social justice values and principles are offered to help ground social workers as they face

1

the realities as well as a discussion of educational issues related to teaching diversity content within the current social and political climate.

In Chapters Four and Five, we turn to in-depth discussion of the fourth component of the educational framework presented in Chapter One, transformative learning processes. Chapter Four provides a conceptualization of the change process, using socialization theory to discuss the difficulties involved in socializing students to assume the dual roles of social justice advocate and social control agent and presents a critical thinking process as a model for preparing students for the social justice advocacy role. Chapter Five conceptualizes a transformative learning process that includes an empowerment process model, attention to the classroom learning environment, and the concept of moral exclusion. The chapter ends with a collection of student journal comments that illustrate transformative changes that can occur in the learning process.

In summary, Part One of this book establishes the context for integrating cultural diversity and social justice content into the curriculum by providing a theoretical foundation and educational framework, defining key issues and concepts, and introducing transformative learning and change processes. Part One sets the stage for the second part of the book that focuses on what students and educators bring to the learning situation and what occurs in the change process for both groups.

REFERENCE

Gil, D. (1998). *Confronting injustice and oppression: Concepts and strategies for social workers*. New York: Columbia University Press.

Chapter One
A Theoretical Framework for Teaching and Learning About Diversity for Social Justice

Effective teaching in higher education in general requires proficiency that includes timing, personal acumen, creativity, commitment, and organizational skill. Teaching in social work programs demands that and more due to the student population profile, the content and mission of professional education, and the need to engage students in the learning process. Core social work values such as social justice, advocacy, and self-determination provide a foundation for the essential thrust of content and teaching methods found in social work curricula.

For almost three decades, social work education has increasingly addressed the need to develop practitioners who are culturally competent. Beginning in the early 1970s, the inclusion of diversity has been mandated by social work curriculum standards for purposes of accrediting educational programs. In 1992, the Council on Social Work Education's curriculum requirements for accreditation specifically mandated content on women, people of color, and gay men and lesbians; on the patterns, dynamics, and consequences of oppression related to these and other vulnerable groups; and on skills to promote change for social and economic justice (Council on Social Work Education [CSWE], 1992). In an increasingly diverse and inequitable society, social work educators now face the additional challenge of not only helping students to understand societal oppression but also helping them to translate that understanding into actions designed to facilitate social change for social justice. The challenges have been found to be daunting for both teachers and students.

Our definition of cultural diversity refers to differences between groups with distinctive characteristics and social identities based on culture, ethnicity, gender, age, sexual orientation, religion, ability, and class. We also see diversity as inseparable from issues of oppression and social and economic justice. The integration of cultural diversity and social justice recognizes the historical and ongoing oppression and privilege that different social identity groups experience in our society. It recognizes economic class as a prime indicator of oppression and, in fact, sees the creation of a class system based on difference as a function of oppression. It further recognizes the intersection and complex interaction of multiple social identities and a continuum of harm and privilege that these identities confer. Our definition of multiculturalism refers to issues of representation and democratic inclusiveness. We also see multiculturalism's roots in the relationship between politics and power, within the context of a historical past and a living present where racist exclusions were "calculated, brutally rational, and profitable" (Goldberg, 1993, p. 105). Our perspective about multicultural education is that its central aim should be to teach students to "interrogate, challenge, and transform those cultural practices that sustain racism" and to "link the struggle for inclusion with relations of power in the broader society" (Giroux, 2000, p. 499). Our definition of culturally competent social work begins with Lum's (1999) definition as "the set of knowledge and skills that a social worker must develop in order to be effective with multicultural clients" (p. 3), and includes a commitment to promote social justice arising from a clear understanding of the impact of oppressive systems on individuals and families.

Ultimately, the goal of cultural diversity education for social justice is to prepare professional social workers to transform oppressive and unjust systems into non-oppressive and just alternatives (Gil, 1998). A context and theoretical foundation for teaching and learning processes aimed at this transformative goal are presented in this chapter. This chapter first examines some persistent issues and obstacles inherent in teaching and learning about cultural diversity and social justice. This examination is followed by presentation of an educational framework that forms the foundation for curriculum development and attempts to address some of the issues and obstacles.

WHY TEACHING AND LEARNING ABOUT CULTURAL DIVERSITY AND SOCIAL JUSTICE IS SO DIFFICULT

While there is a proliferation of creative models for teaching about cultural diversity in the literature and at national conferences, there is evidence of uneven results. Faculty often report resistance to course content and students often express distress and anger in response to cultural diversity course content. There are many issues and obstacles that need to be addressed if we are to become more effective as educators. Three are particularly significant:

1. Fear and anger that make it difficult to listen and talk about issues related to power based on difference.

2. Lack of a coherent conceptual framework that is uniquely formulated on social theory and that is truly inclusive of diversity and social justice.

3. The difficulties posed by current social and political realities such as increased backlash and abandonment of collective social action for social change.

Each of these three obstacles is discussed in more depth below.

1. Exposing our Dirty Secrets and Confronting our Fear and Anger

The first obstacle to teaching and learning about cultural diversity and social justice is related to White privilege. Bob Jensen, a journalism professor, described what White privilege sounds like in an editorial titled, "Wake up to White Privilege":

> I am sitting in my University of Texas office, talking to a very bright and very conservative white student about affirmative action in college admissions, which he opposes and I support.
>
> The student says he wants a level playing field with no unearned advantages for anyone. I ask him whether he thinks that in the United States being white has advantages. Have either of us, I ask, ever benefited from being white in a world run mostly by white people? Yes, he concedes, there is something real and tangible we could call white privilege.
>
> So, if we live in a world of white privilege—unearned white privilege—how does that affect your notion of a level playing field? I ask. He paused for a moment and said, "That really doesn't matter."
>
> That statement, I suggested to him, reveals the ultimate white privilege: The privilege to acknowledge you have unearned privilege but ignore what it means. (Jensen, 1998)

In the editorial, Jensen also wrote: "The dirty secret that we white people carry with us in this world of white privilege is that some of what we have is unmerited" (Jensen, 1998). This dirty secret suggested by Jensen exposes the context in which we approach the subject of cultural diversity and education for multicultural competence in social work. The dirty secret hinders us from the beginning because it keeps us from talking directly and honestly about White supremacy and White privilege.

The Secret of White Privilege: An Obstacle to Curriculum Development

Much of the fear and anger that comes up around discussions related to cultural diversity curriculum issues, we believe, is rooted in this dirty secret of White privilege. In his editorial, Jensen addresses some of this fear when he describes his personal fear of not being special, his fear of not being worthy of his successes, his fear that what he always thought he had earned through his own effort may, in reality, be more a function of being born White rather than brains and hard work. We believe that this kind of fear and anger poses one of our biggest obstacles to teaching and learning about diversity and social justice.

Experience in academia teaches that curriculum changes come slowly and often painfully. We propose that curriculum changes that are linked with issues related to race and difference evoke particularly primitive feelings for all people. Because we are, by and large, basically well-meaning people, the realization of being part of the problem of racism and of simultaneously benefiting from it elicits fervent responses in White social workers, regardless of their status as students, faculty, or practitioners. There is genuine shock about allegations of collusion with a system of dominance, particularly when racism is linked to extremists or institutions. There is a sense of terror that at any moment we might err with respect to racism by revealing something provocative, suggesting that we do not know the rules and therefore do not know how to prevent an insensitive comment from spilling from our lips. White people are confused because they may not know what it means for people of color to navigate through a largely hostile terrain. They do not know what it means to deal with institutions whose cooperation is needed for one's survival and personal efficacy, yet do not function in one's interests. After all, the terrain through which White folks have navigated has operated in their best interests.

The opposite has been the reality for people of color. In an article titled, "Whites in Multicultural Education: Rethinking Our Role," Gary Howard writes:

> Throughout most of our history, there has been no reason why white Americans, for their own survival or success, have needed to be sensitive to the cultural perspectives of other groups. This is not a luxury available to people of color, [whose] daily survival depends on knowl-

edge of white America . . . To be successful in mainstream institutions, people of color in the U.S. need to be bicultural—able to play by the rules of their own cultural community and able to play the game according to the rules established by the dominant culture. For most white Americans, on the other hand, there is only one game, and they have traditionally been on the winning team (Howard, 1993, p. 38).

The differential effects of the misdistribution of power and privilege add up to difficulty in talking about issues related to race. Talking about it is difficult because of the tremendous gulf of experience and meaning between individuals differentially positioned in relation to the system of domination and privilege. So we do not talk about it. Or we do not want to talk about it. Or we talk about it in safe terms, always mindful not to talk about the dirty secret. Or we talk about it in psychological terms, avoiding the institutional nature of the problem. In social work practice we often use the expression, "People are only as sick as their secrets." Not talking directly and honestly about White privilege allows the sickness of racism to fester. Not talking directly and honestly about White privilege allows White people to keep the truth from themselves, which means they do not have to change. It is this resistance to the truth that makes it very difficult for White people to listen to people of color. This resistance also fans interest in placing responsibility on the person of color to tell their story for the purpose of enlightening others.

The Secret of Male Privilege

The dirty secret about a system of advantage for Whites is not the only dirty secret that blocks us in our attempts to teach and to learn about diversity and social justice. Gender in the United States consists of unearned advantage and conferred dominance on males. The dirty secret related to gender is that some of what males have is unmerited. We believe that fear and anger rooted in this secret make it difficult for males to listen to females, just as White privilege makes it difficult for White people to listen to people of color. In an essay titled "White Privilege and Male Privilege," Peggy McIntosh (1995) describes how the system of gender privilege, like racial privilege, becomes invisible to the males who benefit from it, even though it structures the everyday life of both males and females.

The Secret of Heterosexual Privilege

McIntosh further points out that race and gender are not the only advantaging systems at work. The dirty secret is that some of what people in other categories have is unmerited also. Unearned privileges are granted due to a system that advantages some people because of prejudice toward their sexual orientation, class, age, ability, nationality, or religion. In relation to heterosexual privilege, McIntosh asserts that "this is still a more taboo subject than race privilege: the daily ways in which heterosexual privilege makes some persons comfortable or powerful, providing supports, assets, approvals, and rewards to those who live or expect to live in heterosexual pairs. Unpacking [those privileges] is still more difficult, owing to the deeper imbeddedness of hetero-sexual advantage and dominance and stricter taboos surrounding these" (p. 85).

The first obstacle to creating an inclusive curricula is the fear and anger rooted in these dirty secrets of unmerited privilege that keep us from talking honestly and directly about systems of advantage. Delving into feelings about privilege is like roaming into an area rife with emotional landmines.

2. The Need for a Relevant Conceptual Framework

The second obstacle is that we lack a coherent conceptual educational framework that addresses diversity and social justice and can be integrated across all areas of the social work curriculum. We believe this obstacle is the result of adopting educational approaches that ignore or deny the dirty se-crets. The result can at best provide a curriculum framework that is ambigu-ous and evasive in terms of power and privilege dynamics related to difference. At worst this approach creates curricula that negates critical aspects of the experiences of its own student body and clients with whom our students work. Social work education has been unwilling to look at the White side of the racist equation and this has led to an anthropological compromise, a "watered down" version of cultural diversity curriculum. "The anthropological compro-mise approaches the issue of race as essentially a question of subculture. So-cial work education, then, trains workers to perform competently with clients of other races by teaching them about the environment and culture within which those races function" (Edwards-Orr, 1988, p. 7). The anthropological compromise attempts to develop sensitivity toward and understanding of marginalized people without explaining why they are marginalized or who benefits from their marginalization. In other words, such a compromise ne-glects to integrate issues of cultural diversity with issues of social justice.

This kind of approach reinforces the widespread myth that an inclusive curriculum is about and for the others . . . that it is an entitlement program and curriculum movement for African Americans, Latinos, Asians, Native Americans, women, poor people, and gay/lesbian/bisexual/transgendered people. The idea that diversity curriculum in social work is aimed at developing sensitivity to others keeps it marginalized and held apart from our mainstream curriculum. To have a reasonable chance of becoming institutionalized, an inclusive curriculum needs to be regarded as essential for all students. Such a curriculum would critically examine how systems of oppression shape the life experiences of those who are both disadvantaged *and* advantaged by them. An inclusive curriculum would prepare *all* students to work for the transformation of "unjust and oppressive social, economic, and political institutions into just and nonoppressive alternatives" (Gil, 1998, p. 1). Such a curriculum would require exposure of the dirty secrets.

3. Current Social and Political Realities

The third issue and obstacle that we want to highlight is the difficulty of building an inclusive curriculum within current social and political realities. We live in a deeply troubled and polarized nation and world. We should not underestimate the difficulty of establishing inclusive approaches to curricula in the context of continued structural and institutional White leadership. Just as U.S. society and its institutions are controlled by White people, so social work, as a product of its society, is responsive to and reflects that power structure. When it comes to discrimination and oppressive systems, we have been historically more successful in responding to our environment than we have been at setting our own professional agenda. This has been especially true around issues related to race.

It is important to recognize the difficulty of critically examining the role of power and privilege in our society and our profession within the context of today's social climate. The current political atmosphere is characterized by anti-affirmative action and anti-multiculturalism. The myth that multicultural education will divide our country and undercut its unity seems to be gaining in popularity as illustrated by Arthur Schlesinger's 1991 book, *The Disuniting of America: Reflections on a Multicultural Society*. This myth is based on the false assumption that our nation is already united. It ignores the reality that our country is, and always has been, deeply divided along lines of race, gender, class, sexual orientation, and other groupings. Yet the myth persists and is an obstacle that blocks our attempts to build a curriculum that integrates diversity with social justice.

Institutions of higher education continue to follow exclusionary practices that result in a lack of diverse representation at faculty, administrative, and student levels. These normalized practices result in teaching of a primarily Eurocentric perspective that preserves traditional curriculum and reinforces resistance to change in the name of academic freedom. While it is essential that we respect the academic freedom of our colleagues, academic freedom needs to be balanced with the responsibility to provide a curriculum that is sensitive and responsive to the values of the social work profession related to equity and social justice. An indirectly related issue is that of a need for academics to address and distinguish the soundness of empirical work that is espoused and the potential political use (or abuse) to exploit empirical work in the service of self interest (i.e., strengthening dominance). For example, while data suggest that there may be physiological differences that organize differences in the human species, there is no evidence that such differences exist in relation to phenotype. However, the sociobiological argument used to explain dominance has been based on these so-called inherent differences.

Lack of diverse representation in higher education ensures resistance to change in the name of the merit principle. Diverse representation enhances the possibility of vital dialogue characterized by diverse points of view, challenge, and hopefully an attitude of problem solving that can result in change. We need to critically examine how the principle of merit and formal advancement structures maintain the power of White males in institutions of higher education. And we need to work to change such structures.

The three obstacles we have discussed—issues of privilege, lack of a coherent educational framework, and current social and political realities—create substantial barriers to the development of an effective diversity for social justice curriculum. The discussion in the following section addresses the three obstacles by providing four essential components of a coherent educational framework that we believe can help overcome the barriers.

ESSENTIAL COMPONENTS OF AN EDUCATIONAL FRAMEWORK THAT INTEGRATES CULTURAL DIVERSITY AND SOCIAL JUSTICE

In a book titled *Teaching/Learning Anti-Racism: A Developmental Approach* by Louise Derman-Sparks and Carol Brunson Phillips (1997), the authors write that they often begin their first class on racism and anti-racism with the following parable:

> Once upon a time a woman, strolling along a riverbank, hears a cry for help and, seeing a drowning person, rescues him. She no sooner finishes administering artificial respiration when another cry requires another rescue. Again, she has only just helped the second person when a third call for help is heard. After a number of rescues, she begins to realize that she is pulling some people out of the river more than once. By this time the rescuer is exhausted and resentful, feeling that if people are stupid or careless enough to keep landing in the river, they can rescue themselves. She is too annoyed, tired, and frustrated to look around her.
>
> Shortly after, another woman walking along the river hears the cries for help and begins rescuing people. She, however, wonders why so many people are drowning in this river. Looking around her, she sees a hill where something seems to be pushing people off. Realizing this as the source of the drowning problem, she is faced with a difficult dilemma: If she rushes uphill, people presently in the river will drown; if she stays at the river pulling them out, more people will be pushed in. What can she do? (p. 1–2)

The second woman's thoughts suggest that she may be questioning why these people share particular characteristics and if a selection process is underway. If we define racism, sexism, heterosexism, classism, and other forms of oppression as the force on the hill, then this metaphor suggests three alternative solutions for educators and social workers: (a) rescue people in trouble and return them to the oppressive conditions that caused the problem; (b) after rescuing people, teach them how to manage their problems so that if they "get pushed into the river again," they at least will not drown; and (c) organize with people to destroy the source of the problem (Derman-Sparks & Brunson Phillips, 1997, p. 2).

The educational framework that we propose in this book opts for the third position. Social work education needs to do more than prepare students to respond to the symptoms or consequences of oppressive conditions. We need to help students develop strategies for responding to the source of oppression and encourage them to reevaluate their own roles, on personal and professional levels, in its continuation. An inclusive curriculum, in our opinion, must ultimately be about recognizing the problem and learning to understand and to eliminate the problem on the hill.

The metaphor raises several questions that need to be critically examined as part of a coherent conceptual framework:

- If the river represents a situation of oppression or disadvantage, what is it like to be in the river? In other words, what are the conditions and processes of oppression and how do they affect people's lives and life chances?

- Who are the people being pushed into the river? What characteristics do they have in common? What is the singular facet of their experience that puts them at risk?

- What people are *not* being pushed into the river? What are their common characteristics? How do they benefit from having others pushed into the river?

- If the force on the hill that is pushing people into the river represents racism, sexism, classism, heterosexism, and other systems of advantage, how does the force operate? How much of this is to be understood in individual, psychological terms and how much as a business as usual patterning of institutional practices? Is it a mix of this and other factors?

- What happens so that people who used to be in the river and got out then go up the hill to push people who look like them in the river?

- What role can social workers learn to take in helping the people pushed into the river?

- What organizational, collaborative, and advocacy skills can social workers develop in order to eliminate the force that is pushing them into the river? How can social workers differentiate business as usual discrimination from behavior motivated out of personal bias?

To address these questions, we propose that four essential components are required as part of a coherent educational framework. The following framework is grounded in:

1. A foundation of the construction of race and the practice of racism as central.

2. Racism as "a mode of human relations involving domination and exploitation" which, on an economic level, creates a class system (Gil, 1998, p. 10).

3. The complex interaction of racism with the systemic dynamics of oppressions based on gender, class, sexual orientation, ability, and the concept of multiple identities.

4. Processes of teaching, learning, and transformation as an integral part of the framework.

The Centrality of Race and Racism

The first component of our proposed educational framework places race and racism at its foundation. At a time when there is considerable evidence of a widespread wish to retreat from issues of race and racism, why do we propose that they form the basis of a framework for a curriculum that integrates cultural diversity and social justice? We do so because race has always had and continues to have a central role in our country. In his book, *Two Nations: Black and White, Separate, Hostile, Unequal,* political science professor Andrew Hacker (1992) provides overwhelming evidence of exactly how deeply issues of race shape the thinking of everyone in the United States. The concept of race has always been used to assign status and power based on skin color since the first Europeans arrived. Of all the forms of exclusion, discrimination, and power-assignment that exist in this country, and there are many, "none is so deeply rooted, persistent, and intractable as that based on color" (Hopps, 1982, p. 3). Thus, racism is central to understanding the dynamics of oppression.

The Concept of Race: A Social Construct

Our educational framework needs to start by challenging the idea that race is an inherently meaningful concept. Rather, we need to help our students understand race as a socially constructed category linked to relations of power and processes of struggle and as a construct whose meaning changes over time. "Race," like gender and sexual orientation, is *real* in the sense that it has real, though changing effects in the world. It has tangible and complex impacts on peoples' sense of self, experiences, and life opportunities. Thus, to assert that race and racial difference are socially constructed, is not to minimize their social and political reality. It is, rather, to insist that their reality is

---

[1] "Oriental" refers to the French colonialist perspective regarding the Easterner, that is, east of the center, meaning east of France.

precisely social and political rather than inherent and its meaning and function change over time. This will be discussed more in Chapter Two.

Historical research reveals the social construction of racial categorization in our country, for example: "Japanese Americans have moved from categories such as 'non-white', 'Oriental' or simply 'other' to recent inclusion as a specific ethnic group under the broader category of 'Asian and Pacific Islanders'" (Omi & Winant, 1986, p. 3). At the time of their arrival, Jewish people were kept at the margin of "White" America, simply because they were not Christians, and Catholics were not regarded as altogether White as well. Similarly, Italian Americans, Irish Americans, and Latinos, at different times and from varying political standpoints, have been viewed as both White and non-White (Hacker, 1992).

> By this time, it should be clear that the question is not "who *is* white?" It might be more appropriate to ask, "Who *may* be considered white?" since this suggests that something akin to permission is needed. In a sense, those who have already received the "white" designation can be seen as belonging to a club, from whose sanctum they ponder whether they want or need new members, as well as the proper pace of new admissions . . .
>
> The "White club" is, as much as anything else, one of privilege and power and its members have always had the power to expand its domain. While it has admitted people of all ethnicities over time, it has and continues to be particularly reluctant to absorb people of African descent. (Hacker, 1992, p. 9)

While race is a social construct with ambiguous meaning and political utility, racism is real and has haunted this country since Europeans first set foot on the continent. We need to help our students challenge the common misperception that racism is the same as prejudice, which is a personal, psychological phenomenon. They need to understand that racism is an institutionalized system of advantage grounded in social, political, and economic power. Social arrangements of advantage, based on an ideology of White supremacy, serve to deprive and diminish many people of color while offering preparation, support, and opportunity to those considered to be White (Knowles & Prewitt, 1969).

It is our experience that White students' struggle with comprehending racism results in resistance to comprehending the institutional nature of racism. They tend to view racism as an issue that people of color face and have to struggle with (after all, they are the ones being disproportionately pushed into the river). They do not see it as an issue that generally involves or implicates White folks. This view of racism has serious consequences for how antiracist work might be framed in the social work curriculum. With this view, White people can see antiracist work as an act of compassion for an "other" (i.e., they can pull the "others" out of the river). Or, they can see it as an optional, extra project—perhaps even an important social work commitment, but not one intimately and organically linked to White people's own lives. Racism can, in short, be conceived as something external to White people, rather than as a system that shapes the daily experiences and sense of self of *all* of us. Such realization highlights the distortion that all people experience in a racist society, with Whites distorting in the direction of overestimation of self and people of color distorting in the direction of underestimation of self.

Whiteness

Thus, cultural diversity and social justice curriculum must include people with privilege, in this case White people. We must start by acknowledging the fact that race and racism shape White people's lives. Frankenburg, in her book *The Social Construction of Whiteness: White Women, Race Matters* (1993), writes:

> In the same way that both men's and women's lives are shaped by their gender, and that both heterosexual and lesbian women's experiences in the world are marked by their sexuality, both white people and people of color live racially structured lives. In other words, any system of differentiation shapes those on whom it bestows privilege as well as those it oppresses . . . . [Thus] in a social context where white people have too often viewed themselves as nonracial or racially neutral, it is crucial to look at the "racialness" of white experience. (p. 1)

So, the educational framework we propose includes exploration of the question: How does "Whiteness" shape people's lives?

As Frankenburg eloquently describes, using the name Whiteness displaces it from the unmarked, unnamed status that is itself an effect of its dominance. Among the effects on White people both of race privilege and of the dominance of Whiteness are their seeming normativity, their structured invisibility. Institutional racism is hidden behind the standard practices of hard-working, well-meaning White people. Institutional racism typically is not ugly. Rather than being expressed through racial slurs, it tends to be wrapped in noble proclamations of tradition, fairness, and high standards. Rather than being a rare incident, it is woven into the fabric of our historically racist society. The subtle and slippery forms of institutional racism are silently and invisibly tearing at the fiber of our schools and our society. And Whiteness is at its core.

To look at Whiteness, then, is to look head-on at a site of dominance. And, as Frankenburg points out, it is much more difficult for White people to say, "Whiteness has nothing to do with me—I'm not White" than it is to say, "Race has nothing to do with me—I'm not racist" (p. 6).

To speak of Whiteness is to assign *everyone* a place in the relations of racism. It is to emphasize that dealing with racism is not merely an *option* for White people. Rather, racism shapes White people's lives and identities in a way that is inseparable from other facets of daily life. As Frankenburg argues, there *is* a cultural/racial specificity to White people, at times more obvious to people who are not White than to White individuals.

There is a need to insert two caveats here. First, while racism shapes the lives of all people, there is a gulf of difference in the experience of racism between White people and people of color. Second, at this time in U.S. history, Whiteness as a marked identity is explicitly articulated in terms of the "White pride" of the far right. To call Americans of European descent "White" in any celebratory fashion is, in the present political moment, a White supremacist act, an act of backlash. It is only when White activists and culturally competent social workers name themselves racially in the context of antiracist work does naming oneself as White begin to have a different kind of meaning (Frankenburg, 1993, p. 232).

Thus, the challenge inherent in including White people in the cultural diversity curriculum means making visible and undermining White culture's ties to domination. Back to the parable, it means being able to see White people—even well-meaning White social workers—as part of the force that is pushing people in the river.

The Powerful Role of Socioeconomic Class

The second component of the educational framework regards the socio-economic class position of people of color compared with that of White people as a primary indicator of racism and oppression. Essential to an understanding of racism is being cognizant of how oppression functions to create a class system based on skin color. Knowledge of the formation and history of racism in the United States is essential content if we are to understand how the deep roots of its core structures continue to nurture current forms of racism that result in socioeconomic inequity. In the U.S., the colonization and robbing of a flourishing Native American civilization, the importation of Africans as slaves, the expropriation of the land of Mexicans in the Southwest, and the exploitation of Asian labor in the building of railroads and mining of gold combined to lay the economic, political, and ideological foundation for the present structural relationships of racism (Howard, 1993).

As students study the history of peoples of color in this country, the common elements of oppression become clear to them, often for the first time. *Students of color* recognize that exploitation extended historically to people different from themselves with whom they begin to feel a new bond. The recognition of power issues reorganizes thinking regarding oppression based on color by introducing sociopolitical economic factors. When *White students* open themselves to learning about the historical perspectives and cultural experiences of other races, much of what they discover is incompatible with their image of a free and democratic nation. They become caught in a classic state of cognitive dissonance. They see that the success of the European enterprise in this country rests on acts of inhumanity. Yet, they were always taught that their ancestors were building a free and democratic land (Howard, 1993). They often get caught in resolving differences with family members. The cognitive dissonance is not dealt with easily.

Being confronted with the grim realities of history exposes the dirty secret of White privilege and the creation of an economically privileged class. Some students respond with hostility and fear. Well-intentioned students who can understand and behave sensitively, yet harbor ambivalence, often feel guilt. Students need to be helped to move beyond such negative responses and find a place of authentic engagement (i.e., that is personally chosen) in social change. A first step is to approach the past and the present with a new sense of honesty. Facing the realities of history is the beginning of liberation. It is important not to fall into a kind of morose confession about the sins of our ancestors. The healing response for both students who have benefited and students who have been disadvantaged by oppression is action and responsibility (Howard, 1993, p. 40).

We have spent a considerable amount of time presenting the first two components of the conceptual educational framework being proposed. To summarize:

- We stressed the importance of developing a thorough understanding of racism as central to the formation, history, and current realities of U.S. society and that we approach it as an institutional, not psychological, phenomenon.

- We explicitly focused on how the construct of race shapes the identities, experiences, and potential class position of both people of color and White people.

- We emphasized the role of social workers to transform racist systems and institutions into non-racist alternatives that promote social, political, and economic equity.

- And, finally, we stressed that we have all become embedded in the problem of racism in the United States and we will have to deal with it together.

The Complex Interaction of Multiple Social Identities

The third component of the educational framework adds the critical dimension of how racism operates in complex interaction with the systemic dynamics of socioeconomic class and gender oppression. Once the foundation of race and racism is established, the complexities of oppression can be addressed. All people of color are targeted by racism. However, the factors of class, gender, sexual orientation, ability, and other social identities influence the ways and layers in which oppression based on race occurs. Correspondingly, all Whites automatically have institutionalized privilege. However, White people do not reap its benefits equally. Class, gender, and sexual orientation, along with other aspects of identity, influence how much and in what ways individuals experience and benefit from their Whiteness.

The relationship of race, class, gender, and sexual orientation is the subject of considerable, sometimes heated disagreement both in the literature and in our classrooms. Questions arise and arguments abound regarding which of these institutional forms of oppression came first or is worst. This is what we label "competitive oppressions" when students get involved in this kind of conflict. In the educational framework that we are proposing, the response to such arguments is that race remains central as an ongoing theme in U.S. history that divides people who actually share interests. Also, it has proven to be an effective way to weaken resistance to exploitation. The centrality of racism in American society posits it as a dynamic that, once understood, provides relevant and key insights into other oppressions.

Common Ideological Underpinnings of Oppression

We can understand ideological justifications for oppression based on gender, class, and sexual orientation by seeing how they are similar to those justifying racism. The denigration of an entire people on the basis of race is justified by an ideology of White supremacy and racial inferiority. The denigration of an entire people on the basis of gender is justified by an ideology of male superiority that insists that females are less intelligent and logical and more emotional and irrational. The vilification of an entire people on the basis of sexual orientation is justified by insistence on marked mental and moral deficiencies. The defamation of an entire people on the basis of economic status is justified by class superiority; researchers in the 19th century went to great lengths to prove the biological inferiority of poor people and a causal connection between their lack of wealth and their lack of merit.

An inclusive curriculum must examine the effects of the interlocking oppressions of racism, sexism, classism, and heterosexism on individual and group experiences related to power and privilege. In other words, it is important to understand that the force that pushes people into the river does so in a complicated, yet systematic way. The overrepresentation of certain populations among those being pushed needs to be understood as not depicting a chance occurrence. People who are deemed to be inferior or defective in more than one way (e.g., being Black, female, and lesbian) have an increased likelihood of being pushed into the river.

Multiple Social Identities

In learning about the common elements of oppression, we find that students often buy into the "popular wisdom" that one experience of marginality such as being gay or lesbian, being Jewish, or being a woman leads people automatically toward empathy with other oppressed communities. There is a widespread belief that participation in one kind of liberatory movement, such as feminism or gay rights, leads automatically to antiracism. This is not true and needs to be addressed. Understanding the dynamics of oppression in the current historical and political context involves seeing how oppressive systems operate to divide and conquer oppressed populations from each other. It also means understanding the dynamics of internalized oppression, whereby persons may celebrate a part of their acceptable social identity while denigrating their own unacceptable part(s).

The reality is that we all have multiple social identities based on race, ethnicity, gender, sexual orientation, ability, class, and other factors. Thus, most people are both targets of oppression and agents of oppression (Bell, 1997). While people may be vulnerable to being pushed into the river based on one aspect of their social identity, the same people may push others into the river based on a different social identity. The dirty secret gets complicated as one aspect of an individual's identity may confer unmerited privilege while, at the same time, another aspect of that same person's identity creates disadvantages.

More of us get uncomfortable when multiple identities are examined within the framework of power and privilege. Privileges are nice to have. We do not want to notice that we have them because then we will not have to think about giving them up. When power and privilege are threatened, attempts are made to hold on to them. As the population of the United States becomes more diverse, White Americans are becoming nervous about losing their dominant position, as evidenced by an alarming increase in acts of overt and sometimes violent racism. Too many males are uncomfortable with the transition from their dominant gender status and are willing to find both covert and overt ways to hang on to their gender privilege, while not appearing to do so. Too many segments of our heterosexual population remain committed to their position of dominance. This is evidenced by a willingness to defend and legitimize heterosexual privilege, and even justify hate crimes in the name of God. Too many people who enjoy economic advantage do not even consider the possibility of giving up their position of dominance and privilege. Justifications for an unequal class structure remain deeply embedded in our collective psyche.

Even while the world is rapidly changing, the reality of the strong commitment to dominance, power, and privilege by those who have it strongly suggests that a peaceful transition to a new kind of America, in which no group is in a dominant position, will not be easy. The transition to a just and equitable society will require considerable change in education and personal values. It will require deep psychological shifts for all. Those in dominant positions must deal with overestimation of self, and those in subordinate positions, with underestimation of self. The challenge to effect the needed changes is the work of an inclusive curriculum. That challenge leads us to a central question: What must take place in the minds and hearts of White people, of males, of heterosexual people, of economically advantaged people, of able-bodied people, to convince them that now is the time to begin their journey from dominance to diversity, from marginalization and exclusion to inclusion? What are the issues that must be addressed in the current practice climate if social work and professional education is to play an effective role in such change?

Transformative Learning Processes

This question leads to the fourth component of the educational framework. As we stated in the Introduction, we believe that a major transformation is ultimately called for at the level of a paradigmatic shift in our way of thinking about difference that disengages difference from domination and power. Facilitating such a major shift requires an essential and continuous quest to understand the *process* of learning. We need to understand that the process of constructing anti-racist, anti-sexist, anti-heterosexist identity, consciousness, and behavior is a transformative rather than a linear process. It is a process that is influenced by multiple factors, challenges one's sense of self and self-esteem, and takes sometimes unpredictable twists and turns rather than sequential stages. Curriculum content often arouses unexamined feelings about difference and how privilege and power are determined based on difference. Teaching and learning about diversity and social justice requires a willingness on the part of both students and educators to work through any unresolved conflicts in relation to their own role and status in an oppressive society.

The conceptual educational framework we are proposing means that students will inevitably uncover contradictions between the principles they verbalize and their behaviors, between inherited ideas they have been socialized into and new information, between self-image and feedback from others. And when students uncover contradictions, the search for new ways to think and act is ignited. This search motivates continued learning (Derman-Sparks &

Brunson Phillips, 1997). Learning about diversity and oppression involves questioning one's assumptions and exploring alternative ideas in a spirit of critical inquiry. This is not only difficult, but also psychologically explosive (Brookfield, 1990).

Students undergo profound changes in the process and change is inevitably coupled with considerable distress. Ultimately, the struggle requires that students develop a positive social identity in order to better value their clients' identities and related struggles (Pinderhughes, 1989). This struggle for a positive social identity varies depending on the students' experiences and background related to social status and power.

Because students position themselves differently in relation to social relations of oppression, they have different expectations regarding the political positioning of faculty members and the course content. Social relations are often reproduced in the classroom, resulting in difficult challenges for both faculty and students. Difficult events can happen without warning at any moment, with powerful intensity and confrontational interaction. Such situations need to be carefully documented and studied in order to develop creative and constructive strategies to transform them into learning experiences (Garcia & Van Soest, 1999; George, Shera, & Tat Tsang, 1998).

Students' worldviews are challenged by the kind of educational framework that integrates cultural diversity and social justice. Personal turmoil and reevaluation are required to develop a positive social identity in the context of dominant power structures. The challenges of learning and changing can be overwhelming. Students can experience feelings such as debilitating anxiety undergirded by guilt, shame, and confusion. Often these responses can be out of awareness. The effect that can be evoked in students places heightened pressure and responsibility on us as educators to be responsive to process issues that arise in discussion, including students' emotional needs. Without educational interventions that support students through the psychological challenges, such distress can easily result in feelings of resentment, despair, and alienation. Stephen Brookfield (1990), a leading authority on adult education, warns:

> When educators assist people in questioning the assumptions underlying their structures of understanding or in realizing alternatives to their habitual ways of thinking and living, they must act with care and sensitivity. It is no good encouraging people to recognize and

analyze their assumptions if their self-esteem is destroyed in the process. Assisting people to break out of their assumptive worlds without threatening or intimidating them to the point of withdrawal is highly problematic. (p. 179)

Role of Educators

Our role as educators then, is to guide students through a very delicate interaction between challenge and support. In our role as guide we are at the same time in the role of learner because we must pay attention to each student's rhythm of growth. We need to be constantly "reading" the students' openness and level of ability for risk taking to determine how to create a better atmosphere for growth. While we need to do our own work related to oppression and diversity, we need to get outside ourselves in the classroom and get inside the minds of the students. We need to continually ask and probe about: What do students need in order to feel safe? How do they learn best? How do they construct knowledge? How do they make sense of the world? How can we skillfully remind students that this setting is as safe as it gets? How can we create a learning environment that is emotionally and intellectually demanding? How can we provide the support needed to navigate this psychologically explosive terrain?

As educators we face the same contradictions that the -isms (i.e., racism, sexism, ableism) create for our students. Their struggle to become and live as anti-oppressors is our struggle as well. Not to act in the face of oppression and exploitation is to participate. When classroom discussions become heated, the challenges for us intensify. Even when we have the teaching skills to navigate through intense class discussions and keep the focus on learning, the stirrings that we ourselves feel can create a sense of clouded perception that produces doubts about our own judgment.

None of us can do this education work in isolation. It is too complex. It requires multiple voices in dialogue and struggle. It requires knowledge construction. It requires emotional support from people who understand its demands and can help us keep the focus on growing in the midst of a lot of heat. We need to find, develop, and use collegial support. We need support and resources from administrators of social work schools and departments. This book is one attempt to provide support and ideas that can help professors understand more about the process of teaching and learning.

CONCLUSION

In this chapter, we highlighted some of the issues and obstacles we face in building the inclusive curriculum. We then proposed that we need a coherent conceptual educational framework that could be integrated across the social work curriculum. Three essential components of such a framework were then presented. Make no mistake about it. The educational framework that we have proposed aims ultimately at the elimination of oppressive systems. We are proposing transformation on the most fundamental level of knowledge creation. What does this mean? It means exposing the ways in which implicit cultural assumptions, frames of reference, and biases within our profession influence what we think we know about people and their environments and the helping strategies we adopt. It means examining how knowledge is created and influenced by factors of race, ethnicity, gender, class, and sexual orientation. It means identifying and examining the human interests and value assumptions of those who create knowledge. It means creating a learning environment that critically challenges the facts, concepts, paradigms, themes, and explanations routinely accepted in mainstream academic knowledge (Banks, 1993).

When we consider the possibility of our profession becoming firmly and unequivocally committed to the transformation of oppressive systems, it is easy to become pessimistic. We hear about the "me generation," the "Generation X," the increase of campus violence and intolerance, and that many of our students today are apathetic and conservative, that they have disregard for the plight of others, that they lack the kind of social work commitment we desire. Yet, when we read the journals of students in our cultural diversity classes and their reflections at the end of the course, it becomes clear that transformation on an individual level is indeed occurring, even among those who seem the most recalcitrant in relation to issues of power and privilege. We keep learning from our students that personal transformation can lead to actions aimed at societal transformation. Some excerpts from an essay called "Failure to Quit" written by historian Howard Zinn (1997) can give us hope for the future of our work:

I can understand pessimism, but I don't believe in it. It's not simply a matter of faith, but of historical evidence. Not overwhelming evidence, just enough to give hope, because for hope we don't need certainty, only possibility. Which is all history can offer us. When I hear

so often that there is little hope for change from the present generation of young people, I think back to the despair [about the possibilities for change in the United States at the beginning of the 1960s].
Yet, it was on the first of February in that first year of the new decade
that four black students from North Carolina A & T College sat down
at a "white" lunch counter in Greensboro, refused to move, and were
arrested. In two weeks, sit-ins had spread to fifteen cities in five Southern states. By the year's end, 50,000 people had participated in demonstrations in a hundred cities, and 3,600 had been put in jail. That
was the start of the civil rights movement, which became an anti-war
movement, a women's movement, a cultural upheaval, and in its course
hundreds of thousands, no millions, of people became committed for
a short time, or for a lifetime. It was unprecedented, unpredicted, and
for at least fifteen years, uncontrollable. It would shake the country
and startle the world, with consequences we are hardly aware of
today. . . . There is no such uproar today. There is an uncertain mix-
ture of silence and commotion . . . but there is more than silence.
There are thousands of local groups around the country—many more
than existed in the Sixties—devoted to struggling for tenants' rights
or women's rights or environmental protection. . . or to take care of
the hungry and the homeless, or those in need of health care. There
are now tens of thousands of professionals . . . who bring unorthodox
ideas and humane values into courtrooms, classrooms, and
hospitals . . . History does not start anew with each decade. The roots
of one era branch and flower in subsequent eras. Human beings, writings, invisible transmitters of all kinds, carry messages across the generations. I try to be pessimistic, to keep up with some of my friends.
But I think back over the decades, and look around. And then, it
seems to me that the future is not certain, but it is possible. (pp. 656–
661)

It would be a mistake to interpret resistance or lack of action among our
students as lack of thought or feeling. It may be that they are reacting to the
absence of opportunities for transformative knowledge, openings to challenge
one's own and others' privileges, role models to emulate, groups to join, but
when these appear, as we have found throughout history, the silence can change
to uproar.

It is our hope that this book will provide some of the knowledge and skills that social work educators need to be able to provide opportunities for our students to become transformed and to transform oppressive systems into just and nonoppressive alternatives. In the next chapter, basic concepts and definitions are presented, along with discussion of key educational issues. Chapter Three examines in more depth the obstacles for curriculum change presented by the current social and political reality of living in a troubled and polarized country. Chapter Four provides an introduction to learning and change processes. Part Two of the book is aimed at increasing understanding of teaching and learning processes from the perspectives of both students and professors. Part Three provides concrete teaching methodologies and tools.

REFERENCES

Banks, J. A. (1993, September). Multicultural education: Development, dimensions, and challenges. *Phi Delta Kappan, 75*(1), 22–28.

Bell, L. A. (1997). Theoretical foundations for social justice education. In M. Adams, L. A. Bell, & P. Griffin (Eds.), *Teaching for diversity and social justice: A sourcebook* (pp. 3–15). New York: Routledge.

Brookfield, S. (1990). Using critical incidents to explore learners' assumptions. In J. Mezirow and Associates, *Fostering critical reflection in adulthood: A guide to transformative and emancipatory learning* (pp.177–193). San Francisco: Jossey-Bass.

Council on Social Work Education. (1992). *Curriculum policy statements for baccalaureate degree and master's degree programs in social work education.* Alexandria, VA: Author.

Derman-Sparks, L., & Brunson Phillips, C. (1997). *Teaching/learning antiracism.* New York: Teachers College Press, Columbia University.

Edwards-Orr, M. T. (1988, March). *Helping white students confront white racism.* Paper presented at the Annual Program Meeting, Council on Social Work Education, Atlanta, GA.

Frankenburg, R. (1993). *The social construction of whiteness: White women, race matters.* Minneapolis: University of Minnesota Press.

Garcia, B., & Van Soest, D. (1999). Teaching about diversity and oppression: Learning from the analysis of critical classroom events. *Journal of Teaching in Social Work, 18*(1/2), 149–167.

George, U., Shera, W., & Tat Tsang, A. K. (1998). Responding to diversity in organizational life: The case of a faculty of social work. *International Journal of Inclusive Education, 2*(1), 73–86.

Gil, D. (1998). *Confronting injustice and oppression: Concepts and strategies for social workers.* New York: Columbia University Press.

Giroux, H. A. (2000). Racial politics, pedagogy, and the crisis of representation in academic multiculturalism. *Social Identities, 6*(4), 493–510.

Goldberg, D. T. (1993). *Racist culture.* Cambridge, MA: Basil Blackwell.

Hacker, A. (1992). *Two nations: Black and white, separate, hostile, unequal.* New York: Charles Scribner's Sons.

Hopps, J. (1982, June). Oppression based on color (editorial). *Social Work, 27*(1), 3–5.

Howard, G. (1993). Whites in multicultural education: Rethinking our role. *Phi Delta Kappan, 75*(1), 36–41.

Jensen, B. (1998, July 9). Wake up to white privilege. *The Baltimore Sun.*

Knowles, L., & Prewitt, K. (1969). *Institutional racism in America.* Englewood Cliffs, NJ: Prentice-Hall.

Lum, D. (1999). Culturally competent practice: A framework for growth and action. New York: Wadsworth.

McIntosh, P. (1995). White privilege and male privilege: A personal account of coming to see correspondences through work in women's studies. In M. L. Andersen and P. H. Collins, *Race, class, and gender: An anthology* (pp. 76–87). New York: Wadsworth.

Omi, M., & Winant, H. (1986). *Racial formation in the United States from the 1960's to the 1980's.* New York: Routledge.

Pinderhughes, E. (1989). *Understanding race, ethnicity and power: The key to efficacy in clinical practice.* New York: The Free Press.

Schlesinger, A. (1991). The disuniting of America: Reflections on a multicultural society. New York: Norton.

Zinn, H. (1997). Failure to quit. In *The Zinn reader: Writings on disobedience and democracy* (pp. 656–661). New York: Seven Stories Press.

Chapter Two

Key Concepts and Issues in Developing Diversity for Social Justice

Change regarding diversity curriculum usually involves challenges related to maintaining a balance between several factors, such as coherence and standards, faculty creativity, increased relevance, academic freedom, program mission, and integration of core social work values regarding social justice and diversity. The events of September 11 altered our lives in ways that have additional implications for our educational mandate to prepare future social work professionals for effective social practice. They heightened awareness of living in a global community and sharpened our focus on relationships with ourselves and with others different from ourselves.

Even as curriculum change efforts are underway, there are those that criticize diversity curriculum as political correctness, which they characterize as coercive and biased. Such disparagement often represents resistance to "curricular transformation and related change" (Schoem, Frankel, Zuniga, & Lewis, 1995, p. 5) and fuels the perspective that integration of diversity content has the effect of divisive balkanization. Faculty who take the risk to raise diversity concerns and their relevance for curriculum all too often find themselves feeling alone and unsupported in their willingness to bring issues to the table for faculty discussion. Because the integration of diversity content into the curriculum is premised on the social justice roots of the profession, discussions can often provoke dissension arising from a fear that indeed social work has relinquished its social justice mission and moved away from social change and the elimination of inequities (Chambon & Irving, 1999).

Schoem et al. (1995) propose that faculty resistance and conflict are based on an expectation of negative outcomes as a result of faculty confronting parameters of their own knowledge and learning processes and critically evaluating their work. Thus curricular change may be viewed as leading to acknowledgement of imagined or real limitations and deficits. Also, a major obstacle in university settings is teaching from a monocultural perspective (Sfeir-Younis, 1995) that marginalizes and thereby excludes diversity issues.

Yet the inclusion of diversity content is mandated by curriculum standards (CSWE, 2001) and faculty have the responsibility to initiate changes that reflect their program's purpose and needs. They must inevitably deal with diverse and conflictual perspectives while considering proposals for integrating diversity curriculum in a meaningful way. Faculty dialogue must deal with openness to teaching about diverse cultures, unique faculty perspectives about diversity, and differences regarding how to approach curriculum development. Productive dialogue requires that faculty develop and/or have the ability to tolerate the ambiguity associated with exploring new ways to talk about longstanding, often unspoken sensitivities, discomforts, conflicts, and tensions.

The process of curriculum change creates a parallel process among faculty that is similar to what occurs among students in the classroom. The process is facilitated when there is dialogue that is characterized by open inquiry and that is inclusive of all faculty voices. At least two factors influence effective integration of social justice and diversity content into the curriculum: faculty communication to reach understanding of key concepts, and program leadership that is supportive of the sensitive, often intense dialogue that must occur. Critical dialogue is essential in order to acknowledge and work with differing faculty perceptions about diversity and social justice as well as expectations arising from administrative, environmental, and curriculum demands.

This chapter presents fundamental concepts and issues, social justice perspectives, and implications for engaging students in critical thinking processes. It is hoped that this will challenge faculty to examine value assumptions that underlie course conceptual frameworks and program mission statements and ultimately move from diversity awareness to diversity education for social justice action taking.

KEY CONCEPTS AND ISSUES

Multicultural Society Means Change, Not Status Quo

Diversity has always been a fundamental characteristic of American life. There is increased awareness of its presence currently, however. In part this is due to immigration, growth of diverse populations, and greater media attention to diversity-related concerns. Demographic predictions forecast an America comprised of a variety of ethnic and multiethnic individuals and populations that will characterize different geographic regions within the next few decades. Demographic changes enrich communities through the introduction of new immigrant groups, greater integration of diverse cultural contributions (e.g., food, music, art) into the mainstream culture, and increased inclusion of diverse groups into different aspects of community and professional settings resulting from upward mobility. Through increased interaction with those different from ourselves, old perceptions and attitudes are challenged and, in the best of circumstances, new thinking and behaviors are stimulated. To stand still in this ever-changing context is to go backwards.

Shifts in roles and interaction stimulated by demographic social changes have created ambiguous situations that require more interpersonal negotiation than one customarily faces in familiar interactions. While this may be demanding and stressful, it also increases the potential for developing new interpersonal skills that are essential for engaging in diverse interactions. By legitimizing difference as something that is to be appreciated and understood, processes are activated that can lead to increased awareness of one's own value system and behavior in relation to others. Gergen (1991) suggests that different situations elicit different aspects of ourselves and that openness to new interpersonal experiences leads to the development of a relational self that grows and flourishes in relational contexts. When there is curiosity and risk taking, interactions with unfamiliar individuals in new settings can be successful and can stimulate new reactions related to dealing with one's own identity, what one values, and who one wants to get to know. Zuniga and Nagda (1995) suggest that diverse encounters trigger a series of far-reaching questions for students such as "Who am I? With whom do I want to identify? What groups do I belong to? Who are the people different from me? What groups do they identify with? What do they believe in? Why are they behaving that way?" (p. 20). In the presence of diversity, the rules for interaction change and the possibility of gaining understanding of different perspectives is enhanced. This change in conditions of interaction and the makeup of social settings in which we increasingly find ourselves provide a unique type of feedback that fosters curiosity about others and the development of personal and professional awareness of self.

While social work academics are usually well prepared to take on intellectual adventures, bridging differences leads them into new experiential terrain requiring a combination of emotional and intellectual work. It involves active engagement and negotiation with others whose communication and interaction styles are different from one's own. It is easy to be seduced into using initial impressions and knowledge about diverse groups in a boilerplate fashion as if unfamiliar cultures were static or all individuals within that group were homogeneous. We often hear, for example, "Tell me the five things that I need to know to work with a particular population." However, it is essential to treat new information about diverse groups as hypotheses that need to be continually matched to current interactions. Then ongoing interactions and impressions are viewed as a basis for the development of more complex knowledge about other individuals and cultural groups. In summary, the new demographics of society require change and adaptation. Individuals will succeed to the degree that they can process their own experience, value diversity, and sustain a robust curiosity about their experiences with others.

The changing social demographics create new teaching demands in relation both to curriculum content and to teaching methodology. Educational programs must stretch to bring to the center of the curriculum perspectives that have traditionally been at the margins of curricular focus. In addition, the changing composition of the classroom challenges educators to envision and incorporate teaching approaches that engage students in affective and interactive learning. Such challenges are discussed in depth in Part Two of this book.

Racism, Prejudice, Discrimination, Power, and Privilege

Teaching diversity within a social justice perspective, as presented in this book, begins with a focus on racism because of its entrenchment in the history and character of the United States and its formative role in disenfranchising and marginalizing significant portions of the population. We view racism above all as a sociopolitical phenomenon that is characterized by social power. Its attitudinal (i.e., thoughts, feelings, and behaviors) and interpersonal manifestations vary in relation to one's social power.

Racism is defined as the "generalization, institutionalization and assignment of values to real or imaginary differences between people in order to justify a state of privilege, aggression, and/or violence" (Bulhan, 1985, p. 13). As one form of oppression, racism is "a mode of human relations involving domination and exploitation—economic, social and psychological" (Gil, 1998, p. 10). As a form of domination, racism is a means to exploit so that one socioeconomic class benefits from another's resources and capacities, for example through their labor (Gil, 1998). This suggests that social, economic, and political forces determine the social status significance of racial groups based on the meaning of difference that determines social categories (Omi & Winant, 1986). We view institutional racism as business as usual, premised on economic and technocratic means that do not require "psychological mediation" (Kovel, 1984, p. xi). Institutional racism is often manifested out of awareness, even among those who are well intentioned (Gaertner & Dovidio, 1981). Social work education needs to focus on the sociopolitical dynamics that result from power and privilege on both psychological and institutional levels in order to prepare practitioners to intervene on all levels: intrapersonal, interpersonal, and institutional.

Prejudice and discrimination are distinct from racism. Prejudice refers to prejudgments or ungrounded adverse opinions or beliefs about others (Blumenfeld & Raymond, 2000). Psychological explanations about prejudice focus on how it is fueled by the projection of our unowned and unacceptable personal qualities onto people who are targets of oppression (Allport, 1954; Lichtenberg, van Beusekom, & Gibbons, 1997). Because the origins of prejudice "include both the psychological makeup of the individual and the structural organization of society" (Blumenfeld & Raymond, 2000, p. 26), the sociopolitical and ideological context within which individuals are socialized play powerful roles in shaping negative stereotypes about target groups (Garcia-Bahne, 1981). These negative stereotypes can survive even in the face of discrediting evidence.

Discrimination represents an action intended to have a "differential and/or harmful effect on members" of a group (Pincus, 2000, p. 31). It has been characterized as responses that create distance, separation, exclusion, and devaluation (Lott, 2002). Pincus (2000) suggests that individual and institutional discrimination represent behavioral and policy actions that are intended to have a harmful effect, whereas structural discrimination refers to policies and behaviors that may be neutral in intent yet have negative, harmful consequences on target groups. When discrimination is buttressed by social power it represents racism and oppression. When not backed by social power, biased behaviors represent individual discriminatory actions.

By learning and heightening awareness about racism as the foundation, it is our premise that learning about experiences of oppression based on social identities other than race and ethnicity is facilitated. While we see racism as having primacy in American life, our view of diversity education for social justice includes other diversities and oppressions: sexism, classism, ableism, and heterosexism. As with racism, where one facet of an individual having to do with phenotype (e.g., hair texture, skin color, facial features, physiology) is taken as the whole of the individual, likewise, gender, sexual orientation, and physical ability, while only one facet of an individual, are also presumed to be all that a person is.

At the center of discussion about multiple oppressions and multiple identities is the issue of the pervasiveness of oppression. Is it ubiquitous and present in everyone's life? Have all individuals been the target of oppression and also benefited from the privilege of a dominant position as some authors suggest (Miller, 1976)? Further, does this overlapping experience create a structural connectedness among all oppressions (Young, 2000) that provides a basis for bridging differences among all individuals? Or are the sociopolitical forces that buttress social power and privilege sufficiently potent that meaningful dialogue about oppression must keep its focus on societal, institutional levels and on the formative consequences of societal marginalization and devaluation of some social groups? Faculty must resolve for themselves how to approach the uneven experience of oppression in relation to the experience of reaping the benefits of the dominant ideology and practices.

We believe that helping students develop the ability to "walk in the shoes of the other" and suspend their own perspectives as part of learning about other worldviews is one of the most significant aspects of diversity learning. Although it is important to learn about diverse cultures, a core skill in cross-cultural competence is the skill and ability to engage with others for the purpose of developing a working relationship. It is then that we can learn about others meanings, values, and beliefs. Throughout this book, we propose that student awareness and ability to empathize is developed within the context of the cultural, social, and legal realities and the unique patterns of domination associated with each "ism," while keeping perspective on how power and privilege is manifested within each of them (Wildman & Davis, 2000). Just as the system of White privilege, based on an advantage of race, limits access to resources and decision making linked to full participation in society for those considered to be White, and limits access for those not identified as White, a system of privilege operates in similar ways based on other factors such as gender, sexual orientation, or ability (McIntosh, 1989; Tatem, 2000). Educators must deal with validating all students in their classrooms throughout the learning process. How this gets done, we believe, is a function of the creative, imaginative interaction that arises from teaching as both an art and a systematic method.

STRUCTURAL AND INTERPERSONAL DYNAMICS

Oppression

Issues of power and privilege related to social identities must be understood within the context of oppression. Oppression is defined as a situation in which one segment of the population acts to prevent another segment from attaining access to resources or which acts to inhibit or devalue them in order to dominate them (Bulhan, 1985). Young (2000) suggests that oppression is not based on any one group membership and, as a means of distinguishing among various experiences, identifies "five faces" of oppression: exploitation, marginalization, powerlessness, cultural imperialism, and violence. The five dynamics are intended to provide a means to recognize the variety of ways that different groups experience oppression and stay away from hierarchical comparisons about who is most oppressed. Young emphasizes that the presence of any of these five experiences or faces constitutes oppression and that most people experience some combination of these.

There are elements that are common to all oppressions regardless of the target population. First, oppression always bestows power and advantage on certain people who are regarded as the norm and denied to others based on status as the "other" or different. The defined norm (i.e., White, male, heterosexual) is the standard of *rightness* against which all others are judged; the "other" (i.e., not White, not male, not heterosexual) is not only different from the norm, but is also believed and perceived to be inferior and deviant, which then justifies conferring advantage on those who fit the norm and disadvantaging the other.

Discussion of this element of oppression needs to distinguish between social and individual power because students often have notions that racism, sexism, and heterosexism are personal prejudices based on individual power and stereotypes, rather than being sociopolitical phenomena. There is a difference between talking about prejudice and discrimination (personal power) and talking about a system of advantage that confers economic, social, judicial, and political (social) power on people who fit the "norm." To understand oppression, we can look at indicators and patterns in institutional practices and policies. For example, in the political arena, how many senators are Black, Latino, female, or openly homosexual? In relation to economic indicators, who is disproportionately represented among those who are poor?

A second element common to all oppressions is that they are held in place by ideology and violence or the threat of violence. The ideology on which racial oppression is based is that of superiority based on race (i.e., White supremacy). Likewise, the ideology on which sexual oppression is based is that of superiority based on gender (i.e., male) and the basis for homosexual oppression is an ideology of superiority based on sexual orientation (i.e., heterosexual). Violence is used to enforce and maintain all oppressions. Violence comes in many forms and may be physical and direct (e.g., lynching, rape, battering, gay bashing), or personal and psychological (e.g., name-calling based on dominant ideology and negative stereotypes). Violence may be indirect and/or institutionalized. For example, it may be associated with high poverty rates, the predominance of men of color in the criminal justice system and on death row, and the reality of police brutality.

A third common element of all oppressions is that they are *institutionalized.* This means that racism, sexism, and heterosexism are built into the norms, traditions, laws, and policies of a society so that even those who have non-racist, non-sexist, and non-heterosexist beliefs are compelled to act in accordance with institutional interests. Institutionalized racism, specifically, ensures White entitlement and benefits regardless of the intentions of individuals in those institutions. Pinderhughes (1989) proposes that institutional racism ensures that Whites benefit, exonerates them from responsibility, and sanctions the blaming of people of color for those restrictions and limitations imposed by oppression. She points out that there is considerable resistance against comprehending the institutional aspect of racism and that the process of understanding its systemic nature can be very painful. This is especially the case for White people who see themselves as different from Whites whom they view as racists. Pinderhughes writes about how it is particularly devastating for White people who have been involved in civil rights activities to face the implication that they, along with other Whites, are the beneficiaries of racism. There is a sense of injury that stems from recognition of themselves as trapped in the systemic process of racism that benefits them and exploits people of color. This sense of injury is further exacerbated by the realization that, while for many people of color this reality has been obvious, for Whites this has been obscure.

Another common element of oppression is the invisibility endured by groups who are oppressed. By keeping the oppression invisible structurally, how individuals and groups are socially defined inhibits recognition of the group's heterogeneity by the dominant group. In addition, the internalization of external sociopolitical judgments that devalue aspects of one's identity inevitably lead to individuals undervaluing and making invisible to themselves substantive parts of their own origins and history. These issues will be addressed in a later section and will specifically contend with how, on an interpersonal level, the invisibility and exclusion in part is buttressed through moral exclusion.

The issue of multiple identities further complicates the dynamics of oppression. Individual conditions of oppression often involve a convergence between aspects of one's experience where one is a target of oppression (e.g., as a low-income, disabled female; a Latino female, an African American, gay female) with other aspects of one's experience as privileged (e.g., middle- or high-income gay person, disabled Euro-American male) (Rose, 2002). Understanding the presence of power and privilege (advantage) or oppression (disadvantage) in one's life highlights experiences or realities that may have been rejected and also lays the foundation for connecting with others different from us. For example, a gay White male who is coming to terms with his sexuality and is not "out" will continue to exercise White privilege until there is some resolution about his identity. Or someone whose phenotype is Euro-American, yet has another, less socially valued heritage, may choose to underplay the latter until they have resolved and integrated their social identity.

Race, Ethnicity, and Gender as Social Constructs

In this section, we take the position that ascribed social identities such as race, ethnicity, and gender are social constructions produced through sociopolitical meanings that arise from perception and are maintained through social interaction. While culturally we are predisposed to view these meanings as individually constructed, they are intricately tied to the dominant social ideology (Garcia-Bahne, 1981). The historical context presents situational and circumstantial factors that influence how we think about and perceive factors such as race, gender, sexual orientation, and physical disability. The sociopolitical context in which racism and the other "isms" occur has a substantial influence on people's access to power and privilege. Thus, the oppressive effects of racism or sexism do not advance entirely from race or gender but rather through their congruence with socioeconomic class (i.e., power and/or disadvantage). For example, a middle- or upper-class professional Latina will encounter far fewer hurdles in life than a low-income, undereducated Latina who must manage many barriers and, contrary to stereotypes, must do so with little social support.

By focusing attention on changes that have taken place between modernity and the postmodern age, substantial societal transitions can be identified that have implications about the role that difference takes in society. Modernity is a historical period characterized by "individualization, secularization, industrialization, cultural differentiation, co-modification, urbanization, bureaucratization," (Best & Kellner, 1991, p.3) and represents a belief in the view that the "world runs by immutable laws that are knowable and that can be exploited to advance the human condition" (Rifkin, 2000, p. 188). The modern age replaced the 19th century belief based on faith with belief based on facts produced through the scientific method (Gouldner, 1976) and introduced the empiricism of positivism as bringing hope to the world's problems.

The term postmodern has been used in many differing ways that include cultural forms and experiences, sociohistorical perspectives on society, and "critical analysis of theory, society, history, politics and culture" (Best & Kellner, 1991, p. 26; Gergen, 2001). The new technologies, including computers and the media, produced socioeconomic change and major social transformation with worldwide changes related to capital growth. We know this as globalization. Postmodern assumptions about the nature of reality and our knowledge of that reality (Rifkin, 2000) have direct implications for moving discussions of difference to the foreground. New perspectives about global developments engage us in analysis of global dynamics that affect quality of life and legitimize the diversity of worldviews that exist among different cultural groups.

The postmodern approach embodies values and critiques that challenge dominant ideology and culture. What are legitimate questions to ask? What questions or points of view are undervalued and left out? Postmodern scholars reject the notion of an objective and knowable reality (Rifkin, 2000) and even the viability of theory and positivist assumptions (Best & Kellner, 1991). Postmodern theory challenges the view that theoretical formulations can correspond to lived experience as they can only partially grasp aspects of their objects. Postmodernists assert that "all cognitive representations of the world are historically and linguistically mediated" (Best & Kellner, 1991, p. 4). Gergen (2001) observes that for modernists the "world is out there" to know, while for the postmodernists, there is no basis for such an assertion and the task of knowing involves participating "in a textual genre—to draw from the immense repository of intelligibilities" that underlie particular cultures (p. 805). This of course means dealing with the pluralism and ambivalence associated with celebrating the diversity of stories and worldviews found in human experience (Rifkin, 2000).

As paradigms that deal with the creation of meaning in human experience, constructivism and constructionism support the view "that reality is socially and psychologically constructed" through interaction and highlight the significance of the connection between individual and societal influences (Rodwell, 1998). Both constructivism and constructionism recognize reflexivity in understanding meaning, reject the notion of an objective reality, emphasize the multitude of worldviews that co-exist, and purport that there are "many ways to understand behaviors, interactions and events" (Rodwell, 1998, p. 19). Factors such as language and social processes are viewed as obstacles that can interfere with knowing anything other than one's own experience (Maturana, 1988). Constructivist research methodology embodies these principles by utilizing designs that promote collaboration, empowerment, and change toward social justice (Rodwell, 1998). The accent on feedback loops as part of the method of inquiry enhances the possibilities of learning from the participant and engages the researcher in a *mutually oriented way* as a participant in the conditions that they explore.

Constructionism and constructivism diverge, however, in what they see as primary factors in meaning making and understanding how we know what we know. Constructionists place an emphasis on "language, narrative, sociohistorical and cultural processes, whereas constructivists highlight cognitive structures (schemas) and interactive feedback from the environment" (Rodwell, 1998, p.20). Constructivism focuses on individual perceptions and how they affect understandings (Goldberg & Middleman, 1980). In comparison, social constructionism looks at how people's understandings of their experience and beliefs about human development are influenced by changing cultural, historical, political, and economic factors (Lee & Greene, 1999). A central concern is the need for relativist theories to attend to the social context that in some cases determines the evolution of peoples' lives (Minuchin, 1991) and to the link between knowledge and power and access to knowledge associated with privilege (Allen, 1993).

Our intent is not to elaborate on these complex concepts in depth, but rather to emphasize the factors that play a role in the meaning making process related to race. As social work educators, our task is to acknowledge the effects of these processes on the profession's knowledge construction and to develop expertise in deconstructing the professional accumulated knowledge in relation to value assumptions. Both the postmodern and social constructionism approaches recognize that race has evolved as part of the effort to create (i.e., impose) a unified vision of human behavior that is associated with the development of classism and colonialism ideologies (Rifkin, 2000). Race plays a functional role in maintenance of these ideologies. As a social construction, race meets a "historical need to create a hierarchy that would maintain the status quo of white supremacy and privilege in the United States" (Gillem, Cohn, & Throne, 2001, p. 183). Arguments for defining race as a constellation of genes associated with specific populations encounter difficulty in ascertaining the scientific meaning of race and determining its proper application (Yee, Fairchild, Weizmann, & Wyatt, 1993), the existence of real differences, and how useful such categorization would be (Lieberman, Stevenson, & Reynolds, 1989). Socioeconomic factors, parent variables, phenotype, age, gender, and native versus foreign-born information would be far more valuable in strengthening our understanding of population variables, within a perspective that is keenly attuned to the political use of difference. Even if differences exist, it is critical to ask to what end these differences are used.

While perceptions are constructed on intrapersonal and interpersonal levels, the societal context has significant influence on the development of social constructs that reflect dominant ideologies such as racism, sexism, and classism. Foucault's work on understanding power, exclusion, marginalization, and the nature of knowledge (Chambon, Irving, & Epstein, 1999) elucidates the role of institutional forces in delivering truth and normalizing diverse experiences for the purpose of control (Saleebey, 1994). Because ideology represents a social agreement that shapes day-to-day activities and operates through the self-regulation of individuals rather than coercion (Foucault, 1980; Reich, 1970), critical thinking about what is accepted as truth about difference is imperative. What is assumed as real may merely represent political ideology. Two convictions are challenged by this view: that an external world can be empirically validated and that an internal subjective world has sufficient consistency to be known (Irving, 1999).

Foucault's (1980) work illuminates aspects of power that lead to distortions about race, class, and gender and to social constructs, and assists in the deconstruction of internalized societal notions about race, class, and gender. His view of human services as a contemporary system of exclusion that classifies and categorizes people for the purpose of normalizing what has in fact been co-constructed through power relations (Rossiter, 2001) points to a need to watch for how we can unknowingly collude with uneven, unjust institutional practices. This can occur through mere acts of uncritical accommodation to prevalent social constructs. For example, the notion of immigrants as illegal aliens reduces individuals to their national origin and ignores the reality that the majority of immigrants are in fact nondocumented workers who are contributing to the U.S. economy.

In summary, we propose that diversity education for social justice is derived from postmodernist, constructionist, and constructivist concepts in order to address the multitude of voices that often are made invisible. They help us to examine the origins and value base of knowledge construction rather than accepting concepts uncritically. They also provide challenging ideas regarding processes that affect the formulation of practitioner thinking and perceptions.

Culture, Multiculturality, and Social Identity

Social constructions about race and ethnicity make it difficult to understand and/or accept the co-existence of multiple cultural, racial, and ethnic identities. Difficulty in thinking about multiracial or multiethnic individuals in other than monolithic terms regrettably leads to the invisibility of the rich heritage of individuals. In the past, language and thinking about race dealt with "one drop of blood" (Wright, 1994) constructions and either/or thinking about race and ethnic identity that led to the quantification of social identity. Such thinking led to social constructions of individuals as half of one thing and half of something else, as opposed to a whole person who may be struggling with the process of achieving, or has achieved, unique integration of multiple identities. We find that when someone has a number of racial identities that include African American, they are labeled as African American regardless of their racial identity. In short, the growth in the heterogeneity of the American population has essentially outpaced our thinking and language about diversity.

However, in the last few years the diversity discourse has been broadened to include exploration of complex dynamics about diversity and domination that previously had been invisible. The concept of multiculturalism, for example, remains straddled with difficulties regarding the different uses of this concept. Fellin (2000) suggests that multiculturalism is used in at least three ways—all cultural groups, only cultures of people of color, and a combination of people of color and populations at risk—yet it is recognized for its emphasis on social inequality. The challenge in preparing professionals for culturally competent practice lies in whether this can be taught as knowledge content that assumes unfamiliar cultures can be known, or, for example, as ethical principles to guide professional behavior (Walker & Staton, 2000).

Biculturalism and acculturation are two domains that challenge the limits of our understanding. Biculturalism has been assumed to represent the internalization of two or more cultures and the development of diverse cultural lenses. However, constructivist approaches to biculturalism presume that culture is not internalized in a blended form, but rather in terms of a loose network of domain-specific knowledge structures. Thus, individuals may have several cultural identifications with no one culture necessarily replacing another (Hong, Morris, Chiu, & Benet-Martinez, 2000). Three aspects have been proposed as key elements in understanding the meaning of ethnic identity in the experience of individuals. These elements include "cultural norms and values; the strength, salience, and meaning of ethnic identity; and experiences and attitudes associated with minority status" (Phinney, 1996, p. 918). This is in contrast to the view that in postmodern culture, ties to traditional cultures and therefore social identifications with these attachments wane and loosen (Fellin, 2000). This suggests a movement from a linear view of acculturation that sees it as low or high to a more multidimensional view that gives recognition to low or high identifications with different multiple cultures (Ponterotto et al., 2001).

In summary, diversity education for social justice requires openness to the meaning of changing demographics, the societal changes underway regarding the experience of groups that are targets of oppression, and the implications for self-definition. While teaching diversity and social justice content includes many different levels (e.g., individual, family, group, organization), it is crucial to emphasize basic process skills on an individual level such as engagement and developing relationships with those different from ourselves. In the next section, the concept of moral exclusion is presented as a tool to help students examine and change beliefs and behaviors that have been shaped through socialization and other interpersonal processes.

Moral Exclusion

The concept of moral exclusion explains how exclusionary behavior is promoted and maintained on an interpersonal level. Moral exclusion refers to the process of placing those who are different from oneself or one's group outside the boundaries of fair treatment by invoking assumptions about who deserves just treatment and who should enjoy society's benefits (Deutsch,

1990). The concept of moral exclusion presumes that some individuals or populations are subordinate in their level of development on moral, intellectual, or spiritual grounds. This rationalization becomes the basis of exclusion that goes beyond interpersonal interaction through its social and economic consequences of marginalization and exclusion. Persons outside our moral boundaries are seen as expendable or undeserving and thus harming them appears acceptable, appropriate, or just. The process of categorizing groups negatively and excluding them from the realm of acceptable norms or values is linked to stereotypes and prejudicial attitudes related to ethnocentrism. Persons who have been and are excluded from the realm of the norms and values of social justice include people of color, women, gay/lesbian/bisexual/ transgendered persons, people with disabilities, poor people, and others.

There is a considerable body of research on moral exclusion, disengagement practices that make it possible to justify exclusion, and antidotes to exclusion (Opotow, 1990). Thus, the concept of moral exclusion provides a useful framework for helping students understand themselves and their beliefs in relation to different groups in society. While seldom conscious of them, we all have beliefs about which people should be treated justly and the broadness or narrowness of our moral boundaries is influenced by prevailing cultural norms. For example, it is no longer considered acceptable in the United States to own people as slaves or to make interracial marriages illegal, but it is generally considered acceptable to exclude gay men and lesbians from certain benefits such as partner benefits and the right to marry. The identification of and exclusion of an out group from the norms of fairness is a cognitive, affective, and behavioral phenomenon that enables otherwise considerate people to engage in self-serving behavior or inaction in everyday situations in order to gain benefits to themselves even at injurious costs to others.

Social constructionist theories view intrapersonal and interpersonal processes as, whether wittingly or not, being in the service of dominant society's interests. As Foucault pointed out, the alternative to docile acquiescence and buying into socially acceptable truths entails calling into question particular truths and challenging prevalent beliefs (Miller, 1997). Unlike other professions whose purposes are grounded in positivist traditions or service delivery with individuals, social work's historical roots include work with the disenfranchised and a social justice mission. The concept of moral exclusion, by providing a tool for making obvious one's own personal processes of excluding certain people from the boundaries of fairness, provides a viable framework for grappling with addressing diversity and racism within this professional tradition. Analyzing one's own moral boundaries within the context of oppression theory, along with research evidence of antidotes to marginalization, suggests strategies for change.

In addition to holding beliefs about who should be entitled to social justice, we have differing perspectives about what is just. In the next section, a framework is presented for helping students look at their beliefs about social justice and critically assess them within the context of contemporary theories.

SOCIAL JUSTICE PERSPECTIVES

The premise of this book is that diversity education is inextricably linked with social justice. Yet, the term "social justice" is widely used in social work without a clearly articulated and shared definition or understanding of it. Rather than providing a definition, it is our premise that diversity education for social justice involves challenging students to ask critical questions in order to help them examine, challenge, and, if needed, modify or change their perspectives about justice. General questions that need to be raised include the following: What is justice? What is fairness? Is life fair or just? What kind of justice can be expected? Moreover, these questions challenge further thinking about what can and should be considered as basic human rights. What rights are people entitled to as human beings? Alternatively, what are privileges and on what basis should individuals enjoy these? Should privilege be based on merit and to what should merit entitle individuals? What do people have a right to simply because they are human beings and regardless of other factors?

In discussions about social justice, it is important to recognize that conceptually there are different types of social justice and there are different understandings of these types of social justice. Our perspective is premised on the concept of distributive justice, which emphasizes society's accountability to the individual. The issue of how goods and resources are distributed in a society raises questions such as: Who gets what? What is a fair way to distribute goods and resources? Should distribution be based on rights or privileges? If privilege, privilege based on what? Diversity education for social justice includes critical thinking about these questions and more specific questions such as: Is it fair to take (e.g., through taxes) from one group in order to give to another group? When is it fair and when is it not fair to do so? When it is acceptable, should the redistribution be based on rights or privileges? Under what conditions is it a form of justice and fairness and when is it an infringe-ment on people's freedom? In a situation where the goods and services pro-duced are inadequate to satisfy everyone's desire for them, on what basis or according to what principles can these goods and services be distributed justly? For example, if you believe that everyone has a *right* to food and there is an inadequate supply, on what basis do you distribute it? If you believe that hav-ing food is a *privilege*, then what do people have to do to earn it? And what should be done when people who have not earned it get food and those who earn it do not get food? In a situation where the goods and services produced are adequate to satisfy everyone's desire for them, on what basis or according to what principles can they be distributed justly?

By asking questions such as these, we begin to struggle with the question of justice. What is it? Is justice equality? Is justice having freedom? Whether we are aware of them or not, each of us has beliefs in certain principles, theo-ries of what justice is, and certain assumptions related to those beliefs. Per-spectives about what is just and fair are often related to one's own position in relation to power and privilege. And that position is based on facets of one's social identity that are associated with access or lack of access to power and privilege and thus, to resources. When teaching diversity content social work educators need to have clarity about their own position about social justice concepts as well as how they intend to integrate social justice advocacy into diversity content. The following provides a framework that identifies prin-ciples and contemporary social justice theories with which to approach these complex questions and issues.

Five competing contemporary theories of distributive justice illustrate the complexity of examining one's own perspective. Three perspectives—utilitar-ian (Hare, 1992; Sidgwick, 1966), libertarian (Nozick, 1974), and egalitarian (Rawls, 1971)—are prescriptive rather than descriptive in that they present a case for what social justice *should* be or distinct ways that social justice should be defined. A fourth conceptual perspective, the racial contract (Mills, 1997), differs in that it is descriptive rather than prescriptive. The racial contract perspective addresses the situation as it is now, in other words, what the state of our society and the world is in relation to achieving any semblance of social justice. A fifth view, a human rights perspective, is gaining ground because of its assumptions about social justice. Each of these five conceptual perspectives is briefly discussed below. Together, they provide a theoretical framework from which students can examine and critically analyze their own perspectives.

Utilitarian Perspective

The major proponent of the utilitarian perspective of social justice is John Stuart Mills (Sterba, 1985). The key question from this perspective is: What distribution of goods, what principles of justice, what ascriptions of rights are such that their acceptance is in the general interest? Justice is arrived at by weighing relative benefits and harms and determining what maximizes the greatest good for the greatest number of people. Thus, from a utilitarian perspective, it may be determined that social justice exists even if some people have no rights met and others have all their rights met as long as it is determined that it is for the common good. Utilitarian justice tends to produce a distribution of goods and services similar to a bell curve with most people getting their needs met and a small percentage getting none of their needs met while another small percentage gets more than what they need.

The definition of the common good is open to varied viewpoints and the definition determines whether one believes a situation is just or not. For example, some people believe that it is not for the common good if some people are provided for when they can provide for themselves. On the other hand, others may argue that when some groups are not provided for, the common good is not served because there may be unrest or because it harms us morally as individuals and as a society.

Libertarian Perspective

In contrast to the utilitarian perspective, the libertarian position advanced by Robert Nozick (1974) is based on the principle that the distribution of resources occurs by means of a natural and social lottery. Distribution, therefore, is naturally uneven. This theory is considered to be amoral and based on a description of the social contract as it occurs naturally, i.e., that there are laws of nature that regulate distribution. According to the libertarian perspective, people hold certain rights by entitlement. Thus, justice consists in the widest possible latitude of freedom from coercion in what people accumulate and what, how, and when they dispose of it. This view would suggest, for example, that those opposed to taxation should not be coerced into compliance. On the other hand, tax dollars going to the military may be acceptable because the military may be accepted as a protection for this fundamental freedom.

This perspective sees a rebalancing of justice as naturally occurring over time. Thus, when looking at people who are oppressed we are only seeing a snapshot in time. From this view, if we were to look over time we might see that this oppressed group was the oppressor in the past and/or may become oppressors in the future. Also, from this perspective, it is good to give to others and charity is considered a virtue. However, in a just society each person has the freedom to determine how much, to whom, and when to give. No institution or person should interfere with that basic freedom.

Egalitarian Perspective

Egalitarian theory, based on Locke's theory of the social contract and developed by John Rawls (1971), maintains that designing a just society needs to be done under a veil of ignorance, meaning that the designers would not know in advance what their position in that society would be and thus would have a stake in avoiding extreme inequalities at the outset.

In such a just society, two egalitarian principles would rule out accepting inequalities in order to achieve a greater common good (utilitarianism) or to maintain individual freedom (libertarianism). The first principle requires that basic liberties must be equal, because citizens of a just society have the same basic rights to freedom, to fair equality of opportunity, to access to goods and services, and to self-respect. The second principle asserts that although the actual distribution of income and wealth need not be equal, that any inequalities in power, wealth, and other resources must not exist *unless* they work to the absolute benefit of the worst off members of society.

From an egalitarian perspective, in contrast to the libertarian view, redistribution of resources is a moral obligation. The unmet needs that should be redressed first should be of those who are most in need. This means that, to provide genuine equality of opportunity, society must give more attention to those with fewer native assets and to those born into the less favorable social positions. For example, according to egalitarian principles, greater resources might be spent on the education of the less rather than the more intelligent students in our schools, at least in the earlier years, to ensure equality of opportunity in life.

The Racial Contract

In his book titled *The Racial Contract* (1997), Charles Mills provides a way of connecting the previous perspectives about what *should* be with what *is* in terms of the reality of the injustices that are so prevalent in our society and world. Mills' perspective is based on the social contract tradition that is also central to the other three contemporary social justice theories. From this perspective, however, the notion of the social contract being the basis of Western democratic societies is in fact a myth; the actual (i.e., in practice) basis of Western societies is a racial contract. The basic difference between Mills' perspective of social justice and the other three is that the peculiar social contract to which Mills refers is not a contract between everybody (as in "we the people"), but rather is a contract only between people who count, that is the people who are considered to be *people*, as in "we the White people."

Utilitarians, libertarians, and egalitarians use the social contract as a *normative* tool, that is as an *ideal* social contract that explains how a just society, ruled by a moral government, *should* be formed and regulated by a defensible moral code. Mills' (1997) usage of the social contract is different. He uses it not merely normatively, but *descriptively*, to explain the *actual* genesis of a society, a people's moral psychology, and how a government functions. The racial contract thus explains how an unjust, exploitative society, ruled by an oppressive government and regulated by an immoral code, came into existence.

According to the racial contract, it is crucial to understand what the original and continuing social contract actually was and is, so that we can correct for it in constructing the ideal contract toward which social work can then strive. The social contract has always consisted of formal and informal agreements between the members of one subset of individuals who are designated as White (dominant) and thus seen as legitimate. The remaining subset of individuals who are designated as "non-White" (subordinate) and of a different and inferior moral status of subpersons are not a participatory, consenting party to the contract but rather are the objects being acted upon instead of subjects acting on the agreement.

Thus, the moral and legal rules normally regulating the behavior of Whites in their dealings with one another do not apply at all in dealings with non-Whites or apply in an equivocated form. Mills' main point is that the general purpose of the social contract, in reality, has always been the differential privileging of Whites as a group with respect to non-Whites as a group. From the beginning then, race is not an afterthought or a deviation from ostensibly race-neutral Western ideals of the social contract, but rather a formative constituent of those ideals. This view helps us to clarify that, although the social contract is ostensibly committed to moral egalitarianism, the ethical theories that the interests of all matter equally and all must have equal rights are and have always been of restricted scope. In other words, the commitment to moral egalitarianism is explicitly or implicitly intended by its proponents to be restricted to and applied only to those in a dominant position (i.e., Whites).

The racial contract has a strong claim as an actual historical fact. Mills describes specific derivative contracts designed for different modes of exploitation of the resources and peoples of the rest of the world all for the benefit of Europe. For example, the slavery contract, colonial contract, and expropriation contract granted Europeans an absolute dominion over all territories of the world, not by virtue of any conquest of them, but as a right acquired simply by "discovery."

Human Rights Perspective

A human rights perspective also has begun to gain ground in social work as an organizing concept for addressing social justice issues. This view is premised on social work's core values of meeting human needs and developing human potential and resources. From this perspective social justice "encompasses satisfaction of basic human needs and the equitable sharing of material resources" (United Nations, 1992, p. 16). Human rights are seen as inherent in our nature and without them we could not live as human beings because they are integral to a life with dignity and respect. Thus human rights are universal and a basic entitlement, without discrimination. This is a shift from a "defensive stance against oppression to an affirmation of the right to satisfaction of material and non-material human needs and equitable participation in the production and distribution of resources" associated with increased sociopolitical awareness and economic improvement (United Nations, 1992, p. 6). Basic rights include the assurance of freedom, certainty of social justice, and assurance of the social and international order needed to realize one's rights and freedoms. To develop and exercise our human capabilities (e.g., intelligence, talents, and conscience in meeting our needs), qualities are identified that are in people's lives when dignity is present. These include, but are not limited to, life, bodily health, bodily integrity (i.e., freedom to move where one chooses), senses, imagination and thought, emotions (e.g., forming attachments and not having emotional development limited by fear and anxiety), affiliation, play, and control over one's physical and social environment (Nussbaum, 2000, 2001). This perspective broadens the discussion on how the presence of human rights in individual's lives enhances quality of life issues. Further, it stimulates thinking about variation and similarity between and within diverse populations, based on social identity and cultural values, in how these rights might be expressed.

IMPLICATIONS OF DIVERSE SOCIAL JUSTICE PERSPECTIVES: THE ROLE OF CRITICAL ANALYSIS

The diverse conceptualizations of social justice represent differing popular perspectives about what social justice is or should be. When we say in social work education that social workers need to see social problems and individual troubles through a social justice lens, it is important to recognize the various lenses and the underlying value assumptions that provide differing views on what is just. In the classroom, this requires faculty familiarity with social justice concepts, paying attention to value assumptions of the views that are put forward, and challenging students to engage in critical thinking.

While there are differences within the profession regarding the definition of social justice, it is often proposed that the egalitarian theory is closest to traditional social work values and ethics. Wakefield (1988), for example, argues that "social work strives to ensure that no person is deprived of a fair minimum level of those basic social goods to which everyone is entitled," and supports Rawls' inclusion of self-respect in the list of social goods (p. 187). Yet, there is also evidence that, while perhaps holding to egalitarian principles as the ideal, social workers may tend to operate from a utilitarian perspective in practice (Conrad, 1988; Reisch & Taylor, 1983). For instance, terms such as "cost-benefit analysis" and "triage" strategies related to managed care realities might point to a utilitarian approach to promoting justice.

As we prepare students to promote social and economic justice, it is important to address these differing views. The first three contemporary theories (egalitarian, utilitarian, libertarian) are normative and provide a useful tool for thinking about what social justice should be. However, they have serious limitations in that they do not explain why certain groups of people consistently get less justice. They do not acknowledge, tackle, or explain the phenomenon of oppression. The racial contract, on the other hand, is a conceptual bridge between the normative and the reality of race relations. The human rights perspective can be seen as building on the racial contract's description of what is by proposing a universal meeting of the human needs of all as a solution. On the one hand, there is the world of mainstream philosophy (such as the three contemporary theories of distributive justice) that focuses discussions about justice and rights in the abstract. On the other hand, there is the world of analysis and writing that focuses on issues of domination, conquest, imperialism, colonialism, racism, slavery, apartheid, and reparations due to the overwhelming presence of these events in the histories of some peoples.

The racial contract as a concept provides a conceptual tool for integrating issues of cultural diversity, social and economic justice, and the impact of oppression on populations at risk. To endorse and implement an *ideal social contract*, the *non-ideal* contract as it exists needs to be demystified and discarded. A major goal of critical analysis is to identify and acknowledge the reality of oppression. Critical analysis of the way things *are* engages us in normative work, such as advocacy, to work toward a just world. Critical analysis facilitates our understanding of the social contract's real history and how its values and concepts have functioned to rationalize oppression. In its focus on surfacing underlying value assumptions embedded in ideas, critical thinking makes salient the ubiquitous exclusion of oppression in traditional perspectives of social justice.

SUMMARY

In this chapter, we presented fundamental concepts and issues with the goal of providing the foundation for a conceptual framework for diversity education that is aimed at promoting social and economic justice. The beginning point for such a framework is a focus on racism as the fundamental form of oppression from which other forms of oppression can be understood. We proposed that diversity education be derived from postmodernism, constructivism, and constructionism in order to hear the multitude of voices and experiences that have been rendered invisible and to critically examine knowledge construction about issues of diversity. Discussion about multiple identities and multiple oppressions illustrated the complex dynamics related to issues of power and privilege. The concept of moral exclusion was presented as a tool for helping students explore their beliefs about who is deemed worthy of being treated fairly and justly.

Five contemporary perspectives were presented as a way to help students engage in critical thinking about their own perspectives and to challenge them to modify or change those perspectives. Distributive justice theory provides a basis for understanding the complexity of our notions about what social justice *should be* and the reality of social injustice as it currently exists. Analysis of our notions about social justice leads to a recognition that the beliefs we hold about social justice are race- and gender-based. This process illuminates the presence of oppression, its dynamics, and how it shows up differentially in regard to diverse populations. Questions posed about social justice in this chapter included, Is life fair? Is life just?, and through the concept of moral exclusion, addressed the further question, Justice and fairness for whom?

The racial contract reveals that some people are seen as expendable or undeserving and are thus excluded from the realm of social justice. That is to say, some people have not been included in or benefited from the social contract. They are vulnerable to the negative labeling placed on those groups with which they identify. Their oppression and exclusion are thus premised on stereotypes and prejudicial attitudes related to ethnocentrism. Oppressions are characterized by social rather than individual power, institutionalization of norms, practices and laws that maintain their political hold, and are held in place by ideology and violence (real and threatened). A human rights perspective of social justice provides the solution that all people are entitled to the same universal rights, without discrimination.

In the next chapter, we turn to the sociopolitical context in which we live and how it poses challenges for us as we build an inclusive curriculum aimed at promoting social justice.

REFERENCES

Allen, J. A. (1993). The constructivist paradigm: Values and ethics. *Journal of Teaching in Social Work, 8*(1/2), 31–54.

Allport, G. (1954). *The nature of prejudice.* Reading, MA: Addison-Wesley.

Best, S., & Kellner, D. (1991). *Postmodern theory: Critical interrogations.* New York: The Guilford Press.

Blumenfeld, W. J., & Raymond, D. (2000). Prejudice and discrimination. In M. Adams, W. J. Blumenfeld, R. Castenada, H. W. Hackman, M. L. Peters, & X. Zuniga (Eds.), *Readings for diversity and social justice.* New York: Routledge.

Bulhan, H. A. (1985). *Frantz Fanon and the psychology of oppression.* New York: Plenum Press.

Chambon, A. S., & Irving, A. (1999). Introduction. In A. S. Chambon, A. Irving, & L. Epstein (Eds.), *Reading Foucault for social work.* New York: Columbia University Press.

Chambon, A. S., Irving, A., & Epstein, L. (Eds.) (1999). *Reading Foucault for social work.* New York: Columbia University Press.

Conrad, A. P. (1988). The role of field instructors in the transmission of social justice values. *Journal of Teaching in Social Work, 2*(2), 63–82.

Council on Social Work Education. (2001). *Educational policy and accreditation standards.* Alexandria, VA: Author.

Deutsch, M. (1990). Psychological roots of moral exclusion. *Journal of Social Issues, 46*(1), 21–26.

Fellin, P. (2000). Revisiting multiculturalism in social work. *Journal of Social Work Education, 36*(2), 261–278.

Foucault, M. (1980). *Power and knowledge.* New York: Pantheon Books.

Gaertner, S. L., & Dovidio, J. F. (1981). Racism among the well-intentioned. In E. Clausen & J. Bermingham (Eds.), *Pluralism, racism and public policy: The search for equality.* New York: Macmillan.

Garcia-Bahne, B. (1981). *Ideological images: Social psychological considerations on the stereotyping process.* Paper presented at the Conference on Ethnic American Women, Program for the Study of Women and Men in Society, University of Southern California.

Gergen, K. (1991). *The saturated self.* New York: Basic Books.

Gergen, K. (2001). Psychological science in a postmodern context. *American Psychologist, 56*(10), 803–813.

Gil, D. (1998). *Confronting injustice and oppression: Concepts and strategies for social workers.* New York: Columbia University Press.

Gillem, A. R., Cohn, L. R., & Throne, C. (2001). Black identity in biracial black/white people: A comparison of Jacqueline who refuses to be exclusively black and Adolphus who wishes he were. *Cultural Diversity and Ethnic Minority Psychology, 7*(2), 182–196.

Goldberg, G., & Middleman, R. (1980). It might be a boa constrictor digesting an elephant: Vision stretching in social work education. *International Journal of Social Work Education, 3*(1), 213–225.

Gouldner, A. W. (1976). *The dialectic of ideology and technology.* New York: Oxford University Press.

Hare, R. M. (1992). Justice and equality. In J. P. Sterba (Ed.), *Justice: Alternative political perspectives* (pp. 185–199). Belmont, CA: Wadsworth.

Hong, Y., Morris, M. W., Chiu, C., Benet-Martinez, V. (2000). Multicultural minds. *American Psychologist, 55*(7), 709–720.

Irving, A. (1999). Waiting for Foucault: Social work and the multitudinous truth(s) of life. In A. Chambon, A. Irving, & L. Epstein (Eds.), *Reading Foucault for social work.* New York: Columbia University Press.

Kovel, J. (1984). *White racism*. New York: Columbia University Press.

Lee, M., & Greene, G. J. (1999). A social constructivist framework for integrating cross-cultural issues in teaching clinical social work. *Journal of Social Work Education, 35*(1), 21–37.

Lichtenberg, P., van Beusekom, J., & Gibbons, D. (1997). *Encountering bigotry: Befriending projecting persons in everyday life*. Northvale, NJ: Jason Aronson.

Lieberman, L., Stevenson, B., & Reynolds, L. (1989). Race and anthropology: A core concept without consensus. *Anthropology and Education Quarterly, 20*, 67–73.

Lott, B. (2002). Cognitive and behavioral distancing from the poor. *American Psychologist, 57*(2), 100–110.

Maturana, H. R. (1988). Reality: The search for objectivity or the quest for a compelling argument. *Irish Journal of Psychology, 9*, 25–82.

McIntosh, P. (1989). White privilege: Unpacking the invisible knapsack. *Peace and Freedom*, July/August, 10–12.

Miller, J. B. (1976). *Toward a new psychology of women*. Boston: Beacon Press.

Miller, S. (1997). The future of disinterest and Foucault's regime of truth. *Partisan Review, 64*(1), 28-36.

Mills, C. W. (1997). *The racial contract*. Ithaca, NY: Cornell.

Minuchin, S. (1991). The seductions of constructivism. *Networker*, September–October, 47–50.

Nozick, R. (1974). *Anarchy, state, and utopia*. New York: Basic Books.

Nussbaum, M. (2000). *Women and human development: The capabilities approach*. Cambridge, England: Cambridge University Press.

Nussbaum, M. (2001). *Upheavals of thought: The intelligence of emotions*. Cambridge, England: Cambridge University Press.

Omi, M., & Winant, H. (1986). *Racial formation in the United States from the 1960's to the 1980's*. New York: Routledge.

Opotow, S. (1990). Moral exclusion and injustice: An introduction. *Journal of Social Issues, 46*(1), 1–20.

Phinney, J. S. (1996). When we talk about American ethnic groups, what do we mean? *American Psychologist, 51*(9), 918–927.

Pincus, F. L. (2000). Discrimination comes in many forms: Individual, institutional and structural. In M. Adams, W. J. Blumenfeld, R. Castenada, H. W. Hackman, M. L. Peters, & X. Zuniga (Eds.), *Readings for diversity and social justice*. New York: Routledge.

Pinderhughes, E. (1989). *Understanding race, ethnicity and power: The key to efficacy in clinical practice.* New York: The Free Press.

Ponterotto, J. G., Rao, V., Zweig, J., Rieger, B. P., Schaefer, K., Michalakou, S., Armenia, B. & Goldstein, H. (2001). The relationship of acculturation and gender to attitudes toward counseling in Italian and Greek American college students. *Cultural Diversity and Ethnic Minority Psychology, 7*(4), 362–375.

Rawls, J. (1971). *A theory of justice.* Cambridge, MA: Harvard University Press.

Reich, W. (1970). *The mass psychology of fascism.* New York: Farrar, Straus & Giroux.

Reisch, M., & Taylor, C. T. (1983). Ethical guidelines for cutback management: A preliminary approach. *Administration in Social Work, 7*(3/4), 59–72.

Rifkin, J. (2000). *The age of access.* New York: Jeremy P. Tarcher/Putnam.

Rodwell, M. K. (1998). *Social work constructivist research.* New York: Garland Publishing.

Rose, S. (2002). *Social work at the crossroads: A reflection.* Paper presented at the Social Work at the Crossroads Conference, Califronia State University, Fresno, Department of Social Work Education, March 15, 2002.

Rossiter, A. (2001). The professional is political: An interpretation of the problem of the past in solution-focused therapy. *American Journal of Orthopsychiatry, 70*(2), 150–161.

Saleebey, D. (1994). Culture, theory, and narrative: The intersection of meanings in practice. *Social Work, 39*(4), 351–359.

Schoem, D., Frankel, L., Zuniga, X., & Lewis, E. (1995). The meaning of multicultural teaching: An introduction. In D. Schoem, L. Frankel, X. Zuniga, & E. Lewis (Eds.), *Multicultural teaching in the university.* Westport, CT: Praeger.

Sfeir-Younis. (1995). Reflections on the teaching of multicultural courses. In D. Schoem, L. Frankel, X. Zuniga, & E. Lewis (Eds.), *Multicultural teaching in the university.* Westport, CT: Praeger.

Sidgwick, H. (1966). *The methods of ethics.* New York: Dover.

Sterba, J. P. (1985). From liberty to welfare. *Social Theory and Practice, 11*(3), 285–305.

Tatem, B. D. (2000). Defining racism: "Can we talk?" In M. Adams, W. J. Blumenfeld, R. Castenada, H. W. Hackman, M. L. Peters, & X. Zuniga (Eds.), *Readings for diversity and social justice.* New York: Routledge.

United Nations (1992). *Teaching and learning about human rights: A manual for schools of social work and the social work profession*. New York: Author.

Wakefield, J. C (1988, June). Psychotherapy, distributive justice, and social work. Part I: Distributive justice as a conceptual framework for social work. *Social Service Review*, June, 187–210.

Walker, R., & Staton, M. (2000). Multiculturalism in social work ethics. *Journal of Social Work Education, 36*(3), 449–462.

Wildman, S. M., & Davis, A. D. (2000). Language and silence: Making systems of privilege visible. In M. Adams, W. J. Blumenfeld, R. Castenada, H. W. Hackman, M. L. Peters, & X. Zuniga (Eds.), *Readings for diversity and social justice*. New York: Routledge.

Wright, L. (1994, July 25). One drop of blood. *The New Yorker*, 46–55.

Yee, A. H., Fairchild, H. H., Weizmann, F., & Wyatt, G. (1993). Addressing psychology's problems with race. *American Psychologist, 48*(11), 1132–1140.

Young, I. M. (2000). Five faces of oppression. In M. Adams, W. J. Blumenfeld, R. Castenada, H. W. Hackman, M. L. Peters, & X. Zuniga (Eds.), *Readings for diversity and social justice*. New York: Routledge.

Zuniga, X., & Nagda, B. A. (1995). Dialogue groups: An innovative approach to multicultural learning. In D. Schoem, L. Frankel, X. Zuniga, & E. Lewis (Eds.), *Multicultural teaching in the university*. Westport, CT: Praeger.

Chapter Three

Integrating Diversity for Social Justice Content Into the Curriculum Within the Sociopolitical Context of Today

In Chapter One, some issues and obstacles to building an inclusive curriculum aimed at promoting social justice were discussed. One of the obstacles presented was the current social and political reality of living in a troubled and polarized country, which is the focus of this chapter. There is sharp polarization today on a range of issues such as affirmative action and quotas, gay rights, values in public education, and multiculturalism. Such polarization has been described as a culture war that is characterized by two camps: the cultural conservatives or moral traditionalists and the liberals or cultural progressives (Hunter, 1991). The cultural conservatives represent those who have a commitment to an external authority that provides a consistent and unchangeable definition of the truth and of what is good. The cultural progressives, on the other hand, are those who view truth as a process that is ever unfolding and view moral authority as emerging from a variety of inner sources rather than an external authority (Van Soest, 1995). In this chapter, we will first discuss the culture war debate about multiculturalism and social work's ambivalent position in the debate. In order to ground and guide social workers in making decisions about strategies that promote social and economic justice, basic values and principles are then suggested. The chapter ends with a discussion of educational issues related to teaching diversity content within the current social and political climate.

THE CULTURE WARS AND THE DEBATE ABOUT MULTICULTURALISM

The culture war, grounded in such differing moral visions, is a conflict over how our coexistence is to be ordered. As Hunter (1991) purports, "The contemporary culture war is ultimately a struggle over national identity, over the *meaning of America*, who we have been in the past, who we are now, and perhaps most important who we, as a nation, will aspire to become in the new millennium" (p. 50). Among other things, the September 11 terrorist actions at the Pentagon, the World Trade Center in New York City, and in Pennsylvania have touched the foundation of our national identity as Americans, heightened our need for safety, and challenged us to think about our role in the international community and our relationships with other countries. We have seen how fear, anxiety, and anger can lead to unprovoked aggression against the other, specifically those of Middle Eastern phenotypes and backgrounds, even as there is a reaffirmation of resiliency and national unity. Following September 11, there was increased sensitivity about how analyses of the events and causes were framed. It was a difficult time to address the possibility of uneven American foreign policy in the Middle East for fear that one would be perceived as unpatriotic and/or anti-Semitic. In this changing and highly sensitive intellectual and political environment, critical thinking about anti-racism, sexism, classism, heterosexism, and the other isms is more important than ever. In addition, opportunities for change in the unfolding of events can encourage us to face and reevaluate our place in the global community.

It is expected that the culture wars will continue to be at the forefront as we struggle with our responses to the unfolding national and international events of the 21st century. And our educational institutions will be in the eye of the storm because they play a central role in influencing the formation and reproduction of national identity for Americans. Higher education is important symbolic terrain in the broader culture wars as we raise central concerns such as those posed by the following questions: What do we want higher education to be about? What are the values driving our educational institutions? Will the heightened focus on reassuring unity survive the test of time? Will it limit rigorous critical thinking and analysis? As educators we can keep in focus the opportunities for highlighting complexity of race and ethnicity and its implications for practice in the midst of sociopolitical turbulence. When challenges are faced, the controversies that are generated for discussion can strengthen our understanding of diversity and social justice.

The controversy over multiculturalism in colleges and universities that began in the late 1960s and early 1970s continues today. It is within this enduring context of controversy and the current realities of our post-September 11 climate that social work diversity for social justice curriculum is developing. Within the two camps of the culture war context, there are three major themes in the current multiculturalism debate, all of which are relevant to social work education: (a) visions of community, (b) the quality of education, and (c) social change. Opposing perspectives within each of these themes will be discussed in relation to higher education in general and, more specifically, in relation to social work.[1]

Competing Visions of Community

Multiculturalism in higher education raises issues around how people can and should live together. On the one hand, interest in protecting minority group identity is viewed by progressives as a steppingstone to community building. On the other hand, neo-conservatives see minority group identity as a threat to community building. Advocates of multiculturalism promote building a national community with a vision of one nation based on appreciation of differences and unique qualities as sources of strength rather than division. Opponents of multiculturalism see it as tearing the community apart. Each of these perspectives about community and how we are to live together is briefly presented, followed by thoughts about the social work position.

Fragmentation of Community

Cultural conservatives perceive activism and advocacy on the part of marginalized, excluded, and disadvantaged groups as a threat to American identity. The dominant culture promotes a single banner under which all in this nation must join (Hunter, 1991). The push for a national identity, unity, and solidarity has gained tremendous support following the September 11 attacks and subsequent war. Based on the assumption that conflict within our nation is divisive, cultural conservatives fear that the assertion of diverse identities causes fragmentation. There is also a fear that one of the advocacy special interest groups will become dominant over all others. From this perspective, affirmative action is seen as increasing racial tension and violence. A monolithic view of national identity is promoted. In addition, from this perspective curriculum should promote the view that certain accomplishments of Western culture are superior and should be imported into other societies as a resource (Howe & Takaki, 1991).

Protection of Group Identity

The progressive vision of community, on the other hand, is based on the premise that it is not possible to live together in community without a sense of identity and pride in one's uniqueness (Gordon & Bhattacharyya, 1992).

---

[1] This section is adapted from Van Soest, 1995. Used with permission.

The cost of assimilating into one American prototype is deemed to be too high for people of color who have been expected to abandon their distinctive identities and assimilate into the White or European norm, while White Americans have not had to assimilate at all (Powell, 1992). It is maintained that, while people of European origin may have lost their sense of ethnic origin, they have not had to give up their identity as White or European. According to this view, the Western, universalistic depiction of culture in the curriculum excludes different perspectives and truths, particularly those that have been ignored or silenced. Further, learning about and appreciating humanity as a whole makes it possible to learn to live in a community based on cultural pluralism and diversity rather than cultural assimilation.

Social Work Vision of Community

According to Pinderhughes (1989), the assimilationist perspective was the guiding ethic of the social work profession until the 1960s. Problematic definitions about what is deemed pathological and deviant dominated the theoretical constructs that determined assessment and intervention methods, the strategies devised, the programming of services, and the evaluation of outcomes. All of these had been developed in terms of what seemed appropriate for the White American middle class (Pinderhughes, 1989). In this book, we assert that a White, European norm for social work practice is still dominant. A study of articles in four major social work journals during the 1980s revealed the influence of the conservative perspective on our profession and concluded that social work with minorities is a marginal interest for the profession and that the practice literature related to minorities tends to be naïve and superficial (McMahon & Allen-Meares, 1992). It is within the context of this reality that this book proposes that knowledge about race and other diversities has been socially constructed and that diversity education for social justice requires a deconstructionist approach to diversity narratives.

Educational Quality

The quality of higher education is important to both sides of the culture wars debate, but each view differs in terms of what standards are appropriate and what constitutes educational enrichment. The differing perspectives can be characterized by which concern is primary: cultural conservatives fear that educational standards will be lowered while cultural progressives are committed to strengthening and enriching the educational experience through diversity.

Lowering of Educational Standards

Cultural conservatives claim that greater ethnic and racial inclusiveness automatically means either a lowering of standards or no standards at all. This claim is based on two convictions: (a) that there are universal standards that supersede all others, and (b) that certain populations have made lesser contributions to knowledge and have lower academic achievement than others. A blatant statement of this position is made by Bloom (1987) in his writing about race on campus: "The fact is that the average black student's achievements do not equal those of the average white student in the good universities and everybody knows it" (p. 96).

Educational Enrichment

Cultural progressives, in contrast, view society's diversity as a positive source of individual and institutional enrichment. They call for an end to an overemphasis on the European influences in American culture that neglects the contributions made by people of color. They believe that education will be enriched by the inclusion of different experiences, perspectives, and truths. Standards are as important to this side of the debate as they are to the cultural conservatives. The difference is that this perspective takes issue with the fact that standards reflect a European perspective, are not universal, are not the highest, and are not the only standard.

Social Work and Educational Quality

Perspectives that parallel those in the broader societal debate can be inferred from discussions within social work education in the 1960s and 1970s. During that time, the Council on Social Work Education's (CSWE) accreditation standard on nondiscrimination for schools of social work stirred up considerable debate and activity around methods of selection, recruitment, and retention of students of color. A concern about the lowering of educational standards is evident in those debates. For example, a 1966 CSWE-sponsored meeting involving 25 schools of social work addressed the issue of providing graduate education to people disadvantaged by their depressed economic and social status and inadequate academic preparation. Some of the concerns expressed at that meeting were that disadvantaged groups might be better served in ways other than graduate study because they would surely fail. Even though there was sympathy with the aspirations of the disadvantaged, it was felt that it was owed to the profession to give the top students priority for acceptance and that, if disadvantaged students were admitted, they would not only lower the academic standard but also create a double standard (Robertson, 1968). Other meetings revealed similar concerns while, at the same time, the educational enrichment perspective emerged as a vocal and influential force in shaping the curriculum standards.

In light of ongoing affirmative action legal decisions, schools of social work continue to face making decisions related to increasing diversity of their faculty and student bodies. This book is based on the premise that education is enriched by diverse voices, both in relation to knowledge construction and learning processes in the classroom.

Social Change

Early in the development of new multicultural curricula on university and college campuses, there was a strong social justice attitude inherent in discussions about helping students to understand the partiality of traditional studies, the nature of difference and dominance, and the effects of power and privilege (Butler & Schmitz, 1992). Multicultural curriculum provided both critical analysis of underlying assumptions (e.g., what was missing) and introduced content that had previously been excluded and was thus invisible. In today's sociopolitical climate, cultural progressives continue to favor a social justice agenda that emphasizes plurality of voices while cultural conservatives support tradition and the status quo. The core of the disagreement is related to differing views about the role of higher education in relation to social change and, inevitably, power. Both sides call for open inquiry in higher education, but each sees the other as threatening academic freedom of thought that both sides see as the essence of a university.

Political Correctness Versus Social Justice Perspective

The concept of "political correctness" (PC) has evolved into two different and disparate uses. Cultural conservatives use the PC term to describe how they see the social justice agenda changing and politicizing academic curricula by stifling freedom of thought and expression. Their view is that education is neutral, unbiased, and apolitical. They purport that content and ideas about diversity are defined by political criteria that offer a significant example of a presumed distinction between oppressors and oppressed. They allege that the central idea of diversity education is "to give an academic gloss to an implied power struggle and to organize the academy on a political basis without seeming to do so. The net effect is not the encouragement of open inquiry in higher education but attitude adjustment, if not ideological indoctrination" (Hunter, 1991, pp. 218–219). In addition to being attacked on this basis of political correctness, affirmative action programs are seen as violating a conservative sense of social justice. D'Souza (1992) articulates this view by suggesting that the "basic question of 'who belongs' at the university now has two answers: which one you get depends on the color of your skin. Consequently, there is no uniform standard of justice, which, as Aristotle observed, is the only lasting basis for community" (p. 50).

Cultural progressives, by contrast, see traditional education from a political perspective as being inherently political and biased in favor of the status quo and operating under the same repressive assumptions that undergird American society as a whole. According to this viewpoint, the major works of education have come from a patriarchal European perspective that promoted selective attention to what is valid to study and that is infused with racism. Thus, they maintain, only a small part of the human experience has really been studied and because that experience was studied by dominant cultures it can be said to be in part contaminated by dominant world views (i.e., views that are racist, sexist, heterosexist, and imperialist).

Further, social justice advocates criticize proponents of the conservative PC perspective as being "political hypocrites." Some charge that the cultural conservatives' real motive is to advocate for a standardized curriculum designed to exclusively promote capitalist and Christian values (e.g., one true faith). Instead of honestly proposing their agenda, "the new . . . tactic is to claim unbiased objectivity, then to denounce the faults of the present-day academy from that ostensibly non-ideological stance, and finally to demand reforms that turn out to be highly ideological and politicized (although never acknowledged as such)" (Davidson, 1991, p. 10).

It is interesting to note that the original intention of PC was to evoke reflection and curiosity about how certain terms can be laden with biased sociopolitical and historical meanings. The idea behind it was to encourage people to think critically about the language they use, develop some understanding about the complexity of meaning making in the lives of others different from themselves, and probe into the worldviews of others while conveying the same respectfulness that they would want to be accorded. Thus, social justice advocates promote the value of including the voices of those who have traditionally been disenfranchised from the prevailing power structures.

Social Work and Social Change

CSWE (2001) curriculum standards clearly place social work in the social justice camp of the debate. However, in actual practice, the social work profession displays considerable ambivalence about its commitment to social justice. And students often express ambivalence and even outright resistance in relation to appreciating difference. This book is premised on: the fundamental belief that diversity education in social work means education for social justice; advancing inclusion of diversity content by bringing the interests of the disenfranchised to the center; and ending bigotry and discrimination. We believe that, to decrease the ambivalence of the profession about its commitment to social justice, social work education must involve critical thinking and open inquiry. An examination and understanding of how distributive justice has traditionally been defined and how cultural and political power is exercised is central to such critical analysis.

The concepts presented in Chapter Two on racism, oppression, and social justice have clear implications related to strategies for social change. Recently, in parallel with post-September 11 unity movements, there have been movements regarding reparations and mobilization around globalization concerns. These social change movements arise from growing awareness of markets' priorities over social justice concerns and the specter of colonialism framed as international development. In the following section, basic values and principles are offered to help ground social workers in the social justice mission of the profession as they face current change movements and make decisions about their involvement.

SOCIAL JUSTICE VALUES AND PRINCIPLES TO GUIDE ACTIONS FOR SOCIAL CHANGE

Guiding Values

Many problems that social workers encounter at the micro, meso, and macro levels stem from injustices that are grounded in an underlying crisis of values. Social workers need to ground their social change strategies and actions in values and principles that hold out hope for remedying such underlying crises of values. Psychosocial and economic explanations for problems social workers encounter need to be reinforced by an understanding of different and deeper dimensions and by understanding the interrelation of the personal and socioeconomic and value structures and processes. There are many possible actions aimed at promoting social and economic justice. Social workers are faced with complex decisions about which actions to take in each particular situation. To guide their thinking, the following eight values are identified as being central to social workers' decision-making process. They are drawn from the human rights perspective of social justice and are intended to be illustrative rather than exhaustive.[2]

1. Life. Value for life is essential for all social and economic justice and human rights work. The worth of life, human and nonhuman existence, is the fountainhead for all other ideas and values that follow. Social workers are called to actively support positive and life-affirming aspects of all situations. Life is intrinsically connected and interdependent in all its parts and forms. Disruption of any aspect affects the social fabric or threat of life, thereby injuring humankind. Thus, value of life implies that suffering and death are not just individual phenomena but that they touch others. Physical health is an important aspect of the value and quality of life. Environmental deterioration, the water crisis, including pollution, and the nonexistence and curtailment of health programs are some of the major life-threatening factors.

2. Freedom and liberty. All human beings are born free and have the right to liberty. This presupposes that each human being has the freedom of choice in the conduct of his or her life. The enjoyment of this freedom is, however, frequently curtailed by material and other constraints. Freedom is likewise restricted by the principle of not infringing on the freedom of others. Yet freedom, next to life itself, is viewed as the most precious human value, closely linked to human dignity and to the worth of human life. The quest for freedom and liberty has inspired many people to seek release from territorial or geographical domination. The quest for spiritual and intellectual freedom has inspired heroic acts of resistance. Social workers are often in the forefront of the struggle for freedom. In parts of the world where freedom does not exist, they pay a heavy price in oppression for pursuing their principles.

3. Equality and nondiscrimination. The fundamental principle of equality of all human beings is imperfectly applied in everyday life, not least in the manifold aspects of interpersonal relations. For social workers it is a crucial concept related to personal and professional attitudes. It is also the cornerstone for the all-important principle of justice, requiring serious consideration of just and unjust equality and inequality based on biological factors; psychic, social, cultural, and spiritual needs, and on individual contributions

---

[2] The values are drawn from United Nations, 1992, pp. 14–19.

to the welfare of others. Once the principle of equality is accepted, it becomes impossible to discriminate against any person or group of persons.

4. Justice. Various aspects of justice have to be taken into consideration: the legal, judicial, social, economic, and other aspects that constitute the basis of a society upholding the dignity of its members, and ensuring security and integrity of persons. Social workers have long promoted such principles and are conscious of the fact that human rights are best upheld by a law-abiding state. Impartiality in the administration of justice is an important tool to safeguard the rights of the vulnerable members of society who make up the majority of social work clients. The pursuit of justice, however, has wider implications that are less easily codified. Social justice encompasses satisfaction of basic human needs and the equitable sharing of material resources. It aims at universal access to fundamental services in health, education, equal opportunities at the start, protection for disadvantaged persons or groups, and a degree of moderation in the areas of retribution, consumption, and profit.

5. Solidarity. This is a fundamental intrinsic value that implies not only understanding and empathy toward humankind's pain and suffering, but identifying and taking a stand with the sufferers and their cause. Social workers are expected not only to stand by people who are struggling, but also to express their solidarity in words and in deeds in the face of any form of denial of people's political, civil, social, economic, cultural, and spiritual rights. The social work profession must identify itself with victims of violence, torture, expulsion, and curtailment of freedom anywhere in the world.

6. Social responsibility. This is action undertaken on behalf of sufferers and victims: standing for them, championing their cause and helping them. Social responsibility is the implementation corollary of solidarity. The principle of social responsibility is crucial for a profession such as social work because service and commitment to the poor and the needy are its *raison d'être*.

7. Evolution, peace, and nonviolence. The values mentioned so far are determining factors for the quality of interpersonal relations. Peace, as a distinct value, and not simply as the absence of organized conflict, is one additional value. It is to be nurtured and striven for, with the ultimate goal of achieving harmony with the self, with others, and with the environment. While conflicts in human relations are unavoidable, ways to solve them can be peaceful or violent, constructive or destructive. The revolutionary "raze all and build anew" approach has held fascination for people over the centuries, producing untold human suffering. An evolutionary approach is slower, often less immediately rewarding, but in the end, longer lasting and therefore more effective. It is an approach often chosen by social workers in relation to conflicts. Confrontation and resistance in the quest for freedom is not eschewed. Neither is social justice. Violence is. While the world is not ready to abandon the use of arms, and just causes for revolutions clearly exist, it should be recognized that arbitration and conciliation are effective tools to overcome seemingly irreconcilable difference provided they are practiced consistently and with respect, understanding, and knowledge.

8. Relations between mankind and nature. Respect for other species and a quest for harmony with nature are more often permeating human consciousness in the 21st century. Environmental degradation cannot be ignored. The world economic order; faulty development models; inequality with regard to all resources; nuclear, industrial, and other pollution; and consumption patterns in industrialized as well as developing countries are recognized as causes of the earth's serious plight. Excessive consumerism and extreme poverty endanger nature as well as vulnerable groups of people through greed, lack of information, or need for survival. Comprehensive policies to halt and, where possible, repair damage to the environment need to be complemented by comprehensive environmental education programs and advocacy campaigns. Social workers have an important role in this process by linking with other groups.

Guiding Principles

Social workers work with clients on a variety of levels, and concerns about human rights, social inequities, oppression, and other forms of injustice need to be identified on all levels. Because social workers may engage in a variety of social change strategies and actions, the above values were suggested to ground them and the following 10 principles are suggested to guide them:

1. Strategies that represent individual solutions need to be reevaluated to discover the "public in the private" and activities need to be aimed at creating change on larger, structural, sociopolitical levels while, in the process, facilitating the empowerment of individuals.

2. Change strategies need to be collective in nature. People who engage in isolated efforts without social support may become burned out and lose their motivation in the long run to act and/or care.

3. Social justice goals are congruent with participatory leadership that reflects the thinking and voices of the diverse constituencies in the change

efforts and organizational change activities. Selection of leadership must include a participatory process that includes a cross-section of constituents in relation to ethnicity/race, socioeconomic class, gender, sexual orientation, physical ability, and other factors.

4. Coalitions are invaluable because they encourage developing clarity about ones' goals and values as a basis for connecting with other similarly minded social change groups. Also, organizing coalitions is a way to combine diverse special interest groups. This can draw increased attention to common issues and also appeal to individuals who might not be inclined to join large organizational efforts.

5. Social change strategies in the 21st century must deal with knowing media resources in order to heighten the visibility of social issues, educate the public, and engage larger numbers of supporters. Skills with the media include developing contacts with media personnel, preparing media releases, and conducting press conferences (Wallack, Woodruff, Dorfman, & Diaz, 1999).

6. Community development is based on tapping into and building the integrity and leadership of the members of the community. Breaking the cycle of violence and injustice and promoting social and economic justice is a development process that local people must direct and ultimately sustain. No imported scheme can substitute for bottom-up ingenuity.

7. Participatory community development is needed to counter the powerlessness, isolation, and exclusion that is the result of oppression and injustice and is often expressed through violence. Sustainable development must have the participation of community members and successful participation that calls for engaging people, unleashing their creativity, building their capacities, and promoting a sense of ownership.

8. Successful development calls for an equitable relationship between "the givers of help" and "the recipients of help" and a blurring of who receives what from whom. Assisting a community requires one to become involved with it, learn from it, be influenced and changed by it, and in a sense join it. Homegrown strategies to address injustice must be retrieved and exchanged, and new methods must be devised to share learning about what works and why.

9. As budget cuts and managed care change the face of social service delivery, U.S. social workers must become innovative. As in resource-poor de-

veloping countries, accomplishing more with less and pooling resources to achieve otherwise impossible goals is increasingly important. The infusion of more community-wide approaches to treating societal issues must become part of the day-to-day jobs of social workers. Innovation demands that social workers review the root causes of problems so that they can begin to institute positive change for more people at less cost.

10. Social workers need to be involved in global learning. The gap between home and abroad, between "them and us," is rapidly shrinking. Not only do developing nation conditions exist in neighborhoods across America, but also the globalization of the economy, immigrant flows, environmental degradation, and a host of other factors all combine to make interdependency a fact of life. Armed with a more sophisticated knowledge base to analyze and understand current situations and policies, social workers can enhance their effectiveness in practice and at social change. The search for solutions to societal problems should not be limited to U.S. communities and policies.

EDUCATIONAL ISSUES

Responsible consideration of what we want our profession to be and where we want it to go engages us in critical thinking about the assumptions underlying policy and program changes that characterize the development of the profession. We need to keep asking who is at the center, who is at the margins, who should be represented but is not, and what voices are silenced. The indictment that social work imposes truth on clients and allows those truths to dominate the curricula points to the task before us: the reconstruction of meaning that makes room for perspectives that have been marginalized (Chambron & Irving, 1999; Pardeck, Murphy, & Choi, 1994).

Teaching diversity content that is constructed within a social justice perspective directs us not only to examine the social work profession's ability to be relevant to the sociopolitical conditions that we face in the 21st century (Finn & Jacobson, 2002), but also to reconstruct our knowledge base. We need to challenge how we construct knowledge about diversity by examining the assumptions that underlie the dominant social work knowledge base, how we engage students in traditional knowledge, and how we create new knowledge.

How we engage in building knowledge about diversity depends on several variables such as faculty values, a critical thinking perspective, knowledge, and various pedagogical and process skills. In addition, organizational contextual factors such as college/university or program/school climate, mission, and resources must be evaluated for their support or lack of support for critical perspectives in teaching. To realize social justice values in the curriculum, what is required is both familiarity with social justice paradigms and critical thinking skills to address hurdles that may arise in the process. Structural academic factors must also be assessed to determine how they inhibit or promote such examination through providing resources and support that faculty and students need to create knowledge in a diverse climate. In this section, we focus on issues related to knowledge construction and structural academic factors.

Knowledge Construction

Existing knowledge structures can miss hidden factors related to social power, distort what we intend to study, and promote domination and exploitation (Rose, 2002). We propose that a social justice approach to knowledge construction is most effective in developing a relevant diversity curriculum. Such an approach can incorporate concepts from several origins, including those of Freire and Foucault.

Freire's (1970) learning concepts include participatory student engagement; learning focused on issues related to the conditions of one's life; a promotion of consciousness raising about social, political, and economic contradictions; and taking action against oppression as a key element in knowledge building. In addition, Freire's banking concept of knowledge points to the risk of accepting unchallenged accumulated knowledge as leading to collusion with dominant and exploitive forces. It is fundamentally important that students develop a conceptual understanding of social justice, power, and privilege as a basis for formulating advocacy actions.

Foucault's concepts include a focus on the mutual creation of reality resulting from the normalization function of professional disciplines (Gordon, 1977), which highlights the significance of a critical thinking perspective. Several concerns regarding the direction of the profession and the management of the power residing in the social work role illuminate potential domains that bear thoughtful review. One view is that the profession has allowed itself to be increasingly influenced by psychiatry, psychology, and medical models and thus has shifted its focus from working with low-income people to a greater focus on assisting individuals to adapt to conditions rather than to be "agents of change" to change conditions (Gil, 1998, p. 77). Foucault's discussion on how professions exercise power and knowledge in order to exercise social control has direct significance for examining ways that social work maintains oppression (Middleman & Wood, 1993). Foucault proposed that a profession supports objectification and control when it is associated with specific domains of power and truth, promotes a hierarchy in self learning processes such as psychotherapy, and engages in unreflective practices that categorize and classify individuals (e.g., with the American Psychiatric Diagnostic Statistical Manual (DSM)) often at the expense of seeing the client's point of view (Middleman & Wood, 1993). Historically, the social work profession has had a dual focus: to change individuals in order to improve their ability to cope with difficulties and/or to change the societal conditions that cause individual difficulties. This dual focus continues to split the profession into camps that prioritize one focus over the other in either/or fashion. A core value in social work practice is that of framing needs and difficulties in terms of person–environment interaction, a psychosocial orientation, and an ecological systems approach. Thus, the profession has constructed practice knowledge with a focus on systems in interaction and the individual as embedded in multiple systems. Within this conceptualization it tries to integrate its historical commitment to social justice in the midst of charges that social work has actually abandoned its original social justice mission (Specht, 1994).

Conservative, traditional pulls within the profession must be critically evaluated to unearth and counter social work participation in creating and/or maintaining oppression. Acquiescence of the profession to prevailing oppressive ideology as well as trends within the profession itself can be a driving force for oppression. If the charge that social work has abandoned its social justice mission (Specht, 1994) is true, this could result in social work practice colluding with societal oppressive practices. A commitment to social justice means a commitment to engage in critical analysis of oppressive societal trends. A commitment to social justice can be seen in curriculum that promotes a structural approach to practice with an emphasis on responsiveness or lack of responsiveness of social structures to client needs and problems (Middleman & Wood, 1993).

A growing diversification of specialized fields of practice also poses daunting hurdles that impede the integration of diversity for social justice curriculum. For example, formulations of needs and problems in clinical practice tend to focus assessment on attitudinal (i.e., affect, cognition, behavior) factors for the purpose of developing target goals. However, overemphasis on attitudinal factors risks prioritizing them at the expense of factors found in the multitude of systems within which the person lives and interacts. Similarly, overemphasis on organizational concepts and practice can minimize or devalue the contribution of individuals in the alleviation of social justice concerns and potentially undervalue the resilience and strength of individuals even in the most dire of circumstances.

A focus on multi-systems and their interactions provides a method for exploring issues of social justice and oppression by examining elements of the physical and social environment that affect the client system. While macro level concerns most often deal with immediate living conditions such as housing, neighborhood conditions, and access to resources, this domain should also address sociopolitical factors such as racism, sexism, and classism. In principle, a multi-level, multi-system assessment examines all potential factors related to the individual, family, social support, and the physical/social environment that potentially have a formative role in creating and/or maintaining the needs and difficulties that an individual is encountering. Assessment on an individual, micro level should include examination of the social justice issues that limit and shape the person's experience (behaviorally, psychologically) and the resources that can be mobilized to resolve the issues. A person in environment context points to factors in the social and physical environment that contribute to functioning (e.g., family and social networks, low-income neighborhood, lack of access to agency services, sexism, racism, ableism, etc.). By using the multi-level contextual framework of social work practice in the curriculum, application of social justice values and practice with individuals, families, organizations, and communities is facilitated.

Student participation in goal identification, knowledge construction, and grading processes is also an important aspect of the social justice approach to diversity teaching. While faculty need to provide boundaries for relevant course activities, assignments need to be open for discussion. Students often feel anxious that performance and grading will be dependent on their state of awareness of diversity issues and their actions for social justice. It is important to encourage them to see both as an ongoing process rather than as a status. The grading process needs to be based on openness to learning, willingness to wrestle with key issues and listen to others' points of view, and the process of change.

Structural Academic Factors

The university, program, and classroom are microcosms of the greater sociopolitical context. As such, they embody the tensions, values, and perspectives that are present in the larger context. Managing a wide range of perspectives in the classroom places a particular burden on faculty as they try to assure that all voices are heard, that the class engages in inclusive dialogue, and that class members feel that their points of view are heard and respected. Such efforts can only be accomplished through faculty commitment to social justice values coupled with the ability to integrate those values into their teaching and in their interaction with students.

The challenges are tremendous as faculty struggle to manage the potentially explosive terrain that mirrors that of the larger society. Thus, diversity teaching with a social justice perspective requires structural academic support. It is important that the program mission statements and educational climate embody social justice concerns and demonstrate this support through academic practices in committees, faculty activities, and programs. The values and ideals that social work programs embody pave the way for the social construction of diversity that includes social justice and promotes action taking and advocacy.

An educational environment that is characterized by diversity in the student body, faculty, staff, and administration is essential for a wide range of views to be part of the learning process. Unfortunately, national statistics reveal that, although full-time female faculty on university campuses has doubled in the past 30 years (Trower & Chait, 2002; National Center for Education Statistics, 2001), full-time faculty is still predominantly Euro-American (National Center for Education Statistics, 1998). Moreover, the future does not look promising, as the number of ethnically diverse doctoral candidates remains disproportionately low at 17% (Sanderson, Dugoni, Hoffer, & Myers, 2000). Although we cannot assume that ethnic faculty perspectives on diversity and social justice concerns are more developed compared to other faculty, a balanced and inclusive faculty profile brings in a diversity of voices and views and conveys a message about the commitment of the program to diversity goals.

Graduates often are dismayed when they discover a gap between social work values and actual practice, suggesting that students need both social justice perspectives and strategies for countering injustices in the real world. Thus, preparing students for practice that emphasizes cultural competence for social justice involves preparing them to critically examine the role of power and privilege in each situation and to identify the status quo tendencies of many social service agencies. The challenge is enormous. Universities and professional schools can function as important mechanisms of oppressive and unjust societies or they can prepare students who have a vision for change and a commitment to work organizationally and individually toward change. When teaching about oppression and injustice, educators need to acknowledge and analyze the oppressive and unjust aspects of their institutions. They further need to transform their own classes into liberated spaces to the extent that academic freedom permits. This does not mean giving up responsibility. Rather it means clarifying the responsibilities of students and those of teachers and fulfilling their respective roles in a shared undertaking (Burstow, 1991; Freire, 1970, cited in Gil, 1998, pp. 113–114).

To implement and maintain a social justice perspective of diversity, faculty must make certain decisions and commitments. The first decision is whether diversity for social justice content should be infused across the curriculum or presented in discrete courses. This consideration is most often directly related to the program mission and how faculty interprets that mission. Infusion of social justice curriculum in all courses can illuminate how social justice issues manifest themselves on individual, family, group, and organizational levels. A combination of both infusion and discrete courses can benefit students through increased horizontal integration of program curriculum thus amplifying a sense of direction and purpose. Which option gets chosen may depend on program resources such as funding, number of faculty, and faculty expertise. It particularly depends on faculty willingness to support social justice and diversity goals. A second decision is related to the resources that must be made available for faculty development. There must be support for the time, effort, and development of skills for teaching this content.

We believe that all faculty, regardless of ethnicity and expertise, should be encouraged to teach diversity for social justice content. This conveys to the student body that the program is serious about its commitment to social justice and facilitates more continuity across classes. Diversity content does not belong in only one part of the curriculum. Social justice issues are raised in all courses, whether they are related to clinical practice, policy, research, administration, or any other content area. For example, in clinical practice workers see the effects of privilege or oppression in the lives of individual clients; in making policy decisions, questions are raised regarding how some budgets benefit some people more than others; and in research, it is essential to examine the values that underlie how a research question is framed by asking questions such as: How is the topic approached? How is the social construction of the objectivity versus subjectivity dichotomy managed? How are participants chosen, engaged in the project, informed? To what degree does the methodology reflect participatory research designs?

A key to successfully teaching diversity content across the curriculum, however, depends on the program providing support, such as encouraging team meetings of faculty who teach diversity courses and facilitating dialogue in faculty meetings regarding the integration and implementation of diversity curriculum. Faculty who lack experience or familiarity with social justice and diversity teaching particularly need a supportive environment, in part due to anxieties and fears about being labeled racist or sexist that automatically get triggered when teaching this curriculum.

SUMMARY AND CONCLUSIONS

Our vision for social work education is the transformation of both curriculum and programs so that students will become transformed by their professional preparation and will, in turn, work to transform oppressive systems into just alternatives. To realize this vision, it is essential to understand the social and political context. The polarizations and conflicts in the broader U.S. society, as well as in the global village, are reflected within our institutions of higher education, in our schools of social work, and even in our classrooms.

Conflicts regarding inclusion of diversity and social justice content need to be dealt with openly and directly, with all faculty feeling that they have been able to communicate their viewpoints. This includes identifying and dealing with competing visions of community within the faculty body. It also includes revisiting social work values regarding social change related to program mission and goals as structural academic factors are addressed. Structural factors that inhibit or support such efforts and resources that faculty need to teach this content need to be explored and strategies for change discussed across the curriculum.

The challenges of developing diversity curriculum are great for faculty in social work programs. The challenges for students are also great as they engage in the transformative process that we envision. In the next chapter, we conceptualize the change process in depth. In Chapter Five, an empowerment process is presented that is characterized by transformative change.

REFERENCES

Bloom, A. (1987). *The closing of the American mind.* New York: Simon and Schuster.

Burstow, B. (1991). Freirian codification and social work education. *Journal of Social Work Education, 27*(2), 196–207.

Butler, J., & Schmitz, B. (1992). Ethnic studies, women's studies, and multiculturalism. *Change, 24*(1), 37–41.

Chambron, A. S., & Irving, A. (1999). Introduction. In A. S. Chambron, A. Irving, & L. Epstein (Eds.), *Reading Foucault for social work.* New York: Columbia University Press.

Council on Social Work Education. (2001). *Educational policy and accreditation standards.* Alexandria, VA: Author.

D'Souza, D. (1992). *Illiberal education: The politics of race and sex on campus.* New York: Vintage Books.

Davidson, C. N. (1991, September–October). "PH" stands for political hypocrisy. *Academe: Bulletin of the American Association of University Professors, 77*(5), 8–14.

Finn, J., & Jacobson, M. (2002, February). *Just practice: Steps toward a new social work paradigm.* Paper presented at the Annual Program Meeting, Council on Social Work Education, Nashville, TN.

Freire, P. (1970). *Pedagogy of the oppressed.* New York: Herder and Herder.

Gil, D. (1998). *Confronting injustice and oppression: Concepts and strategies for social workers.* New York: Columbia University Press.

Gordon, E. (Ed.) (1977). *Power/knowledge: Selected interviews and other writings 1972–1977, Michel Foucault.* New York: Pantheon Books.

Gordon, E. W., & Bhattacharyya, M. (1992). Human diversity, cultural hegemony, and the integrity of the academic canon. *Journal of Negro Education, 61*(3), 405–419.

Howe, I., & Takaki, R. (1991, May/June). The content of the curriculum: Two views—The value of the canon and the value of multiculturalism. *Liberal Education, 77*(3), 8–10.

Hunter, J. D. (1991). *The culture wars: The struggle to define America.* New York: Basic Books.

McMahon, A., & Allen-Meares, P. (1992). Is social work racist? A content analysis of recent literature. *Social Work, 37*(6), 533–539.

Middleman, R., & Wood, G. (1993). So much for the bell curve: Constructionism, power/conflict, and the structural approach to direct practice in
social work. *Journal of Teaching in Social Work, 8*(1/2), 129–146.

National Center for Education Statistics. (1998). *Fall staff in postsecondary
institutions, 1995.* NCES-98-228. Washington, DC: U.S. Department of
Education, Office of Educational Research and Improvement.

National Center for Education Statistics. (2001). *Digest of education statistics
2000.* NCES-2001-034. Washington, DC: U.S. Department of Education, Office of Educational Research and Improvement.

Pardeck, J. T., Murphy, J. W., & Choi, J. M. (1994). Some implications of
postmodernism for social work practice. *Social Work, 39*(4), 343–346.

Pinderhughes, E. (1989). *Understanding race ethnicity, and power: The key to
efficacy in clinical practice.* New York: The Free Press.

Powell, J. (1992, July). The debate on multiculturalism. *Poverty and Race, 1*(3).
Washington, DC: Poverty and Race Research Action Council.

Robertson, M. E. (1968). Social work education's responsibility to minority-
group members. In *Educationally disadvantaged students in social work education,* (pp. 132—136). New York: Council on Social Work Education.

Rose, S. (2002, March). *Social work at the crossroads: A reflection.* Paper presented at the Social Work at a Crossroads Conference, Department of
Social Work Education.

Sanderson, A., Dugoni, B., Hoffer, T., & Myers, S. (2000). *Doctorate recipients
from United States universities: Summary report 1999.* Chicago: National
Opinion Research Center.

Specht, H. (1994). *Unfaithful angels: How social work has abandoned its mission.* New York: The Free Press.

Trower, C., & Chait, R. P. (2002, March/April). Faculty Diversity: Too little
for too long. *Harvard Magazine, 104*(4), 33–37.

United Nations. (1992). *Teaching and learning about human rights for schools of
social work and the social work profession.* New York: Author.

Van Soest, D. (1995). Multiculturalism and social work education: The non-
debate about competing perspectives. *Journal of Social Work Education,
31*(1), 55–66.

Wallack, L., Woodruff, K., Dorfman, L., & Diaz, I. (1999). *News for a change.*
Thousand Oaks, CA: Sage.

Chapter Four
Conceptualizing the Change Process

This book is based on the assumption that it is critical for educators who teach diversity content within a social justice context to understand learning and change processes. To help students move from information and ideas to beliefs about injustice and ultimately to action for social justice, educators need to understand some of the psychological barriers students may face when their worldview and self-concept are challenged. Socialization theory is useful as an underlying conceptual framework for such understanding, particularly in relation to social work education as the formal organization charged with preparing students for the role of social justice advocate.

In this chapter, we first discuss the difficulties involved in socializing students to assume the dual roles of social justice advocate and social control agent. A critical thinking process is then presented as a model for what might be more accurately characterized as "re-socializing" students for the social justice advocacy role. Cognitive dissonance is discussed as a key component of critical thinking. The process is conceptualized as beginning with a trigger event that creates a discrepancy between student perceptions of how the world is and how the world is supposed to be. The result is inner discomfort and feelings of distress related to issues of racism, sexism, heterosexism, and other forms of oppression. Such distress—seen as the hallmark of an educational environment that encourages critical thinking—is expected to lead to questioning and assessing one's identity, beliefs, and behaviors in relation to social injustice. The ultimate goal of the socialization and critical thinking processes presented in this chapter is transformative learning that includes a new contextual awareness that recognizes the importance of understanding the context within which oppressive assumptions, and the actions that spring from those assumptions, are formed (Brookfield, 1987).

SOCIALIZATION THEORY AND EDUCATION FOR SOCIAL JUSTICE ADVOCACY

Socialization of Adults

Socialization is the process through which persons acquire the knowledge, skills, and dispositions that are needed to function as capable members of society. The study of socialization is concerned with how society transforms individuals into engaged, working members. This involves understanding society's status structure and the role prescriptions and behavior associated with different positions in that structure (Brim, 1966). Different stages of human development involve different statuses with corresponding roles and behavior expectations. Childhood socialization cannot adequately prepare people for all the roles they are expected to fulfill throughout the life cycle due to the complexities and fluctuations of modern U.S. society, such as geographic and social mobility, cultural diversity, and rapid social changes that occur during a lifetime (Brim, 1966). Moreover, rapid societal change creates new, unforeseen expectations and roles.

Role acquisition is probably the most important aspect of adult socialization and socialization into various roles is increasingly a function of large-scale bureaucratic organizations. Schools and universities are examples of what Wheeler (1966) calls "developmental socialization systems" whose formal purpose is the training, education, and further socialization of students. Such systems are contrasted with "re-socialization systems" whose purpose is to compensate for or correct some deficiency in earlier socialization. Social work educational programs are considered developmental socialization systems in which educators are formally charged with the task of influencing adults so that they will leave with different skills, attitudes, values, and other qualities from those with which they entered. The socialization role of social work education, however, involves unique problems and complexities, which are discussed in the next section.

Socializing Social Work Students for the Role of Social Justice Advocate

While socialization theory is concerned with how society changes the individual, social work is also concerned with how the individual changes society. The profession's person-and-environment orientation creates unique problems regarding whether social workers are agents of social control or advocates for social change. With a focus on the interactional dynamics of the person with his or her environment, social workers help clients function effectively within society and at the same time they work to change society when it is unjust. Thus, three interrelated aspects of socialization for professional commitment to social justice require special attention: (a) goal ambiguity and potential goal conflict, (b) education for social justice and societal sanction, and (c) student motivation and values for social justice advocacy. While the three aspects of professional socialization are interrelated, each will be discussed separately.

Goal Ambiguity and Potential Goal Conflict

For a person to perform satisfactorily in a role, the expectations of what is required in terms of both behavior and values must be clear. However, a distinctive problem that frequently arises in socializing organizations is related to lack of consensus about purpose, assignments, and efforts (Brim, 1966). Wheeler (1966) points out that organizational capacity to provide clear and unambiguous norms depends to some extent on the absence of contrary definitions of the norms. Within the learning context of preparing students for professional social work practice, there sometimes seem to be contradictory messages about what is expected of social workers. Ambiguity about goals and potential goal conflicts in social work education revolve around whether students should be socialized into the social control or social justice goals. In other words, should educators prepare students to learn effective ways of resocializing clients to function as capable members of society and, at the same time, prepare them to question unjust societal conditions and to work for social change in order to make society more functional for clients? Which should have precedence when the two goals conflict? Which goal should be emphasized as a guiding value or principle for social workers?

The social justice purpose of social work is clearly articulated in accreditation statements of the Council on Social Work Education (CSWE) and the *Code of Ethics* of the National Association of Social Workers (NASW). However, when social workers influence people to conform to societal norms or to adjust to institutional needs, they also act as agents of social control, a function that is frequently performed in prisons, welfare institutions, schools, and probation and parole agencies. It is also performed in less obvious settings such as therapy sessions, hospitals, and nursing homes (Macht & Quam, 1986). While the social control function has been seen as complementing other social work functions such as caring and rehabilitation (Day, 1981), the issue of social control versus social change continues to be contentious and conflictual within the profession.

Social work education may not be atypical in relation to this type of goal conflict and ambiguity. Brim (1958) suggests that a systematic description of the aims of education in general would undoubtedly reveal that many of them conflict with each other, making some unachievable. Significant questions for social work educators and practitioners are how to manage their efforts toward achievement of one or another aim and how the inherent conflict between the two goals influences morale and career satisfaction.

Educating for Social Justice Advocacy and Societal Sanction

Traditional sociological analyses have focused on the relation between educational goals and the general values of society, with special reference to the social control over educational aims (Brim, 1958). While education is seen as possessing legitimate power to pursue its goals only to the extent that such goals are considered desirable by society, this does not mean that educational goals are always conservative in terms of maintaining the status quo. Because higher education is important symbolic ground for a broader societal conflict over competing moral visions of what constitutes the ideal American, there continues to be basic disagreement about the role of the university in society. The current question that is hotly debated in and out of academia remains unresolved: Is the role of higher education to educate for social justice by advancing the interests of the oppressed and ending bigotry and discrimination through critical thinking and open inquiry, or is its role to uphold moral and political traditions that are seen as providing a universal, consistent, and unchangeable definition of the truth and of what is good (Hunter, 1991)? In social work, this question translates into whether the primary goal of professional education is socializing students to be social justice advocates or social control agents. This is a conflict that has its origins in the historical roots of the profession.

If the social justice aims were to gain priority in social work education, it is important to recognize that they would still derive their legitimacy from societal sanctions. Brim (1958) cautions that it is a mistake to treat the educational system "as a means whereby a social revolution is effected through production of a new generation of adults seeking new values . . . . In fact the educational system of a society is the means whereby traditional culture is preserved, and . . . any new values it transmits within one generation are fractional compared to the massive tradition it imparts" (p. 16). This view of the socialization role of education does not deny that existing conditions of society are unrealistic and unjust, that the demands of society may make impossible the personal satisfactions of many if not most of its members, or that the demands may be so irrational as to bring about disintegration of the society itself (Brim, 1966). Because social work is concerned both with how society is changed to better meet individual needs as well as with how individuals meet the needs of society, socialization for social work practice ultimately leads to the question of what is the desirable and just society.

Student Motivation and Values for Social Justice Advocacy

Brim (1966) maintains that the purposes of socialization are to give a person knowledge, ability, and motivation. Organizations tend to screen out those who do not have the appropriate motivation and values for anticipated roles. This ensures that those who enter the organization will not experience conflicts with its goals and thus futile resocialization efforts can be avoided. Because values and ideology have a particularly powerful effect on professional practice, knowing what values and motives best fit social work makes it possible for educational programs to sort out and place students. However, the question arises for social work education as to whether the appropriate motives and values for the profession differ depending on which role is assumed, that of social justice advocate or social control agent.

This question is grounded in two conflicting views that are held within the profession about social work values. One opinion is that professional values are simply reflections of the prevalent cultural values, i.e., social work values are "only preference patterns shared by the general population" (Meinert, 1980). Lappe and Collins (1977) support this view with their contention that, because society funds and sanctions the profession, social workers are society's agents and must reflect the prevailing values, assumptions, and attitudes of the social system. Based on this idea, social work values seem more congruent with the role of social control agent than with the role of social change agent. The other view, endorsed in NASW's 1987 *Encyclopedia of Social Work*, is that social work has, over an extended period of time, developed a value base that is deeply imbedded in professional culture and is thus less vulnerable to societal value changes. Those enduring social work values are widely accepted as "a commitment to human welfare, social justice, and individual dignity" (p. 801). According to this viewpoint, social workers should function as social change agents.

On an individual level, it seems that social work students who uphold the dominant value system of society would be motivated to assume the role of social control agent and those who are critical of dominant North American values would be motivated to assume the role of social justice advocate. It is generally understood, however, that a middle-of-the-road liberal perspective dominates the profession, perhaps mediating the two potentially dichotomous value orientations. The liberal perspective sees the present social system as basically benevolent and assumes that the central values of capitalism—individualism, acquisitiveness, and competitiveness—automatically serve society's best interests (Ephross & Reisch, 1982; Macht & Quam, 1986). Macht and Quam (1986) point out that even though liberals are committed to decreasing inequality in society, they also fear that true equality would decrease productivity and efficiency and thus they do not seek fundamental change in the economic system itself. The dissonance that social workers often experience in relation to values may stem from the profession being pulled by both conservatives and radicals away from this centrist position. Radicals criticize the profession for facilitating oppression and conservatives call for social workers to be the moral agents of society and to stop supporting such immoral behavior as homosexuality and single parenthood (Siporin, 1982). Perhaps the centrist ideology reflects the reality that the values required for social justice advocacy and fundamental systemic change are tempered, in practice, by the profession's role as an agent of society.

Resocialization and Social Work Education

The discussion thus far has focused on the educational goal of socializing social work students to assume the roles of social control agent and social justice advocate. We now turn our attention to the resocialization function of social work education. The purpose of resocialization is to compensate for or correct some deficiency in earlier socialization (Merton, 1968). The social control function involves resocializing clients who deviate from societal norms in some way in order to help them adapt to the social system and thus enhance their social functioning. It is inferred that implementing this resocialization function requires that social workers themselves be effectively socialized into the dominant societal norms.

The role of social justice advocate, however, involves critical questioning of societal norms and structures. It is difficult to engage in such questioning when one has been effectively socialized to adopt the dominant norms and structures. Thus, to successfully prepare students to assume the social justice role, social work education may need to resocialize students to agitate against dominant societal values in order to envision and seek change in the social structure. Some students may need to be resocialized to assume attitudes and behaviors that are consistent with critical questioning and promoting social justice.

Social Control Function and Resocialization

Lappe and Collins (1977) assert that the basic concern of social work has been to help the victim rather than alleviate the systemic causes of problems. Based on the parable in Chapter One about people drowning in the river, this assertion implies that social workers tend to opt for the action of rescuing people from the river and then teach them how to manage their problems so that they either do not end up in the river again or, if they do, that they at least will not drown. According to this assertion, the focus of practice is often on the social work goal of promoting, restoring, and maintaining improved social functioning. One aspect of helping clients improve social functioning is resocializing those who deviate in some way from the commonly shared norms of the dominant society. Societal norms related to capitalism, meaning individualism, acquisitiveness, and competitiveness, have particular significance for understanding social workers' tendency to uphold mainstream cultural precepts rather than focusing on social change.

Merton (1968) maintains that in U.S. society there is an exceptionally strong emphasis upon achieving certain goals even when the institutional means to achieve them is absent. He purports that U.S. culture socializes people into acceptance of three dominant principles:

1. The same lofty success goals are open to everyone and thus all people should strive for the same goals;

2. What appears to be failure is only a temporary barrier to ultimate success; and

3. Genuine failure only comes from insufficient ambition or withdrawal of ambition, not from lack of institutional support.

The result, from Merton's structural functionalist perspective, is that (a) those who do not have full and equal access to opportunity criticize themselves rather than the social structure; (b) the structure of social power is preserved by having those in the lower social strata identify with those at the top (who they will purportedly join); and (c) pressure to conform to the cultural dictates of unslackened ambition is provided by threatening people with less than full membership in society if they fail to conform. Back to the parable of Chapter One again, this means that if people end up drowning in the river, it is their own fault.

When a differential emphasis upon goals and the means to achieve them consistently focuses on the goals, a significant question becomes how to achieve the culturally approved goal regardless of whether the procedure is culturally legitimate or not. Merton (1968) purports that a persistent emphasis on wealth as a basic symbol of success without a corresponding emphasis upon legitimate approaches to achieving financial success results in what Durkheim called "anomie" or normlessness in society that is characterized by deviance. Merton further hypothesizes that deviance is a normal response to the social situation in which some groups find themselves. He suggest five types of adaptation taken by individuals who occupy different positions in the social structure:

1. Conformity—to both the cultural goal and institutionalized means of achieving the goal.

2. Innovation—assimilating the cultural goal without equally internalizing the institutional norms governing ways to achieve the goal (e.g., criminal behavior).

3. Ritualism—lowering one's achievement goal in order to experience satisfaction while continuing to abide almost compulsively by institutional norms (e.g., the conforming bureaucrat).

4. Retreatism—putting little value on either the success goal or institutional practices.

5. Rebellion—visualizing and seeking to bring about change in the social structure.

Both social workers and clients can be found in the ranks of each type of adaptation. Social workers who have assimilated the three cultural principles listed above and conform to both societal goals and dominant institutional norms may be inclined to focus on resocializing clients who deviate from the principles and to blame those who fail to achieve financial success and/or adhere to institutional norms. While clients who are victims of the discrepancy between the cultural emphasis on financial or material aspiration and social barriers to opportunity are often aware of a disparity between individual worth and social rewards, they are not always aware of the structural sources of their frustrated aspirations. According to our parable, the structural source is the force on the hill that is pushing them into the river. Merton (1968) points out that the result is to either attribute their failure to bad luck or to blame themselves for not being intelligent or ambitious enough to succeed. When social workers also lack awareness of the structural roots of inequity and focus exclusively or predominantly on changing the client, they too may blame the client, and they become vulnerable to the charge of collusion with injustice.

Social Justice Advocacy and Resocialization

When clients are aware of the structural roots of injustice, they may become alienated from the social system and thus become "ready candidates for the adaptation of rebellion" (Merton, 1968, p. 201). Social work intervention for social justice facilitates awareness of the systemic origin of inequity that empowers those who are victims of social barriers to full opportunity. A corollary to this idea is that social work education may need to resocialize students into the rebellion role so that they adopt the values and attitudes necessary for the promotion of social justice. Such resocialization involves withdrawing allegiance from aspects of the prevailing social structure that are unjust and transferring one's allegiance to values, standards, and practices that have not yet been institutionalized but are envisioned as an as-yet-to-be-realized normative system (Merton, 1968). According to our river parable again, social workers then opt for the alternative of organizing with people to eliminate the source of the problem.

Distinguishing Between Criminal and Nonconformist Behaviors

Depending on which social work role is assumed—the societally sanctioned role of social control agent or the rebellion role of social justice advocate—intervention is aimed at either resocializing those who are deviant or aimed at supporting and joining with those who are considered deviant because they do not accept the dominant norms and practices. As social workers struggle with making a choice about which intervention is appropriate in each particular case, they must be able to distinguish between deviants, i.e., the behavior of the criminal, and that of the nonconformist. The idea of a criminal is one who operates covertly out of self-interest and makes every effort to evade punitive consequences of his or her actions. Nonconformists, on the other hand, overtly challenge injustice based on principle and caring for others and try to change societal structures in accord with deeply felt sentiments and values in the face of likely punitive consequences. In both cases, the dominant social system operates to try to bring the deviants back into line with established behavior expectations and the nonconformist is, in fact, frequently declared to be a criminal. However, as Merton (1968) writes: "To lump together these functionally . . . different forms of conduct in the one concept of 'deviant behavior' is to obscure their sociological import. After all, it seems safe to suppose that, unlike John Brown's, Al Capone's soul will not go marching on" (p. 420).

Failure to distinguish between types of deviant behavior, as acts of criminality or as acts of rebellion for social justice, can result in social work practice that implicitly views virtue only in social conformity. Social work interventions differ based on the type of deviant behavior. With criminals, the intervention is aimed at resocializing the deviants to conform to noncriminal behavior. With nonconformists whose rebellion is directed toward social justice, the intervention is aimed at supporting them and participating with them in actions for social justice. Social workers whose interventions uphold the social justice function need to be aware, however, that they may be subject to criticism, even within the profession itself, and that their nonconformity may be derided as radicalism, utopianism, or even personal pathology.

Nonconformity and Social Change

While society must develop members who conform and fit into the existing order, it also needs those who, although considered deviant now, may influence societal change in a positive way. Brim's (1966) discussion of what happens when the social system fails to bring nonconformists back in line with societal norms points to the potential for social change. He maintains that, at first, the social system is divided as nonconformists withdraw from the groups in which they are involved (e.g., activists form alternative client advocacy organizations to challenge social welfare injustices; pacifists refuse to pay taxes). The social system continues for awhile under conditions of stress characterized by both hostility and mistrust because of its precarious nature and also by suppression of antagonistic feelings in order to maintain social relationships. In the final stage of the process, the expectations of others in the system are changed to accord with the formerly deviant persons' behavior or objectives; the definition of what is deviant has changed, the new behavior or values are accepted, and others comply with the deviants' wishes. The nonconformists have "transformed the system, the rebel has won his cause, the innovative aspects of his behavior have been accepted as legitimized, and the socializing agency has been forced to reconsider its objectives" (Brim, 1966, p. 45). This is the goal of educating students about cultural diversity for social justice: to ultimately transform unjust and oppressive systems into just alternatives.

LEARNING AND CHANGE PROCESSES

Transforming oppressive systems into just alternatives and bringing about lasting social change that involves a new way of collective thinking takes a long time. Social work educators need to convey to students that the business of social change is for the long haul, more like a marathon than a sprint. Thus, perhaps the most valuable skill for the social justice advocacy role is the ability to think critically. Critical thinking is a skill that serves not only as a way of thinking but also as a way of living. Critical thinkers pay attention to the assumptions underlying ideas and actions and the context in which ideas and actions are generated. They ask what feel like awkward question such as "Why are nearly all faculty at my college white, and nearly all the service staff Black or Hispanic?" (Brookfield, 1987, p. 67). This kind of debunking skepticism often leads to nonconformity with established norms, laws, and institutions and to alternative ways of looking at, and operating in, the world.

Cognitive dissonance can potentially open the door to critical thinking. In this section, discussion will focus on critical thinking processes and the significance of creative cognitive conflict as a trigger to critical thinking. Both are seen as essential if we are to achieve the goal of transformative learning that involves life-altering change in the direction of commitment to social justice advocacy.

Critical Thinking

Brookfield (1987) describes a five-phase process that people go through in becoming critical thinkers. The process considers the affective as well as cognitive nature of learning. It has particular relevance for understanding the difficulty inherent in socializing (or resocializing) students for their role as social justice advocates and provides a conceptual background for the remainder of this book. The critical thinking process is frequently initiated by a trigger event that creates inner discomfort and perplexity, often related to a perceived contradiction between how the world is and how the world is supposed to work based on the student's current belief system and experiences. During professional education, social work students are presented with alternative ways of thinking about social issues and with examples of social injustice that may create a sense of disbelief and immobilization that are often characteristic of this initial stage (Hopson & Adams, 1977).

The second phase involves a period of appraisal, during which the student alternates between minimization and denial and often broods about the perplexing discrepancies (Hopson & Adams, 1977). During this self-examination period, concerns are identified and clarified. The student may engage in distressing examination of his or her own identity and role in relation to the problem under study.

The third stage involves exploring new ways of explaining the discrepancies or of living with them. In an attempt to reduce the sense of discomfort and distress related to oppression and injustice, students may try out new social identities, consider new role models, take some kind of action, talk with family and friends about the problem, pay attention to the many manifestations of injustice that present themselves in day-to-day life, find ways to rationalize injustice to reduce discomfort, etc. New ways of thinking and behaving are tested that seem more congruent with the new perceptions about oppression and the student's own role in relation to social change.

During the fourth stage, alternative perspectives are developed from the social identities, role models, and philosophies explored in the previous stage. Students may begin to develop confidence in the new roles they wish to play in relation to social change. During this transition stage, leaving behind familiar but now inappropriate beliefs or behaviors often involves a wrenching sense of loss. As Brookfield (1987) points out, "a common tendency is to hang on to the assumption or behavior, but to try to modify it to fit the situation more closely" (p. 27). For example, some students may realize that privileges derived from the present social structure are valuable to them and thus they modify rather than completely change their philosophy and behavior in order to hold on to their benefactor status. Others may experience alienation from their primary reference group and thus modify their beliefs and behaviors enough to ease the perplexity and distress caused by the trigger event but not so much that they lose family and friends.

The fifth and final stage involves integrating new ways of thinking or acting into one's life. At times this involves radical transformation of attitudes and assumptions; at other times it involves a renewed sense of conviction about previous positions. It is at this stage that some integration of conflicting feelings and ideas is achieved. Internal actions, such as affirming one's own social and ethnic identity, may be taken. Visible actions may involve joining advocacy groups or proposing reforms in one's field placement.

At any of the above stages, the critical thinking process can become blocked. The critical role of educators is to serve as a guide and prodder at each stage. While stages are not necessarily sequential or all-inclusive, what is important is that educators become comfortable with the idea that students will experience distress and cognitive dissonance and that they develop skills for helping them navigate through the sometimes deeply disturbing terrain. As students engage in the transformative learning process, their social identities often change. This change process is further discussed in the next two chapters.

Cognitive Dissonance and Change

Educators can set the stage for creative cognitive conflict that can potentially open the door to critical thinking. Haste's (1988) study of how and why people make moral commitments to social causes reveals that, in the cases studied, there was always a "triggering event" that led up to a crisis of meaning. Support from knowledgeable others was then required in order to translate the crisis into personally meaningful terms that, in turn, led to the need for action. Research on commitment to movements of social transformation (Gerlach & Hine, 1970) shows that commitment for some people begins with an "identity-altering" experience that changes one's view of self and produces some degree of cognitive restructuring. Support from others provides encouragement to consequently turn away from the old way of living or thinking.

Educational methods that emphasize critical thinking and psychological reflection encourage students to talk about their emotional responses and to acknowledge the real difficulty of facing the overwhelming reality of oppression. Facilitating empowerment and a sense of political efficacy through personal commitment in a particular issue and providing positive role models can lead to belief in the possibility of social change.

Success in addressing attitudes and beliefs that impede progress toward effective social change actions depends on educators' success in eliciting and understanding students' beliefs. Joy (1990) proposes six pedagogical building blocks that provide underpinnings for designing teaching strategies. They are not guidelines for changing attitudes but for "creating educational interventions" that make it possible for learners to reassess aspects of their shared social beliefs. The building blocks include the following suggestions:

1. Bring pre-existing beliefs and assumptions into the open in a nonjudgmental atmosphere.

2. Provide opportunities for group collaboration and group bonding.

3. Set the stage for cognitive conflict (i.e., a triggering event) to engage the learner in critical thinking. This is based on the idea, which is supported by research, that changes in beliefs occur "simply by virtue of discovering contradictions between our conceptions of self and our values, attitudes, and behavior" (p. 32).

4. Raise provocative questions, rather than providing answers.

5. Emphasize relationship and connectedness.

6. Invite students to be co-creators of the educational process.

This book is based on the conviction that education about social issues is as dependent upon the instructor's ability to uncover student's beliefs, hear the affect stimulated, and inspire students to re-examine them in a safe environment as it is on having something didactic to teach. Education for social justice by necessity involves affective learning. Concerns about social justice cannot, in fact, be separated from belief systems, those cognitive structures that dominate every facet of our lives and evoke intense emotion.

Deep-seated, primitive beliefs are the social beliefs we share with various in-groups with which we identify and these shared beliefs are influential determinants of how we think and act (Aronson, 1988; Joy, 1990). Such fundamental beliefs are often least apparent and most resistant to change. Joy (1990) points out that our deeper beliefs usually remain unaffected by exposure to information that runs contrary to them. For example, in a study at Stanford University (Moyer, 1989), students were divided into two groups: those who strongly believed in capital punishment as a deterrent and those who just as strongly believed the opposite. After hearing a balanced presentation in which evidence both for and against their beliefs was cited, both groups were even more opposed to the other's views than when they began. The researcher came to the conclusion that "the 'information antidote' approach is not very effective against firmly held beliefs" (pp. 15–16). Aronson (1988) cites several studies that show that people are not inclined to take in information that is dissonant with their beliefs.

Realization of the pervasiveness of oppression challenges firmly held beliefs about fairness and raises self-doubt about social identity and one's role as benefactor or perpetrator of injustice. Educators may experience considerable student resistance as a result of information that disrupts such primitive belief systems. As Garb (1990) points out, "This disruption often engenders quite a profound disorientation: students are overwhelmed by the immensity, complexity, ubiquity, and seeming intractability of the problems."

Students need educational interventions that support them through such psychological challenges. When students are exposed to a fairly intense dose of evidence of an unjust system in a discrete course on oppression, the cognitive dissonance that they may experience may be so great that, as a result, they hold on to their former beliefs even tighter in order to cope with the distress. In such a case, it is important to understand that we are not dealing with a linear, short-term process. After the intensity of dealing with social injustice issues in a discrete diversity course, student resistance to new ideas about injustice and fairness may be reduced and openness to challenging former beliefs may be increased when oppression content is infused into other courses.

While deep-seated beliefs are very resistant to change, they do change with transformative learning processes that are affective, cognitive, and experiential. Both classroom and field education are ideal vehicles for addressing the shared social beliefs that impede effective social change. To socialize or resocialize students to be advocates for social justice, educators "must be willing to understand and then to probe the various layers of shared beliefs that both we and the learners we teach invariably bring" (Joy, 1980, p. 16). Thus, teaching and learning processes are needed that go beyond the cognitive level to understand the psychological barriers to assimilating and integrating knowledge that challenges one's worldview.

Transformative Learning

The educational framework proposed in this book aims ultimately at the elimination of oppressive systems and transformation on the most fundamental level of knowledge creation. In this chapter, the focus has been on learning processes that critically challenge the facts, concepts, paradigms, themes, and explanations routinely accepted in academic knowledge (Banks, 1993). The process of constructing an anti-oppressive social identity, consciousness, and behavior is a transformative rather than a linear process. As the previous discussion illustrates, such change involves critical thinking that is not solely rational but that involves, in a central way, emotive aspects. In fact, the ability to imagine alternatives to current ways of thinking and living in relation to difference often involves a conscious break with rational modes of thought in order to inspire forward leaps in creativity (Brookfield, 1987). For example, nonsequential learning experiences, the use of dreams, surprising moments of insight, and extraordinary linkages between ideas and experiences may occur in unexpected ways. The process is complex and often perplexing as students challenge their own and others' belief systems and jettison assumptions previously accepted without question. Educators play a vital role in the transformative learning process; they act as "sympathizers, empathizers, reactors, devil's advocates, initiators, and prompters" (Brookfield, 1987, p. 11).

Transformative learning is emancipatory learning, "which frees people from personal, institutional, or environmental forces that prevent them from seeing new directions, from gaining control of their lives, their society and their world" (Apps, 1985, p. 151). Transformative learning is evident when students become aware of the forces that have brought us all to the current situation of institutional racism and other forms of oppression and take action to change some aspect of the situation. Transformative learning is evident when students see the world and their place in it in a different way and act on this new vision (Habermas, 1979).

SUMMARY

At the beginning of this chapter, discussion of the issue of socializing students for commitment to social justice advocacy highlighted the inherent conflict between the social control and social change functions of social work. Resocializing students to question unjust societal norms and structures involves a difficult learning process that challenges personal and professional self-concept, creates cognitive dissonance and distress, and requires the engagement in critical thinking processes. What is required is a transformative learning process that involves testing out new ways of thinking and behaving and integrating such newness into one's life. The outcome may be radical transformation of attitudes and assumptions or a renewed sense of conviction about previous positions. As stated in the first chapter, the ultimate goal of cultural diversity education for social justice is to prepare professional social workers to transform oppressive and unjust systems into non-oppressive and just alternatives (Gil, 1998). To achieve this goal, the learning process itself must be a transformative one. In the next chapter, we present an empowerment process aimed at personal transformation and the expansion of moral boundaries.

REFERENCES

Apps, J. W. (1985). *Improving practice in continuing education: Modern approaches for understanding the field and determining priorities.* San Francisco: Jossey-Bass.

Aronson, E. (1988). *The social animal* (5th ed.) New York: W.H. Freeman.

Banks, J. A. (1993, September). Multicultural education: Development, dimensions, and challenges. *Phi Delta Kappan, 75*(1), 22–28.

Brim, O. G. (1958). *Sociology and the field of education.* New York: Russell Sage Foundation.

Brim, O. G. (1966). Socialization through the life cycle. In O. G. Brim & S. Wheeler, *Socialization after childhood: Two essays* (pp. 3–49). New York: John Wiley & Sons.

Brookfield, S. D. (1987). *Developing critical thinkers: Challenging adults to explore alternative ways of thinking and acting.* San Francisco: Jossey-Bass.

Day, P. (1981). *Social work and social control.* London: Tavistock.

Ephross, P. H., & Reisch, M. (1982, June). The ideology of some social work texts. *Social Service Review, 56,* 273–291.

Garb, Y. J. (1990). *Responding to the environmental crisis: The pedagogic challenge.* Paper presented at the symposium "Educating for Moral Responsibility Across Societal Contexts," at the meeting of the American Educational Research Association, Boston, MA.

Gerlach, L. P., & Hine, V. H. (1970). *People, power, change: Movements of social transformation.* Indianapolis, IN: Bobbs-Merrill.

Gil, D. (1998). *Confronting injustice and oppression: Concepts and strategies for social workers.* New York: Columbia University Press.

Habermas, J. (1979). *Communication and the evolution of society.* Boston: Beacon Press.

Haste, H. (1988). Moral responsibility and moral commitment: The integration of affect and cognition. In T. Wren (Ed.), *The moral domain.* Cambridge, MA: MIT Press.

Hopson, B., & Adams, J. (1977). *Transition: Understanding and managing personal change.* Montclair, NJ: Allenhald & Osmund.

Hunter, J. D. (1991). *The culture wars: The struggle to define America.* New York: Basic Books.

Joy, C. (1990). *Believing is seeing: Attitudes and assumptions that affect learning about development.* New York: National Clearinghouse on Development Education.

Lappe, F., & Collins, J. (1977). *Food first: Beyond the myth of scarcity.* New York: Ballantine.

Macht, M. W., & Quam, J. K. (1986). *Social work: An introduction.* Columbus, OH: Charles E. Merrill.

Meinert, R. (1980, Spring). Values in social work called dysfunctional myth. *Journal of Social Welfare, 6*(3), 5–16.

Merton, R. K. (1968). *Social theory and social structure.* New York: The Free Press.

Moyer, R. (1989). On annihilating enemy images: Some American reflections on a Soviet proposal, *Building Bridges: US-USSR*, Bridges for Peace, 15–18.

National Association of Social Workers. (1987). *Encyclopedia of social work.* Silver Spring, MD: Author.

Siporin, M. (1982, December). Moral philosophy in social work today. *Social Service Review, 56*(4), 516–537.

Wheeler, S. (1966). The structure of formally organized socialization settings. In O.G. Brim & S. Wheeler, *Socialization after childhood: Two essays* (pp. 53–116). New York: John Wiley & Sons.

Chapter Five
Personal and Professional Advocacy for Social Justice: Is Transformative Change Possible?

We can begin anywhere—everywhere. 'Let there be justice,'
says a bumper sticker, 'and let it begin with me' . . .
Let there be transformation, and let it begin with me.[1]

In the previous chapter, we discussed how socializing students for commitment to social justice advocacy by necessity involves an inherent conflict between the social control and social change functions of social work. Our discussion of learning and change processes that help students address this conflict focused on critical thinking skills. It is our premise that in order to prepare social workers to transform oppressive and unjust systems into non-oppressive and just alternatives (Gil, 1998), the learning process itself must be a transformative one. In this chapter, we conceptualize how students learn to translate their understanding of the patterns, dynamics, and consequences of societal oppression into actions designed to facilitate social change. An empowerment process model is presented that includes issues related to personal connections, the grieving process, the necessity of actions, barriers to change, and the benefits of empowerment. The role of the classroom is then discussed, both in terms of the kind of learning environment that is necessary to facilitate the empowerment process and the methods used. Finally, the concept of moral exclusion is introduced as one way to understand how the empowerment process results in students seeing the world in a new way. The chapter ends with a collection of student comments, excerpted from their journals, that reveal the kind of significant transformative changes that occur in the learning process.

---

[1] Adapted from Ferguson, 1980, p. 1.

EMPOWERMENT PROCESS[2]

Dictionary definitions of empowerment include phrases such as "to give power or authority to," to "authorize," "enable or permit," or "license." When students become empowered to advocate for social justice, they affirm the authority that already belongs to them as human beings and as citizens. This power is both internal, in terms of how they experience their own efficacy, and external, in terms of the power they have to persuade others in interpersonal encounters and relationships. This power enables them to protest injustice and to seek alternatives to oppression at the levels of organization, community, country, and world.

Empowerment is a process of discovering within ourselves and in others the capacity to bring about change. Empowerment means accepting personal responsibility to act. As students realize their power, they become free to transform themselves and to discover untapped strengths. Their individual actions of protest and creativity create a ripple effect that empowers others. At the heart of the empowerment process is the phenomenon of helping someone to see something that he or she has not seen before and subsequently, to act upon that insight. It is a power to help others see new things as possible.

In the model that we propose in this chapter, students are encouraged to see the empowerment process as beginning with the smallest of individual actions. When joined with other actions, these efforts create a chain reaction that releases human energy. Over time, this energy can build to become a critical mass that results in social change. Each person's awareness and actions will increase the likelihood that a critical mass will develop and lead to change.

Creating a just society and world is a global issue of overwhelming proportion. A transformation from injustice and oppression to just alternatives will not come about easily or quickly. Giving birth to social justice will be a long and painful process. It requires personal commitment and social transformation on a massive scale. Despite the magnitude of the problem, if social change for social justice is to take place it will grow from the grassroots, at the level of the individual, the small group, local organizations, and communities. By starting at this level, the empowerment process provides a bridge that connects the person and the smaller group with larger social change movements. This bridge becomes a vehicle for change as students join with others

---

[2] This section is adapted with permission from White & Van Soest, 1984.

in crossing over to yet uncharted terrain. If we trust the process, empowerment will provide the energy needed for creating a just society.

Personal Transformation and Connections

In the 1980s it became clear that if social movements were to grow, organizations needed to focus on the individual. It became clear that individual needs must be met if the larger cause is to flourish. In *The Aquarian Conspiracy,* Marilyn Ferguson (1980) describes how social activism stems from personal transformation. In the empowerment process, first steps toward such personal transformation take place when students acknowledge their deep feelings about injustice and oppression and the role they play as privileged or oppressed based on their social identities. Personal connections are critical. Problems of injustice and oppression at first seem so large and removed from their everyday lives that students may not feel personally responsible. However, once they begin to accept their feelings of shame, guilt, anger, and other feelings of distress as normal human reactions to the horrors of injustice, they can become free to see other ways in which we are all personally connected to the issues.

Personal connections to issues of diversity and social justice can be many and varied. Awareness and/or acknowledgement of their feelings about racism in the United States often begins the change process for students. They may begin to feel personally involved with racism in a variety of ways. Perhaps the most basic connection between students comes from shared fears about being victimized by racism and other forms of oppression. For others who have benefited from an oppressive system based on race, concerns about being viewed as a racist can cause some students to take action. While some students feel defensive and attempt to prove they are not racist, connecting with the issue of racism in such a personal way can nonetheless open the door to exploring new ways of thinking. Some students become enraged when they learn about historical events of which they had previously been unaware and make new connections through those feelings of anger at not having been taught all aspects of our country's history. Some become outraged at the lack of vital human service programs for certain populations in the United States. Other students make a connection to the issue of social justice in a more direct, political way through an analysis of how economic and political interests operate to maintain inequities. Some students begin to question laws that sanction and create oppressive conditions and realize that horrors can be unleashed legally as, for example, when slavery in the United States was legal. They realize that the Nazi Party in Germany, based on creating a superior race, was able to implement its genocidal program legally and with the approval of citizens and the establishment. For these students, such questioning compels them to begin to respond to higher principles such as valuing all life and respecting the uniqueness of each individual. Some students feel a deep sense of commitment based on a moral or philosophical principle regarding the value of human life, a perspective that transcends traditional differences between people based on race, ethnicity, religion, etc.

Education about cultural diversity for social justice calls upon students and faculty to look within to identify connections such as those described above. The process of making connections between injustice and oppression and their personal lives leads students to begin to consider ways to respond. Thus, the empowerment process starts with where each of us is on the issues and awareness of the personal connections that create feelings of conflict and distress.

During the process of exploring diversity and oppression, students often make an important personal connection when they discover a gap between what they want to see in themselves and what they actually find in themselves. Students may experience a loss of or threat to self-respect and question the self-image they want to hold as they struggle to come to terms with effects that privilege and oppression have had in their own lives (Pinderhughes, 1988). It has been proposed that such a sense of loss is triggered by a "discrediting of familiar assumptions" that creates a "crisis of discontinuity" (Marris, 1974, p. 21). Thus, transformative learning initiates a process similar to the grieving process. By understanding the grieving process and appreciating it as a normal response, both students and faculty can support and validate each person's personal journey toward change. In the next section, we apply concepts related to loss and grief to transformative learning.

The Grieving Cycle

As students begin to share their experiences and reactions, they may experience a process that is similar to the grieving cycle described by Elisabeth Kubler-Ross (1975) and others in relation to death and other losses. The five stages of grieving are summarized below with examples of how each may be experienced by students in relation to racism and other forms of oppression.

1. *Denial.* While many students believe there is injustice in our country and the world, they deal with their feelings by denying that a problem exists at this stage of the process. This protects them from making personal connections that thus do not need to be felt and creates a state of "psychic numbness." In this state, students are protected against a feeling of being out of control and against feeling responsible or accountable. The denial stage helps cushion the impact of the horrors of injustice and oppression under which we all live. Students are resistant to information about injustice to protect themselves from discomfort. Their response is often automatic and unemotional. For example, upon hearing about racism as an institutionalized phenomenon, students may experience confusion and express an incapacity to comprehend what that means. They may perceive such ideas to be propaganda. There is a desire to hold on to a belief that the world as they perceive it is a just place and to maintain faith in our "experts" and leaders to uphold justice.

2. *Anger/Rage.* In reaction to loss, whether it is loss of innocence, of belief that the world is just, or of self-image, denial is often followed by anger or rage. Students react with intense feelings, for instance, as they share stories of oppression such as a racial profiling incident, a hate crime, an innocent Black man living on death row for decades before his innocence is proved, or any number of other stories personally experienced or learned about through friends or in the media. As a Euro-American student wrote in her journal: "I am angry when I realize that I have always lived in a racist and sexist society and that everyone lied to me about it . . . I am furious when I discover that our country was founded on violence, slavery, and annihilation of indigenous people when I have always been taught that it was founded on truth and justice . . . . I am angry when I consider that some people are considered to be expendable by the powers that be." A student of color expressed his anger when he wrote: "I could strangle some of the privileged white students in this program and in this class! They don't *know* about police brutality? What in the world do they think slavery was about? Are they stupid or do they just choose to put their heads in the sand? I am so sick of hearing them be shocked about injustice that I want to scream!!" This stage of the grieving cycle is perhaps the most uncomfortable for many students and faculty, especially those who have been taught that it is not socially acceptable to be angry and who may cringe at seeing anger in others.

3. *Bargaining.* In the bargaining stage, students may be aware of the seriousness of injustice and oppression and at the same time try to protect them-

selves from understanding the full impact on themselves and other people. One student's journal reflects such a desire to strike a bargain to minimize his pain and sense of responsibility: "I understand that the world is unjust and that there is work to do. Yet, it is important that we understand that things are not anywhere near as serious now as they used to be. We no longer enslave people, for example, and everyone has the right to vote. While there are still problems with some people accessing what they need, there are laws that now protect people from unfair and unequal treatment." While the bargaining stage may help students manage their pain and provides some hope, it is difficult to be completely consoled by bargaining because they now see the injustices and how much more needs to be done.

4. *Depression.* The magnitude and ramifications of oppression, when truly faced directly, can be so overwhelming that thinking about it can produce feelings of extreme helplessness and even despair. Some students have described their dismay at recognizing the disparity between personal anguish over the realities of oppression and injustice and the social reality of "business as usual." Some students express feelings of self-blame, suggesting that they feel that it is they who are insane and overreacting rather than society that is perpetuating and allowing such injustices. When students begin to experience such feelings, they often retreat back to a state of denial in which they refuse to acknowledge the problems and resist becoming involved with the course content.

Apathy characterizes the depression stage of the grieving cycle. Students may report withdrawal symptoms and feel that they have no energy left to hear anything else about injustice. They feel hopeless, helpless, and alone. It is a state of despair. As one student wrote: "Something has changed for me at this point in the semester. My optimism has vanished and all I see is pain and separation between all humans, only ignorance, prejudice. I don't see any point in having a course like this when there is no hope for changing the conditions we are learning about."

5. *Acceptance and Reorganization.* At this stage, students refuse to accept the inevitability of injustice. Instead, they accept responsibility to act and are able to reorganize their behavior and purposefully work toward finding solutions. They have an increased awareness of reality and are able to act on that reality. They are empowered to bring about change. Through taking action, they have hope in the possibility of change.

The grieving cycle, as described above, can provide a useful guide for students to understand what they may go through as they face the realities of racism, injustice, and oppression. The cycle is not absolute—not everyone goes through every stage in a linear fashion, or at the same predictable pace. Yet the model can help both faculty and students comprehend their own feelings and behavior and those of others. It is important also to recognize that the cycle, as applied to our reactions to learning about cultural diversity and oppression, differs from other types of grieving in that we cannot imagine a final resolution of the problem, nor of our grieving, in the foreseeable future. As long as problems of injustice are ongoing, students may find themselves recycling through stages. In other words, feelings of denial, apathy, despair, anger, and helplessness may return as they continue to learn of new situations of injustice through their heightened awareness. Students need to be prepared for that eventuality and to understand that, although feelings of grief can be overwhelming at times, hope cannot be bought with a refusal to feel.

The empowerment process helps students to accept the fact that experiencing feelings in the grieving cycle is a sane reaction to facing the realities of an unjust world. It helps them to know that they are not alone in their feelings. Students can help each other by acknowledging their mutual feelings and by talking about the problems. It is important to discover that we are all in this together. The fact that our situation is a collective one, bearing on us all, albeit in different ways depending on the status conferred by our social identities, has tremendous implications. It means that in facing oppression together, openly and deeply, people can rediscover their interconnectedness in the web of life, and this brings personal power and resilience (Macy, 1983).

The Necessity of Actions

Actions give students the energy to work through the grieving cycle. Callahan (1982) writes about the effectiveness of actions: "New and different actions can change thought and feeling just as new and different thoughts can change behavior. Taking even one small step on a journey changes one's perspective on the landscape, as well as changing one's self definition to that of a person who is able to move out toward new goals. Action, either practical or symbolic, overcomes the learned helplessness, inertia and apathy correlated with the absence of hope" (p. 1). By taking action, commitment to effecting change is strengthened as well as chances for making social change possible.

Actions become the steps on the empowerment journey. Often the first steps are the most difficult. To act in response to social injustice involves an evolutionary process. What students are able to do today may be radically different from what they can do next month or next year. Students learn that small steps lead to larger actions in a natural progression. As first steps, students usually think more about racism and other forms of oppression and begin to talk about it with their families, friends, and others in their immediate circles. Gradually, they move to reading more about the subject on their own, to speaking out at public gatherings, to writing letters, to educating others, to wearing a button, to circulating and/or signing petitions, to lobbying their political representatives, to advocating for agency policy changes in their field placements, to peaceful demonstrations, to organizing actions with others. It is important that students' efforts are acknowledged, including the smallest effort, because social justice is accomplished by laying one brick at a time, taking one step at a time.

We can suggest to students that to be advocates for social justice, they need to weave the issues into their daily lives. They can be most effective by bringing their advocacy work with them wherever they go—in their own families, neighborhoods, workplaces, social gatherings, and field placement agencies. Everyone has a skill or talent that can be used in the empowerment process. Faculty can suggest that students focus on the present and ask themselves what it is they do in their daily lives and then consider how they might do it for social justice. Thus, their lives are changed but not rearranged.

Students' actions become the impetus for their growth. The more they do, the greater their desire to know and to share what they have learned. Because they choose their actions, they can set their own limits and control their rate of change. To get started, all that is needed is a strong commitment to work for an end to racism and other forms of oppression and injustice. Students learn from the examples of others. When they begin to act, their actions join with the actions of others to provide the energy for the journey.

Barriers to Change

Part of the learning process involves students looking at the barriers that keep them from being advocates for social justice. A common block for many students is personal fear of taking risks, standing out by making a personal statement, being embarrassed in public, losing security or the respect of people they had thought were friends, or being alienated from family.

Students are often deterred from social justice advocacy actions by a fear of stepping outside their personal safety zones. We all have spheres of operation in which we feel safe. Stepping outside this area is risky for when we confront issues in a public way, we may be subjected to the ridicule, misunderstanding, and anger of others. For example, interrupting a racist joke can be a terrifying and thus courageous action for a student to take when he/she would quite possibly receive a negative response or ostracism from others for doing so. The empowerment process, however, generates confidence and courage. As students become more involved and are sustained by the support of others, they discover that their safety zones expand.

A significant barrier for many students is the fear of creating communication gaps, tensions, and conflict within their own family if they identify the prejudice within that system. Applying the process of empowerment to that of family change can be helpful for students in this regard. Students can be encouraged to be sensitive to each family member's attitude toward the issues. Unrealistic expectations about the family's response usually increase the tension. Communicating consideration for others while respecting one's own stage of involvement can help reduce resistance to open discussion about the issues.

Some students speak quite honestly about another barrier: that of losing the privileges conferred on them based on their own social identities in an oppressive system. As one student wrote in his journal, "I feel terrible about the inequities I am learning about and I want to work to change the system. I must admit, though, that I am quite ambivalent about what I might have to give up in terms of the privileges and benefits I currently get from the system as it is since I am a white, heterosexual male. It is easy to think theoretically about social justice but when I think in practical terms—like maybe I wouldn't get preferential treatment in a job application situation if there were truly equal opportunity—I am ashamed to say that I have to think twice." It is important to acknowledge the courage it takes for students to be honest about this and to challenge them to face their cognitive dissonance rather than slipping back into denial. Positive role models of people throughout history who were advocates for social justice can help in this regard as well.

Two additional barriers frequently impede progress in becoming social justice advocates: the fear of speaking out in public and the fear of not being sufficiently informed about the issues. By encouraging small steps, the empowerment process can be used to overcome these fears. Speaking out in public will seem less frightening if students are encouraged to first talk to those with whom they feel most comfortable. Then, when they are ready, they can begin to speak to other people in small groups and at public meetings. It can be very rewarding to find that acquaintances and even strangers are willing to talk about issues of racism, poverty, and oppression of other kinds. Often the message on a pin or button (e.g., "Stop Racism," "Another student for justice") will help begin a conversation. Speaking out is a natural outgrowth of increased commitment and involvement.

To reduce the fear of being uninformed, it is helpful to tell students that we can never have enough information or remember all the facts. Statistics change and one fact can counteract another. What is most important is having an understanding of underlying concepts. Once students develop a point of view as a framework for their own thinking, the facts will fall into place. A preponderance of information exists in books, articles, and videotapes. To make sense out of the facts, it is helpful to absorb only small amounts of information at one time and take time to process it. Students will soon be surprised by how much they know.

Benefits of Empowerment

As advocates for social justice, social workers are enriched and strengthened by the friendships that are made with others who share common goals. We get to know and appreciate others whose backgrounds and lifestyles may be quite different from our own. People who work for social justice are old and young, rich and poor, religious and nonreligious, heterosexual and homosexual, and bisexual and transsexual, and come from a variety of cultural and ethnic backgrounds. Our strength grows as we celebrate this diversity and face our differences honestly. In the process we learn to trust each other enough to live justly on a personal level.

Throughout the empowerment process, our actions become seeds that germinate best within a supportive environment. As the seeds grow, we discover that we have developed previously untapped strengths and talents. Some students report taking actions that they thought they could never take, when the opportunity to act presented itself. Like wildflowers, our actions spread, affecting those in the world around us. One student reported that as a result of her actions, her husband became involved in a community civil rights group. Another reported that, because of her new involvements, her children were engaging in dinnertime discussions of issues that they never seemed interested in before. Thus, there is a ripple effect and the circle of awareness continues to grow. As personal transformations become interwoven with social change, lives take on new meaning and deeper purpose.

What sustains us in our social justice advocacy work is the belief that our actions can and will make a difference. Although individual acts may seem insignificant, they have tremendous power when joined with the efforts of countless others. Historically, we know that social and political changes have always stemmed from the grassroots. The abolition of slavery, the right to unionize, women's rights, and civil rights, to name a few, all came about as a result of grassroots efforts. If social justice is to become a reality, a collective commitment to change must be made at the local level. As more and more people unite, we gain the strength to change both the world and ourselves.

> Actions are clearly effective when those involved in them experience their capabilities and their strength. That exciting feeling of empowerment is something that cannot be taken away. It becomes part of how we think about ourselves, as purposeful, effective people who can express ourselves clearly on an issue of vital importance.[3]

THE ROLE OF THE CLASSROOM

Joanna Rogers Macy (1983) writes that the discovery of the vital interconnectedness of our lives has largely been made through working in groups. It is in groups that people have the opportunity to experience and share with others their deepest responses to incidents of injustice. Through experience and sharing in the classroom as a group, students are enabled to move beyond numbness and powerlessness into action, from denial into awareness, and from hopelessness into hope. Each classroom becomes an opportunity for students: to meet in a small group to educate themselves and each other about oppression; to discuss their feelings, attitudes, and values; and to commit themselves to actions that advocate for social justice. The empowerment group process emphasizes making personal connections in a trusting environment. This approach encourages the kind of personal transformations necessary to bring about social change.

Personal growth and empowerment can come about when the climate within the classroom is respectful and supportive. Students must feel safe and

---

[3] From Cook & Kirk, 1983, p. 18, as quoted in White & Van Soest, 1984.

accepted if they are to work through their grief and move from despair to action. A safe environment can be created when class members try to understand empathically each other's feelings and personal meanings. The professor plays a key role by serving as a model of empathic listening, with an understanding that the more personal a statement is, the more universal it is. By listening to understand on a deep level, the professor can begin to experience the feelings and connections of the students. As students in the classroom develop an attitude of acceptance and appreciation of each other, they can come to feel safe enough to expose themselves. A positive outlook about each other as persons is especially important when there is disagreement or differing points of view and experiences.

It is important for the professor to keep in mind each student's feelings, perceptions, and readiness for action. The direction of each student in the empowerment process will be different and unique. Some of them are at the beginning stages of assuming the role of social justice advocate, while others are more seasoned activists. In an atmosphere of nonjudgmental acceptance, students can more freely disclose their feelings, ideas, and struggles. They can experience the conditions that help them overcome the limits imposed by socialization. They can learn to become free and have their energies released for action. Such individual change and growth is facilitated within a classroom environment in which the professor balances individual concerns and class processes. Within the context of a nurturing environment, the classroom as a source of empowerment does three things: share information, provide support, and mobilize for action.

Sharing Information

Sharing information can take many forms. In a formal course, students read and discuss books and articles as assigned. New information is presented through lectures, panel presentations, videotapes, and guest speakers. In addition, students can inform each other of social justice activities in the community, share knowledge obtained from individual research, and bring in their life experiences. As students learn more, they are able to overcome their tendency to deny injustice and oppression.

Providing Support

A key element in the empowerment classroom is providing support for each other as students go through the grieving cycle described earlier. A student may have read an article that plunged her into a state of hopelessness or anger; in the classroom those feelings are recognized and discussed. Another student may experience alienation from family members and in the classroom those feelings can be aired. Someone may have taken an action that felt exhilarating and freeing. The support of the classroom can be further affirmation of the joys of empowerment. Sometimes, the students as a group may experience mutual feelings and in the classroom it is safe to rage, to cry, to sing, or to laugh together. The class becomes a place where students can be themselves—where they can share their ignorance, loneliness, despair, and anger, as well as their joys and hopes about their personal journeys.

Mobilizing for Action

A natural part of the group empowerment process is taking action. While acquiring information and gaining support from their peers, students can take the first steps of involvement. Some students may wear a button to work or to their field placement, some may talk daily to others about the issues. Others may read an alternative news source or periodical each week (e.g., *The Nation, In These Times, Sojourners, Mother Jones*) or write letters to congressional representatives, or bring a family member, neighbor, or friend to a lecture on campus. The opportunities for action taking are unlimited. As students become empowered, they change. With the group providing a lifeline of support and information, personal transformation begins.

The empowerment group as a whole or a subgroup within the larger group, whether in a classroom, continuing education, or small discussion group environment, can organize small group actions. These events involve a few people making a significant statement. Handing out materials in public places, attending a rally together, setting up a literature table at events, organizing a letter writing campaign to public officials, organizing an event for students in an elementary school—these are examples of small group actions. Large group actions, such as conferences and public lectures, are activities that students can participate in together.

It is important not to discourage small actions—every action is an important step in the empowerment process. Not everyone may be ready to engage in the same type of action. Some students, for example, may want to study the issues more and start with self-reflection while others may be eager to take a public action. Students learn about empowerment from the examples of each person's actions. The actions flow from and in turn strengthen the empowerment process. Because the activities vary according to the interests and talents of the students, the possibilities for actions are unlimited.

Individual, small group, and large group actions (or a combination of all three) are used in the empowerment classroom; the result of those actions is an overcoming of the inertia and helplessness that can immobilize students. With each step and each action, students move farther along their empowerment journey. As students learn to trust the process, they become more courageous and confident in the face of opposition. They begin to trust their perceptions and let them guide their actions. When students feel discouraged and weak, the group can be there to help them. As students become more aware of their connectedness with others who are working for social change, they find that they are an integral part of a larger effort to create a just society.

EXPANDING MORAL BOUNDARIES

Through the empowerment process, students begin to transform themselves and to discover their capacity to bring about social change. The transformation process involves seeing the world in a new way. Once they have had the courage to look directly at the forces of injustice and face their own positions as oppressed and/or privileged, students are free to also look at the beliefs they have about which people should be treated justly. The concept of moral exclusion (Opotow, 1990) provides a useful framework for students to understand themselves and their beliefs in relation to different groups in society. As students become transformed, their moral boundaries expand and become less and less exclusive.

Moral exclusion occurs when persons or groups are perceived as being outside the boundary in which values, rules, and considerations of fairness apply. Persons outside our moral boundaries are seen as expendable or undeserving and thus harming them appears acceptable, appropriate, or just. The process of categorizing groups negatively and excluding them from the realm of acceptable norms or values is linked to stereotypes and prejudicial attitudes related to ethnocentrism. It is linked to the notion that the process of determining who is entitled to social justice has always been and is an exclusionary one (i.e., a process that has always applied the rules of justice and fairness to certain people and not applied them to others). Diversity courses address the wide range of groups whose rights have been invalidated and delegitimized because of their exclusion from the scope of justice.

While seldom conscious of them, we all have beliefs about which people should be treated justly and the broadness or narrowness of our moral boundaries is influenced by prevailing cultural norms. For example, it is no longer considered acceptable in the United States to own slaves but it is generally considered acceptable today to exclude gay men and lesbians from certain benefits and entitlements that all others have, such as partner benefits and the right to marry.

The exclusion of an out group from the norms of fairness is a cognitive, affective, and behavioral phenomenon that enables otherwise considerate people to engage in self-serving behavior or inaction in everyday situations in order to gain benefits to themselves even though at injurious costs to others. We live in a world where certain groups of people benefit from an implicit and explicit contract that disadvantages other groups. According to Mills (1997), our world is built on the Racial (Sexual, Heterosexual) Contract, which is simultaneously quite obvious and also nonobvious, because most Whites (males, heterosexuals) do not think about it or do not think about it as the outcome of a history of political oppression.

The concept of moral exclusion provides a mechanism for making obvious one's own personal processes of excluding certain people from the boundaries of fairness. By helping students analyze their own moral boundaries within the context of understanding oppression, the professor provides a tool that can be used to increase understanding and thus to promote personal change. The empowerment process helps students expand their moral boundaries in order to be authentic social justice advocates.

PERSONAL JOURNEYS: STUDENT VOICES OF CHANGE

Empowerment is the discovery and unlocking of individual power for new ways of thinking, acting, and being. It is a transformative learning process. Under what conditions is such transformative change possible for our students? The following excerpts from student journals—ungraded, uncensored, free writing—reveal that profound changes can occur in the process of taking just one course on cultural diversity for social justice. The student voices speak for themselves, revealing common themes the authors have heard from students over the years.

"At the beginning of the semester I thought that I was not racist, did not have many negative stereotypes about minorities, and that this class would not change my opinions. Now I realize that oppression is *my* problem. I am part of the problem, and therefore need to be part of the solution. I need to act to bring about change. I have started a growth process and will continue it throughout my life. I am committed to addressing the issues of injustice and not hide from them."

"I feel this class has opened a whole new worldview for me. I thought I knew about oppression and was rather informed about diversity issues. I was very wrong. I was a covert oppressor. I did not understand the depth of oppression. I never thought of myself as having privileges just for being white. Viewing myself as an oppressor strongly influences my ability to change. Instead of being defensive, I can be open to what my part is and take responsibility to take action. I must always speak up or take action when I see an injustice. And I now see injustice."

"I have undergone tremendous personal change over the semester. I am amazed at how naïve I was at the start. It scared me to see the racism in myself. There was a point in the semester when I was ready to give up and I was numb to the topics. But the class wouldn't let me quit even though I was very pissed off that I had to come to class and read the assignments. Now, while I am still disgusted with myself for being an oppressor, knowing that has definitely influenced me to change. I have to take action. I have to share my new knowledge with others and let them know that racism is still strong. I am committed to stay on the path of self-discovery. Challenging my old views will not end with this class."

"I began the school of social work with a strong sense and appreciation for diversity. However, I had never paused to consider the basis for the systems of oppression. I had no idea that I was part of the problem. I initially vehemently rejected this idea. This class has changed my life tremendously. I confronted my own oppression as a Black person, a woman, and a lesbian. I have tapped into a depth of emotion that is now available to use to make change. It is vital to know that I am connected to others and myself. It is my lifelong goal to become more empowered on a personal level and to not stand for injustice at the macro and institutional level. I now know that none of us are truly free until we are all free."

"This class has been like a huge magnifying glass that was looking at every aspect of my life. In my entire educational career, never has a class changed me in the numerous ways this class has. Weeks, months, and even years from now, the effects will still impact me. I am on a profound journey of understanding my responsibility as a privileged, non-oppressed person all my life to work to eliminate oppression of all kinds. This journey is not going to stop with the end of this class."

"Some people are overtly racist; for some it is more covert. One way that people can be racist is by thinking of themselves as non-racist people with no prejudices and not part of the oppressive structure. This was me coming into the School of Social Work. I learned most of the ideas in the course with my mouth open in disbelief. Boy, do I fit in to the opportunity structure of this oppressive system! The responsibility is thus mine to change. I am leaving this course feeling inspired. I must fight for social and economic justice."

"Over the course of this semester, I have changed my perceptions dramatically, become aware of denial, and faced some contradictions between my stated principles and my daily practices. My self-image has gotten shaken up. I'm not sure I can adequately communicate the enormity of the perspective change that acknowledging the privilege, unearned advantage, conferred dominance, and power of my status as an Anglo has brought to me. A whole new way of seeing the world and my place in it has occurred. Until I was able to see the privileges I live with, I had excuses for stereotypical views and excuses for being powerless to change society. Learning that I am part of the problem and that I have the power to address injustice, both personally and in social systems, has been very liberating! The world has become a much bigger place in this short semester and my role in it has expanded."

"I have undergone a transformation. When I came into this class I assumed exaggeration of oppressed populations when explaining the depths of that oppression. How scary is that? Especially since I am a

member of one of those oppressed populations! I have been socialized to believe 'it is not so bad,' when in actuality it is worse. What
has changed is that I am no longer afraid and I have made some
changes. I had never thought about taking a stand before. I will march.
I will speak out. I will educate others about the issues. I will not think
that I cannot make a difference. I will teach my son that everything is
not as it seems. I will teach him to read between the lines. I will teach
him to be strong and speak up. I will teach him to go against the
grain if he feels it is important to do so."

"I am unbelievably changed in one semester! The connection to my
role as an oppressor was a tough pill to swallow since such a large
aspect of my identity has been as a 'helper.' At first I completely rejected the concept of institutionalized racism and of my own part in
perpetuating it. In my mind the world was still a fair place. Slowly I
came to understand that our prized institutions and cultural norms
are oppressive and as a part of those systems, I am colluding. A flood
of emotion has been opened in me. I have been forever changed and
now I must act."

"This semester has radically affected the way I view the world and
myself. I have uncovered some uncomfortable truths about the ugly
racism that lives inside of me. I will never be able to see things in
quite the same way again and I am grateful. I am a better person. I
now realize how deeply rooted the problem of racism is. I now realize
that I have to be proactive. I need to be willing to critically examine
myself for deeply engrained racist beliefs. I will keep reading the literature that reveals the ways that oppression thrives. I have friends
who support and challenge me not to give up fighting injustice."

"This course has had a profound effect on me. Being able to stand up
and be gay in front of the class and to have the support of professors
and peers was a powerful experience. I am no longer afraid that someone will think I am gay. I have been able to explore things that I
would have been afraid to do before coming out. On the other side,
viewing myself as the oppressor has been the hardest thing for me
this semester. My sense of social justice has really been awakened—

so much so that I am seriously considering how to make fighting for it a career."

"This is incredible. Viewing myself as an oppressor has actually given me some power. Since I am part of the problem, rather than the innocent bystander I have always felt I was, I have the ability, indeed, the requirement to do my part to make changes. I have also been oppressed and I have hidden my Jewish identity in certain situations. I am going to try to stop doing this and learn to educate people about how they are being oppressive. After leaving this course, I will continue to question, read, spread the word, be a good listener, and never forget that we have been brought up in this racist society and we must change it!"

"What I have learned goes against everything I learned growing up. If I can change my way of seeing things to such a great extent in such a short time, then there is hope for the world. I truly want to promote social and economic justice and I am a persistent person."

CONCLUSION

In this chapter we presented an empowerment model as a framework for the kind of transformative learning that is required to help students develop or deepen their commitment to their role as social justice advocates. Students' journal comments demonstrate that deep change is possible through diversity education for social justice as eyes are opened, hearts are touched, moral boundaries are expanded, and courage is discovered.

This book is an attempt to provide research-based information about the learning process and teaching methodologies that address how students are moved from ideas to an examination of deep-seated beliefs that can lead to the internalization and implementation of social justice values. Part One established the context for integrating cultural diversity and social justice content into the curriculum by providing a theoretical foundation and educational framework, defining key issues and concepts, and introducing learning and change processes. In Part Two, we will provide information about what both professors and students bring to the learning situation and what occurs in the change process for these two groups. Chapter Six focuses on students, Chapter Seven on professors, and Chapter Eight on the interactional dynamics in the classroom. In Chapter Nine, three professors dialogue about teaching and learning processes.

REFERENCES

Callahan, S. (1982, November 19). Peacemaking strategies for inertia. *National Catholic Reporter*, 1.

Cook, A., & Kirk, G. (1983). *Greenham women everywhere*. Boston: South End Press.

Ferguson, M. (1980). *The aquarian conspiracy*. Los Angeles: J. P. Tarcher.

Gil, D. (1998). *Confronting injustice and oppression: Concepts and strategies for social workers*. New York: Columbia University Press.

Kubler-Ross, E. (1975). *Death: The final stage of growth*. Englewood Cliffs, NJ: Prentice-Hall.

Macy, J. R. (1983). *Despair and personal power in the nuclear age*. Philadelphia: New Society.

Marris, P. (1974). *Loss and change*. London: Routledge and Kegan Paul.

Mills, K. W. (1997). *The racial contract*. Ithaca, NY: Cornell.

Opotow, S. (1990). Moral exclusion and injustice: An introduction. *Journal of Social Issues, 46*(1), 1–20.

Pinderhughes, E. (1988). Significance of culture and power in the human behavior curriculum. In C. Jacobs & D. D. Bowles (Eds.), *Ethnicity and Race: Critical Concepts in Social Work* (pp. 152–166). Silver Spring, MD: National Association of Social Workers.

White, M. S., & Van Soest, D. (1984). *Empowerment of people for peace*. Minneapolis, MN: WAMM.

Part Two
Teaching and Learning Processes: The Student, the Teacher, the Interactions

INTRODUCTION TO PART TWO

This part of the book is aimed at increasing understanding of teaching and learning processes. Research and experience-based information is presented about what both professors and students bring to the learning situation and what occurs in the change process for them. Part Two thus dissects aspects of the fourth component of the educational model provided in Chapter One, transformative learning processes.

Chapter Six focuses on students: their experiences and outcomes from learning about diversity-for-social-justice. It highlights three empirical studies that were conducted in courses that were based on the educational model presented in Part One. The studies present evidence of how students are moved from ideas, beliefs, and new awareness about equality and justice to operationalizing them into actions for social change.

Chapter Seven focuses on professors: what they bring to the learning process and challenges they encounter in the classroom. Three paradigms or perspectives with which to frame the teaching experience are presented and their usefulness discussed.

In Chapter Eight, the focus shifts to interactional dynamics among students and professors in the classroom related to various constellations of racial identities. The discussion focuses on racial identity development models and how they contribute to understanding the lenses through which both students and faculty view the learning process and the interactions that result. This chapter emphasizes how a process orientation premised on racial and social identity frameworks can provide a perspective for faculty to work with their own learning about diversity and to understand and facilitate the journey that their students are expected to engage in as they learn about diversity and social justice.

Finally, Chapter Nine is devoted to the description of some challenges encountered in teaching a course on cultural diversity, power, and oppression. Candid dialogue among three tenured professors is used to provide a practical understanding and awareness of the impact of the course on both students and instructors. Thus, Part Two ends with a unique view of the impact of the teaching and learning process on its participants and the implications of this impact on the profession as well as on the curriculum.

Chapter Six
Research: Student Experiences and Outcomes

Faculty often report that class discussions related to social, cultural, and ethnic diversity arouse strong emotions and strained interactions among students, both in courses that focus on diversity issues and courses that integrate the issues into other content (Tatum, 1992; Van Soest, 1994). Classroom discussions about issues such as power, privilege, social identity, and empowerment often provoke deepened student awareness of social justice issues, the multilevel aspects of oppression, historical legacies, and culture-based identities. Facing the social and psychological consequences of injustice, however, can be difficult. Regardless of whether students have lived lives of privilege or marginalization, they may find exploration of these topics painful—and they may resist it.

It is thus important for educators to be aware of and seek to eliminate the cognitive and emotional barriers to student learning that often emerge during classroom discussions and student interactions. Empirical research is needed to measure both the process and outcome of educational models in order to help educators understand student experiences and thus be in a position to promote positive change. In this chapter, three such studies conducted by the authors are highlighted.

Each investigation was conducted in courses that were based on the model presented in Part One. The first study (Van Soest, 1994) attempted to understand, in an exploratory way, how students experienced the learning process and outcomes of an MSW course aimed at developing knowledge and awareness of cultural diversity and societal oppression. The second study (Garcia & Van Soest, 1997) focused on understanding more specific issues and processes related to student change in a similar MSW course, including changes in students' understanding of their social identity, cognitive and affective changes related to the effects of discrimination and oppression on their own lives, and barriers to and/or resources for confronting oppression that they discovered during the learning process. The third study (Van Soest, 1996) focused on deep-seated beliefs that influence students' thoughts about social justice and about actions that demonstrate students' level of commitment to advocacy on behalf of oppressed populations. This study also measured the distress that may be experienced when examining one's worldview and activities as part of the educational process. Recommendations are made based on the results of each study, as well as suggestions for further research.

STUDY 1: A FIELD STUDY OF HOW STUDENTS EXPERIENCE THE LEARNING PROCESS[1]

This exploratory study focused on student experiences in an MSW course on Societal Oppression and Cultural Diversity. The course aimed to prepare students for their role in working to eliminate oppressive hierarchies, for equality, and to provide culturally sensitive services. Course content focused on power and inequality in addition to culture. Thus, the course involved an examination of important issues on three levels: personal identity and prejudices, institutional oppression, and structural causes and consequences of oppression.

The learning process in the course began with promoting awareness and understanding of the student's own cultural background and its meaning and significance in interaction with others. The model was based on Pinderhughes' (1989) premise that social workers with a positive ethnic identity are better able to value their clients' identity. The course moved beyond the personal and direct practice level to expose the pervasive influence of race, gender, ethnicity, and power on the social worker's own identity. "Beginning with where students are" involved helping them develop empathy for themselves as a first step in understanding the pervasive nature of oppression. This approach was based on the idea that one's own experience as a target of disempowerment provides resources for developing empathy for others who have been oppressed on different grounds. The course centered on generic experiences that have an effect on diverse populations in order to facilitate an understanding of the common elements of oppression.

A major course requirement was participation in a group presentation that focused on the strategies used to oppress a specific population and the micro and macro practice implications. Students were also required to keep a weekly journal in which they were to record their thoughts, feelings, and per-

---

[1] This section draws from Van Soest, 1994. Used with permission.

sonal connections. The journals were not graded and anonymity was assured. Students were encouraged to use a "free writing" style, with the idea being to carry on a conversation with themselves as a way to learn through writing.

To explore how students experienced the learning process and outcome of the course, data were collected from a total of 97 students in two phases of the study. In the first phase, a content analysis was conducted of 30 student journals and in the second phase a questionnaire was completed by 67 students.

Research Questions

Three exploratory questions guided the study: (a) how do students view their own role position or identity in relation to oppression—as victim, benefactor, and/or participant? Do they experience multiple roles or identities?; (b) How do students experience the change process?; and (c) How are students influenced by interactions with other students and the classroom environment?

Methodology

In Phase 1 of the study, a content analysis of 453 entries from all 30 student journals from one section of the course was used to discern how often and in what manner students wrote about three themes: student self-image/social identity in relation to societal oppression content; the change process; and the learning environment, particularly interactions with others students and the professor. Within the range of 5 to 43 journal entries per student, students averaged 15 entries of from one to 10 pages in length. Student diversity included: gender—24 female (80%) and 6 male (20%); race and ethnic identity—21 Euro-American (70%) and 9 persons of color (30%), with 4 African American, 2 Latino, 1 First Nations (Native American), 1 Asian American, and 1 Latino-Native American; and self-designated sexual orientation—16 heterosexual (53.3%), 1 gay/lesbian (3.3%), 1 bisexual (3.3%), and 12 not indicated (40%). All of the students were first year non-advanced standing MSW students in their first semester of graduate studies.

In Phase 2 of the study, which was conducted a year later, an anonymous questionnaire was completed at semester's end by 67 students from three sections of the course (89% response rate) as a follow-up to the Phase I content analysis. Student demographics in Phases 1 and 2 did not differ significantly. Narrative responses to the following three open-ended questions were subjected to a content analysis using the same three themes as Phase I:

1. Please describe what you learned about oppression and how you person-
    ally related to oppression during the course.

2. How did interaction with others students affect your learning?

3. How did interaction with the professor affect your learning?

Phase I Results: Content Analysis of Student Journals
Self-image/Social Identity Theme

There were 120 journal entries out of the total of 453 entries (27%) in which students identified themselves as either victims or benefactors of oppression. Of the 101 entries written by females, 50% addressed their role as victim and 50% addressed how they were benefactors of oppression. Of the 19 entries written by males, 14 (74%) were about their status as benefactors and 5 entries (26%) were about their role as victims. Students of color were three times as likely to write about their role as victims rather than benefactors, while Euro-American students wrote more often about their role as benefactors than as victims (3:2). Students described their experiences with multiple identities in diverse ways as illustrated by the following examples: experiencing oppression due to race (African American) and gender (female) while being in the dominant group based on sexual orientation (heterosexual); being disadvantaged based on gender (female) and ethnic heritage (Irish) while receiving privileges based on race (White) and political party membership (Republican); colluding with and benefiting from oppression due to race (White), gender (male), and class (upper class) while experiencing oppression as a recovering alcoholic.

The Change Process

Of the journal entries related to change, high emotional involvement of students with the issues was particularly striking in 188 entries (42%). A larger percentage of females (46%) and Caucasians (47%) wrote about their affective process compared with males (24%) and students of color (28%). The entries indicate that many students struggled on a deep level with their sense of identity in relation to oppression, as almost all of the entries were about experiencing feelings such as shock, anger, and despair.

Increased awareness was a significant part of the change process as indicated by 132 (29%) of the journal entries. Of these entries, 53 (40%) addressed students' awareness of their own negative attitudes and prejudices, with an equal number being disturbed about their prejudices against African

Americans and homosexuals. Of the 132 entries, 34 (26%) indicated aware-ness of the oppression of groups that seemed to have been outside students' consciousness previously. This was particularly the case in relation to lesbians and gay men, Latinos, and African Americans. In addition, 11 students wrote about becoming aware of their own oppression as women or as students. A significant number of the entries (23%) indicated a strengthened acceptance of responsibility to work to eliminate oppression. The emotional tone of the entries is captured in the following example:

> I have been on an emotional roller coaster since day one. Many times I wanted to return to my former role in a world that seemed so *nice,* neat, and pure. I still tend to want to do that. But I have this compel-ling urge to make things better. I want my children to know how devastating oppression is and how it must be beaten with social jus-tice, fairness, and being able to respect every human being for being themselves; to respect self and all that each person is!

The Learning Environment

The process of interacting with students who were different from them was significant in facilitating learning and change as indicated in 177 journal entries (39%). Such interactions were reported as being difficult and even painful, even though they resulted in positive change. One particular incident in class, involving a student who came out as a lesbian and openly shared her experiences, was particularly influential for 15 of the 30 students. Ten of the 30 students wrote of learning significantly from a student who shared her experiences as a person with a disability. The significance of learning from each other was often powerfully stated:

> It must have been quite frightening for that student to admit she was a lesbian in front of the class. What courage! She is the genesis for my taking a closer look at other cultures and climbing out of my ivory tower to smell the roses. So I guess the adage goes "if you can save one person, then you will be successful" ...well, I have been saved!

Fifty-eight journal entries (13% of the total) related to the environment of the classroom. Four themes emerged as significant. First, concerns about political correctness in the classroom were expressed in statements such as: "I felt I wasn't angry enough to prove that I wasn't a racist"; "I was intimidated by so many women in the class and didn't want to appear sexist so I didn't say what I really felt"; and "I feel constrained sometimes as if I have to watch every word for fear of offending someone." A second theme involved making comparative contrasts between groups of people in terms of who is more oppressed, as illustrated by statements such as: "I am uncomfortable when someone feels their group is more oppressed and thus feel they are entitled to more" and "suffering and discrimination are not a unique [black or Hispanic] experience." The third theme was concern about conflict between students from different oppressed populations that emerged in classroom discussions. And finally, trust issues were important to students, with 2 students indicating a distrust of certain people in the class and 8 students indicating that they experienced a high level of trust and openness.

Phase II Results: Preliminary Confirmation

Responses to the open-ended questionnaire completed by 67 students in three subsequent sections of the same course resulted in qualitative information comparable to that obtained in the Phase I journal analysis. There were three significant responses to the question about what students learned from the course: (a) the pervasiveness and subtleties of oppression; (b) oppression concepts and theory; and (c) the institutional and systemic nature of oppression.

In response to the question about how students personally related to oppression during the course, responses were comparable to the journal entries about the change process; they were involved emotionally to a high degree and their self-image was challenged. Two significant themes emerged: (a) students felt they had personally changed in terms of feelings, attitudes, and behaviors and used their own experiences as a member of an oppressed group to empathize with other oppressed people; and (b) students expressed feelings of guilt and shame about their collusion with oppression and how they benefit from it.

In response to questions about interactions with students and the professor, the significance of such interactions for student learning was confirmed. Similar to the journal entries, student comments indicated that hearing about other students' experiences as victims of oppression had the most impact. Professor behaviors reported as most helpful included demonstrating respect for students, being supportive and available, challenging students, providing insights, being sensitive, and providing a safe environment "where feelings and views could be dealt with and discussed without judgment." Professor behaviors reported as hindering learning involved students feeling intimidated by the professor's strong point of view, a politically correct environment, and feeling that the classroom was not open to all points of view.

Discussion and Implications

This study provides some insights about the combination of multiple and sometimes contested roles and identities that can begin to be uncovered by students in a course that focuses on cultural diversity for social justice. The concept of moral exclusion that was discussed in Chapter Four provides a framework for understanding some student experiences in the classroom. In this study, some students became aware for the first time that they had exercised moral exclusion by marginalizing others, as illustrated by a journal entry: "It is remarkable to me that for the *first* time, I am finding that I feel empathy for homosexuals and their situation." Others realized that, due to denial, self-blame, and internalizing dominant norms, that they had not been aware of their own exclusion and the injustice done to them, as illustrated by a Latina student's journal entry: "I had never before considered that I was 'down there' or 'excluded' or 'marginalized' in some other people's eyes. I have become aware of the pain I experienced growing up as an immigrant. This has been quite a lesson!"

This study also highlights the high level of emotional involvement in which students may engage in a course on cultural diversity for social justice. In Chapter One, the educational framework that was presented included an understanding that the process of learning is a transformative one, influenced by multiple factors that challenge one's sense of self and self-esteem. Insights from this study about the change process that students undergo reveal how curriculum content on diversity aimed at promoting social justice often arouses unexamined feelings about one's role in the societal context of oppression.

Much of the student journaling in this study focused on experiences of loss and feelings related to that loss. In Chapter Four, the empowerment process was presented, including conceptions of loss and grief as part of the change process. Such concepts may provide a useful guide for helping students to successfully engage in the change process when confronting difficult issues. Students in this study seemed to experience loss on several levels, for example, a loss of self-image or social identity as they became aware of their own oppression and a psychological loss as they began to let go of their bene-factor status and its corresponding power. Some students experienced loss in relation to no longer identifying with reference groups that were once signifi-cant, as the following entry illustrates: "I just had a very upsetting phone conversation with my father about a racial situation in my hometown. I felt so disappointed about my father's prejudiced opinions. I am faced with seeing my father as a racist and I am grieving for the perfect father who I thought was just toward all human beings."

In this study, a powerful element of the learning environment was the sharing by peers of their personal experiences with oppression. This is consis-tent with data from other studies that show that when representatives of a dominant and subordinate social group interact, the result is a more favorable attitude of the dominant group toward the subordinate group and a greater willingness to extend social justice principles to them (Cook, 1990). While more intellectual debates seem to result in conflictual discussions around which group is more oppressed, the ability to empathize seems to be facilitated by personal sharing. The power of classroom interactions to facilitate or hinder learning is clearly suggested in the student responses. This highlights the need for educators to pay special attention to the creation of an open and safe class-room environment that is characterized by respect, empathy, and an honoring of each student's individuality and process, while at the same time challeng-ing them to engage with difficult material in a meaningful way. When stu-dents (particularly those who are White) discuss their feelings of shame and guilt, it is important to empathically accept what they are experiencing and, at the same time, provide direction that helps them to move on. When stu-dents assume a talking position that focuses the discussion on their own feel-ings of shame and guilt, it is important to not succumb to the covert request that others listen to or forgive or take care of them by not holding them accountable for their behavior. When students say they feel unsafe in an at-mosphere of "political correctness," it is important to help them examine what that means in terms of their own expectation of having the privilege of feel-ing safe before taking risks, i.e., focusing on safety can be not only a way for White students to avoid acknowledging their racism, but also a way to pro-tect their privileged position rather than addressing issues of power and op-pression honestly and directly.

STUDY 2: STUDENTS' CHANGING PERCEPTIONS OF DIVERSITY AND OPPRESSION[2]

In this study we explored how 43 MSW students experienced the learning process in two sections of a required course on diversity and oppression that was based on the same model as the first study. Questions that guided the research were: How did students' understanding of their social identity change over the course of the semester? What cognitive and affective changes accompanied their consideration of the effects of discrimination and oppression in their own lives? What barriers to and/or resources for confronting oppression did they discover during the learning process?

The Study

At the beginning of the semester, the 43 students audiotaped a self-administered interview patterned after a taping project[3] developed by Tatum (1992). The approximately hour-long interview inquired into the development of their social identity. The interview questionnaire had six sections that asked students to:

1. Provide demographic information.

2. Discuss their experience and contact with those different from themselves.

3. Describe their personal identity.

4. Explore their attitudes toward current race/racism issues.

5. Examine the cost of oppression.

6. Describe their feelings about doing the assignment.

The taped interview was intended to challenge students to examine their own social identity, social status, and roles as oppressors/oppressed. The tape recordings were collected and held until the end of the semester, without being heard by the instructor. Near the end of the semester, the tapes were returned to students along with an assignment to listen to the tape and write a paper reflecting how they felt hearing their views from the beginning of the semester. An optional assignment was to write the story of their racial and social identity in narrative form, beginning with "My name is, . . . and I was born . . . ."

---

[2] This section draws from Garcia & Van Soest, 1997. Used with permission.
[3] A version of the taping assignment is provided in Chapter 11.

The information gathered from the end-of-semester papers was used as qualitative data for the study. Investigators used content analysis to discern themes and patterns in four areas: students' description of their responses to doing the taping project; their examination of the development of their social identities; their exploration of the changes in that identity over the semester; and their identification of barriers to and/or resources for confronting oppression. Based on the premise that students' learning processes would differ depending on their perception of their own social status and their identification with the dominant culture, the papers were categorized for analysis based on the students' membership in three groups: (a) White, non-Jewish students, (b) students of color, and (c) multiethnic/multicultural students. Because many students identified more than one social identity in their papers, and sometimes used distinctions other than race/ethnicity in defining these identities, the multiethnic/multicultural category covered nationality, religion, and sexual orientation as well as race/ethnicity.

The 43 students included 38 females and 5 males, 23 (54%) of whom were members of the first group. Of the 7 students (16%) who were members of the second group, 5 were African Americans, 1 was Puerto Rican, and 1 was American Indian. The 13 (30%) members of the third group included 7 Jewish/White students (one of whom was gay), 1 Jewish/Christian/White, 1 Argentinean/Italian/White, 1 Jewish/Turkish/White, 1 Latina/White, and 2 Native American/White students. The students ranged in age from 23 to 50, 21 (49%) were age 23–30, 13 (30%) age 31–40, and 9 (21%) age 41–50.

Student Responses to the Project

Twenty-six (60%) of the 43 MSW students described their thoughts and feelings about doing the taping project in their end-of-the-semester papers. These included 14 (64%) of the White/non-Jewish students, 2 (29%) of the students of color, and 10 (77%) of the multiethnic students. Their responses fell into two general categories: self-critical and enlightened.

Self-Critical

In all, 24 (92%) of the 26 students reported experiencing intense negative emotions as they listened to their taped interviews at the end of the semester. They reported feeling shock or amazement at how naïve and ill-informed they were about race and racism at the beginning of the semester; feeling guilt or shame upon listening to their biased responses; and feeling sadness, dismay, or pain when reflecting on their internalized negative stereotypes, the nature of their socialization, and their experiences of oppression in childhood. Students also reported feeling embarrassed, uncomfortable, angry, and confused. Six of the 14 White/non-Jewish students and 8 of the 10 multiethnic students made self-censuring comments. The following examples indicate the force with which these students were overly critical of themselves: "Here I thought I was a liberal, thinking I was not prejudiced but I do and say things to the contrary on a daily basis without even knowing it!" "I realized in listening to my tape how socialized I was into the dominant White view about minorities . . . ironically, I had always considered myself a progressive liberal." "My racism stared me in the face! Now I am shocked to see how snobby and closed-minded I can be . . . I hold prejudices I never thought existed!" "I cringe to think of the insensitivities I display!" Neither of the two students of color who responded to the taping project made self-censuring comments.

Affective responses differed depending on students' backgrounds. White/non-Jewish students frequently reported feelings of shock, amazement, guilt, and shame. Multiethnic students most frequently reported feeling dismay, sadness, and pain. One student of color expressed anger and offense at the nature of the interview questions. The high level of affect denotes the pain involved in acknowledging and processing one's own attitudes about oppression. It also demonstrates students' willingness to confront strong emotions and work them through in the learning process.

Enlightened

Fourteen of the 26 students (54%) who wrote about the taping project indicated that their answers to the interview questions were vague and tentative compared to how they now felt. Students commented, for instance, "I lacked awareness at the beginning of the semester that discrimination is built into our institutions," "I was uncertain about the pervasiveness of racism and this is no longer the case," and "There was so much I couldn't answer or didn't have much to say about; I thought race was not an issue and I never thought about being White." Several students reported that listening to their tapes made them realize they had difficulty responding because of a need to give socially desirable answers, as in the following example: "I see now that what I said was not true; I exaggerated to prove I wasn't prejudiced."

At the beginning of the semester, many White students seemed unaware of the significance of privilege and oppression in shaping social identities. Helms (1990) suggests that this ignorance of or unwillingness to challenge social inequities can prevent White people from being aware that they have a racial and social identity.

Social Identity Development Process

All 43 students discussed their social identity development process in the assignment paper and their responses varied according to their ethnic/cultural group membership.

White/Non-Jewish Students

All 23 students in Group 1 characterized their exposure to diversity when discussing their racial identity. Most of the exposure was positive, such as growing up in ethnically or racially diverse environments, participating in exchange programs, and being introduced to readings or speeches by African American civil rights leaders. Most of the White/non-Jewish students discussed White privilege and how it had distorted their thinking and led to expectations for deferential treatment throughout life. Their parents' influence was described as mixed in terms of being positive or negative, with 7 presenting this influence as positive and 10 as negative. On the positive side, one student wrote that her parents refused to join an organization that did not allow African Americans or Jews as members. Negative personal influences ranged from parental teaching that White is the "norm" to passing on extreme prejudice.

Students of Color

Descriptions written by students of color of their social identity development differed significantly from those of the White/non-Jewish students. They tended to discuss their development in terms of personal experiences with oppression and the sources of strength that they drew in coping with these experiences. There was considerable examination of how they gained strength to face prejudice and discrimination from mothers, grandmothers, Black universities, and their religious beliefs. Some students described how their family's sense of pride and integrity was invisible to others, in stark contrast to their own perception. Three students of color wrote about their initial identification with members of the dominant culture and the pain provoked by their subsequent rejection.

Multiethnic Students

All but one of the students in this group focused on their experiences of being oppressed due to being Jewish; Jewish and female; Jewish and gay; Native American, a person with a disability, and an atheist; a foreigner living in the United States; or a Latina. Several students described how they had internalized their oppression and felt self-hatred. Most of the students in this group described their conflicts and confusion about trying to integrate aspects of their diverse backgrounds. Their stories conveyed both the pain they felt about societal devaluation of one facet of their identity and guilt about the privilege they enjoyed due to another facet of their identity. Several students wrote about coming to terms with their minority identity, but few had come to terms with their White identity. One example poignantly demonstrates this:

> I am a member of the Cherokee nation and at the same time I look like a member of Hitler's youth (my German part) . . . I am a stereotypical white liberal with a black boyfriend who is still struggling to have a positive identity as a white person.

How Stories Changed Over the Semester

White/Non-Jewish Students

All 23 students in this group described how their social identity stories had changed since making the tape recording at the start of the semester. Their changes fell into three areas: (a) an increased awareness of their White privileges and their feelings of disadvantage when they cannot use these privileges; (b) a deepened understanding of oppression, including its ubiquitousness, its institutional nature, its historical roots and present-day interaction into society and culture, its damaging effects, and its grounding in power and violence; and (c) greater hope and a plan to take actions for social change. Several students characterized the changes in their social identities as "transformative."

Students of Color

Six of the 7 students of color described how their social identities had changed since the beginning of the semester. They reported having gained a better understanding of their own oppression, they were more reflective and self-confident, they developed positive plans for social change, and they had increased awareness of the oppression of groups other than their own.

Multiethnic Students

Twelve of the 13 multiethnic students commented on how their social identities had changed since the taping. The three categories of change identified by the White/non-Jewish students emerged for this group as well. Students in this group also expressed an increased understanding of their own ethnic identities, specifically discussing the significance of establishing a positive ethnic identity in terms of personal liberation and empowerment. Some discussed the pain involved in this process, particularly when they had to give up unearned privileges or a false, albeit comfortable or socially desirable, sense of identity. This suggests the students' awareness of the grief that can accompany the development of an authentic self-identity.

Barriers to and Resources for Confronting Oppression

Fifty percent of the White/non-Jewish students and 71% of the multiethnic students reported that their own White privilege poses a barrier for them in confronting oppression. Some explained that it blinds them to the presence of racism, while others expressed a reluctance to forgo their position of advantage. A barrier reported by students in all three groups is the pervasiveness of oppression—a belief that the problem is too big and too institutionalized to be changed. In addition, White/non-Jewish and multiethnic students identified fear as a barrier to confronting oppression—fear of losing friends and family, of being seen as a race traitor, or of being rejected by members of the dominant culture. They also reported that their internalization of racist beliefs, their fears, and their distaste for conflict acted in combination to pose a significant barrier to confronting oppression.

Various resources for confronting oppression were also described by members of each group. For example, students of color listed family and religion as significant sources of strength and multiethnic students said their own experiences of being treated unjustly motivated them to confront racism. White/non-Jewish students identified the fewest resources, though as a group they expressed the most hope for the future and planned to work for change.

Implications and Recommendations

The findings from this study suggest the importance of reaching beyond the cognitive level in course content intended to teach students about diversity for social justice. Analysis of students' papers related to the taping assignment indicates the struggles involved in developing a positive identity within the context of issues of power and privilege. Further, the nature of this struggle varies depending on students' experiences and backgrounds. Diverse personal experiences with oppression often result in different perceptions of diversity course content, a potential source of strain in the classroom.

The MSW students in this study were encouraged to analyze their social status and power, to reevaluate their worldviews, and to perceive their social identities in the context of racist power structures. The guilt, shame, and confusion expressed by all of the White students contrasted with the more positive feelings expressed by students of color. This suggests that educators must look for ways to help students move from self-censure to alternative beliefs and behaviors that reduce the dissonance they feel when confronted with the oppression embodied in the dominant culture and their own privileged status in it. Educators must be willing to help students with the personal turmoil so they can engage in the kind of reevaluation process that is required to develop a positive White racial identity. Because White students may be prone to defend themselves as not being like "other White people" to cope with feelings of guilt and shame, it can be helpful to provide them with models such as Helms' (1990) White racial identity development process. This can begin to normalize their experiences and allow them to be less judgmental with themselves. It is important to provide models of White people effectively engaged in anti-racist work. While educators need to help students understand that the development of an authentic social identity varies depending on ethnicity/race, culture, gender, sexual orientation, and socioeconomic class, it is very important to not allow students to avoid dealing with their own power and privilege.

This study also reveals that loss and grief are inherent in the struggle to confront oppression. Educators need to be mindful of the feelings of loss that often accompany the development of an authentic identity and the assumption of responsibility for reducing oppression. Part of the educational process should involve helping students grieve for the world they thought they lived in and for the person they thought they were. Educators can help with this process by eliciting student stories about their own experiences with oppression and helping them to interpret and understand their experiences on a societal level. It is important to invite students to acknowledge, discuss, and work through their feelings in relation to course concepts and to appreciate that grieving is a normal part of the process.

STUDY 3: BELIEF IN A JUST WORLD AND COMMITMENT TO SOCIAL JUSTICE ADVOCACY: THE IMPACT OF SOCIAL WORK EDUCATION ON STUDENT ATTITUDES AND BEHAVIOR[4]

The first two studies focused on students' social identity development and changes they experienced when taking courses that focused on diversity for social justice. This third study takes a different approach by focusing on belief systems and advocacy actions related to social justice and fairness.

A study of 222 MSW students from two universities examined the impact of a course, Societal Oppression and Cultural Diversity, on student beliefs about justice in the world and their commitment to be advocates for social justice. The educational model for the required course followed the general educational framework presented in Part One of this book. The course was intended to prepare students to provide culturally sensitive services, work for equality, and promote the elimination of oppressive societal hierarchies. Course content emphasized power and differential treatment based on difference and focused on both oppressive systems and the internalization of oppression (Pinderhughes, 1989). The course readings highlighted ubiquitous power issues related to race, gender, ethnicity, and sexual orientation on the levels of belief systems, personal identity and prejudices, and institutional systems. Students were exposed to the pervasive influence of power on their own personal identity, on the social work profession, and on society as a whole.

The course included both didactic and experiential components, in order to provide opportunities for both cognitive and affective learning. A major course requirement was participation in a group presentation that focused on the origin and history of beliefs and stereotypes about an oppressed population; economic, political, educational, and legal strategies used by the dominant group to ensure societal subordination of the target population; strengths and resilience of the target population to endure oppressive conditions; and implications for social work practice, particularly professional responsibility to work for social justice, eliminate oppression, and promote just alternatives. Several presentations focused on various oppressed groups, thus helping students identify the common elements of oppression that have an impact on diverse populations.

An essential element of the course involved student exploration of their own cultural backgrounds and the meaning and significance of their own po-

---

[4] This section draws from Van Soest, 1996. Used with permission.

sitions in a racist, sexist, and heterosexist society. Students were challenged to look at their side of the oppression equation and analyze how self-image and social status are related to prejudice and injustice. Students were required to keep an anonymous weekly journal that would not be graded, whereby they could record their own thoughts, feelings, and the personal connections they made with the course content.

Theoretical Framework for the Study

The study investigated student responses to course material about social justice and oppression on two dimensions: belief in a just world and a commitment to social justice advocacy, as grounded in the concept of moral exclusion.

Just world thinking was conceived as the belief that the world is a just place, where a person's merit and fate are closely aligned (Lerner, 1980). Studies indicate that a strong belief in a just world is related to acceptance of status quo social and political institutions, nonparticipation in social change activities, and denigration of oppressed populations (Peplau & Tyler, 1975; Rubin & Peplau, 1973; Rubin & Peplau, 1975; Smith, Ferree, & Miller, 1975; Walster, Walster, & Berscheid, 1978).

Commitment to social justice advocacy was conceived as everyday advocacy on behalf of members of oppressed populations. The concept of moral exclusion is a component of this dimension based on the assumption that a person's concern for justice and actions for advocacy are focused only on those who are perceived to be in that person's moral community. In the moral exclusion literature, perpetrators and benefactors of injustice are defined as individuals or groups that harm others, societal institutions that justify harm, and bystanders who condone harm (Opotow, 1990). Even small and seemingly insignificant acts that cause limited harm such as telling jokes that denigrate devalued groups can cause psychological changes in individual perpetrators and bystanders that make further harmful acts possible (Bandura, 1990; Staub, 1989). Social justice advocacy in this study included the power of bystanders to either reduce harming behavior or increase helping behavior (Lerner, 1980; Lerner & Lerner, 1981).

Because students in the study were predominantly White and middle class, it was assumed that most of them entered social work school with the belief that on some level they lived in a just world. It was speculated that exposure to the course on Societal Oppression and Cultural Diversity would reduce their acceptance of the just world ideology and increase their understanding of the harmful effects of moral exclusion, awareness of the power of bystander behavior, and their personal advocacy behavior on behalf of oppressed groups. It was expected that contradictions between students' deep-seated belief in a just world, upon which their self-concept depends, and information presented in the course could trigger student distress and resistance.

Research Methodology

A quasi-experimental research design, with pre- and post-measurements for two comparison groups and a posttest for two additional comparison groups was used. Three sets of research questions examined differences between students who just completed the course and students in the two comparison groups:

1. What were students' beliefs about the world being a just place (a) compared with their beliefs prior to taking the course, (b) compared with the beliefs of students who took the course in the past, and (c) compared with those of students who did not take the oppression course?

2. What were students' self-reported advocacy behaviors on behalf of oppressed populations (a) compared with their self-reported behaviors before taking the course, (b) compared with those of students who took the course in the past, and (c) compared with those of students who did not take the oppression course?

3. What is the relationship between the distress they experience during the course and their belief in a just world or their advocacy behaviors?

Study Population

The pool of subjects included MSW students at the National Catholic School of Social Service at The Catholic University of America (CUA) in Washington, D.C., who took the oppression course, and MSW students at the School of Social Work at St. Thomas University and College of St. Catherine (UST/CSC) in St. Paul, Minnesota, who did not take an oppression course. Ninety-two (92) first-year CUA students who were enrolled in five sections of the oppression course completed the study instruments at the beginning and again at the end of the fall 1993 semester; 93 second-year CUA students who had taken the oppression course in the past one to two years completed the study instruments at the end of the same semester; 16 UST/CSC first-year students completed the study instruments both at the beginning and the end of the semester; and 21 second-year UST/CSC students completed the instruments at the end of the semester. No advanced-standing students were included in the sample.

Of the 222 students who participated, the majority were White (91%), female (89%), and enrolled full-time (70%). Analysis of variance, used to determine statistical similarity of the two groups of first-year students, revealed only one statistically significant difference: first-year CUA students were in field agencies that served a higher percentage of African American clients than did the agencies for the UST/CSC students. There was no statistical difference between the groups on any other demographic or educational variable or on any of the pretests.

The second-year students from the two schools were compared using student's t tests to ensure statistical similarity. The CUA students were somewhat younger (average age 32) than the UST/CSC students (average age 38). Field placement agencies for CUA students again served a higher percentage of African American clients and had more diversity of both clients and staff than those for UST/CSC students.

Study Instruments

The following three instruments were used in the study.

1. Belief in a Just World Scale (BJWS) was administered to measure students' acceptance of a just world ideology. The BJWS is a 20-item standardized instrument developed by Rubin and Peplau (1975) that uses a 6-point Likert continuum of 3 degrees of agreement or disagreement. The BJWS is based on the assumption that just world thinking is an attitudinal continuum ranging from total acceptance to total rejection of the idea that the world is a just (i.e., fair) place. It has been shown to have high internal consistency (coefficient alpha or K-R 20 equal to .80). Using Cronbach's Alpha in this study, the BJSW had a reliability of .77 for the pretest and .71 for the posttest.

2. A Social Justice Advocacy Scale (SJAS) was originally constructed to measure self-reported advocacy behavior. The SJAS consists of 80 items comprised of 5 subscales that measure self-reported advocacy behaviors on behalf of African Americans, other racial/ethnic minorities, women, gay men and lesbians, and persons with disabilities. Each subscale explores the frequency with which students engage in 15 advocacy behaviors. The instrument was field tested for validity and reliability with 90 MSW students, social work faculty, and practitioners, with reliability analysis resulting in Cronbach's Alpha for the 5 subscales ranging from .63 to .76. In this study, Cronbach's

Alpha for the total SJAS (all 80 items) was .92 for the pretest and .93 for the posttest. Cronbach's Alpha for each of the subscales at the pre-/posttests was: African Americans, .72/.77; other ethnic/racial minorities, .69/.76; women, .69/.72; gay men and lesbians, .77/.80; and persons with disabilities, .65/.72.

3. Level of Distress, defined as student self-perception of affective engagement with curriculum content related to oppression, was measured by a semantic differential format that was originally constructed and field-tested along with the SJAS. Nine pairs of "polar opposite" feelings were listed: uneasy–comfortable, insulted–gratified, guilty–guiltless, discouraged–exhilarated, pained–relieved, denounced–affirmed, powerless–empowered, depressed–happy, and anxious–assured. For each pair, students were asked to indicate which feeling they experienced and to what degree (on a 5 point scale, with the middle choice indicating "neither"). CUA students were asked to indicate their feelings specifically in relation to the content in the oppression course; UST/CSC students were asked to indicate their feelings in relation to oppression content in the overall curriculum. Average scores close to 5 indicated a high level of distress and scores close to 1 indicated a low level. Using Cronbach's Alpha, reliability was .79 at the posttest.

Results

The mean BJWS score on the pretest for first-year CUA students (3.67) indicates a solidly moderate acceptance of the just world ideology. Pre- and posttest scores were compared using a paired difference t test. Although first-year CUA students' belief in a just world was expected to decrease through taking the oppression course, Table 1 shows there was a small yet statistically significant *increase* on posttest mean scores. The student's t test was used to compare the posttest scores for first- and second-year CUA students. Table 2 shows that second-year students who had previously taken the oppression course had a significantly lower acceptance of just world ideology than first-year students who had just completed the course. Table 3 shows that UST/CSC

Table 1. Paired Difference t Test of Pre- and PostTest Scores on the Belief in a Just World Scale, First-Year CUA Students ($N=92$)

Pretest Mean	Posttest Mean	Degrees of Freedom	t
3.67	3.96	91	-5.16*

Note. Scores above 3.0 indicate acceptance of the just world ideology; scores below 3.0 indicate rejection of it (Rubin & Peplau, 1973).
*$p < .01$

students (none of whom took the oppression course) had a statistically significant lower acceptance of the just world ideology than both first- and second-year CUA students who had taken the oppression course.

In terms of Social Justice Advocacy results, the paired difference t test findings on the SJAS were significantly higher for first-year CUA students on the posttest than on the pretest. On the subscales, there were statistically significant increases in self-reported advocacy behaviors on behalf of African Americans and gay men and lesbians, but no significant increase in advocacy on behalf of the other three populations, other racial/ethnic minorities, women, and persons with disabilities. The only significant difference between first- and second-year CUA students on the posttest scores was that second-year students reported engaging in fewer advocacy behaviors on behalf of gay men and lesbians. Statistically significant but small differences were found between students from the two schools on the total posttest SJAS scores and the subscales measuring advocacy behavior on behalf of other racial/ethnic minorities and gay men and lesbians, with the UST/CSC students reporting more advocacy behaviors than the CUA students.

Using Pearson correlations between BJWS and SJAS posttest scores and level of distress for all students in the study, level of distress was positively associated with BJWS posttest scores but negatively associated with SJAS posttest scores. In other words, students who experienced higher distress in relation to oppression content had higher acceptance of the just world ideology and engaged in fewer advocacy behaviors. There was a significant asso-

Table 2. Students' t Distribution Comparing Post-Test Scores on the Belief in a Just World Scale, First- and Second-Year CUA Students

Group	Posttest Mean	t
First-year CUA students ($n=92$)	3.96	3.13*
Second-year CUA students ($n=93$)	3.76	

*$p < .01$ one-tailed test, $df = 182$

Table 3. Students' t Distribution Comparing Post-Test Scores on the Belief in a Just World Scale, CUA and UST/CSC Students

Group	Posttest Mean	t
CUA ($n=185$)	3.86	1.90*
UST/CSC ($n=37$)	3.70	

*$p < .05$ one-tailed test. $df = 220$

ciation between higher level of distress and lower advocacy behavior on behalf of other racial/ethnic minorities, women, and gay men and lesbians.

Discussion and Implications

The findings reveal that social work students in this study tended to accept the just world ideology and that this acceptance increased after taking an
oppression course that demonstrated injustices that contradict just world beliefs. While students' self-reported advocacy behaviors increased somewhat
immediately after completing the oppression course, the results were uneven
and inconsistent among the five populations. Moreover, advocacy behaviors
on behalf of gay men and lesbians were significantly lower for students who
had completed the oppression course in the past than for students who had
just completed the course, and were significantly higher for students who had
not taken an oppression course at all. This study also revealed that students
who had a stronger tendency to accept the just world ideology and who engage in fewer advocacy behaviors reported greater distress when confronted
with evidence of injustice in curriculum content.

It is important to note that the social work students in this study had a
stronger tendency to accept the just world ideology than did students in other
disciplines in other studies (Merrifield & Timpe, 1973; Rubin & Peplau, 1975).
This raises concerns, as studies have shown a negative correlation between
acceptance of just world ideology and political and social activism (Rubin &
Peplau, 1973). Other studies indicate that those who have a strong belief in a
just world will blame victims of social harm or unfairness even in the absence
of evidence suggesting the victims were responsible for their misfortune (Rubin
& Peplau, 1973). On the other hand, when evidence suggests that a victim's
suffering has been caused by some other entity, strong just world believ-
ers often turn from blaming the victim to demanding vengeance against
the perpetrator—another way to restore their idea of social justice (Rubin
& Peplau, 1973).

Another noteworthy finding in this study is the statistically significant
increase in first-year students' belief in a just world following the oppression
class. Just world ideology is viewed as a deep-seated, primitive set of beliefs
that play a central role in a person's life to the extent that it has an impact
similar to the belief that one is a decent, worthwhile person (Lerner, 1980).
Such fundamental beliefs are often resistant to change; they may remain unaffected by exposure to information that contradicts them or they may be

embraced even tighter. The shift to even stronger acceptance of just world ideology by CUA students immediately after completing the oppression course may reflect a tendency to screen out information that does not conform to one's beliefs. Nonetheless, the possibility of a shift in fundamental beliefs, even if it means hanging on to them even tighter, may be a necessary stage in the process of personal transformation, similar to the denial stage of the grieving process. For students, beginning to confront their own position (as advantaged or disadvantaged) in an oppressive system may be part of fundamental self-identity change.

Interpretation of the lower acceptance of just world ideology by second-year CUA students than by their first-year counterparts, as well as the somewhat lower just world beliefs of the UST/CSC students than of the CUA students, is speculative. One possible explanation is that completing more of an MSW program contributes to the development of a different world perspective. Further, given the positive association between distress related to oppression content in the curriculum and scores on the BJWS posttest, perhaps students recently exposed to a fairly intense dose of evidence that the world is *not* a just place (in the oppression course) experienced greater dissonance than their counterparts, and reacted by embracing their beliefs more tightly. When the intensity of dealing with social injustice issues decreases during the second year of course work, resistance to abandoning the just world ideology may be somewhat reduced. The UST/CSC students, who were not exposed to a concentrated examination of oppression in a discrete course, might experience both less resistance to the idea that the world is not so just and less cognitive dissonance that might lead to a change in beliefs.

Deep-seated beliefs, such as the just world ideology, are shared by various groups with which we identify; as such, they are influential in how we think and act (Joy, 1990). Although such beliefs are deeply embedded, they can and do change. Education is an ideal vehicle for addressing the shared social beliefs that impede effective social change. To socialize (or resocialize) students to be advocates for social justice, social work educators "must be willing to understand and then to probe the various layers of shared beliefs that both we and the learners we teach invariably [hold]" (Joy, 1990, p. 16).

Success in addressing attitudes and beliefs that impede progress toward effective social change actions may depend on educators' ability to elicit and understand students' beliefs about justice in the world. Educators must understand that students encounter psychological barriers when assimilating and integrating knowledge that challenges their world view, and that they often experience profound disorientation, feeling "overwhelmed by the immensity, complexity, ubiquity, and seeming intractability of the problems" (Garb, 1990).

Educators can set the stage for creative cognitive conflict that helps reduce students' distress and encourages them to critically examine their beliefs. Educational approaches that emphasize psychological reflection encourage students to talk about their emotional responses, including the profound difficulty of facing the reality of oppression in our society.

In this study the statistically significant changes in self-reported advocacy behaviors, though very small and uneven among the five oppressed populations, suggest that social work education may influence student behavior. The negative correlation found between self-reported distress level and self-reported social justice advocacy suggests that students who engage in fewer advocacy behaviors may experience more distress when confronted with examples of the effects of injustice on oppressed populations, especially if they disapprove of those populations or think of them as inferior (i.e., morally exclude them). Without educational interventions that support students through psychological challenges, such distress may easily result in feelings of resentment, despair, and alienation. By demonstrating how empowerment and political efficacy can be achieved through personal commitment and advocacy, educators can encourage student trust in the possibility of social change.

The results of this study suggest that the often-reported student dissatisfaction with diversity courses may be based in the deep-seated dissonance and distress that they can cause. This interpretation raises profound questions about curriculum development: (a) If a course focused on oppression *invites* cognitive dissonance and distress as is suggested by the data, what are the implications for faculty comfort and ability to teach successfully?, (b) What follow-up efforts in subsequent courses might be required to help students through the change process?, and (c) What are the implications of *not* addressing belief systems and self-identity/self-concept issues related to oppression in the social work curriculum?

SUMMARY AND CONCLUSION

All three studies that were reported in this chapter investigated student experiences and outcomes as a result of taking courses that were based on the educational model presented in Part One of this book.

The first study provides some insights into how students experience the learning process in relation to three themes: self-image and self-identity issues related to one's role as victim or benefactor (or both) of oppressive conditions; the change process; and the learning environment. The study results suggest the possibility that, as a result of exposure to course content related to societal oppression and social justice, some students may expand their moral boundaries; undergo a change in perceptions of themselves and their identity as benefactor, perpetrator, and/or victim of oppression; and develop empathy for others who were previously outside their realm of consciousness, including developing empathy for themselves.

The second study explored several questions related to students' learning process and how their understanding of their social identity changed as a result of taking a diversity course with a focus on social justice. The findings point to the struggle involved in developing a positive identity and suggest that the nature of the struggle varies depending on students' experiences and backgrounds.

The third study focused on deep-seated beliefs that influence students' thoughts about social justice and about actions that demonstrate their level of commitment to advocacy on behalf of oppressed populations. It also measured the distress that may be connected to examining one's worldview and activities as part of the educational process. Although the results raise many questions that call for further research, they also have implications for social work education, particularly in relation to the importance of belief systems and their inseparability from concerns about social justice.

In Chapter Five we presented an empowerment process model of how students are moved from ideas, beliefs, and new awareness about equality and justice to operationalizing them into actions for social change. The studies reported in this chapter presented evidence of what students bring to this process and what happens to them as they engage in the learning endeavor. They provided information that can increase our understanding of how students experience the learning process and some of the possible outcomes. In the next three chapters, we discuss what professors bring to the learning process and what they experience in interaction with students.

REFERENCES

Bandura, A. (1990). Selective activation and disengagement of moral control. *Journal of Social Issues, 46*(1), 27–46.

Cook, S. (1990). Toward a psychology of improving justice: Research on extending the equality principle to victims of social injustice. *Journal of Social Issues, 46*(1), 147–161.

Garb, Y. J. (1990). *Responding to the environmental crisis: The pedagogic challenge.* Paper presented at the symposium, "Educating for Moral Responsibility Across Societal Contexts," American Educational Research Association Meeting, Boston, MA.

Garcia, B., & Van Soest, D. (1997). Changing perceptions of diversity and oppression: MSW students discuss the effects of a required course. *Journal of Social Work Education, 33*(1), 119–129.

Helms, J. E. (1990). *Black and white racial identity: Theory, research and practice.* Westport, CT: Greenwood Press.

Joy, C. (1990). *Believing is seeing: Attitudes and assumptions that affect learning about development.* New York: National Clearinghouse on Development Education.

Lerner, M. (1980). *The belief in a just world: A fundamental delusion.* New York: Plenum Press.

Lerner, M., & Lerner, S. C. (Eds.). (1981). *The justice motive in social behavior.* New York: Plenum.

Merrifield, C., & Timpe, R. (1973). Local revisions and additions to the Just World Scale. Oklahoma State University: Unpublished manuscript.

Opotow, S. (1990). Moral exclusion and injustice: An introduction. *Journal of Social Issues, 46*(1), 1–20.

Peplau, L. A., & Tyler, T. (1975, April). *Belief in a just world and political attitudes.* Paper presented at the meeting of the Western Psychological Association, Sacramento, CA.

Pinderhughes, E. (1989). *Understanding race, ethnicity and power: The key to efficacy in clinical practice.* New York: The Free Press.

Rubin, Z., & Peplau, L. A. (1973). Belief in a just world and reactions to another's lot: A study of participants in the national draft lottery. *Journal of Social Issues, 29*(4), 73–93.

Rubin, Z., & Peplau, L. A. (1975). Who believes in a just world? *Journal of Social Issues, 31*(3), 65–89.

Smith, E. R., Ferree, J. M., & Miller, F. D. (1975). A short scale of attitudes towards feminism. *Representative Research in Social Psychology, 6,* 51–56.

Staub, E. (1989). *The roots of evil.* New York: Cambridge University Press.

Tatum, B. D. (1992). Talking about race, learning about racism: An application of racial identity development theory in the classroom. *Harvard Educational Review, 62*(1), 1–24.

Van Soest, D. (1994). Social work education for multicultural practice and social justice advocacy: A field study of how students experience the learning process. *Journal of Multicultural Social Work, 3*(1), 17–24.

Van Soest, D. (1996). Impact of social work education on student attitudes and behavior concerning oppression. *Journal of Social Work Education, 32*(2), 191–202.

Walster, E., Walster, G. W., & Berscheid, E. (1978). *Equity: Theory and research.* Boston: Allyn & Bacon.

Chapter Seven
Affective, Behavioral, and Intellectual Challenges in Diversity for Social Justice Teaching

Our job as educators is to help students become aware, reflect, and critically examine diversity through a social justice lens. The goal is to help students translate the knowledge they acquire into effective strategies for social change. This requires proficiency in both pedagogy (e.g., syllabus conceptualization and formulation) and managing classroom dynamics. Faculty must have expertise in self-knowledge and process skills. They need to engage in negotiating interpersonal dynamics between self and students and between students. They need to be prepared for predictably intensive, disruptive quality of class discussions. They must model social advocacy. In short, extraordinary expectations are placed on them. It is thus not surprising that some faculty may avoid teaching this content. Some experience "catastrophic fears" (Stevens, 1975) that they will be accused of being racist, sexist, classist, ableist, or another oppressor label. It is essential that faculty who teach diversity for social justice confront and come to terms with how they will approach such ubiquitous dynamics that are endemic to the work.

What this means is that faculty who teach diversity for social justice content must engage in the emotional/cognitive work that we require of students. While it may seem that we, as faculty, understand the complex social, political, and psychological influence of diversity on individuals, we need to be mindful that the nature of diversity learning is more than increasing one's cognitive, intellectual comprehension of oppression. The affective and intellectual preparation requires that faculty explore how we see ourselves and how we perceive others. Most importantly, it requires a willingness to work with personal reactions that arise in teaching. This work involves suspending judgment of oneself and instead fostering curiosity about past and current experiences. How we manage our experiences, combined with the teaching style that we bring, includes learning to manage ambiguity and to bear the ambivalence that comes with exploring gray areas. We need to allow process to develop among students and between students and ourselves. We need to develop comfort with strong affect. Diversity teaching can feel like walking through a landmine field as we discover in the process that we harbor feelings or are discomforted by strong affect in ourselves.

This chapter explores the various affective, behavioral, and intellectual challenges involved in teaching diversity and social justice content. It addresses several aspects of faculty experience, including teaching skills, life experiences, perceptions of students, challenges encountered in classroom dynamics, and relevant personal responses. All of these areas are evoked in the teaching experience. Their immediate and personal quality triggers some degree of discomfort for us, just as for students. The teaching thus builds on and pushes our comfort with complexity and ambiguity and where we are in the process of integrating our own social identities. Perspectives with which to frame the teaching experience are also presented.

WHAT FACULTY BRING TO THE LEARNING PROCESS

Process and dialogue are at the heart of diversity teaching for social justice. These are prompted by a combination of lecture and interactive modes of teaching such as experiential exercises, small group discussions, role plays, and panel presentations. The affective component in the learning process is central, requiring that faculty ascertain how they will manage the occasional intensified interaction. This includes assessing the trade-offs that might result from not engaging with and processing these heated moments. When managing classroom dynamics, faculty need to be cognizant of the possible costs of not moving students beyond a safe comfort zone and thus losing opportunities for meaningful discussion. They need to consider what bigger meaning and learning the student might take away from the classroom if exchange and dialogue, as heated as they may be, are aborted. What is conveyed to students in how educators respond or do not respond to classroom interactions? What message is conveyed about the professor's personal understanding of course concepts and comfort level? And what are the implications of the professor being uncomfortable with course issues when students are expected to confront their discomfort when doing the personal work the course entails?

Conveying values such as direct communication, open inquiry, and willingness to identify underlying value assumptions and to validate student participation and diverse perspectives is instrumental in creating and maintaining an effective learning environment. Key skills are needed such as mentoring, self-awareness, and engagement. When such skills are modeled well, a learning environment can be created that helps students become aware of and work with their biases, begin to internalize sociopolitical concepts, and explore what taking action means in their personal and professional lives. In this section, we address factors that faculty bring to the learning process, including teaching skills, life experiences, and perceptions of students.

Teaching Skills Pertinent to Diversity Teaching

The goals of teaching, traditionally, are to inspire and motivate students through course activities that increase their knowledge and critical thinking, relate the knowledge to student experience, and create attitude change (McKeachie, 1986). These basic goals, we believe, need to be coupled with strong teaching skills, as faculty need to manage the ambivalence, anger, and other uncomfortable feelings that can be generated in relation to diversity issues. Students often experience vulnerability, which increases the need for faculty to recognize and honor diverse learning styles. Attention to different learning styles is an effective way to get students "on board." By including all channels of learning—hearing, doing, and seeing—the pace and intensity of content are individualized for students. Such individualization communicates concern for students and their learning needs. Faculty must also have some degree of comfort in managing intense affect in themselves and others. And they need to integrate both didactic and process methods of teaching.

Life Experiences

We promote student awareness of beliefs, values, and perceptions relevant to our course goals when we use ourselves, our life experiences, and our observations of our change process in teaching. By integrating our personal perspective, we bring to life what otherwise may seem remote. Self disclosure that focuses on exploration of our past and current experiences related to diversity and oppression helps to make the content immediate and provides a role model for learning from personal experience. We must expect of ourselves the same emotional, intellectual, and advocacy work that we expect of our students. Our experience is that most faculty have done considerable work to make personal explorations an organizing value in their lives and see social justice and diversity issues as being at the heart of social work. Nonetheless, the nature of this content continues to unexpectedly stir untouched or even deeper elements of our experience. The mere act of reading someone's narrative aloud as part of a presentation or screening a video can generate an unexpected welling up of powerful feelings of which we were unaware or thought we had resolved. Such reactions are opportunities to further enhance our teaching as they bring into awareness previously minimized experiences associated with our experience and understanding of difference.

Teaching in this area thus means having to take our unexpected reactions seriously. This means recognizing our life experiences with diversity, exploring our own socialization and values related to socioeconomic class and family values, and examining stereotypes, biases, and social identity issues. Sometimes our strong responses arise from feelings about past hurts associated with target status (i.e., oppression) or from our parent's behavior as recipients of privilege with an attitude of entitlement. Strong feelings may arise in relation to childhood memories, family values, and/or cultural beliefs. Strong reactions may arise from awareness of the impact and importance of particular historical events on our lives, such as the social advocacy associated with the 1960s and 1970s. It is both an opportunity and responsibility to work with students in a similar way to help them comprehend and analyze the formative influence of the political events that have unfolded since the September 11 attacks. Clearly these events constitute a watershed and have direct implications for how difference is viewed within the United States. Many questions are raised as we mutually explore perceptions of the role of social work in this new age. What is the nature of the post-September 11 events? What are the particular consequences of those events for race relations and our conceptualizations of social justice? And what are the differential psychosocial effects on students' personal and professional lives?

At some points in our teaching, we may lack personal awareness about how our constellation of social identities, experiences with power and privilege, and values influence the very topics that we teach and how we teach them. At those times, our minimization or lack of awareness of those influences means that we risk being shaken, confused, or overwhelmed by our own responses to the material or to the students. We may find that we avoid encouraging classroom dialogue and therefore potentially lose a teachable moment. This kind of reaction is predictable and provides information about where we are in the process of learning about the meaning of difference in our lives. Our reactions need attention and affirmation even though there may be a discrepancy between how we see ourselves and the meaning we give our reactions. They remind us that something is unresolved. They compel us to name and process our feelings in the interest of improving our teaching. Effective diversity teaching is contingent on our doing this work. It is a parallel process that provides us with deeper insight into students' sensitive and conflictual feelings that often surface as defensiveness or aggressiveness. Figure 1 lists faculty issues, several of which are discussed further below.

Our effectiveness in teaching diversity for social justice is aided when we explore the effects on us of being socialized in a certain socioeconomic class. This exploration includes experiences with privilege and entitlement, as the target of oppression, of feeling invisible or having choices limited based on group membership, etc. We need to reflect on our life experiences with diverse groups based on socioeconomic class and the messages that we got in our families about others different from ourselves. Often we lived in homogeneous neighborhoods, which meant we did not have any contact with diverse others until our college years or as adults in the workplace. We need to explore the observations and insights that we have as a result of these experiences.

Exploration of our life experiences also needs to encompass socialization related to gender, ethnicity/race, and disability. These explorations can probe into the benefits of privilege and entitlement that were bestowed because of our particular statuses as well as the limitations imposed through experiences as targets of oppression. For example, did our family standing or activities in the community afford access to community organizations and/or local significant figures who were professionally, socially, or religiously based? Was our community multicultural, yet segregated socially so that friendships or social ties did not span group differences? How much opportunity was available in college to expand our friendships and social interactions beyond those available during our formative childhood and adolescent years? How did these experiences familiarize us with new social settings and interactions?

Reflections on our current perspectives regarding our parental and family values and biases and their influence on our racial and social identity bear particular exploration. As social identity issues were dealt with in adolescence and early adulthood, what was the nature of our experience in owning, modifying, or rejecting the values that we learned in our families? Did we have differences with family or friends and how were those differences managed? Last, but not least, where do we stand today regarding our racial or social identity? Have we honored our historical and cultural legacies by acknowl-

Figure 1. Faculty Factors

Life Course Experiences

Family Values/Attitudes Toward Difference

- Beliefs, values, practices, rituals (intergenerational, contemporary)

- Feelings and perceptions about core family values

- How dealt with these with self? With family members?

Socioeconomic Class Socialization—Power and Privilege

Neighborhood—Low/Hi Diversity? Exposure to Diversity? Friendships?

Adolescent Friendships, Social Activities

Mid-School and College Friendships, Social Network, Social Settings

Social Identity and Feelings Related to Entitlement or Target Status

- Aspects of social identity that are comfortable

- Aspects of social identity that generate conflict

- Beliefs that activities that promote development of racial/social identity represent "balkanization" and are divisive

Use of Self in Teaching

Comfort with intense affect in self and in others. Self disclosure as part of teaching. Use of self in teaching.

Reflective process in teaching.

Teaching Style—Pedagogy and Androgogy

Comfort in engaging in mutual consultation with other faculty teaching similar content; use of other faculty as a resource for ongoing development and learning.

Management of ambiguity and ambivalence.

Acknowledgement and naming of one's own strong feelings.

Ability to suspend judgment of student reactions and to respond to angry and/or aggressive student behavior without becoming defensive.

Comfort in using a combination of didactic and experiential teaching approaches.

Ability to maintain dual focus: attending to individual student responses and keeping focus on larger classroom dynamics.

Use of Parallel Process

Constructions on Difference, Power, and Privilege

Understanding of convergence/overlap between socioeconomic class and race/ethnicity, gender, sexual orientation?

Values self reflection and critical analysis leading to insight.

edging values, practices, and perhaps rituals that have been passed on through the family intergenerationally or through lived and current family experiences? What feelings do we have about various aspects of our racial or social identity? In instances where there are aspects of our social identity that were not as socially "respected and visible" as others, how have we managed those multiple legacies? Were some aspects ignored and others prioritized? If so, what is our understanding of our different responses and perceptions? How we deal with such concerns and experiences influences how we present ourselves to and interact with students as we engage them in learning about diversity for social justice. While there is no right or wrong in these processes, it is critical that faculty take responsibility to fully and authentically interact with students on these sensitive, potentially emotionally laden concerns that are embedded in intellectual learning about difference.

Faculty Perceptions of Students

Our interactions and teaching styles are shaped, in part, by the kinds of relationships we have with students and our perceptions of them. Because of the stronger interpersonal role that we take in teaching about diversity, we may come face to face with internalized negative stereotypes whose vestiges still have some emotional pull on us. Some of these stereotypes may come from unresolved personal experiences that make it difficult to see the individual student within the group. However, some may also come from societal projection (Bowen, 1978; Pinderhughes, 1989). Projection is a means of perceiving strong feelings that would generate discomfort (i.e., anxiety) by virtue of their intensity were we to see them ourselves. Projection makes it possible to not own these feelings as our own but to attribute them to others (Lichtenberg, van Beusekom, & Gibbons, 1997). Both individual and societal projection are phenomena that mediate transactions between individuals and between groups and identify dynamics that by definition are out of awareness. Yet they have tremendous implications for our perceptions of our students. Projection highlights the importance of faculty being aware of their responses to students and their consequences.

The concept of transference also helps us to understand distortions we may have of students. Transference phenomena can easily come into play depending on how a student may appear to us or interact with us. Although we are often more alert to negative responses, transference concepts can remind us that the distortion can also be positive. An example might be a situation in which we feel an urge to rescue students from the struggle they find themselves in with other students. Such dynamics are ubiquitous and predictable in diversity teaching. They are best dealt with when we suspend judgment of ourselves.

Through discussion and supportive dialogue aimed at improving our teaching, we will find many variations of these dynamics as well as other snares. One of our responsibilities as faculty is to confront the consequences of our coping mechanisms because of the formative influence that our interactions can have on students. Unexamined classroom interactions can result in lost learning opportunities. Certain faculty characteristics promote growth: awareness and direct assertion of our feelings, needs, and thoughts and engaging in the personal work of integrating them (Lichtenberg, van Beusekom, & Gibbons, 1997). Maintaining perspective on this highly subjective level of affective work is integrally connected to our effectiveness as teachers of diversity for social justice content.

Constructions of Difference That Faculty Bring Into Teaching

Some provocative propositions have been identified by Llerena-Quinn (2001) through her application of constructivist concepts to teaching. The social constructions of difference from which faculty teach have implications for power relations in the classroom and for both what and how we teach. Llerena-Quinn (2000) suggests that faculty may construct difference as meaning inferiority, as something to minimize because "we are all the same," as something to understand in others, or as something as valuable for the knowledge it provides of multiple perspectives and truths. These constructions then shape what content we choose to emphasize and the degree to which we view the learning process as a participatory one.

Faculty fears that diversity teaching will bring out differences and create divisiveness bear earnest attention. When meaningful discussion evolves in the classroom, we will get into potentially controversial areas such as traditional versus nontraditional family structures and values, exploration of various types of coping, strengths associated with different cultures, etc. Often diverse perspectives that students bring to these discussion are unspoken. In the face of the discomfort that some students may feel, faculty must be prepared to nurture contentious topics with a belief that this activity in fact builds a foundation on which diverse individuals can relate to one another and respect differences.

CHALLENGES ENCOUNTERED IN THE CLASSROOM

Attention needs to be paid to the combination of intellectual and affective feats that faculty are expected to master in teaching diversity curriculum. Many of the required tasks are similar to those in anti-racist workshops, including conflict resolution, maintaining empathy and patience when dealing with verbal crossfire, navigating anger and conflict, and managing personal attacks and scapegoating (Ring, 2000).

Deutsch (1993) suggests that faculty recognize the type of conflicts that may be evolving in classroom discussions (e.g., zero sum, mixed-motive, pure cooperative) and face conflicts rather than trying to avoid them. It is especially important that faculty recognize their anxiety about conflict and their tendency to avoid it. It is important to notice the typical defenses that they use to evade conflict and become aware of the negative consequences of evasion such as irritability, tension, and persistence of the problem. Several factors are important when facing conflicts: maintaining respect for yourself, your interests, and the interests of others; engaging in exploration of similarity; defining the conflict as a mutual problem to be solved; and being aware of how your tendency to distort or misjudge may be heightened during heated conflict (Deutsch, 1993). It is important to monitor tendencies toward extreme responses to conflict situations such as being too hard or too soft, too rigid or loose, too intellectual or emotional, tending to escalate or minimize, and feeling compelled to reveal or conceal. In this section we focus on ways that faculty use themselves in the classroom and the inherent challenges.

Negative Emotion and Learning

The affective quality of learning about diversity for social justice thrusts faculty into staying on top of a variety of challenging, highly fluid, and potentially rigid dynamics in the classroom. When relatively untouched and value-laden topics are probed, we are certain to trigger affective reactions. By definition, feelings represent an appraisal of something as positive or negative based on a person's goals, standards, and/or attitudes (Davidson, 1994). They function to direct actions and assist in coping (Frijda, Kuipers, & ter Schure, 1989; Lazarus, 1966; Lazarus, 1991). Affect colors the mood of the classroom and thus it must be dealt with. Faculty need to be aware of student differences in affective style and reactivity (Davidson, 1994) as well as personality differences such as conscientiousness and extraversion versus introversion.

The complex tasks of self exploration can lead students to excessive self criticism, feeling they are being evaluated on their attitude, and defensive behavior. Individuals interpret situations and form appraisals based on individual and social factors such as esteem, values, ideals, meanings, and ideas that shape how they react (Lazarus, 1991). Thus the subjective appraisal by the student, based on interactions with faculty and other students as well as observation of interactions in the classroom, is key.

Because dealing with emotion is a ubiquitous charge, it is important that faculty learn to accurately read classroom dynamics and remain goal-directed in their perspective. Classroom interactions reflect individual patterns, while the group also develops as trust and class identity evolve. The art of teaching involves balancing individual and group dynamics. This means reading the moment and making a judgment about where and how to challenge either the group, or individuals, or both.

PERSPECTIVES ON TEACHING

Social work programs gain when all faculty participate in teaching diversity courses and have an inclusive perspective based on an appreciation for the richness of diverse worldviews. This requires attention to faculty development. Teaching expertise can be enhanced through the application of several significant yet divergent paradigms. In this section we present three paradigms that contribute to our effectiveness in teaching diversity for social justice content: reflective practitioner (Schon, 1983), constructivism (Goolishian & Winderman, 1988; von Glasersfeld, 1984) and social constructionism (Gergen, 1985), and critical social theory's (Agger, 1998) emphasis on knowledge and relations of power (Foucault, 1977, 1980).

The Reflective Practitioner

Schon's (1983) concept of the reflective practitioner addresses the ability of practitioners to create practice wisdom in the midst of acting. This view asserts that the technical rational model of theory as guiding practice is deficient because it does not deal sufficiently with the complexity of the real world, which is characterized by nonrational processes. To know in practice and reflect-in-action represents a perspective that acknowledges (a) a spontaneous emergence of tacit knowledge in action, (b) the reality that people's perceptions and beliefs influence what they attend to and that these are influenced by social context, and (c) that knowledge building develops through reflective practice that utilizes experiments in action (Papell & Skolnik, 1992). While the idea of reflection in action is premised on systematic inquiry and emphasizes cognitive processes, it fails to adequately integrate the affective component of learning (Papell & Skolnik, 1992). Yet the focus on tacit knowledge illuminates an aspect of knowing that can promote faculty confidence to draw from their immediate experience in dealing "on the spot" with uncomfortable exchanges and content.

Active engagement in class interaction about difference inevitably raises questions about the best use of the teachable moment. Is it possible to reflect while acting due to the affect that faculty may feel and the diverse and impassioned perspectives that students bring? In moments when we are in the midst of interactions with one or a few students, for example, the effect that this interaction has on the remainder of the class looms as something to be dealt with in the future. Complexity arises from being aware of and working with the intensity and discomfort of our responses (e.g., values, beliefs, feelings, spontaneous reactions). It also resides in acknowledging and engaging with the distinctively different points of view expressed by different students. Schon and Rein's (1994) work on policy formation addresses this fundamental question about whether it is possible to reflect in the midst of action taking, doing, and implementing. They assert that frames, that is, assumptive structures, are tacit in nature. Thus they are exempt from mindful attention, influence what individuals perceive as self interest (e.g., what constitutes conflict), and shape how we formulate problems as well as solutions.

This doubt and ambivalence, arising from the complexity of a situation, is especially relevant to diversity teaching. Faculty are confronted with complexity in at least two ways: they must learn about new paradigms, perspectives, and approaches and they must manage diverse student perspectives when they are articulated in the classroom. It is critically important that faculty be willing to be open to new paradigms that broaden and deepen cognitive and affective understanding of other cultural worldviews. Methods for enhancing our teaching of that content are also critically important. Sometimes faculty refrain from exploring new intellectual territory because of perceived differences with conceptual approaches. Sometimes they may be unwilling to stretch intellectually and engage in efforts to deal with new formulations that challenge current beliefs and could lead to shifts in thinking. Even when faculty are open to grappling with understanding diverse student views and the resulting dynamics, there can still be considerable ambivalence about the best means for using that teachable moment. Thus, looming big on the scale of best teaching methods with diversity content are the ability to bear ambivalence and doubt, to sustain openness to complexity, and to allow process to unfold.

Schon & Rein's work (1994) normalizes the doubt and ambivalence experienced by faculty in relation to the complexity of their own reactions and the diverse viewpoints in the classroom. More needs to be understood about the nature of the doubt and the ways that faculty manage this reflective process as they guide students in managing their own conflicts as they learn. The reflection in action concept gives meaning to what emerges out of the classroom interaction, goals of learning, and theoretical content. It enhances students' appreciation of their own contributions, wisdom, and creativity in the classroom and supports students' creative reflexivity (Papell & Skolnik, 1992; Weick, 1993). While the reflective practitioner perspective can guide faculty in their discovery of effective teaching strategies, its positivist emphasis on inquiry via experiments in action contradicts several basic constructivist and critical social theory tenets, to which we now turn.

Social Constructionism

In Chapter Three we discussed some similarities and distinctions between constructivism and constructionism. We emphasized that both approaches counter the positivist view that an objective reality exists that can be known through empirical methods (Hoffman, 1992). The discussion also pointed out how constructionism looks at the influence of language and concepts on thinking and how constructivism examines the descriptions and explanations that we use to account for events (Goldstein, 1993). We agree with the view that ideas, concepts, and memories arise from social interaction and are "mediated through language" (Hoffman, p. 8). Thus we refer to social constructionism when discussing the effect of social context on behavior. Contributions from social constructionism that are relevant for teaching diversity include (a) having students focus on analyzing the relationship between private difficulties and public issues as they emerge in case studies and role plays (Allen, 1993; Sessions, 1993); (b) focusing on the historical context in understanding interpersonal dynamics; and (c) addressing the power dynamics in the profession's construction of professional knowledge (Sessions, 1993).

Social constructionism can inform faculty interactions with students in several ways. Students can be encouraged to see that many approaches are valid and expertise is not the exclusive property of the teacher. They can be encouraged to question theoretical and personal assumptions and apply multiple theories to understanding behavior. They can be encouraged to examine value assumptions underlying theories about human nature and change. And they can be encouraged to focus on multiple perspectives to practice (Dean, 1993). By engaging students in these activities, social justice and social change are furthered through evaluating how professional theories shape and create data (Dean, 1993); examining the relationship between personal problems and public issues; and acknowledging ambiguity, multiple meanings, and theory as metaphor (Middleman & Wood, 1993).

Critical Social Theory

Critical social theory refers to both distinct theories and a body of theory that shares a critique of positivism; concern for questions of power, difference and domination; attention to the dialectics of structure and human agency; and a commitment to social transformation (Agger, 1998; Finn & Jacobson, 2002). Readers are referred to Finn and Jacobson's (2002) work for a comprehensive discussion of the range of theories that are included under the rubric of critical social theory. Critical social theory offers a critique of positivism, gives credence to the possibility of progress away from present day oppression, and promotes social change. It posits that domination is structural and identifies people's "false consciousness promoted by ideology, reification, hegemony, and one-dimensional thinking" as the means for reproducing domination (Agger, 1998, p. 4). Most important, in line with social justice work, Agger (1998) suggests that the structural roots of oppression can be undone by using the knowledge of that structure as a foundation for changing social conditions.

There is postmodern criticism of the assumptions of coherence and truth that accompany metatheory, such as critical social theory. The value of critical social theory is thus challenged based on its "totalizing and positivist currents" (Best & Kellner, 1991, p. 257). Yet the criticism becomes muted as Best and Kellner (1991) point out that the type of sociopolitical analysis that is needed for contemporary issues must be grounded in an approach that examines the subject matter within the context of factors that include the nexuses of power and knowledge and micropower in human services (e.g., psychiatry, medicine, prisons).

Usefulness of the Three Paradigms for Diversity Teaching

Twenty-first century challenges such as social injustice, denial of human rights, multiple levels of violence, and growing inequality that is both national and global in nature pose difficulties that are beyond the reach of social work paradigms (Finn & Jacobson, 2002). Each of the three paradigms that we briefly presented—reflective practitioner, social constructionism, and critical social theory—contribute valuable perspectives that faculty can bring to their teaching as a way to work with the subjective dimension that builds on their life experiences and emphasizes processing and integration of affective and intellectual teaching experiences. It also promotes "beginning with where the student is" regarding their constructions of diversity and social justice and furthers their movement toward social justice action. Our perspective is that often difficulties with the positivist approach arise from imposing knowledge building through method at the cost of recognizing and valuing knowledge through experience (Rose, 2002). Thus, a problem with the reflective practitioner model lies in its belief in the systematic application of inquiry and empiricism. However, we propose combining constructivist/constructionist and critical theory approaches with the reflective practitioner framework to create a paradigm for exploring the questions identified by those approaches.

The learning goals for diversity education are constructed to provide faculty with the structure to challenge students' limits of awareness and engage them on a journey that promotes racial and social identity development. In this process, students are expected to develop an ability to manage greater complexity in others and openness to difference in the service of becoming a social change agent. The tasks for faculty are immense. They can be facilitated by faculty's prior experience in teaching ethnicity-based courses and a balance of experiential and didactic teaching methods. They are also facilitated by exercising judgment regarding defensive reaction, possible distortion of communication, and use of appropriate self-disclosure (Gloria, Rieckmann, & Rush, 2000; Goldstein & Benassi, 1994). A combination of reflecting-while-acting, coupled with asking the kinds of challenging questions modeled by constructionism and critical social theories, can help faculty effectively accomplish the required tasks.

CONCLUSION

The goal of engaging students in the development of sociopolitical self-awareness evokes a parallel process for us as faculty. This is both daunting and challenging. It offers an opportunity for our own personal and professional growth. It pushes us to build connections with colleagues who are committed to this teaching in order to be valuable resources for each other. By engaging in the process of co-learning with other faculty and with our students, we give ourselves the supportive context that makes it possible to bear our responses to our subjective lived experiences and keep going. Such a supportive context provides the foundation for increasing our capacities for learning about diversity and social justice teaching. In the next chapter we discuss the classroom interaction and dynamics within a framework of racial identity development on the part of both faculty and students.

REFERENCES

Agger, B. (1998). *Critical social theories: An introduction*. Boulder, CO: Westview Press.

Allen, J. (1993). The constructivist paradigm: Values and ethics. *Journal of Teaching in Social Work 8*(1/2), 31–54.

Best, S., & Kellner, D. (1991). *Postmodern theory: Critical interrogations*. New York: The Guilford Press.

Bowen, M. (1978). *Family therapy in clinical practice*. New York: Jason Aronson.

Davidson, R. J. (1994). On emotion, mood, and related affective constructs. In P. Ekman, & R. J. Davidson. (Eds.), *The nature of emotion*. New York: Oxford University Press.

Dean, R. (1993). Teaching a constructivist approach to clinical practice. *Journal of Teaching in Social Work, 8*(1/2), 55–76.

Deutsch, M. (1993). Educating for a peaceful world. *American Psychologist, 48*(5), 510–517.

Finn, J., & Jacobson, M. (2002, February). *Just practice: Steps toward a new social work paradigm*. Paper presented at the Annual Program Meeting, Council on Social Work Education, Nashville, TN.

Foucault, M. (1977). *Discipline and punish*. New York: Pantheon Books.

Foucault, M. (1980). *Power/knowledge: Selected interviews and other writings, 1972–77*. New York: Pantheon Books.

Frijda, N. H., Kuipers, P., & ter Schure, E. (1989). Relations among emotion, appraisal and emotional action readiness. *Journal of Personality and Social Psychology, 57*, 212–228.

Gergen, K. (1985). The social constructionist movement in modern psychology. *American Psychologist, 40*(3), 317–329.

Gloria, A. M., Rieckmann, T. R., & Rush, J. D. (2000). Issues and recommendations for teaching an ethnic/culture based course. *Teaching of Psychology, 27,* 102–107.

Goldstein, H. (1993). Field education for reflective practice: A re-constructive proposal. *Journal of Teaching in Social Work 8*(1/2), 165–182.

Goldstein, G. S., & Benassi, V. A. (1994). The relation between teacher self-disclosure and student classroom participation. *Teaching of Psychology, 21,* 212–217.

Goolishian, H., & Winderman, L. (1988). Constructivism, autopoiesis and problem determined systems. *Irish Journal of Psychology, 9,* 130–143.

Hoffman, L. (1992). A reflexive stance for family therapy. In S. McNamee & K. Gergen. (Eds.), *Therapy as social construction.* Newbury Park, CA: Sage.

Lazarus, R. (1966). *Psychological stress and the coping process.* New York: McGraw-Hill.

Lazarus, R. (1991). *Emotion and adaptation.* New York: Oxford University Press.

Lichtenberg, P., van Beusekom, J., & Gibbons, D. (1997). *Encountering bigotry: Befriending projecting persons in everyday life.* Northvale, NJ: Jason Aronson.

Llerena-Quinn, R. (2001). How do assumptions of difference and power affect what and how we teach?. *NMTP Newsletter, 5*(1). Retrieved from http:// www.nmtp.org/newsletters/nmtplettervol5-1.htm.

McKeachie, W. (1986). *Teaching tips: A guidebook for the beginning college teacher* (8th ed.). Lexington, MA: D.C. Heath.

Middleman, R., & Wood, G. (1993). So much for the bell curve: Constructionism, power/conflict, and the structural approach to direct practice in social work. *Journal of Teaching in Social Work, 8*(1/2), 129–146.

Papell, C. P., & Skolnik, L. (1992). The reflective practitioner: A contemporary paradigm's relevance for social work education. *Journal of Social Work Education, 28*(1), 18–26.

Pinderhughes, E. (1989). *Understanding race, ethnicity and power: The key to efficacy in clinical practice.* New York: The Free Press.

Ring, J. F. (2000). The long and winding road: Personal reflections of an anti-racism trainer. *American Journal of Orthopsychiatry, 70*(1), 73–81.

Rose, S. (2002, March). *Social work at the crossroads: A reflection.* Paper presented at the Social Work at a Crossroads Conference, Department of

Social Work Education, California State University, Fresno.

Schon, D. (1983). *The reflective practitioner*. New York: Basic Books.

Schon, D. & Rein, M. (1994). *Frame reflection*. New York: Basic Books.

Sessions, P. (1993). Private troubles and public issues: The social construction of assessment. *Journal of Teaching in Social Work*, *8*(1/2), 111–127.

Stevens, J. O. (1975). *Gestalt is*. Moab, UT: Real People Press.

von Glasersfeld, E. (1984). An introduction to radical constructivism of reality. *Dialectica, 33*, 37–50.

Weick, A. (1993). Reconstructing social work education. *Journal of Teaching in Social Work*, *8*(1/2), 11–30.

Chapter Eight
Diversity Focus: Implications for Classroom Interaction Dynamics

Throughout this book, we emphasize the significance of intensified interaction that emerges when classroom discussion turns to issues of difference. Thus, some of the most significant expertise and skills a professor needs for effectively teaching diversity and social justice concepts involve understanding and working with classroom dynamics. In this chapter, we propose some frameworks for understanding the intrapersonal, interpersonal, and societal dynamics that influence and kindle what might otherwise be benign, uncomplicated exchanges in the classroom. The discussion focuses on racial identity development models and how they contribute to understanding the lenses through which both students and faculty view the learning process. The chapter ends with discussion of dynamics that arise in relation to various constellations of racial identities in the classroom.

INTRODUCTION

This chapter is based on the assumption that the racial and social identity development of both students and faculty play a role in shaping classroom interactions. It is also based on a belief that individual behavior needs to be understood in the context of both an individual's history and the sociopolitical factors that have been formative in that person's life. We assume that the meaning that individuals assign to an event or situation influences their behavior. In other words, individuals respond to each other's behaviors based on the meaning that they attach to those behaviors, rather than responding to the behavior itself (Blumer, 1962; Mead, 1934). This meaning making activity leads to individuals creating a view of themselves that is, in part, based on expectations others have of them. This includes larger societal expectations. Due to the centrality and prevalence of racism and classism in the history of the United States, that socialization includes internalization of dominant ideological values that include racism, sexism, classism, ableism, and other isms based on social power differences.

We propose that racial and social identity development models provide useful frameworks for understanding how social psychological processes of meaning making are shaped by oppression, privilege, and racial and social categorization related to race, gender, sexual orientation, and class. Following up on our earlier discussion of race as a social construction, in this chapter we discuss the related social, psychological, and political consequences that result from socially constructed views of race and difference. Because of the depth of the affective learning about difference that diversity teaching involves, the ways in which students and faculty construct race and difference contribute to unique classroom dynamics that are not found in other courses. While there are many cases where students learn and grow by leaps and bounds, there are many disappointing accounts as well. Faculty can become discouraged that they are not reaching more students or by student overreactions to the curriculum and to the professors themselves. The hardest part of the learning process is that it involves students in changing how they view society, how they view themselves (Edwards-Orr, 1988), and how they see themselves as agents of change. It is an emotional and intellectual change process that engages them in reflecting on how oppression has influenced their lives and their relationships. It involves making connections between social, political, and institutional factors and their personal experience. We have much work to do to better understand how differential teaching methods can engage students effectively in this affective and highly sensitive learning process.

Racial and social identity models can help identify some key considerations for faculty and serve as useful tools as they engage in this classroom journey. The models are based on developmental dynamics associated with coming to terms with racism and oppression in society and the internalization of their effects. Faculty awareness about their own racial and social identity and their attention to students' racial and social identity needs can help them make decisions about teaching methods. For example, by paying attention to students' racial identity needs, we can engage them first in their comfort zones or cozy boxes (Koch, 1995) and then move them into more challenging subject matter at a pace that does not intimidate or create overwhelming anxiety.

For faculty to be prepared to bring students through an effective change process, however, they need to confront the issues in their own personal and professional lives. This means taking time to do the emotional and intellectual work involved in addressing the complex concerns that arise from our own racial and social identity development processes. The rewarding result is gaining a variety of new perspectives about diversity. It is essential that faculty have their bearing on where they want to go with the learning activities. They need to remember that this is a process. Thus, for a class to reach a point of shared commonalities, this may first mean traversing the jagged and uneven terrain of students' perceptions and experiences. The old adage of starting where the client is offers faculty a particularly useful guide for engaging students in learning about diversity, oppression, and social justice. It is essential to validate their struggles and intentions. When needed, it is important to support them to suspend judgment of themselves. We need to remember that this is a lifelong process of integrating the political into the personal.

Social identity development models address the change process that individuals go through as they work through and reject oppression throughout their lifetimes. In the next section, we present racial identity development models for African Americans and Euro-Americans. The models include tasks involved in personally confronting racism and undoing its effects on one's identity. Both models address the internalization of dominant ideological belief systems, the realization of an identity based on privilege or marginalization, and movement toward the formulation of an identity that no longer needs a self-definition that is contingent on the "other." According to the models, when people have a wholesome identity they have the capacity to own characteristics that had been projected onto others in the form of negative stereotypes. They are free of distortion that comes from privilege or target status. The distortions to be undone for those in a dominant position involve undoing the overestimations of self that come from a status of privilege and entitlement. The distortions to be undone for those in a subordinate position involve undoing the underestimations of self and giving up the devaluation of their group that was projected on them by dominant ideology and internalized by them as members of the devalued group.

RACIAL AND SOCIAL IDENTITY DEVELOPMENT MODELS

Racial and social identity models address developmental dynamics that are associated with the process all individuals go through, regardless of background and identity, as they recognize racism and oppression in their environment and in themselves. These models highlight the tasks involved in confronting our experiences as either privileged and/or oppressed. This can mean dealing with multiple identities that embody both privilege and target status. For example, someone with both a European and a Hispanic heritage must deal with the meaning of these identities for him or herself. The models identify various points of awareness on a proposed continuum of development that color our perception and experience. The models raise provocative questions about how faculty awareness of their own racial and social identity influences their interaction with their students and vice versa.

Racial identity development models propose that people move through a series of points or statuses. People transition from one point to another on a continuum of development through successive statuses that represent attitudinal (i.e., behavior, affect, cognition) processes that regulate how an individual interprets racial information (Helms, 1999). Helms (1999) suggests that movement from one status to another is influenced by how an individual copes, i.e., what information processing strategies individuals use. The models propose that change is triggered when existing perceptions are too limited to help the person cope with a personally meaningful racial event. Coping responses are seen as varying between different racial groups based on the effects of social categorization and dissimilarities in social power.

Racial identity development models offer frameworks for understanding personal change that begins with lack of awareness of dominant societal oppression and moves toward the development of an integrated wholesome identity. This identity is free of being defined in relation to the "other"—an identity that is defined on its own terms rather than being defined by a context imbued with a biased distribution of power and privilege. While there is still little empirical work on these models, they provide provocative paradigms for grappling with the psychological consequences of social ideology and for thinking critically about classroom interactions.

Racial identity development models focus on factors related to intrapersonal and interpersonal processes that are identified as unique to individuals of Euro-American, Black, Latino, and Asian identity. Race, as a social construction, fulfills particular economic and social functions and plays a formative role in psychological experience and psychosocial development. It plays a role as well in the manifestation of violence on interpersonal, cultural, and institutional levels (LoCicero & Trimble, 1997). Hence, diverse racial identities bring to light the consequences of racism on individual awareness depending on one's racial group identity. Three racial identity models are briefly described below for White, Black, and multiracial people and social identity development.

Black Racial Identity Development

The Cross (1995) Black Identity Development Model outlines personal movement through points that begin with devaluation of self and one's group and end in self confidence based on internalization of a new racist-free identity. The change process is initiated either by an event that devastates one's identity or worldview or a "series of smaller eye opening episodes" that elicit anger and guilt. This results in less engagement with dominant society and more immersion into one's own group, followed by the development of an identity that meets new personal needs (Cross, 1995, p. 105).

The model outlines personal and social change through points conceptualized as "ego statuses" that include pre-encounter, encounter, immersion/emersion, internalization, and internalization/commitment. Racial identity development is proposed to involve a renunciation of internalized racism and the emergence of a positive racial social identity. *Pre-encounter* consciousness and behavior is characterized by an out-of-awareness devaluation of self and one's group, along with efforts to "fit into" dominant cultural life. The *encounter* stage is a two-part process that involves the person experiencing an event that challenges their current worldview and precipitates an interpretation of the event from a new perspective. Sue and Sue (1999) suggest that an event, such as the death of Martin Luther King, Jr., can stimulate a shift in worldview because one's prior worldview cannot explain his death. The shift can be accompanied by feelings of anger and guilt. In the *immersion-emersion* stage, individuals focus full attention on their own culture and an increasing sense of cultural pride develops. In the final stage of *internalization*, the individual integrates the old and new social identities, has a greater sense of confidence, and is more flexible with and appreciative of difference. The new racist-free identity is one that meets their new personal needs and is reflected in a commitment over time to Black community concerns (Cross, 1995).

White Racial Identity Development

White racial identity development models point to racism as a significant aspect of being a Euro-American. They highlight how Whites are socialized into perceiving that they are entitled to privileges. Further, they are socialized into maintaining their privileged status through mechanisms such as denial, distortion, and aggression (Hardiman, 1982; Helms, 1999). The models also illuminate how movement through the developmental continuum points or statuses involves recognition of how, by exercising privilege, one has participated in oppressive practices. They move to confrontation of one's biases and prejudices and ultimately to taking responsibility for personal and social change.

Helms' (1999) proposes a model with two phases, each with three levels, called statuses. Phase I involves the abandonment of racism and Phase II involves defining a nonracist identity for oneself. Phase I includes:

1. Contact, where the person is characterized by colorblindness about difference and accepts White supremacy.

2. Disintegration, where the person begins to see the consequences of racism and feels conflicted; the breakdown of denial can mean anxiety and psychological pain.

3. Reintegration, where the person regresses into the dominant ideology as a retreat and has a "bootstrap" perspective about poverty with an "I did it, they can too" attitude.

Phase II includes:

4. Pseudo-Independence, where the person experiences events that trigger insight into racism and compel more understanding of diversity differences while still valuing solutions that support the status quo.

5. Immersion/Emersion, where the person moves into dealing with their Whiteness, privilege, biases, and oppression, which involves undoing distortion and denial. This is a major shift away from focusing on people of color to understand racism to changing oneself.

6. Autonomy, where the person's increased awareness of their own Whiteness involves "reduced feelings of guilt, acceptance of one's role in perpetuating racism, and renewed determination to abandon White entitlement" (Helms, 1999, p. 152).

Multiracial Identity Development

The growing numbers of individuals who identify as multiracial bears particular attention. They experience societal pressure to identify as being of one racial group when, in fact, their heritage includes several groups. Some attention has been given to the unique tasks of identity development for multiracial people, primarily those of African American and Euro-American backgrounds (Kerwin & Ponterotto, 1995; Root, 1992). Several unique considerations related to their multiracial heritage arise for people in this population. For example, based on the "one drop rule" (Wright, 1994), dominant society classifies African Americans as Black when their parents are Euro-American and African American, and individuals with multiple racial identities are categorized as having one overriding, monolithic racial identity.

Tremendous work is involved in order to integrate multiple racial and social heritages that enjoy varying degrees of societal legitimization. It falls on the shoulders of the individual to work through conflicts and validate their background in ways that sometimes are not present even within one's own social support network. Differential societal valuations of different origins in one's multiracial background make the developmental tasks of racial identity development more difficult. This is particularly the case when racism leads to avoidance and ultimately invisibility of some aspects of one's identity. Biracial identity models explore issues such as the possible relegation to marginal membership in one's primary groups (Stonequist, 1937, as cited in Kerwin & Ponterotto, 1995), self esteem, feelings of disloyalty, racism, experiences with society's uncertainty regarding race, and factors that support functioning in more than one culture (Jacobs, 1992; Kerwin & Ponterotto, 1995; Kich, 1992; LaFromboise, Coleman, & Gerton, 1993; Poston, 1990).

Social Identity: An Overarching Concept of Oppression

Our stance in this book is that diversity education for social justice starts with racism as the fundamental oppressive system in the United States and then expands to include other forms of oppression. Racial identity development models address the process of coming to terms with one's identity based on race within the context of a racist society. Similarly, social identity development processes address coming to terms with one's identities based on membership in other groups. Social identity refers to an overarching concept of oppression that is experienced on the basis of race, ethnicity, gender, sexual orientation, physical ability, socioeconomic class, age, religion, and other groups with which individuals identify. These identities are fundamental elements of one's self-concept and their combination with one another in different configurations can have a powerful influence on how one understands life experiences (Robinson & Howard-Hamilton, 2000).

Jackson and Hardiman (n.d.) propose that the considerable work that has been done on racial identity and oppression collectively identify "what is known about the social identity development process for individuals and groups with what is known about the effects that specific manifestations of oppression have on individual and group development" (p. 1). Their model is generic to oppressors and oppressed and describes the tasks involved in achieving a liberated social identity. Points of transition proposed for both individuals and groups are characterized by attitudinal change (i.e., thinking, feeling, behaving) that begins with a naïve stage of awareness that is either accepting or resisting of the dominant ideology. Jackson and Hardiman (n.d.) point out that both acceptance and resistance can either be passive or active, which accommodates heterogeneity among individuals in coping with increased awareness of social injustice. These points of awareness are followed by redefinition of self and internalization or integration of a new identity. Transition from one stage to the next is initiated when one's way of thinking is no longer adequate to explain one's observations or is "detrimental to a healthy self concept" (Jackson & Hardiman, n.d., p. 2). The attitude change reflects coming to terms with social power, taking responsibility for feelings, and self-definition.

Contributions of Racial and Social Identity Models to Diversity Teaching

The array of models that address racial identity development in relation to general minority identity development (Atkinson, Morten, & Sue, 1998) and specific racial/ethnic groups (Helms, 1999; Ruiz, 1990; Sue & Sue, 1999) illustrates the nature of internalization of negative stereotypes, how individuals devalue and make invisible aspects of themselves, and the emotional and intellectual work involved in undoing the distortions of self and others.

As people try to cope and adapt to diversity situations, the racial identity development process is a tool that can help them develop the ability to manage increasingly more complex data. The ability of faculty to handle complex racial and diversity information in social justice curricula is essential for teaching effectiveness. By dealing with their own racial and social identity development tasks, faculty can gain increased access to feelings about difference and oppression. This means they will be less intimidated by their own powerful reactions and the overreactions of others (such as accusations of being racist!). This is essential in order to connect with students as they identify and engage in difficult work on their personal issues and begin to explore where and how social change fits into their lives.

IMPLICATIONS OF RACIAL IDENTITY DEVELOPMENT MODELS FOR UNDERSTANDING STUDENT PERSPECTIVES

Racial identity development models can help faculty understand the diverse lenses with which students see and thus interpret both classroom interactions and course content. They provide a perspective from which to view student responses by helping identify where they might be in the process of confronting and working with the effects of oppression and dominant ideology in their lives. Just as we get a "reading" on where our class as a group is for the purposes of pitching our teaching approach to our students, it is also useful to get a reading on where students may be on the journey of racial identity development. This is important both for teaching purposes and as a perspective from which to try to understand student reactions to us and to other students. Racial identity development models provide a framework for understanding what might be happening when students perceive faculty as hostile or angry. The models address the societal influences that contribute to the complexity of what is going on in the classroom.

While racial identity is a powerful determinant of behavior, classroom dynamics are influenced by a combination of factors such as the ethnic and/or racial critical mass in the classroom, program climate, and student experiences with diversity. Faculty appreciation of heterogeneity within racial, ethnic, and other diversity groups is an important factor. Such appreciation involves more than recognizing stereotypes. It also seeks to learn about sameness and difference between and within groups.

It is essential that faculty understand the tremendous amount of heterogeneity within any group in order to discern what students might be dealing with in relation to race, ethnicity, regional culture, socioeconomic class socialization, spirituality, religion, and other factors. Some examples illustrate exploration of heterogeneity within Latino, African American, Asian American, and White groups. With Latinos, consideration needs to be given to what they choose to call themselves: Latino, Hispanic, Chicano, Mexican American, or identification by one's national origin, all of which have unique meanings that can be understood only on individual terms. Latino heritage should at least generate curiosity for others about native-born versus foreign-born status, immigration experiences, level of acculturation, language dominance, national origin, socioeconomic class, and racial/social identity. Similarly, exploration and discovery about African Americans involves regional culture, urban/rural differences, family life, and religious/spiritual connections. Heterogeneity among Asian Americans involves differences regarding national origin, generation in the United States, family experiences with war and/or camps, and many other factors. Finally, the lack of visibility to the dominant group of its heterogeneity has often led to White students indicating that they "do not have a culture" because their family does not perceive its practices and values as reflecting culture and little attention has been paid to the distant immigrant background with its rich heritage. In sum, contextual, historical issues need to frame our inquiry as groups learn about one another. This includes issues such as intergenerational dynamics, emigration, immigration, genocide, slavery, social marginalization, and exploitation of labor.

What Students Bring to the Classroom

Students influence dynamics in the classroom depending on their racial identity and their experience in addressing racism, classism, sexism, ableism, and other isms. They may encounter many hurdles in the affective learning process. Sometimes difficulties arise from the course structure and how the course is presented and set up. Hamilton (2001) found that students of color, in particular, encountered difficulty with a "lack of clear objectives about how the course would be taught and what roles [they] would have in the classroom" (p. 76). Jackson (1999) suggests that students of color may feel in a double bind about being expected to be spokespersons for their own and other ethnic groups and may experience anxiety and doubt about doing so. They may also feel discomfort about discussing racism in a public setting. Speaking out in class may feel like risking being criticized. This can be particularly difficult for those who have self-esteem issues or are in the midst of struggling with racial or social identity or acculturation issues.

Often, Euro-American students' efforts to be liberal can be motivated by guilt, of which they might be unaware. An intellectual level of learning can be complicated by lack of awareness about White privilege. LoCicero and Trimble (1997) suggest that this lack of awareness can prevent students from taking responsibility for changing institutionalized power relations between and among racial and ethnic groups. As Euro-American students begin to see how White privilege operates, new ways of coping are required. For example, they must adjust and adapt to the reality that the option of denying the existence of privilege is a type of privilege itself. White students who see themselves as social change agents may experience particular confusion and distress when they discover that, as a sociopolitical phenomenon, White privilege cannot be relinquished and that individuals have few choices about institutionalized, patterned social processes. The task of White students is to identify how to be accountable in responding to social processes that support White privilege.

Such student dynamics point to the need to create and maintain an open, respectful learning environment in the classroom. The lack of such an environment can affect the classroom in ways that give rise to stereotypic perceptions of the professor. Commonplace classroom responses such as unresolved conflict between faculty and student(s) or lack of faculty responsiveness to student inquiries take on heightened magnitude in the context of diversity teaching.

What Faculty Bring to the Classroom

Professors influence classroom dynamics by their awareness and use of self related to their personal experience in understanding the effects of diversity, oppression, social justice, privilege, and entitlement in their own lives. It is important for faculty to be role models by sharing personal experiences and emphasizing that there are no experts here and that we are all on this path of learning together. In doing this, they convey to students that the process of making sense of diversity and social justice in one's life is a collective classroom activity and one that is worked on together (LoCicero & Trimble, 1997). This communicates what is expected of students and normalizes their experiences. It also stimulates thinking about taking responsibility. For example, when White students understand diversity as the experiences of people of color and expect or need students of color to speak on behalf of their group or to educate them about oppression, faculty can encourage the White students to take responsibility for their own learning and feelings. They can reframe such encounters in terms of understanding their experiences of Whiteness as well as the experiences of people of color.

An issue that is approached in different ways depending on the social work program is who should teach diversity courses. While it is generally assumed that diversity content across the curriculum is the responsibility of all faculty, there are different points of view about who should teach discrete diversity courses. Faculty who are members of historically oppressed groups (e.g., based on race, ethnicity, gender, sexual orientation, physical ability) are often viewed as having special expertise and thus may be relegated to teach diversity courses. Depending on individual preference and perspective on diversity and social concerns, however, they may view this as prejudice. Faculties of color, in particular, are often perceived as spokespersons within the program for their racial and ethnic group issues and concerns. As with other program decisions, individual differences among faculty of color regarding their interests, experiences, and preferences need to be explored as part of the decision-making process related to diversity curriculum and program formulation.

Increasingly we are seeing social work programs where all faculty contribute to and teach diversity courses and content. This is an achievement that conveys a message to the student body that the program values and practices diversity and social justice. However, Euro-American faculty may often feel unsure of themselves when teaching something that they feel is best taught by someone who has been the target of oppression and knows more about it personally. They may also be uncomfortable because they feel that they are still in the midst of learning about oppression themselves. Understanding privileged and targeted status touches everyone's lives and a central aspect of teaching diversity curriculum is to integrate intellectual content with personal awareness, regardless of where one is at in the journey of personal awareness.

Students may assume differences regarding ethnic, racial, or socioeconomic class in a negative way based on perceptions that faculty are not aware of oppression or do not understand the nature of the struggles they have experienced. Depending on their perceptions, students may be more sensitive to an apparent lack of faculty responsiveness to diversity and social power issues and may view faculty attitude as dismissive.

Due to the historical presence of anti-Semitism, students who are in settings where they do not have exposure to or are unfamiliar with people who are Jewish may have stereotypic views of Jewish faculty. They may not recognize heterogeneity within the Jewish community, for example the continuum between orthodox practice, nonpracticing Jews, and those who identify as an ethnicity and not a religion. The location of the program may make a significant difference in terms of regional demographics and their implications for negative stereotypes. However, tenacious and negative stereotypes can exist whether a population is visible or not in a particular region. Extensive media coverage of international or national events can ignite veiled biases. Also, when a social group is not visible in a region, the negative stereotype can be buttressed by discomfort arising from individuals not knowing what to expect for lack of experience with that group.

The point is that many different dynamics can evolve based on configurations of the racial and social factors represented by faculty and students related to power and privilege issues. There are many possible configurations of differing levels of racial and social identity development between faculty and students and each plays a role in the evolution of classroom dynamics and patterns. Perspective about predictable classroom twists and turns is possible when faculty are aware of possible pitfalls that can occur.

What follows are some transactions in relation to possible racial and ethnic classroom constellations between faculty and students. The aim is to suggest possible dynamics that arise in relation to racial and social identities of faculty and students. While we are only focusing on racial identity, our intention is to generate discussion about possible dynamics related to other constellations as well, for example, faculty characteristics such as physical ability or sexual orientation and reactions from students who may not have deal with ableist or heterosexist biases. Our application of racial and social identity models to faculty–student interaction is not intended as an evaluative exercise about low or high awareness. Such a use would surely defeat and go against the very aims of diversity teaching to facilitate awareness and action. It is suggested, however, that the discussions can be used as paradigms to identify tasks and processes that all individuals face in undoing oppression in their lives, to pose provocative questions for self-inquiry, and to suggest ideas for faculty preparation in teaching. In the interest of identifying possible dynamics below, we may err on the side of overgeneralization of the models. We trust that specificity can be suspended in the interest of exploring forces that come into play when individuals are in the beginning and/or middle of their efforts to confront their racial and/or social identity and how this can influence the classroom environment.

A significant issue for all professors is the perceptions of and interactions with both students of color and White students. The amount of contact and exposure to other ethnic, racial, and diversity groups, for instance, depends on the individual professor's formative life experiences, such as the degree of segregation in childhood neighborhoods. Several scenarios may get played out in the classroom depending on group configuration, as illustrated by the examples that follow: professor of color with primarily White class, professor of color with high diversity class, White professor with primarily White class, and White professor with high diversity class.

Professor of Color and Primarily White Class

Depending on the geographic location of the school or its public/private nature, some faculty of color find themselves teaching a class of White students who, in general, may have had little experience with people of color or with the professor's ethnic or racial heritage in particular. When there is a lack of connection between faculty and students in such cases, routine differences such as a poor match between student learning style and teaching approach can rapidly escalate into angry, aggressive reactions by the class. Where White students are in their social identity development can be a significant factor. Studies by Martinez and George (2001), for example, found that White individuals at early stages of racial identity development express more anger in response to racial minorities or racial issues compared to those with greater awareness in later stages of development. Professors of color may sense, from indirect behaviors and attitudes, that the White students lack respect for their knowledge and skill as teachers. Criticism of the professor by White students can also be very direct as the students play out their White privilege and superiority in the classroom.

When faculty of color experience such intensified overreactions, it is useful to explore systemic issues such as the program climate, the school's view of difference, and even perhaps the function that professors of color serve in the school. The outcomes of difficult classroom events are influenced by how professors of color interpret them, the support they get from colleagues, and whether they deal with the events directly with the class. Successful outcomes depend heavily on a process orientation in class that will identify interactions and probe into their dynamics.

Professor of Color and High Diversity Class

Class dynamics are influenced when either students or a professor of color make assumptions about similarities between them. There are many differences, however, based on a wide range of factors that include socioeconomic class, acculturation, urban/rural differences, and other factors. Thus, the risk of creating conflict is greater when professor and/or students assume similarities when they share the same race or ethnic background. Assumed similarities can lead to positive projections that can inhibit learning. In such cases, the professor may feel overprotective of students and identify with their struggles, life experiences, or achievements. When faculty experience a positive connection with students from groups with which they identify, they may not challenge these students to engage in the level of exploration needed in affective learning. There may also be negative projections that lead to irritation generated by culturally based stereotypes about behavior.

Negative interactions can also arise between students of color and a professor of color when students are in early stages of dealing with their own racial and social identity and may project unresolved issues onto the professor. Students of color who are beginning to deal with internalized negative stereotypes about their own group may make harsher judgments of faculty of color than of Euro-American faculty, based on beliefs of White supremacy. Jackson (1999) suggests that students of color may have difficulty trusting professors of color who are evenhanded with all students and do not take sides.

White Professor and Primarily White Class

A number of issues arise for a White professor when the classroom is primarily White. Some of the issues are similar in nature to those that faculty of color experience with high diversity classes. The assumption of homogeneity among the students and similarities between professor and students always need to be explored. This is particularly the case in regard to differences such as urban/rural experience, sexual orientation, physical ability, religion, and other factors related to social identity. For example, there is a potential opportunity that students with disabilities or Jewish identity (i.e., national or religious) may come with life experiences that can assist in bridging differences. At the same time that students with experiences of oppression may have a basis for bridging differences and learning about racism, it is important to not assume that such connections will be automatic.

In an all-White class, students may express a need to have people of color present in the classroom in order to ground diversity and oppression learning in the lived experience of people of color. While the professor has a role in working to increase the diversity of the student body, the class before him/her in the present needs to be dealt with. The challenge for the professor is to bring to life and make meaningful the personal work that the White students must engage in as they deal with White privilege and entitlement. Because oppression affects all members of society in regard to access to social power, the professor needs to focus the learning on the differential effects on students' lives. This emphasizes that dealing with racism is not merely an option for White people but rather, that racism shapes White people's lives and identities in profound and unavoidable ways. When we challenge students to deal with their "Whiteness," as we emphasized in Chapter One, we assign everyone a place in the work to be done.

Efforts to deal with and integrate one's racial identity involve tremendous work. The work involves integrating multiple racial and social heritages, each of which enjoys varying degrees of societal legitimization. It is on the shoulders of the individual to work through conflicts. White students may find themselves conflicted when they discover, through their White professor's experience and teaching, that it is in fact possible for Whites to take on anti-racism and deal with internalized racism in their own lives. While this realization is facilitated by the White professor's modeling, they may consequently have to deal with a myriad of intense feelings that get stirred up for White students when they face the prospect of having to go further in their personal confrontation than they expected. On another note, Jackson (1999) suggests that in cases in which students idealize a professor through over-identification, while the professor may feel flattered, an opportunity can be lost if this results in not challenging the student. White professors with predominantly White students have a unique opportunity and responsibility to challenge the students in a powerful way through sharing their own White identity development process in relation to power, privilege, and internalized dominance.

White Professor and High Diversity Class

Diverse classroom demographics provide an opportunity for both faculty and students who have little experience with diversity to learn about the tremendous heterogeneity within groups as well as commonalities across groups. Diverse classrooms also pose challenges because they become a microcosm of real world tensions and conflicts. Professors need to develop comfort in talking about oppression with students who have experienced it. This is particularly challenging for White faculty who feel that their lives have not been significantly limited by oppressive experiences. It can feel daunting if professors expect that they have to speak about someone else's experience because this is an impossible task. Professors can convey an attitude of exploration rather than expertise when they maintain a focus on their own observations, questions, processes, and struggles as a means to lay a foundation for classroom dialogue. They can also emphasize to the students how classroom experience parallels the client's experiences with oppression and how classroom dialogue and learning can be insightfully applied to work with clients.

Ghosts in the Classroom

In addition to the interactions between professor and students and between students in the classroom, several other sources of tensions from outside can permeate interactions. A range of formal and informal interactions that students engage in outside of the classroom can spill into it. Faculty need to be attuned to interactions that cohorts of students may engage in during other classes. Tensions related to difference that began in other classes may spill out in a diversity class. When conflict that is generated in a diversity course is not dealt with in class, it can spill over into other classes as well. It is not unusual for a class that encourages dialogue to find itself dealing with spillover from another class when the issues were not dealt with in that class. When the professor explores the issues and dynamics that are operating, students have a forum in which to think critically about tensions related to difference and how they are dealt with.

SUMMARY AND CONCLUSION

Affective learning involved in diversity teaching touches on aspects of faculty and student experience that are not ordinarily stimulated in other academic courses. The learning process is facilitated by faculty awareness of and comfort in talking about difference and challenging student conceptions of diversity. A process orientation premised on racial and social identity frameworks provides a perspective for faculty to work with their own learning about diversity and to understand and facilitate the journey that their students are expected to engage in as they learn about diversity and social justice.

While it is important to understand dynamics and reactions, it is also important not to force students to engage in processes for which they are not ready. The content can be highly anxiety-arousing for all. It requires faculty self-awareness and sufficient mastery of conflictual material to model and engage students in a collective effort. In the next chapter, three professors dialogue about their experiences in teaching a diversity course and how they engage in a learning process themselves as they develop their awareness, knowledge, and skills.

REFERENCES

Atkinson, D. R., Morten, G., & Sue, D. W. (1998). *Counseling American minorities: A cross cultural perspective.* (5th ed.). Dubuque, IA: William. C. Brown.

Blumer, H. (1962). Society as symbolic interaction. In A. M. Rose (Ed.), *Human Behavior and Social Processes.* New York: Houghton Mifflin.

Cross, W. E. (1995). The psychology of nigrescence: Revising the Cross Model. In J. G. Ponterotto, J. M. Casas, L. A. Suzuki, & C. M. Alexander (Eds.), *Handbook of multicultural counseling* (pp. 181–191). Thousand Oaks, CA:

Sage.

Edwards-Orr, M. T. (1988, March). *Helping white students confront white racism.* Paper presented at the Annual Program Meeting, Council on Social Work Education, Atlanta, GA.

Hamilton, J. (2001). *Transactional learning and double consciousness: The voices of students of color in required racism courses.* Unpublished dissertation. Smith College, North Hampton, MA.

Hardiman, R. (1982). White identity development: A process oriented model for describing the racial consciousness of White Americans. *Dissertation Abstracts International, 43,* 104A. (UMI No. 82-10330)

Helms, J. (1999). White racial identity development: Therapeutic implications. In D. Sue & D. Sue, *Counseling the culturally different.* (3rd ed.). New York: John Wiley & Sons.

Jackson, L. (1999). Ethnocultural resistance to multicultural training: Students and faculty. *Cultural Diversity and Ethnic Minority Psychology, 5*(1), 27–36.

Jackson, B., & Hardiman, R. (n.d.). *Social identity development model.* Unpublished manuscript.

Jacobs, J. H. (1992). Identity development in biracial children. In M. P. P. Root (Ed.), *Racially mixed people in America* (pp. 190–206). Newbury Park, CA: Sage.

Kerwin, C., & Ponterotto, J. G. (1995). Biracial identity development: Theory and research. In J. G. Ponterotto, J. M. Casas, L. A. Suzuki, & C. M. Alexander (Eds.), *Handbook of multicultural counseling* (pp. 199–217). Thousand Oaks, CA: Sage.

Kich, G. K. (1992). The developmental process of asserting a biracial, bicultural identity. In M. P. P. Root (Ed.), *Racially mixed people in America* (pp. 304–317). Newbury Park, CA: Sage.

Koch, S. (1995). The human agency of science. In F. Kessel (Ed.), *Psychology, science and human affairs: Essays in honor of William Bevan* (pp. 17–33). Boulder, CO: Westview Press.

LaFromboise, T., Coleman, H. L. K., & Gerton, J. (1993). Psychological impact of biculturalism: Evidence and theory. *Psychological Bulletin, 114,* 395–412.

LoCicero, A., & Trimble, D. (1997). Teaching from a multicultural stance. *Network for Multicultural Training in Psychology Newsletter, 1*(3). Retrieved

March 25, 2002, from http://nmtp.org/newsletters/mntplettervol1-3.htm.

Martinez, L. J., & George, W. H. (2001). *White racial identity attitudes, emotion and multicultural competency.* Paper presented at the meeting of the American Psychological Association, San Francisco, CA.

Mead, G. H. (1934). *Mind, self and society.* Chicago: University of Chicago Press. Ponterotto, J. G., & Pedersen, P. B. (1993). *Preventing prejudice.* Newbury Park, CA: Sage.

Poston, W. S. (1990). The biracial identity development model: A needed addition. *Journal of Counseling and Development, 69,* 152–155.

Robinson, T., & Howard-Hamilton, M. (2000). *The convergence of race, ethnicity and gender.* Columbus, OH: Prentice Hall.

Root, M. P. P. (1992). Within, between, and beyond race. In M. P. P. Root (Ed.), *Racially mixed people in America.* Newbury Park, CA: Sage.

Ruiz, A. S. (1990). Ethnic identity: Crisis and resolution. *Journal of Multicultural Counseling and Development, 18,* 29–40.

Stonequist, E. V. (1937). *The marginal man: A study in personality and culture conflict.* New York: Russell & Russell.

Sue, D. W., & Sue, D. (1999). *Counseling the culturally different: Theory and practice.* (3rd ed.). New York: John Wiley & Sons.

Wright, L. (1994, July 25). One drop of blood. *The New Yorker,* 46–55.

Chapter Nine
Three Professors Dialogue About Teaching and Learning About Cultural Diversity and Societal Oppression

Darlene Grant and Dorothy Van Soest

This chapter is devoted to the description of some challenges encountered in teaching a required, master's-level foundation year course on cultural diversity, power, and oppression.[1] Candid dialogue among three tenured professors is used to provide a practical understanding and awareness of the impact of the course on student and instructor alike. This dialogue is important because in the social work profession, an understanding and sensitive negotiation of diversity in relation to socioeconomic class, gender, race and ethnicity, physical and mental ability, sexual orientation, and religion have become a characteristic *sine qua non* of effective service delivery.

The purpose of this chapter is to present a unique view, not on how diversity should or could be taught, but rather the impact of the teaching and learning process on its participants—both instructors and students—and the implications of this impact on the profession as well as the academy. Given this purpose, the chapter is meant to serve as a guide by providing information to help professors meet the challenges of communicating and processing diversity material among themselves as well as communicating and processing effectively with students. The chapter begins with a description of how three professors set the context for their dialogue and the corresponding reflections. The chapter ends with a summary of some of the lessons learned from the taped dialogue, along with recommendations.

CONTEXT AND EVOLUTION OF THE DIALOGUE

A basic premise of the cultural diversity course as we teach it is that by encouraging social work students to unearth and examine the influence of

---

[1] The authors appreciate the contributions of Dr. Rosalie Ambrosino, who participated in the dialogue sessions with us.

power, privilege, and oppression in their own lives, including areas of comfort and discomfort, they will be more effective in assessing and understanding how the same influences work similarly and differently in the lives of others. This approach involves encouraging students to explore their own experiences, perceptions, attitudes, beliefs, values, and perspectives about difference, power, privilege, oppression, and social justice. Our teaching and practice are guided by the National Association of Social Workers' *Standards for Cultural Competence in Social Work Practice* (2001). The standard related to self-awareness, in particular, supports our efforts to encourage professors and students alike to "seek to develop a personal understanding of their own cultural values and beliefs as one way of appreciating the importance of multicultural identities in the lives of people" (NASW, 2001, p. 2).

Over the span of six years, we have used increasingly demanding teaching techniques that invited master's-level social work students to confront their own personal experiences related to difference and privilege. We have done so in the context of teaching a course on cultural diversity and societal oppression that is required for all first-year MSW students. Four sections of the course have been taught simultaneously and collaboratively. Because several of the professors were concerned and often disheartened by students' responses to the learning experiences provided in the course, a habit of having lunch together right after class for the purpose of debriefing and support evolved. As each professor brought her concerns, successes, and disappointments to the table each week, a system of learning expanded to allow the dialogue to become the vehicle through which course assignments and expectations were consistently fine-tuned and revised.

At the end of a particularly brutal 15-week semester in the course and after several iterations of the lunch support process, the idea to tape-record and transcribe the dialogue was agreed upon. As three of us talked, four specific themes or issues arose including (a) course methodology, (b) management of tensions in the classroom, (c) creating a safe environment (i.e., responding sensitively and empathically to all students), and (d) managing the impact of the repetitive pressure and intensity of the course on the professors.

PROFESSOR DIALOGUE BY THEME

While the focus in this chapter is on dialogue among professors teaching a particular required cultural diversity course in a CSWE-accredited master's degree program, an attempt is made to address content that might be relevant across programs, disciplines, and approaches to teaching diversity content. Below are excerpts of the taped dialogue, each of which addresses different aspects of the four general themes in turn. Each short excerpt is followed by proscriptions and prescriptions for teaching cultural diversity and/or our responses to the challenges professors encounter in the classroom.

Course Methodology

The course is built around a framework with a dual focus on valuing diversity and understanding power and oppression. Using small group discussion sections, we attempt to create an environment for relationship building between professor and students and among peers with the goal of increased comfort and freedom to discuss historically difficult issues. Small groups also provide greater opportunity for members to "practice" newfound skills related to verbalizing and reflecting on misinformation, stereotypes, and prejudices that they might hold and that they are interested in modifying given new information gained from the course and new experiences. Through the use of a variety of assignments and course experiences (such as self-interview techniques, an ethnic roots assignment, panel presentations, journaling, novels, and immersion assignments) students are asked to examine and subsequently transcend biases that may be internalized due to normative family, community, cultural, educational, and socialization processes and media exposure.

Each of the following dialogue excerpts addresses a concern or issue related to one of the course assignments. After each dialogue excerpt, we discuss the assignment under discussion.

G: My concern is that we find a way to fairly assess and use our assessment to intervene/teach when students are so rigid in their beliefs that their assessments and practice with those who are different from them tend to be culturally insensitive.

V: Sure. But while it's easy for us to detect rigidity, it may be more effective for students to assess themselves over time. Student self-assessment in combination with instructor feedback regarding flexibility and openness to learning and accepting the culture and worldview of others may be the most effective approach we can use given our framework for this course.

The above excerpt was related to assessment of student openness to learning about difference. An opportunity is provided for students to do a self-assessment through a taping assignment. At the beginning of the semester, students are asked to conduct an interview-style initial self-assessment of their own ideas and attitudes about diversity and oppression. An interview guide is provided. They are asked not to prepare in any way for this self-assessment. They are asked to record their responses on a cassette tape. At the end of the semester, students are asked to listen to the tape and to reflect on their responses to the initial assessment. The purpose of the assignment is self-reflection and processing, not extensive discussion of the readings.

As professors we also have opportunities to assess students' openness to learning by observing class interactions and reading their journals and other papers. An important teaching goal is to help students open themselves to learning opportunities in relation to clients who are different from them, to grow in their "plasticity," and to become more "malleable" in terms of issues related to cultural diversity, power, and oppression (Ridley, et al., 1994). As three professors who have taught this course over time, we borrow from physics in our definition of plasticity. That is, it is our contention that the social work practitioner who demonstrates cultural competence through plasticity is someone whose view of the "other," power, and oppression undergoes continuous deformation and reformation, given the introduction of new information and experiences with the other and as an advocate of the other, without the basic belief in the other's humanity, dignity, and worth rupturing or relaxing.

Openness to continuous learning, through critical reflection and thinking processes, is essential. Professors need to continuously find ways to assess students' openness and to create ample opportunities for students to engage in meaningful self-assessment. One of our ongoing challenges is related to how to create a balance between providing students with feedback of our assessments and respecting their own processes of self-assessment and discovery. The challenge is particularly great with students who demonstrate rigidity and lack of openness to learning. In some cases we have found it necessary to intervene by exploring with the student his or her fit for the profession.

G: I had an Asian student in my class who at a young age had been adopted by an Anglo American family and brought to the U.S. It was not until the end of the semester that she shared how transforming this class was, as she had never thought of herself as Asian American. For all intents and purposes she considered herself to be White. When I asked what transformed her into seeking information about her cultural identity, she talked about the impact of hearing African American and Mexican American students tell stories about the impact of their own cultural heritage on how they viewed the world and themselves and how empty and sad she felt in response to their sharing. She admitted to being unable to share how much she appreciated their taking the risk of sharing such personal information in class because she was so jealous and at one point almost immobilized by sadness and grief over not knowing much about her own heritage. Not only did the African American and Mexican American students support her in her desire to find out more about herself, several White students joined in too. The class discussion that day evolved around concern that her adopted parents and extended family would see her new-found interest in her identity as an Asian American woman as denial of the family identity they'd worked so hard to cultivate for her over the years.

V: Okay, stop the presses, hold everything. Let's mark this date. G. admits to students actually taking risks in her cultural diversity class and that those risks actually resulted in growth and further sharing. See, it can happen. These are the instances that I think we have to recall and cherish when we're on that treadmill of students with limited diversity skills and knowledge coming into the class every fall semester and our subsequent feeling that the world's not getting any better at this diversity thing.

G: I learned the importance of giving students an opportunity to explore their own cultural ethnic roots that semester.

There are two issues related to the above excerpt. One is the importance of faculty recognizing and celebrating the positive results of their efforts. When classroom relations are strained and there are struggles with the course, such successes help put the difficult times in perspective and provide hope and motivation to continue.

The second issue is related to an assignment that we use in the course. In further keeping with the NASW standard related to self-awareness, students are asked to personally explore their own cultural values and beliefs through writing an ethnic roots paper. This is an opportunity for them to carefully trace their ancestral roots and the assimilation experiences of parents, grandparents, and/or other significant influential relatives in their lives. The purpose of this assignment is to assist students in gaining insight about how they've come to the worldviews they hold in relation to multicultural identities in the lives of colleagues, coworkers, and clients they will interact with as social workers. For many students, the assignment provides an opportunity to learn, for the first time, about their roots and it is often a profound experience. For some adopted students such as the one discussed above, the assignment provides an opportunity to explore what it means to them to know or not know about their roots, to integrate that with their life experience in their adoptive family, and to take action to learn more about their racial/ethnic identity.

> A: I had an African American middle class female student in my class and I also had two other African American students in that class.
>
> G: No kidding! We must have done a good job in recruitment that year. I hope we keep it up.
>
> A: Ha. Well, this particular student talked a lot at the beginning of the semester about how she hadn't had a lot of experience with African Americans and had been raised in a predominately White familial, educational, and social environment. What was interesting was that she always spoke on behalf of all African Americans. I mean, every time she spoke she spoke with such authority that I watched as her predominately White classmates nodded their heads in agreement with her and some even wrote down her prescriptions for dealing with African Americans while her African American peers in the class looked on in what seemed like shock.
>
> G: It seems her African American peers didn't want to address their differences of opinion and experience with her in the broader class context, as that might have also been terribly misconstrued as intragroup conflict by the predominately White class. I bet we've all experienced that dynamic in class! It's tenuous to deal with at best. I've used my responses to journal entries to encourage students to see that

in many ways their experiences are unique to the experiences of others in their same cultural ethnic group and that they must be attentive to both subtle and blatant differences instead of overgeneralizing. I'm sure that we can emphasize the error of overgeneralization of characteristics and prescriptions. Using panel presentations is one approach.

V: Panels are great, and they reduce the pressure on class members and us for feeling like we have to be the spokespersons for our group.

Two interrelated issues are touched on in the above excerpt. One is the paucity of diversity within the social work student body and the pressures that puts on students of color, because White students tend to look to the few students of color for information and modeling. Second, the excerpt highlights the danger of reinforcing rather than eliminating stereotypes, which is more likely to occur when students have little interaction with individuals from racial and ethnic backgrounds different from their own. The sarcastic tone that is evident in our dialogue represents frustration with the lack of diversity within our classrooms. This lack can stir up uncomfortable emotions related to not practicing what we preach. While promoting diversity and social justice in the course, we are faced with the reality that our school is not being successful in doing so in practice. While the following approaches are ways we try to address the issues inherent in this reality, we recognize the importance of our responsibility to be part of active recruitment efforts to increase diversity of the student body. However, because our current student body is predominantly White, we address the related challenges in three ways.

First, panels of speakers invited from outside the classroom provide a source of experiential expertise and an example of intragroup diversity, as well as a break from lecturing and a break from circular discussion among class members who have nothing but cognitive/intellectual information about certain diverse groups. When most students in the class are Euro-American and middle class, as in our experience, panel presentations also serve to relieve the pressure on the one or two African American, Mexican American, or Asian American students to serve as the spokespersons for their race/culture (Walker, 1993).

Second, we incorporate two free writing opportunities into the course to provide students an opportunity to reflect on the readings, topics, and issues brought up in class discussions, videos, and speaker panels. The assignments are consistent with our emphasis on self-analysis and awareness. The first assignment is an interactive online forum that, by using pseudonyms, offers an opportunity for anonymous dialogue among students, teaching assistants, and the professor and allows class participants to read each other's thoughts (see Chapter Thirteen for more information about this approach). In addition, an interactive online journal that also uses pseudonyms is a confidential dialogue between the individual student and professor that allows the professor to cultivate and capitalize on teachable moments as much as possible. These writings are not graded. And while students are not expected to follow APA Style or to follow rules of grammar, courtesy and sensitivity are expected in the online forum.

Third, we use novels as a way to counteract the lack of diversity in class and to increase understanding of diversity within populations. The use of novels (i.e., fiction and/or autobiographical material) in teaching about diversity has been discussed in the literature. In her discussion of teaching about race, gender, and class diversity, Walker (1993) suggests that diversity "material may be more easily understood by students than academic treatises. Novels and short stories are powerful tools with the ability to place individuals and families in carefully drawn social context. They may reflect sympathetic portrayals that can lead to increased understanding and acceptance of difference. And they can minimize tension by temporarily shifting the focus onto fictional characters rather than real persons" (p. 346).

> G: As professors we represent several diverse cultures and I believe students are hungry to understand our cultures through knowing more and more about us.
>
> V: The down side of it is that they can discount things about our different cultures by saying things like "that's her stuff," or they can overgeneralize what might be unique to our individual experiences as something that is more universal.
>
> A: I don't think we can totally avoid that. All we can do is keep emphasizing the importance of seeing people as unique while also considering the broader context of their experience.

The above dialogue addresses two issues. The first issue is related to the social identity of the professor and how it can be both a source of curiosity and a source of information that can be used by students in diverse ways. If the professor's experiences do not support students' deeply held stereotypes, they may discount the information as unique or atypical and thus can hold onto their beliefs. Conversely, students may "swallow whole" the professor's experiences and generalize them to everyone else with the same social identity. From our experience, both student responses seem to be more prevalent when the professor's social identity is related to ethnicity/race or sexual orientation.

The second issue is also related to social identity of the professor. It has to do with how to help students understand that, although there are strategies used on a societal level to oppress particular groups of people, lives are lived and people develop as unique individuals who may find community with others of the same cultural/social identity and yet be quite different from others in that group. We use an immersion assignment to help facilitate this learning. The purpose of the immersion assignment is to provide students the opportunity to interact with a member or members of a group about which they have discomfort and a fundamental lack of knowledge. Students are asked to (a) write a brief paper about the group they have chosen and to candidly discuss preconceptions and beliefs they hold about that group, (b) write an in-depth research paper on the history and current-day consequences of oppression for the group they have selected and the privilege other groups enjoy in relation to that group's oppression, (c) shadow a person from that population for five different events including religious, family, work, celebration, and recreation, and (d) write a paper reflecting on the shadowing experience and implications for social work practice.

The dialogue about course methodology changes direction in the following excerpt by addressing broader curriculum issues rather than focusing on assignments.

A: We all agree that it's safer to approach diversity from an infusion perspective, because you're integrating the diversity, but you're not doing it every single week, so the emotional impact is not as intense.

G: And we agree that while detailed and accurate information about different cultures is important because many students and faculty come to this course without accurate information, the anthropological approach is similarly "safe."

V: I'm interested in whether our more immersion-driven approach to teaching this course is spilling over into other classes, thus influencing the kinds of questions students are asking, say, in research methods and policy classes. That has implications related to influencing our colleagues to pay more attention to diversity in their classes.

G: I think this is certainly something to keep an eye on. We may even need to bring it up as a point of discussion in faculty meetings or our annual faculty retreat. Our choice to teach cultural diversity using an experiential, self-awareness framework has broader implications for the entire faculty. While we've decided as a faculty to have a discrete course, we must also talk about the impact of this discrete course on us all, as it may be seen as a way to concentrate the issues in one place while in reality it's heightening the focus across the entire curriculum.

V: Or it should be. We need to know if students are actually asking better or rather more culturally grounded/sensitive questions in their other classes before we can assume the rest.

In the above excerpt, we touch on three important issues that point to the need and opportunity for broader dialogue among faculty from our entire program: (a) infusion of diversity content throughout the curriculum versus a required discrete diversity course, (b) an approach to diversity that focuses on culture versus an approach that focuses on diversity education for social justice (see Chapter One), and (c) the impact of an intensive, discrete diversity course on student behavior in other courses. We agree in our dialogue that a discrete, intensive course with a focus on power and oppression related to diversity presents more challenges for professors and students alike (i.e., is less safe) than courses that infuse diversity issues and/or focus on understanding and appreciating culture without linking culture to power and oppression. Yet without research evidence, the jury is still out as to which approach—infusion versus discrete course—is more effective in terms of student learning.

As professors who teach an intense diversity for social justice course, our hope that there will be a positive overflow effect in other courses is clear from the above dialogue. As students develop their critical thinking skills, it is our hope that a positive influence of the course will be that they will continue to ask critical questions about diversity in other courses as well as other aspects of their lives. On the other hand, the overflow effect from an intense diversity course may be negative. For example, students who leave a diversity course with a high level of distress or who "shut down" (or who never opened up) to the learning process may be aversive to hearing anything else about diversity in other courses. Even students who leave a discrete diversity course with increased knowledge and understanding may feel that they have now learned what is needed and resent having the issues raised again in other courses. When either our hopes or our fears about overflow effects are realized, there are implications related to the readiness of faculty in those other courses to address the corresponding challenges. The point is that diversity education for social justice involves all aspects of the curriculum. As noted in the above dialogue excerpt, discussion among all faculty about managing diversity curriculum in the program is needed.

Creating a Safe Environment

The second theme that emerged from our taped dialogue was related to class environment. Our overall goal in the diversity course is to create an environment where tensions are acknowledged and where students can remain open to learning even as their core belief and value systems are constantly challenged and brought to their attention and often revealed to their peers. Beyond learning from texts, journal articles, panel presenters, and the professors who also model the process of wrestling with the issues raised in class, students are encouraged to think critically about how they have arrived at their beliefs and values and their subsequent philosophies of social justice (i.e., who is deserving and who is not in a society of diverse lifestyles, behaviors, and beliefs). A part of this goal is for students to be able to track how their understanding of diversity and social justice issues change during the semester and subsequently their sense of agency in a profession dedicated to an appreciation of cultural diversity, rather than efforts to facilitate assimilation and conformity to a socially acceptable prescribed norm. The following excerpt is related to safety, risk-taking, and pain in the classroom.

> G: After six years of hearing students complain that they don't feel safe enough to share in the class I find myself chiding them with the questions, "How much safety is enough safety? How long do we permit ourselves the luxury of avoiding the issues in a 15-week semester before sharing of the tough stuff occurs?" I've finally started telling students that "This is a hard topic and by definition most of us will never feel fully safe. So, the choice as I see it is to share a little, learn to deal with the response of peers and professors, seek support for the

effort and taking the risk to share, applaud yourself for the effort, and then share some more."

V. But I see their use of sharing as a camouflage for the pain they're really experiencing in struggling with these issues. Some of it is pain of realization that they've bought into a value system and beliefs that actually hurt other people. This is hard when they come into social work, in general, thinking they're good people who would never purposefully hurt anyone. I think it's important for us to let them know that we don't create their pain in this course. That pain is already there and it is tapped just by virtue of attempting to be a conscious member of this society. And they have a choice to be conscious or not in relation to issues of diversity, power, and oppression. But we must constantly reassure them of the value of being conscious, and that it is not always painful.

G: Okay. I agree with you on the underlying pain. I've got to continuously remind myself of this issue too. It reminds me that being in the academic classroom setting, where a grade will eventually be assigned for students' performance in the course, serves as a significant barrier to feelings of trust and safety to share disparate views and opinions, or to air one's prejudices and stereotypes held about the "other." So, if a student is focused on her/his grade, she/he will never get to feel the pain you talk about.

The above excerpt addresses the presence of pain and fear in the classroom. While such feelings cause discomfort for both professors and students, they are natural reactions to the kind of transformative learning processes we are promoting. The kind of critical learning that we are asking students to engage in is hard work that involves risk. The creation of a safe classroom environment in which to do this work is essential. Yet, it is important to communicate to students that topics of diversity related to power and oppression are not safe topics and they will cause distress. In discussing issues of privilege and power with students, it can be pointed out that one of the privileges of members of a dominant group (e.g., White, heterosexual) is to feel that they cannot talk about such topics until they feel safe to do so. In the above excerpt it is noted that students should be encouraged to take risks in spite of not feeling safe. With students who are members of the dominant group, this is a way of encouraging them to give up their privilege of feeling entitled to safety or staying in a comfort zone.

The above excerpt ended with mention of the issue of grades and students "playing it safe" in order to get a good grade. We are continuously challenged to find ways of rewarding students for engaging in the difficult work in order to counteract a tendency for them to feel that their academic achievement will be compromised if they are honest in the learning process.

Managing Tensions in the Classroom

The third theme extracted from our dialogue related to managing the inevitable tensions in the classroom. Discussion of societal oppression elicits a variety of responses from students who, whether they are conscious of it or not, are members of the dominant groups that have historically had a role in oppression (racism, sexism, heterosexism). The reactions can range from defensiveness and anger to guilt and shame. The following excerpt addresses the issue of how to manage the resulting classroom strain and conflict.

V: Related to managing tensions in the class, I frequently struggle with how to be open to students' process and yet remain true to my position on the issues without preaching and giving the impression that there's an agenda that students have to buy into. Yet if I don't let them know where I stand on the issues, then I risk them not trusting me and lowering the level of safety they feel in sharing their stances.

G: Yeah. I frequently have a sense that a lot of students feel compelled to "go underground" with their beliefs. The big underground issues include political party affiliation, religious orientation, and feelings about homosexuality. The questions for me are (1) how to help students manage tensions among themselves (i.e., conflict resolution), and (2) how to help students see the parallel process between learning how to manage conflict around diversity, power, and oppression issues in the classroom and subsequently doing the same in the treatment team, agency, and client–therapist relationship.

A: That parallel process idea is really important. If students hold onto the perception that if they say what they really think they will be judged by their peers and punished by their professors, they'll take that same perception into the social work practice world and essentially be immobile. You can't advocate for disenfranchised people if you fear being criticized!

Three issues related to classroom tensions are touched on in the above excerpt: professor self-disclosure in the face of conflict, what tensions students experience, and the concept of parallel process. In relation to the first issue, professor self-disclosure, an ongoing struggle is how to find a balance between facilitating a process of student self-discovery and sharing one's own position on the issue under dispute or causing distress. With the professor in a position of power and authority in the classroom, his or her self-disclosures carry considerable weight. There are diverse ways of handling the issue of authority that we have tried over the years. One way is to let the students know in the beginning of the course what your position/beliefs are and emphasizing that you are doing so in a spirit of openness that includes openness to their holding different positions and beliefs. This approach aims to alleviate students' possible concerns about what to expect from the professor and it puts considerable pressure on professors to be hyper-vigilant in their openness to opinions that are different from their own. Another approach is for professors not to inform the students of any of their positions or beliefs during the course. This approach aims to allow for complete student freedom of discussion without fear of offending the professor. Yet another approach is for the professor to self-disclose on a situation-by-situation basis. This approach aims to determine what response would be most likely to enhance student learning in each particular case.

The second issue that emerged in the above dialogue excerpt is related to what causes students to experience classroom tension. From our experience of teaching a discrete cultural diversity course, three tension themes seem to emerge over time: (a) tension related to a fear of being perceived negatively, (b) tension related to class composition, and (c) tension related to difficulty with difference. Given these themes, tension in the classroom may manifest in myriad ways. For example, during one semester students became polarized on the Monica Lewinsky–Bill Clinton sex scandal. Regardless of the topic of the week and instructor efforts to keep the class focused, in-class discussions and anonymous online forum entries for the majority of that semester quickly moved back to the same topic. The class seemed unable to sit comfortably with their differences of opinion and were thus unable to move on in their learning. Another way that tensions may manifest themselves is through students who make unpleasant, disparaging, or intimidating responses outside of the classroom that carry over and muffle the interactional dynamics in the class. This dynamic usually occurs outside the range of the professor's immediate radar, thus direct instructor-level intervention is often difficult.

Whatever conflictual feelings or behaviors are manifesting themselves, one approach is to openly discuss them and address how they limit our ability to address issues of diversity. Feelings of guilt, shame, anger, or defensiveness, as well as conflicts between students, tend to shift the focus of learning away from diversity, power, and oppression and toward the subjective experience of the dominant culture. By focusing on and allowing personal feelings and behavior to block learning in this way, we personalize and psychologize what is essentially a societal phenomenon. It is important to acknowledge that the feelings of distress that students may have are natural and a part of a grieving process that they may be going through when there is a discrepancy between the way they thought things were and the way they are learning they really might be. However, it is also important to let students know that learning cannot progress if they become stuck in a feeling or reaction or interpersonal conflict. We need to encourage students to move beyond the tensions, both intrapersonal and interpersonal, to seek knowledge of diversity for its own importance rather than to prove a point, protect one's self-esteem, or alleviate an uncomfortable feeling.

In the last part of the above dialogue excerpt, a third issue is brought into the discussion: the concept of the parallel process. It is important that professors communicate with students that by successfully navigating and resolving the tensions in the classroom, they are also preparing themselves to live and act more fully in the world. As professors, it is important that we not protect students from the classroom tensions but rather that we find ways to use the tensions to promote the knowledge and skill that will be required in social work practice.

In the following excerpt, we discuss the panel presentations both as a source of valuable learning and of classroom tension and conflict. Perhaps because panels are powerful in terms of personalizing the experience of oppression, they are also powerful in eliciting strong student reactions.

G: I have one thing to say about panels. We're damned if we do and we're damned if we don't.

A: I agree. Remember when we had the disability panel? It was totally embarrassing for us as a school to realize that the auditorium in our building wasn't wheelchair accessible. The students really laid into us for that. Remember how I tried to get the students to move away from blaming the school to figuring out ways they could use their voices to advocate to the proper authorities to make the building and subsequently the entire campus fully wheelchair accessible? So, that's my comment. Panels leave us open to criticism from students with new-found fervor related to power and oppression and we have to be able to help them find their role in taking action instead of colluding with them in blaming others for the way things are.

V: Isn't that the goal of this school of social work in general, to graduate students who can effectively take action against oppression and on behalf of disenfranchised and oppressed people?

G: Remember the women's panel we had this semester? The panel included young dynamic professors from psychology and theater and they talked about the history of how women have been assessed, diagnosed, and treated clinically and in the media, and subsequently how women have fought for the right to define what's healthy and what's not healthy from a women's point of view, not men's. Wow!

V: We got at a lot of issues as a result of that panel. The theme I remember so powerfully was violence and how my students responded to that. One student talked about her sister being raped and we all had tears after she shared that personal experience. And then later in the semester, in their final papers and in the student evaluations I encountered the criticism that we didn't spend enough time focused on women. I got angry. We made it a point to make sure that we infused gender and class across each of the panels (disability, gay/lesbian/transgendered, religion, and people of color) but suddenly they didn't see it that way. It's as if they have selective memory or something.

G: What I think that criticism really speaks to is their desire to experience the same heightened emotions, counter transference, and catharsis, if you will, as with all the other groups. They didn't feel it (related to gender) so it must've been the topic that engendered it, so the resulting request is "give us more of that topic." I don't know if this is something we'll ever be able to escape.

A: Remember the African American panel with the clearly middle-class woman who talked about her religious belief that the husband is the "head of the family." What an uproar that caused.

G: Yeah. That's when I intervened to caution students that while they jump to defend someone offending their feminist and empowerment of women sensibilities, they totally overlook the sociopolitical context of the Black family where men have, in many instances, been emasculated by an oppressive society, so religious and familial efforts to empower the man are important to the survival of the family. Or, at least that's my take on it.

V: That's an example of an opportunity to emphasize the need for flexibility and plasticity of thought and analysis. Students often look for information from representatives from different groups to confirm their stereotypes and affirm their prejudices. We can use the framework of this course as a framework for their practice, i.e., how to listen fully, consider the context of the person and her/his cultural ethnic group before jumping to conclusions, and use the literature and colleagues similarly committed to cultural competence to avoid falling into old ways of thinking about difference.

The dialogue excerpt above captures the kinds of reactions that are elicited by the panels. Regardless of what issues are addressed by students in their small discussion groups following a panel presentation, a high level of emotional intensity and a reactive stance appear to be consistently present. As professors who struggle with whether the panel strategy is the best learning experience to offer students, we speculated about possible reasons for this response. Because there is limited diversity among our student body, the introduction of diversity into the classroom by the presence of people who are members of oppressed groups puts real faces on the exploration of diversity. And when the panelists tell their personal stories, the exploratory process becomes more difficult, and even painful. We have observed a variety of strategies used by students in possible attempts to alleviate discomfort. For one, they focus on issues that are peripheral to the real pain and distress they may be experiencing. They look for ways to minimize the complexities (e.g., of multiple identities, contextualizing responses to life experiences, etc.) of difference related to power and privilege. They take a self-righteous, blaming position against others (e.g., the school, "less enlightened" peers, etc.). They criticize the affect of panelists (e.g., too angry, too passive, too intellectual). And they criticize the professors for not addressing all groups adequately.

Whatever intense reaction students experience, as instructors we experience discomfort as well. It is tempting to minimize the feelings by engaging in the peripheral issues or colluding with strategies aimed at alleviating the fear and pain. It is important to resist seeking premature resolution or comfort in such ways. Instead, we advocate engaging in a discussion with the students about the pain itself. It is important to normalize it. In a society that is founded on and maintained by oppressive structures, acknowledging the pain inherent in that system is not only appropriate but encouraging. Feeling and acknowledging that we carry pain about oppressive conditions and what they do to people, is a sign of growth and openness to new perspectives and new knowledge. Just as the panelists share their stories, it is important to provide space for students to tell their stories as well. When listening to each other, students often look for (and find) similarities in their stories. However, it is important to encourage them to look for the differences and to fully hear the lived experiences of their peers. Listening to each other's stories and the stories of the panelists often requires a willingness to walk through the pain and students are to be commended for doing so. By opening themselves to the uniqueness and diversity of the lived experiences of others, they also can begin to understand in a very real sense that in no group are the members all the same.

What Happens to Professors

Social work faculty who teach cultural diversity courses face numerous challenges, as illustrated by the three themes addressed thus far. In addition to incurring the negative affective response of students, colleagues may sometimes be threatened by efforts to engage them in wrestling with this sensitive subject matter. This leads us to the fourth theme from our taped dialogue: how professors experience the challenges.

> G: The most difficult thing about teaching a discrete course on cultural diversity is withstanding the pain, anger, frustration of students that manifests in the form of constant criticism and negative evaluations.
>
> A: Another difficult thing about teaching this course is trying to find validation for the importance of the process in students' lives and in their practice when they're busy criticizing, which makes making legitimate and effective course corrections difficult.
>
> G: It never ceases to amaze me how heightened my senses are to overt as well as covert, direct and indirect discrimination, and racism

and heterosexism, etc. during the semesters I teach this course. Like the other night. My sister called me and said my four-year-old nephew says, "Mommy, I want to be White." She responded, "No you don't, and don't you dare tell your father." And I said, "Well, you know, being White in our society does have a few more perks than being Black, so he's just showing you that he's picked up on that little fact. Why don't you tell him that he's wonderful just the way he is, and maybe that his White friends need to have a nice African American friend to help them see that being Black is important and fun too." My sister laughed and asked if I was teaching cultural diversity this semester. I wondered if that negated everything I'd recommended to her.

V: While we're laughing in agreement about this hypersensitivity we experience, I do sometimes wonder if there's something wrong with me during this process. Why can't I teach this and not have this happen? And what will other people think if I let them know how viscerally and pervasively teaching this course affects me. I can't see a cashier treat a Mexican American customer differently than me without making a big deal out of it and asking to speak to the manager anymore. I can imagine that my family members and other faculty are just saying "Oh, God, there she goes on her little soapbox again."

G: Do you mean to say that after a while we're defined by what we teach to the degree that the substance of what we teach gets discounted?

V: I think this dynamic may not be peculiar to cultural diversity, but it sure doesn't result in a long line of faculty wanting to teach the course, does it?

A: Maybe we should think of rotating out of this course every few years. That way we can spread the wealth and other faculty have the rotten student evaluations related to teaching this course and they can then join us in figuring out how to practice our vision of cultural competence as a school instead of a few professors.

G: Rotating out is not a bad idea. We'd have to do it separately so that the entire dynamics of the course aren't lost every few years. At the same time we get the benefit of fresh points of view that might keep us from imposing our personal perspectives on the course without checks and balances.

V: You know, I want students to see how insidious oppression really is. I want them to move from thinking that they have earned everything that they have and that by virtue of being graduate students in a prestigious research university, they are in a privileged group. I thought most of our students would readily understand this, but I forgot that to have privilege is to fight to keep privilege using tactics including denial, and immobilization due to fear of being criticized as we've discussed earlier. I'm really committed to students getting it and actually would have a hard time rotating off of this team of teachers.

In the above excerpt, we take turns articulating the profound impact teaching the diversity course has on us, both personally and professionally. The challenges of moving social work students who come with a broad range of beliefs, values, knowledge, and skills towards the poor, people with disabilities, people of color, gays and lesbians, and religion are indeed often great. They in fact can contribute to faculty refusal to teach cultural diversity courses, the marginalization of faculty who teach these courses, general student dissatisfaction with the course, and poor student evaluations that may impact tenure and promotion. Although those of us who have been teaching the required diversity course over the years actually receive high course evaluations from students, we are often left feeling that teaching the course still took its "pound of flesh" in other ways.

On the positive side, the challenges of moving social work students toward cultural competence through such dedicated courses provides an opportunity for us to engage in important social justice work through teaching. We also learn a tremendous amount ourselves around issues that require a commitment to lifelong learning and action. The diversity course also offers the entire faculty in the school an opportunity to dialogue and expand its understanding of diversity and oppression. Engaging in the challenging teaching and learning process represents an opportunity as well to have schools of social work reflect a needed depth of understanding in their curriculum, policies, and services.

In the following and final excerpt, we extend our conversation about what happens to us as professors to a consideration of cross-cultural and intercultural communication. As the dialogue shows, we each bring our own culturally laden ways of decoding and interpreting student actions, reactions, and interactions with the material and with each other. We agree that part of our role as instructors is that of interpreters for the purpose of providing rich learning opportunities. Embedded in this discussion is a concern that we need to understand the means by which we instill in our students, through this course, the broader mission of social work.

G: Have you ever considered that a part of what we do is manage the communication and interaction between people from up to four or more different cultures and how ludicrous that "management" process becomes?

V: What do you mean by "ludicrous"?

A: I think it means how impossible it is even on our best days to track everybody and all the stimulus we're getting thrown at us.

G: Yeah, the subtle and not so subtle stuff. Like the student who would stare at me the entire class session. She'd even move her chair if her view were obstructed.

V: Oh, I remember. I thought she was busy attempting to catch you being incongruent with the philosophy of diversity that you were espousing in class so that she could say, "I knew it, I knew she was just like every other African American I've run into."

A: So, when you were busy decoding and interpreting her behavior and figuring out how to respond so that she had a growth opportunity in class, you also had up to 30 other students presenting their own stimuli into the environment for our analysis and response too. How do we do it semester in and semester out?

G: Part of the how goes back to the importance of these weekly debriefings with each other. This constant assault on the senses is heavy with emotions and values, especially since these same students will evaluate us at the end of the semester—scores that the university takes seriously. Another part of the how is related to "selective attention" and what we attribute to ourselves versus what we attribute to the students.

V: Are you suggesting that during cross-cultural interactions, like the ones we have every week, we interpret students' behaviors as fitting the value system we're prescribing or going against it and thus possibly going against us?

G: Hhhhhuuummmm. I certainly think that's worth thinking about. And I think our students and colleagues are thinking about this to a degree also. Consider the student who shared that she thought we wanted everybody in class to have an epiphany and cry at some point during the semester. We've never said that! Nor do we limit our affirmations to students who cry or have "ah ha" experiences. We applaud wrestling with the material in whatever shape it happens to come in.

A: But we also come to these debriefings, on occasion, upset with the negative emotions from our interaction with students and it really does upset our assessments of ourselves. I know I've taken this course home many nights and weekends, struggling with what I could have or should have said to help shed light on a particularly difficult topic.

V: And sometimes we don't. We just chalk the negativity of the interaction up to our expectations of students who are appropriately struggling with some difficult material and depend on their need to struggle for their own growth and development of new ways of thinking and being in this complex world. This doesn't free us from constant self analysis, but it sure helps us be more compassionate with ourselves during this grueling process.

G: We certainly should talk more about the complexity of cross-cultural and intercultural communication in class to better contextualize for the students and ourselves the environment we create with this class. And like V. suggests, it might actually reduce judgmental attitudes and negative emotional reactions, and possibly increase willingness to work for understanding and effective communication.

In the above excerpt, we explore the potential benefits and pitfalls of viewing teaching cultural diversity from a cross-cultural or intercultural perspective. One issue is related to what is often referred to in clinical circles as "trusting the process." To manage the constant bombardment of stimuli, instructors naturally use selective attention. They trust that what, in gestalt terms, comes to the forefront and needs immediate attention will serve the individual and group learning needs for the moment and will translate to other situations and contexts as needed. We strongly feel that instructors must commit, however, to exploring how their culture and values interact with the stimuli being presented by students. We need to ask ourselves tough questions, such as: What assumptions am I making about this Mexican American student who just shared a painful experience with a person from my own racial background? Why is it that I have such a negative reaction to whatever this particular student says? Why is it that I caretake this student instead of giving the group room to confront her judgmental stance?

Another issue implied in the last excerpt is a stance that we consider an imperative for those teaching diversity courses. We need to build in collegial support for processing classroom dynamics as well as the emotional material in the course. We need to agree to create a nonjudgmental yet honest environment in which to provide support for each other. The final issue that emerges from the above dialogue is that we need to work to avoid making negative judgments or assessments of individuals or the entire class based on what we perceive to be negative content in their interactions with each other, their assessment of the class, or their assessment of us. It is the very act of wrestling with this material that brings out negativity. And we have thankfully learned that it is this same wrestling that brings out a commitment to personal and professional learning, growth, and advocacy for disenfranchised and oppressed people.

SUMMARY AND IMPLICATIONS

We believe that students who examine their own ethnic cultural lives in relation to diversity, power, privilege, and oppression, including areas of comfort and discomfort, will be more effective when assessing and understanding how those influences work similarly and differently in the lives of their coworkers and clients. Further, we believe that students should demonstrate an ability to be open to learning opportunities in relation to clients who are different from them, to grow in their plasticity and to become more malleable in terms of issues related to cultural diversity, power, and oppression. While many students come into social work demonstrating plasticity and openness to learning, for others these skills are new and must be learned. Discrete courses may be the most important factor contributing to practice competence that these students and subsequently their clients have.

This learning process for students presents new and demanding challenges. The learning is both affective and intellectual and class discussion can be intense and conflictual. The challenges for professors are demanding as well. We have learned the importance of support and consultation with each other in order to face the challenges and develop teaching skills that help students engage in reflection and discussion related to tension-ridden issues. In this chapter, we have shared some of the dialogue and a little of what we have learned from teaching a required diversity for social justice course. We end with a summary of a few of the lessons learned, along with some recommendations in four interrelated areas: facing the challenges for professors, helping students navigate the challenges, classroom tensions, and challenges for social work programs.

Facing the Challenges for Professors

1. A discrete, intensive course, with a focus on power and privilege related to diversity, presents more challenges for professors and students alike (i.e., is less safe) than courses that infuse diversity issues and/or focus on understanding and appreciating culture without linking culture to power and oppression.

2. Professors need to continuously find ways to assess students' openness to learning that is critical, and to create ample opportunities for students to engage in meaningful self-assessment.

3. Professors need to provide support and consultation for each other on a regular basis in order to face and learn from the challenges of teaching cultural diversity.

4. It is important for faculty to recognize and celebrate the positive results of their efforts.

5. The challenges of moving social work students toward cultural competence provides professors an opportunity to engage in important social justice work through teaching and to enhance their own learning.

Helping Students Navigate the Challenges

1. We need to inform students that the kind of critical learning that we are asking students to engage in is hard work and inevitably involves risk.

2. We need to find ways of rewarding students for engaging in the difficult work in order to counteract a tendency for them to feel that their academic achievement will be compromised if they are honest in the learning process.

3. While the creation of a safe classroom environment in which to do the work is essential, it is important to communicate to students that topics of diversity related to power and oppression are not safe topics and that they will cause distress.

4. It is important to find a balance between facilitating a process of student self-discovery and the professor sharing his or her own position on issues under dispute or causing distress.

Managing Classroom Tensions

1. Whatever conflictual feelings or behaviors are manifesting themselves, it is important to openly discuss them and address how they limit our ability to address issues of diversity. Feelings of guilt, shame, anger, and defensiveness as well as conflicts between students tend to shift the focus of learning away from diversity, power, and oppression and toward the subjective experience of the dominant culture.

2. It is important to acknowledge that the feelings of distress that students may have are natural while at the same time letting them know that learning cannot progress if they become stuck in a feeling or reaction or interpersonal conflict.

3. When there is pain and fear in the classroom, it is important to engage in a discussion with the students about the pain itself. Encourage them to see that feeling and acknowledging the pain we carry about oppressive conditions indicates an openness to new perspectives and new knowledge and is a sign of growth.

4. We need to encourage students to move beyond the intrapersonal and interpersonal tensions to seek knowledge of diversity for its own importance rather than to prove a point, protect one's self-esteem, or alleviate an uncomfortable feeling.

5. It is important that professors communicate with students that, by successfully navigating and resolving the tensions in the classroom, they are also preparing themselves to live and act more fully in the world.

Challenges for Social Work Programs

1. Faculties have a responsibility to be part of active recruitment efforts to increase diversity of the student body.

2. Diversity education for social justice involves all aspects of the curriculum and discussion among all faculty about managing diversity curriculum in the program is needed.

REFERENCES

National Association of Social Workers. (2001). *Standards for cultural competence in social work practice.* Washington, DC: Author.

Ridley, C. R., Mendoza, D. W., Kanitz, B. E., Angermeier, L., & Zenk, R. (1994). Cultural sensitivity in multicultural counseling: A perceptual schema model. *Journal of Counseling Psychology, 41*(2), 125–136.

Walker, A. J. (1993). Teaching about race, gender, and class diversity in United States families. *Family Relations, 42,* 342–350.

Part Three
Teaching Methodologies

INTRODUCTION TO PART THREE

Part Three builds on Part One in relation to the context for integrating cultural diversity and social justice content into the curriculum, dynamics related to injustice and oppression and their relationship to topical areas such as race, ethnicity, gender and sexual orientation. Concepts developed in Part Two on the contribution of professors and students to the learning process and their unique change processes are developed further in Part Three. This section is the most pragmatic. It provides content, methods, strategies, and processes for creating and maintaining the safe classroom environment that is essential for the development of open dialogue and learning.

The first three chapters offer specific approaches for faculty in their planning and for dealing in class, at the moment, with classroom interactions. Chapter Ten addresses how the affective nature of the learning process requires the utilization of both didactic and experiential teaching methods. Particular attention is given to structure that can be introduced in the first meeting to facilitate building a safe classroom environment. Course concepts, their implications for faculty disclosure, and contracting with the class are also discussed. Chapter Eleven further focuses on how faculty can transform critical incidents in the classroom into teachable moments. Themes identified in data gathered from 16 faculty using a Faculty Critical Event Survey are presented. Also, a critical incident debriefing protocol is proposed as a means for faculty to reflect on their classroom encounters. Chapter Twelve proposes a process approach for teaching that attends to classroom developmental processes and emphasizes faculty development of relational skills aimed at validating student experience. Proposals for syllabus development, interaction, and safety guidelines are presented. Attention is given to the selection of classroom activities in relation to the purpose they are intended to serve. This is followed by a listing of activities in the context of function, such as foundational interaction, icebreaker, building awareness about power and privilege, and social work practice skill building.

The next three chapters provide further resources for faculty learning and teaching. Chapter Thirteen presents journal writing in pairs as a methodology for developing dialogue for dealing with reflections and actions about white racism at personal, interpersonal, and sociopolitical levels. Data are presented from faculty journaling pairs as well as recommendations for use by other faculty. Chapter Fourteen presents an interactive website used as a teaching methodology and aimed at increasing student safety, providing instructors with ongoing information about students' levels of awareness and knowledge, and identifying areas of confusion in the student learning process. Teaching challenges related to cultural competency and an educational model are also discussed, and recommendations are made regarding use of computer technology in teaching oppression courses. Chapter Fifteen elaborates on the relevance of literary sources, such as autobiography and memoir, as a basis for learning about the meaning of difference, others different from oneself, and about oneself. A format for an assignment as well as references on several populations of color and Euro-Americans are presented.

Finally, Chapter Sixteen identifies and discusses teaching resources related to web-based teaching and provides assignments and handouts relevant to a diversity and social justice framework. Several recommended references, such as sourcebooks for faculty and simulations, are identified.

Chapter Ten

Concepts and Methods in Teaching Oppression Courses[1]

Betty Garcia and Michael Paul Melendez

The opening chapters in this book identify fundamental diversity and social justice course concepts. The development of critical thinking, engagement in classroom dialogue, and viewing learning as a process necessitate thoughtful attention to class structure and instructor modeling. This chapter further elaborates on foundation concepts, their application in the classroom and, in particular, focuses on strategies for faculty managing the strong affect arising in classroom interaction. Issues such as faculty disclosure and contracting with the class are addressed. In addition, experiential exercises are presented in the context of their relevance for building a safe classroom environment.

Courses on oppression and diversity have been developed in social work and psychology programs for over 30 years (Fox, 1983; Melendez, 1994; Nakanishi & Rittner, 1992). This has been in response to the need for increased competencies for working with diverse populations. To understand diversity and the dynamics of oppression, students must examine their own attitudes and values (Garrett & Thornton, 1993) as well as affect and behavior (Fox, 1983). They must confront their experience and understanding of their own ethnicity and culture (Comas-Diaz & Jacobsen, 1991; Pinderhugues, 1989). Optimally, courses should be designed so as to transform knowledge into social action at the professional, personal, and institutional level.

The pedagogical approach most often used to build knowledge and enhance personal awareness integrates didactic and experiential methods (Romney, Tatum, & Jones, 1992). Both methods are needed to engage students in the intellectual and affective processes that are necessary to learn about oppression and diversity. The importance of integrating both aspects will help avoid overdependence on one process at the cost of the other. This imbalance, which often develops in oppression courses, can result in dry intellectual ab-

---

[1] This article originally appeared in the *Journal of Progressive Human Services*, Volume 8(1), 23–40. Reprinted with permission from Haworth Press.

stractions or impassioned vitriolic polemics. One important aspect of skill building for dealing with diversity is engaging the student in developing critical thinking. Cognitive and affective learning is instrumental in enhancing critical thinking skills (Brookfield, 1987). This learning process is effectively approached by facilitating participation as an active learner (Bonwell & Eisen, 1991). A major goal in this learning process is to enhance students' ability to identify assumptions in their thinking and to challenge students' thinking for the purpose of increasing their understanding about the meaning of difference.

We also propose that teaching on diversity must be based on a conceptual framework that addresses the dynamics of oppression. The experience of minority communities within U.S. history has not simply been one of the experience of difference but has involved subordinate treatment (Atkinson, Morten, & Sue, 1989; Pharr, 1988; Rothenberg, 2001).[2] A major purpose of oppression curricula is to build practice competencies for working with diverse populations based on factors such as ethnicity, race, class, sexual orientation, gender, and ability. With our backgrounds as clinical practitioners we bring this perspective to our teaching practice, however, we believe that diversity issues are relevant to all social work practice roles such as group work, community organizing, or policy administration. To meet that aim, course objectives need to address the development of the following:

1. Knowledge regarding how social justice issues (historical, socioeconomic, and political implications) relate to diversity and the development of individual identity.

2. Awareness regarding one's value assumptions resulting from one's own socialization and biases and the consequences of those biases on our interactions with similar and different others.

3. Management of intense, difficult, and painful feelings in oneself and in others.

4. Deepening an understanding of the multiple levels (personal, interpersonal, cultural, and institutional) in which oppression operates and the variety of ways that one can act against oppression and value diversity.

This article presents guidelines for teaching oppression and diversity content by focusing on organizing course concepts, faculty preparation, class con-

---

[2] "Minority" is used to refer to ethnic groups often referred to as racial groups (i.e., African American, American Indian, Asian, and Latino).

tracting, and sample exercises. It represents a synthesis and integration of our teaching an MSW course on racism for approximately eight years in a private northeastern college. During this period, both authors taught classes on racism and social work practice. Although the course was taught individually, we have engaged in formal, ongoing dialogue on the evolution of this course with all faculty engaging in teaching this course. This article is based on a paper copresented at the 1994 Bertha Capen Reynolds Society Meeting. We are particularly indebted to Tatum's (1992) work, having refined and adapted her conceptualizations and methodology for inclusion in social work curricula.

ORGANIZING CONCEPTS

The challenge of oppression/diversity courses is the use of a contextual, multilevel focus in a way that validates personal experience, builds insight, and promotes action taking. It is essential to understand sociopolitical patterns of power and privilege and one's accessibility to structures of socioeconomic opportunities. Course content deals with social power and examines history, politics, and economics so as to understand the marginalization, invisibility, and devaluation of some individuals based on their group membership. Intellectual appreciation for the "structures of opportunity," which are taken for granted by some individuals or seem beyond the reach of others, leads to deepening awareness of the ways in which this power imbalance results in distorted perceptions of self.

The following concepts facilitate intellectual and experiential learning. These concepts are seen as crucial for courses addressing oppression and diversity and have implications for the various roles and interventions of social work. The objective is to assist in the recognition, analysis, and undoing of dominant ideologies and the empowering of the self to choose freely alternative ways of analyzing, understanding, and intervening. These concepts are generalizable and thus helpful for the tasks of examining discrete types of oppression such as racism, heterosexism, sexism, and anti-Semitism. We view social workers' understanding of these core concepts as valuable for practice in all settings, regardless of a direct or macro focus to services.

Social Power

Social power endows individuals with social, cultural, and institutional validation of their social identity. Unlike individual power, which is negotiated situationally, social power legitimizes and fosters an individual's social, psychological, and physical appearance. Our use of the concept of social power is similar to that of Lott and Maluso (1995), who define power as access to resources, free movement, and opportunity. It involves the aesthetics of communicating our uniqueness and the respect bestowed in unfamiliar, formal interactions.

In some circumstances, individuals cannot act on choice simply because choice is not present or conditions impose powerful restraints. Historical examples with which to acquaint students include the genocidal policies directed toward Native peoples, the experience of slavery and Jim Crow laws, the Nazi Holocaust, and the current attempt to legislate against gay men and lesbians. We do not suggest that low social power precludes individuals from having choices, but rather that individual behavior be interpreted from a transactional perspective in which choice is contextualized by access to opportunity and the presence of constraints. Acknowledgment of how social power differentially shapes individual development creates a framework for validating diversity rather than unintentionally denying someone's social identity with the "we're all human beings" perspective.

This notion of social power is crucial for social work practitioners to understand as it permeates every level of interaction with clients and client systems. As Pinderhughes (1989) asserts, practitioners need to come to terms with their own experience with power, and their own need for power, to appreciate the implicit and explicit power differential that exists in all helping relationships. Our own experience of the use and misuse of social power is mediated by such factors as race, ethnicity, gender, class, and sexual orientation. In the helping dyad our experiences interact with those of our clients. An understanding of these dynamics can facilitate an appropriate intervention and help to avoid painful misunderstandings.

Privilege

Closely associated with ideas of social power are the advantages conceptualized as privilege that McIntosh (1989) suggests ultimately confer individuals with the entitlement of not having to deal with issues of diversity. This is premised on the "myth of meritocracy"—that individuals have what they deserve. It denies the presumptions predicated on the experience of being a member of a dominant group such as male, White, or heterosexual. Privilege is not about deliberateness or fairness. Rather it explains the sociological concept of ascription as opposed to achievement (Miller, 1992). What is significant for many is the realization of how the often unacknowledged presence of privilege shapes their sense of self and interactions with others. Again, for practitioners this self-awareness is crucial for the helping relationship. An inability to appreciate the experience of our privilege can impede an analysis of the very real constraints that impact the lives of our clients.

Social Identity/Racial Identity Development

A number of theorists have proposed and refined a stage model theory of identity development. Cross (1971) and Jackson (1975) began with the concept of Black Identity Development. Hardiman (1979) explored White Identity Development and Atkinson, Morten, and Sue (1989) propose an inclusive model called Minority Identity Development theory. This stage theory postulates that individual identity development progresses through stages that begin with unawareness and acceptance of the dominant ideology, and moves through stages of active awareness, active rejection, and eventual culmination in synthesis and integration of preceding tasks. Implicit in all stage theories are notions of uneven development, differential progression, duress and stress, and regression to previously mastered stages.

Access to social power has a powerful effect on one's identification with dominant values regarding difference. Three issues arise in learning about how we have been affected by the uneven distribution of social power and how that shapes the stage of identity development that an individual might find her/himself in:

1. Everyone faces working through how they have first benefited from the presence of social power. The flip side is examining how they have internalized negative stereotypes about self and different others.

2. Each individual faces and examines these concerns when they are ready and at their own pace. This process can be encouraged and facilitated by participation in these types of courses. Many distinct factors in individual's lives, such as anxiety, fear, lack of support, crisis, lack of insight, and lack of conceptual analytical tools, take a formative role in someone's "readiness" to deal with these issues.

3. It is important to frame the experiential learning by relating it to the unique learning involved in the particular stage one is in, as well as how to facilitate and contend with obstacles that impede one's further development.

Dealing with these issues normalizes the struggles encountered in dealing with difficult and painful affect. In this way, a student can hopefully accept his or her own place as well as accept and understand where others are in their dialogue with these issues. An understanding of stage theory can help avoid scenarios of name-calling, self-righteousness, or withdrawal that can occur in these types of courses.

One important aside is that we view this stage theory as taking its place alongside the multiple stage theories that social work students are expected to master, such as Erickson's stages of development, Freud psychosexual stage theory, Mahler's separation-individuation developmental theory, and Hoffman's family developmental theory. This integration needs to be deliberate and intentional in that it addresses the issues of students who think that content that focuses on diversity and/or oppression is not relevant to their goals as practitioners.

Empowerment

Empowerment is a term that remains elusive and ambiguous (Hegar & Hunzeker, 1988). Within social work, it has undergone a number of revisions, articulations, and applications to various populations (Browne, 1995). Pinderhughes (1983) views empowerment as the individual's feeling of increased power and the capacity to influence those forces that influence one's life. It has implications for internal experience as well as an ability to intervene in the environment. While empowerment is seen as a value applicable to our clients, rarely do we consider it for the social work practitioner. In short, it is the ability to choose among alternatives, to act, to intervene, and to change. It involves an appropriate use and sharing, and not the abnegation, of power.

A typical reaction of students in these courses is to feel disillusioned, overwhelmed, and disempowered. The sheer pervasiveness and complexity of the dynamics of oppression invite many students to think that they are powerless to intervene or to change the existing situation. Encouraging students to validate self, expand their range of choices, and to act on concerns that are unjust occurs on many levels and reflects an individuals' needs, motivation, preparedness, and learning styles, both cognitive and affective.

Becoming aware of the role of social power, the presence of privilege, and an appreciation of social and racial identity are all learning tasks that facilitate the development of strategies to promote change and help students experience empowerment. Initially, the connection may need to be made explicit.

In time, however, students begin to appreciate the possibilities of intervening that are congruent with the range of social work practice interventions. It is essential that class members provide social support for one another's growing awareness of the personal consequences of oppression and for action taking.

It is also important to place the students' experience of disillusionment and discouragement within the context of their individual developmental process. Often they are also experiencing similar feelings in their Behavior, Social Policy, and Practice courses. This intellectual crisis needs to be identified as a developmental stage that leads for most to clarity of thinking and understanding. Above all, individuals need patience, perseverance, openness to dialogue, and the acceptance of the process of change for self and others.

Communication of these core concepts can lead to the development of a series of competencies including the development of self-awareness, mastery of analytical and conceptual tools, and formulating and implementing interventions at appropriate levels (i.e., intrapsychically, interpersonally, and within large systems). These competencies can be obtained through a number of components: readings, didactic material, videotapes, journal writing, written assignments, and experiential exercises. The next section will focus on faculty preparedness for implementing these teaching methodologies and is followed by how to contract with the class and the use of experiential exercises. This is one component of a well-integrated syllabus.

FACULTY SELF-DISCLOSURE

The dual emphasis on intellectual and experiential learning places unique demands on faculty regarding managing group dynamics, exercising good timing by being tuned into a variety of passage points during the course of the semester, and time management. This is in addition to the normal demands of competency with content and process. Faculty development and strengthening of group skills are integral in this process. It requires the faculty's ability to tolerate and mediate strong affect, theirs as well as the students. It is helpful to remind ourselves and our students that the learning expected in these types of courses is an ongoing process that occurs over time—during, and hopefully beyond, the course.

Teaching courses on oppression and diversity may involve a measure of self-disclosure by the faculty member that may differ from other courses. Our sense is that faculty modeling self-disclosure is an important element of the presumed collaborative process we are attempting to engender. This self-disclosure can be accomplished in two ways: by providing information about yourself and by clarifying your expectations as a professor.

Giving personal information about oneself is a charged activity for most professors. Determining what information about yourself you are comfortable sharing with the class is important. You may have to set some limits in answering the questions that students may put forth. Significant aspects to share can include aspects of your own social/racial identity, ethnic and racial background, sexual orientation, class background, professional training, and biases. It has been our experience that instructors in these courses often have to establish their legitimacy to teach this content. We have found that no matter what categories the instructor represents—of color or White, male or female, gay or straight—issues arise from students as to your personal experience and values regarding the content. Sometimes this exploration can feel like an attack. For example, a White male dean at a school of social work in the Northeast was asked how he could teach such a course and what did he know about oppression. On one level, this was a reasonable question, on another level it is somewhat undermining and hostile. The dean responded to his students by pointing out that all members of the school took active ownership of oppression issues, that it is everyone's concern and responsibility and not exclusively an issue for those perceived as "victims."

It is apparent that faculty may need to set some limits on the questions that they entertain. In part, questions are requests for information, ways of orienting and familiarizing oneself with something unfamiliar. At other times, they serve to deflect attention from the content, or are meant to avoid painful interchanges. This negotiation of self-disclosure has an added benefit of modeling a set of behavioral skills we wish students to develop: appropriate self disclosure in treatment. Modeling self-disclosure is an opportunity to practice boundary setting that is going to occur in every helping relationship. It is important to be genuine rather than defensive and reactive. Each question posed to the instructor or comment made about an aspect of the instructor represents a teaching moment in the negotiation and acceptance of difference.

You may ask "why even put myself through this?" Our belief in modeling what we expect from students compels us to seriously consider this approach. Remaining cognizant of the power difference and the evaluative aspect between students and ourselves is helpful in keeping perspective on students' experiences and responses. If relevant, you may want to share with the class your ongoing learning and struggles and outlook of evolving development. We feel it is an abuse of power to ask students to do something that we are unwilling to do, namely to struggle in dialogue for understanding, with all the potential for mistakes and misunderstanding that arise in these situations. The power differential and our evaluative role as faculty suggest that we can also participate and maintain clarity about being in charge and responsible for conducting activities. We want to model the ability to manage multiple roles. A caveat for professors is to watch out for presenting ourselves as the "redeemed," that is, that we have arrived at a place in which the dynamics of oppression do not influence us. Let the class know about the ways in which you are thinking, developing, and struggling with oppression issues in your own life.

Another type of faculty disclosure involves being explicit with the class about your expectations as a professor. Clarifying your explicit expectations about how you will conduct the course, class participation, and mechanisms of evaluation can do this. The following are some expectations whose clarification can facilitate creating a "relatively" safe environment.

Be clear about what is being graded. Even in pass/fail arrangements, we cannot deny that students worry about grades. An added dilemma in these courses is that of student awareness that certain positions and thoughts are contrary to the goals and values of social work. It works against the notion of change and process if students feel too intimidated to explore ideas and concepts into which they have been socialized. Emphasize the expectations that students demonstrate: (a) critical thinking, knowledge about conceptual and analytical models in understanding oppression (rather than whether they agree or not with the course concepts), and (b) an ability to produce coherent written material that reflects both an integration of didactic and experiential material, and an understanding of oppression as a multilevel phenomenon (i.e., psychological, sociological, economic, and political).

Have a discussion about the fear that many students hold that they will be graded on being racist, sexist, homophobic, ableist, or conservative. It is true that we have a set of values that we are trying to impart and a set of goals that we are striving to move students toward. This is no different from other required subject matter that students are attempting to master in the areas of policy, research, and human behavior. For example, we do have certain ideas about what constitutes sound ethical practice. In keeping with the ideas of the social/racial identity development theory, we explicitly inform the class of our assumptions that class members are all at varying points in the continuum of developmental stages. Our goal is to increase their awareness, and promote movement in a desired direction. We understand and accept that individuals may express oppressive notions that will become the subject of analysis and discussion. Having an opinion does not exempt an individual from feedback about that opinion. For a student to assert that it is their right to hold a position without having to experience the impact it has on others is an example of privilege. While they may hold certain positions they should be expected to be challenged. A refusal to participate and to master particular conceptual frameworks would not be permitted in other courses, and it should not be here. Acquiescence to this by faculty would invalidate the learning contract, which we will explain below.

Related to the above, clarify your thinking about "political correctness." You may point out that the term originated among progressives as a way to probe each other to analyze situations and that its usage focuses discussions on form (how people present themselves) as opposed to the more substantive concerns of meanings and action taking. We do not find it a contradiction to state our values and the goals we have for student development and attempt to promote a critical analysis of their own position. Again, we do not view this course as different from other courses.

Emphasize that disagreement is expected and welcomed and that the skill that students are mastering in this dialogue is the ability to give and receive critical feedback. Growth involves a certain amount of tension and it is reasonable to expect that this content area will produce a significant amount of it. This cannot become an excuse to avoid the dialogue.

Also, clarify your expectations about class participation. Suggest that at certain times all students may wish to "pass," meaning that they are unwilling to share at a certain point. Individual process needs to be respected, however, it is important to comment on how anxiety impedes individual growth and that they are making decisions about their own learning for which they must take ownership. Most students pass to get a moment to regroup, and to process and internalize difficult experiences and affect. Should a student feel overwhelmed, that person has a right to stop the process, without harassment and with support to complete their point. No one has to reveal more than they are comfortable with. Each student has control and responsibility over what they disclose.

There is a difficult balance between respecting individual development and promoting the professional development we desire. We are proposing that some strained interaction can be avoided, as in the following example: a young and naïve student will share an idea that is clearly perceived as racist and is then assaulted by her/his peers for holding such a notion. The conversation is then moved away from a focus on helping an individual to think through a position. Instead, it is organized by students' discomfort, their own suspect notions, and the wish to externalize it onto another person. We propose that there is value in remaining focused on class dynamics, and acknowledge that there are no right answers to these difficult moments. Ultimately, judgment must rest on what best facilitates learning for the class as a whole.

Our responsibility as faculty to earn student trust can be facilitated by encouraging some caution in the beginning of the semester and stressing that each student is at a different point in the learning process and has a different pace for addressing this sensitive content. Explain the rationale for supporting the right to selectively refuse to participate as a measure to limit our potential abuse of power as faculty. Coercing students to engage in something that they are not ready for can produce resentment, distress, and/or fear both in those who feel pushed and those who witness how these students are managed. We are not suggesting that there be no discussion of students' apprehension in sharing. We are, however, proposing that a student's refusal to participate can become part of the class dialogue. The focus is not on why this particular student is reluctant to engage, but rather students can reflect on what happens in a process when someone withdraws, refuses to dialogue, or in some way is unavailable to negotiate. Again this is a generalizable social work skill that we are modeling for students. In their career, students will often encounter clients who are mandated to services, do not wish to engage in treatment, or are uncertain as to how to make use of help. Learning how to gently make demands for work and developing a range of interventions motivating individuals is a skill that all social work practitioners need to develop.

Finally, a professor can encourage students and model for them the use of "I" statements that encourage accountability, are descriptive, and speak to an individual's experience. This experiential aspect of learning, reflecting on, and discussing an ongoing process requires tremendous amounts of sensitivity and tact on the part of faculty.

CONTRACTING WITH THE CLASS

Much of what has previously been discussed is also related to contracting with the class about the learning that will occur. Creating a class atmosphere that facilitates the mastery of core concepts and the building of competencies requires preparing students (and self) for the dual activity of intellectual and experiential learning. A balance between didactic and affective learning allows for moving from unique individual experience to a more abstract and generalizable knowledge. Because students usually focus on conceptual content, the experience of using course concepts in classroom settings in ways that involve self-disclosure can create a significant amount of anxiety. Experiential activities serve several functions in learning about oppression that cannot be achieved through cognitive learning. For example, students engage in examining and confronting their assumptions, meanings, and feelings about difference. The experiential component allows students to learn to recognize and deal with strong affect (their own and others), and supports their development of self-awareness and differential use of self (Pinderhughes, 1989; Romney, Tatum, & Jones, 1992).

As a way of beginning to create an open dialogue in sensitive areas, we recommend that two course assumptions be explained in the first class meeting. First, emphasize that everyone's life has been touched by oppression because we grew up in and were socialized by a society that values the "myth of meritocracy" (McIntosh, 1989). This has differential consequences for the process of an individual's racial and social identity formation and integration. There are no "neutral" observers or "innocent" bystanders and so the content will have direct meaning and experience for everyone. It is essential to remember to begin "where the students are." This is done by eliciting and validating their experiences with respect to the many forms that oppression takes (i.e., racism, classism, sexism, heterosexism, anti-Semitism, ageism, and ableism). Make explicit that the privilege of validation and the hurdles that are introduced by social devaluation are played out and processed differently in individual lives. This means that they can expect that they and their peers may be at very different points in their understanding and awareness of these issues. Developing social awareness can trigger a process of self-learning that is characterized by particular tensions regardless of background identity (i.e., power, privilege, marginalization). By anticipating this, faculty can normalize a process though students experience a range of uncomfortable affect—guilt, shame, anger, frustration, anxiety, resentment, and fear. Do not forget to emphasize the positive aspects of growth—excitement, mastery, and growing intellectual rigor.

Learning in oppression courses focuses on the ideological environments in which we have been socialized, the values underlying those beliefs, and the consequences for the perception of self and others. This approach allows the class to engage in examination of the unique perceptual screen that each has developed through life experiences and that functions to help interpret and process personal experience. Again, it is important to note that self-awareness is critical to being a skillful social work practitioner.

Second, emphasize to the class the significance of the experiential learning that is to occur and how it may differ from other courses in the program. Review some of the points that were raised earlier about the nature of experiential learning. In this way students may feel more prepared for what will occur and there will be fewer expressions of surprise when asked to participate in a given activity. In identifying the importance of experiential learning, it is important to establish conversation parameters particularly around self-disclosure. First-year MSW students may feel particularly nervous and uncertain. They may be unclear about what constitutes appropriate sharing. If they share too much too quickly, they may feel overexposed and less likely to participate in further activities. This can certainly impede the process midway through the course as you move to more demanding and "riskier" activities of self-disclosure and reflection. Creating a relatively safe environment should begin in the first class, after logistical tasks such as explaining content, course assignments, texts, and instructor's expectations. We will now provide some examples of experiential activities to be used in the course.

USING EXPERIENTIAL EXERCISES

It is important to monitor the class dynamics along different points in the semester as a guide for introducing low- to high-risk (increased vulnerability and disclosure) experiential exercises. An important first step is to involve students in a mutually developed exercise that creates a set of conversational parameters referred to earlier. This is a very simple exercise of brainstorming with which many instructors are familiar. The purpose is to co-create a set of rules to be observed throughout the semester. Ask the class, "What do people think is important to establish at the beginning of a course like this so that people feel free to have a dialogue?" Write the suggestions that are volunteered on the board. This activity requires attending to several tasks that include communicating an attitude of acceptance about their points, rewording and reframing their suggestions in an affirming manner, doing some reality testing and clarifying about course content, and declining a suggested rule.

For example, a rule articulated by an individual may be overly protective and interfere with the process. Many students say they want to feel "safe," which usually translates into not experiencing any uncomfortable affect. This is an unreasonable expectation for the course and cannot be supported. One can promote a feeling of safety by being respectful and taking responsibility for self-learning, but that does not include not experiencing discomfort. Emphasize that when something new is experienced it is often accompanied by feelings of anxiety. Relate this to their future professional development by pointing out that at times we will simply not accept contracts posed by clients because while they may provide a feeling of safety for the client, this may violate ethical and legal standards. For example, consider a client who says that the condition of their involvement in treatment is that the provider swears they will not hospitalize them no matter how depressed or suicidal they become. In regard to their future professional identity you can remind the class of the need as professionals to have an ability to give and receive critical feedback. Practitioners need to be able to tolerate evaluations from clients that may communicate a less-than-perfect response as well as fit on the part of the practitioner.

Once the exercise is completed, distribute a list of communication guidelines such as found in *Guidelines for Cross-Cultural Conversations* or *Dynamics of Racism and Oppression Classroom Guidelines*.[3] The guidelines are prepared prior to the class, although another manner is to have a student create the handout from the board list and distribute it in the subsequent class. These guidelines can be referred to throughout the course. Establishing these parameters gives students beginning experiences with experiential exercises, critical feedback, and a sense of mastery with a concrete finished product.

Following this initial brainstorming activity, an instructor can introduce a number of low-risk experiential exercises that reflect the content of the course and build an experience of group cohesion. For example, a very simple low-risk exercise is called "Stand Up."[4] This exercise involves the faculty reading off a series of descriptive statements that range from very general to very specific aspects of individuals. If the student's response is yes to the descriptive statement, the student stands up. Statements focus, for example, on where people were born, what type of music they prefer, where they were raised, how they identify ethnically, and so forth. This exercise introduces the idea that most, if not all, people negotiate difference all of the time (i.e., each student will most likely stand up for more than one statement). Some descriptive statements are significantly less charged than others. This can segue into a discussion examining why some aspects seem more charged or threatening than others.

As the semester progresses, one can introduce more challenging and demanding exercises. An example is a version of Creighton and Kovel's (1992) "Power Shuffle." This involves placing students physically in positions of domination and subordination as the instructor takes the class through a series of oppressions: racism, sexism, classism, heterosexism, anti-Semitism, ableism, and ageism. This is a very powerful exercise that produces a tremendous amount of affect. An instructor should carefully monitor the time to ensure debriefing at the end of the exercise. Do expect to return to this exercise throughout the remainder of the semester as material will be surfaced as time goes on. While it is unreasonable to expect that one will have complete closure on an issue by the time a class session ends, it is unwise to simply let students go without some debriefing. Do anticipate that they may experience a range of feelings subsequent to the class, including feelings of distress. These issues can be revisited as needed by the individual in a class discussion, through their journal writing (when programs require these), or in an individual conference with the instructor.

Here we make two points about the use and selection of exercises. First, a wide range of exercises have been developed for this content area and are available to instructors. Additionally, exercises from other content areas, such as those used in certain family therapy or group work courses lend themselves to use in these courses. It is our suggestion that you do not attempt to initiate an exercise with which you are personally uncomfortable. For example, some exercises are highly confrontative, and may be contrary to your own values and philosophy about the educational process. An exercise that "does not fly" can have a disastrous impact on the class process, not to mention the instructor's self-esteem. When attempting a new exercise in the class, it is sometimes

---

[3] Guidelines for Cross-Cultural Conversations were developed by Spirit of Survival, Boston, MA. Dynamics of Racism and Oppression Classroom Guidelines were developed by Patti De Rosa (1993), Boston, MA.

[4] This exercise is an integration of three sources: Creighton & Kovel, 1992; P. De Rosa (personal communication, Simmons College, Boston, MA, 1988); and Njeri, 1989.

helpful to explicitly involve the class in the evaluation of its implementation. Identify that this is the first time you are implementing the exercise and that you will want students' input and suggestions regarding its effectiveness and further development. Second, be clear and descriptive about the points that you are attempting to illustrate with these activities. Students need to understand the purpose of activities in order to freely engage.

It is helpful to have a summary sheet for distribution to the class following the debriefing of an exercise. One can attend to this in two ways. One way is for the instructor to prepare the sheet prior to the class. A second way is to use the debriefing to generate a summary that is distributed to the students in a subsequent class. For example, there are a number of possible summaries of the "Power Shuffle," and Pharr's (1988) "Common Elements of Oppression" also provides some. Some summaries are syntheses of the readings that students are expected to have done for the class. A written summary is important for two reasons. One reason is that it provides an opportunity to integrate the readings with the class exercise. Do not assume that students have gotten the major points upon completing the exercise. Having the sheet allows students to reflect at different points on the learning that has or will occur. Preparation by the faculty of a summary sheet helps the faculty member to be clear about what he or she is attempting to accomplish with the use of an exercise. It forces a reflection and choice around appropriate activities.

Another example of exercises is that of making use of opportunities that are provided by current situations in one's environment. Sometimes an oppression course can have an overly historical perspective with little exploration of the current complexities of these issues (Melendez, 1994). One semester, a local regional high school experienced a significant violent racial conflict involving several hundred Black and White students. The high school was closed for a period of time to allow for a cooling-off period. A class activity was organized around dividing the students into teams of four or five members and giving them the role of a consulting team that has been contracted to prepare the school for reopening subsequent to the conflict. The teams were given a certain amount of time to struggle with how they would go about intervening. This lead to a very rich discussion on assessment, constituencies to approach, long- and short-term goals, the consequences of the particular make-up of a given team, and countertransference issues. It offered the students an opportunity to draw on the material that they had been examining and attempt to integrate it into a practice situation.

A final example is that of providing a closing ritual for the semester. There are a number of possible variations. One possibility is the use of a Native American ritual known as "smugging," which involves acknowledging the end of the course using the Native people's metaphor of breaking up the camp and the notion of the sacred hoop. While there is an end to this location, this event, and the class, the ritual suggests an ongoing connection and continued process and development.

SUMMARY

Mindful preparation and planning for courses on oppression integrates didactic and experiential methods into the learning process. This article has focused on the issues of experiential learning activities in these courses. The success of these courses depends on the instructors' presentation of these activities. It is critical in the first class to define experiential learning and take students through an initial low-risk activity that formalizes the contract through the articulation of a set of conversational parameters. The meaning making and value-laden aspects of oppression will generate strong affect in the class. While some key concepts can assist professors in conceptually organizing this content, a significant part of ensuring success depends on the preparedness by faculty, including awareness of our own comfort level with strong affect. In this manner, faculty can use personal indicators as guides to determining how to organize class activities. The professor's clarity about the class process and expectations is an initial step at creating a relatively safe learning environment. Normalizing where each student is in relation to the learning about oppression, and conducting the class in a way that is respectful of diverse student needs, are both essential. The educational demands may at first seem quite daunting. We have found the returns for our investment to be worth the effort. A future direction is to develop an ability to measure the intended outcomes of these activities. This remains a significant challenge that requires the further attention of educators and practitioners.

REFERENCES

Atkinson, D. R., Morten, G., and Sue, D. W. (1989). Proposed identity development model. In *Counseling American minorities* (3rd ed.) (pp. 35–52). Dubuque: W.C. Brown.

Bonwell, C. C., & Eisen, J. A. (1991). *Active learning: Creating excitement in the classroom,* ASHE-ERIC Higher Education Reports, Report No. 1.

Washington, DC: George Washington University, School of Education and Human Development.

Brookfield, S. D. (1987). *Developing critical thinkers: Challenging adults to explore alternative ways of thinking and acting.* San Francisco: Jossey-Bass.

Browne, C. V. (1995). Empowerment in social work practice with older women. *Social Work, 40*(3), 358–364.

Comas-Diaz, L., & Jacobsen, F. M. (1991). Ethnocultural transference and countertransference in the therapeutic dyad. *American Journal of Orthopsychiatry, 61*(3), 392–402.

Creighton, A., & Kovel, P. (1992). It's about power. In *Teens need teens* (pp. 12—20). Oakland, CA: Oakland Men's Project/Bridges.

Cross, W. E. (1971). The Negro to Black conversion experience. *Black World, 20,* 13–27.

Fox, J. R. (1983). Affective learning in racism courses with an experiential component. *Journal of Education for Social Work, 9,* 69–77.

Garrett, K. J., & Thornton, S. (1993, March). *Crossing cultures with sensitivity: Teaching ethnic diversity in social work practice.* Paper presented at the Annual Program Meeting, Council on Social Work Education, New York.

Hardiman, R. (1979). *White identity development theory.* Amherst, MA: New Perspectives.

Hegar, R. L., & Hunzeker, J. M. (1988). Moving toward empowerment-based practice in public child welfare. *Social Work, 33,* 499–503.

Jackson, B. (1975). Black identity development. *MEFORM: Journal of Educational Diversity and Innovation, 2,* 19–25.

Lott, B., & Maluso, D. (1995). *The social psychology of interpersonal discrimination.* New York: The Guilford Press.

McIntosh, P. (1989). White privilege: Unpacking the invisible knapsack. *Peace and Freedom,* July/August, 10–12.

Melendez, M. P. (1994). *On the teaching of difference: Cross-cultural competence.* Unpublished manuscript, Case Western Reserve University.

Miller, J. B. (1992). Domination and subordination. In P. Rothenberg (Ed.). *Race, class and gender in the United States: An integrated study;* pp. 57-62. New York: St. Martin's Press.

Nakanishi, M., & Rittner, B. (1992). The inclusionary cultural model. *Journal of Social Work Education, 28,* 27–35.

Njeri, I. (1989). Facing up to being white. *Los Angeles Times,* pp. 12–28.

Pharr, S. (1988). *Homophobia: A weapon of sexism* (pp. 53—64). Inverness, CA: Chardon Press.

Pinderhughes, E. (1983). Empowerment for our clients and ourselves. *Social Casework, 31,* 214–219.

Pinderhugues, E. (1989). Understanding race, ethnicity and power: The key to efficacy in clinical practice. New York: Free Press.

Romney, P., Tatum, B. D., & Jones, J. (1992). Feminist strategies for teaching about oppression: The importance of process. *Women's Studies Quarterly, 20.1-2,* 95–110.

Rothenberg, P. S. (2001). *Race, class and gender in the United States* (5th ed.). New York: North Publishers.

Tatum, B. D. (1992). Talking about race, learning about racism: An application of racial identity development theory in the classroom. *Harvard Educational Review, 62*(1), 1–24.

Chapter Eleven
Transforming Critical Classroom Events Into Teachable Moments

Throughout this book, there has been considerable discussion about the demands on faculty who teach diversity for social justice content. They frequently face strained classroom interactions and strong affect as students' deep-seated beliefs, worldviews, and self-concepts are challenged. In Chapter Three, the critical thinking process was presented as a model of preparing students for their role as social justice advocates. An integral part of that process is the ability to critically reflect on one's assumptions and behaviors, particularly in relation to significant events (Brookfield, 1990). A significant event or critical incident, as we are using the term, is a trigger event that creates a discrepancy between one's perceptions of how the world is and how the world is supposed to be. Such events can occur in the classroom, the student's field placement, or other aspects of the student's life. Regardless of where or when they occur, the cognitive dissonance can result in inner discomfort and distress that has the potential to open the door to critical thinking.

In this chapter, we focus on how educators can transform critical incidents that occur in the classroom into "teachable moments" aimed at facilitating critical reflection. The chapter includes two major sections. First, we begin with discussion of some possible themes that characterize strained classroom interactions and faculty responses to them. The discussion is based on faculty reports of actual critical events that occurred in the classroom (Garcia & Van Soest, 1999). We believe that before educators ask students to be critically reflective of their own assumptions and meanings, they must be able to do this for themselves. Thus, a critical incident debriefing process is presented in the second major section of this chapter as a method for faculty to critically reflect on the challenges they face when teaching and learning about diversity for social justice. Reflections on a case example of a critical incident debriefing is included.

CRITICAL INCIDENTS IN THE CLASSROOM

Classroom discussions that either intentionally or unpredictably touch on oppression content can easily trigger feelings of denial and resistance, shame, guilt, anger, and anxiety (Pinderhughes, 1989; Tatum, 1992; Tatum, 1994). To better understand how to transform the resulting strained classroom interactions into teachable moments, we asked faculty to share their experiences of dealing with critical events. The investigation was based on two basic assumptions: (a) that managing emotionally laden class dialogue requires that faculty have skills in recognizing and managing their own affect as they work with student feelings and course concepts, and (b) that examination of classroom interactions in the context of systems and ecological perspectives enables identification of the multiple factors that play a part in influencing classroom encounters (Garcia & Van Soest, 1997).

Sixteen faculty who were participants at a conference workshop or who were identified through professional networks as having an interest in and/or having taught diversity content were asked to complete a Faculty Critical Event Survey on diversity issues in the classroom (Garcia & Van Soest, 1999). We asked them to write about a difficult incident, situation, or pattern of interaction that arose in a cultural diversity course or in another social work course where the discussion focused on diversity issues. They were asked to describe the event, what they did, the segment of the course in which the event occurred (beginning, middle, end), the role contextual factors may have played (e.g., class dynamics, students, professor response, department/school context), what concerned them the most about the event, with whom they consulted and why, and what they learned or gained from the experience. Analysis of the critical incidents revealed four themes: use of the teachable moment, process-oriented teaching, use of self in teaching, and use of life experiences to promote learning. A brief discussion of each theme, including what we learned from analyzing the incidents, follows.[1]

Use of the Teachable Moment: Faculty Readiness to Deal Comfortably With Strong Emotional Responses

By far the most prevalent and powerful theme that emerged from analysis of the critical events was related to faculty readiness to translate strong student affect into a meaningful learning experience. A range of diversity issues,

---

[1] This section draws from Garcia & Van Soest, 1999. Used with permission.

such as bilingualism, immigration, racism, male-female relationships, gay and lesbian parenting, and other issues related to homosexuality, triggered emotional responses in both students and faculty in 14 of the 16 critical incidents. Some of the conflicts involved diverse student pairs or subgroups in class: male/female, White/Black, international/U.S. citizens, Mexican American male/White female, gay White male/African American male. In some cases, faculty noted that students expressed volatile conflicts around issues that were personally experienced by the faculty themselves. Faculty also reported feeling strong emotional responses to students such as anger at student projection and their judgment of the students as racist. Eight of the critical events involving strong emotional responses were identified as having positive outcomes when the situation was converted into a teachable moment, as illustrated by the following:

> In the middle of a course on Issues in Social Work, in which the topic under consideration was racism, a small group of White students became increasingly silent. When asked by the professor about the silence, they said they were "sick of talking about issues of racism" and wanted to move onto other issues. When the professor asked if others felt the same, half of the students agreed while the other half felt the focus on racism was very important to social work practice. An African American woman, who was encouraged to speak by the professor, said she could never stop talking about racism because it followed her every day. The professor then reminded the class that they had all agreed that discussion of racism would bring up lots of emotion and wondered if such emotions were stirred up and, if so, were students finding it difficult to bring up their feelings in class. The White students were then able to talk about their feelings of guilt and other strong negative feelings. The professor congratulated the students for bringing the issue forward in class and the class was able to move to continue the learning process.

Positive outcomes that were reported by faculty about the class included the following students moved to deeper exploration of demanding issues, student respect for each other increased, the professor was more motivated to learn about how to help students with difficult issues, candid communication between students was established, and student worldview was stretched and enhanced to include viewpoints previously not seen. Faculty behaviors that appeared to contribute to the positive outcomes included setting and adhering to class ground rules and promoting a safe and open environment, lack of condemnation in a context of support and encouragement of student perspectives and personal growth, validating students' hard work, supporting balanced participation among the class members so that all students were encouraged to speak, self-disclosure and openness, and student-centered teaching and learning processes.

Six of the 16 critical events involving strong emotional responses were categorized as having negative outcomes, as illustrated by the following:

> In the middle of a master's level course on diversity, students were discussing Spanish-speaking clients and their comfort level when others conversed in a language the rest of the class didn't understand. This was the first animated discussion to occur among the students, who had been resistant to engaging in meaningful discussion up to that point. A student confronted another student who had been extolling the values of bilingualism by asking if she was bilingual herself (the answer was no) and then stated that she had no right to act righteous when she was not bilingual herself. The professor stopped the discussion by stating that it was getting into a level of personal attack, which would not be tolerated and then attempted to summarize points of the discussion and to invite continuation. Both appropriate and inappropriate discussion stopped from that point on. The professor reported that attempts to consult with peers about the situation resulted in sympathy and empathy but no guidance for action.

Negative outcomes that were reported when faculty were unable to convert difficult situations into teachable moments included discontinuation of all student discussion, antagonism and dysfunction within a student work group, student disengagement, class polarization, and unresolved conflict. Faculty identified some reasons for the negative outcomes as delayed intervention (i.e., poor timing), lack of preparation for an outburst that seemed to occur without warning, inadequate skill to work effectively with the situation, lack of anticipation and prevention strategies, inability to help students work through their pain and anger, and letting the professor's own feelings of anger and impotence block the creative use of teachable moments.

Summary of Learnings

The above reports reveal that faculty can expect strong emotional responses when discussing diversity issues, both from students and from within themselves. Faculty can be prepared for such emotional outbursts by acknowledging that it is normal for diversity and oppression issues to activate previously existing pain and conflicts that are deep-seated and personal for both students and faculty. To promote growth and change through use of the teachable moment, faculty need to (a) be willing to acknowledge their own strong emotions and unresolved conflicts; (b) come to terms with their own social identity struggles and development in relation to role, status, and privilege in an unjust society; (c) develop insight and androgogical skills into how to help students come to terms with their social identity and social status issues; and (d) develop support systems for processing critical events in order to get assistance/ideas about how to handle them.

Process-Oriented Teaching: Communication Dynamics

The second most prevalent theme is closely related to the first. In 13 of the critical events, faculty discussed the influence of communication dynamics on student willingness to engage with difficult content. Nine events occurred in discrete diversity courses (of which four resulted in satisfactory and five in unsatisfactory outcomes) and four occurred in other courses (two of which resulted in positive and two in negative outcomes). Regardless of whether the event occurred in a diversity-oriented course, certain professor behaviors seemed to facilitate student willingness to stay with difficult issues. These included pushing students to persist while guiding the dialogue, making positive use of student diversity to promote learning from each other, engaging in appropriate self-disclosure while maintaining student focus, and consulting with colleagues to explore alternative strategies for dealing with class dynamics. The following critical event illustrates the value of process-oriented teaching in helping students deal with content that is difficult for them:

A panel of gay and lesbian leaders from the community was brought into a course on cultural diversity and oppression. The professor noticed during the discussion that one of the students, who was known to be very religious and from a very fundamental denomination, was literally turning red even though she was amiable to the panel and asked significant questions concerning their spiritual lives. The professor sought out the student after class and acknowledged that he knew that the discussion had been difficult for her. The student looked relieved in response to the professor's acknowledgement of her process and said that she was trying hard to understand. The professor supported her willingness to expand her worldview and once again acknowledged her efforts to stay with the process. The professor reported that his biggest concern when reflecting on the event is that this point of growth in the student could have gone unnoticed and unsupported and that he learned that reinforcement, support, and acceptance of students' processes of growth are crucial to learning.

Professor behaviors that seemed to inhibit student willingness to engage with difficult content included pushing one's own opinion, scolding students, intellectualizing feelings, insensitivity or lack of awareness of student issues, allowing or inadvertently contributing to student divisiveness, and colluding with injustice. These experiences raise questions regarding how faculty can more actively integrate process-oriented teaching into the classroom, and equally important, develop a style of teaching that represents a balance of content and process (i.e., high structure and high facilitation).

Summary of Learnings

It is important to encourage students' free expression of thoughts, beliefs, and ideas on difficult issues while maintaining a safe classroom environment. This may mean more effective expression of a professor's own feelings, self-disclosure, and containment of inappropriate student behavior. Reinforcement and support of the development of a student's own social identity and acceptance of others is crucial. The use of small groups in the classroom is extremely helpful because it provides students with more opportunity to process difficult material and to normalize their experiences.

Use of Self in Teaching: Faculty–Student Profiles

Nine of the 16 critical events involved the influence of the faculty–student profile as a factor in classroom interactions. This was particularly true when the professor was of a minority sexual orientation or ethnicity in a primarily Euro-American class of students. Three of these situations were reported as having positive outcomes. In one case, the instructor used strong helping skills (e.g., empathy, summarizing, clarifying) to facilitate student interaction around issues of racism. In another situation, the professor modeled appropriate use of anger and confrontation by using his own anger constructively in class. The following summarizes that situation:

> A Latino professor taught a required racism course to a class of all White students. During a presentation to the class, a White male student said, "let's face it, all we have learned in this course is propaganda and how to act out in our agencies" and proceeded to argue that racism is not about institutional structures but only about individual psychology. After a few minutes of a poorly organized monologue by the student, the professor stopped him and expressed anger about the provocative presentation. The student responded by saying that the presentation had been deliberately planned to demonstrate an alternative point of view. After acknowledging his disclaimer, the professor noted that it was nonetheless unacceptable. The rest of that class session and the next session were used to debrief about the experience of the confrontation between student and professor. The professor reported that the outcome was positive in that students processed their experiencing of the professor's anger and the confrontation. The professor reported that his major learning was that he could handle an angry confrontation in a professional manner, i.e., his anger was controlled and he was very careful not to attack the student but to model constructive anger and confrontation.

In six situations where the majority of the students were Euro-American and the professor was a person of color, classroom interactions seemed to be influenced by student perception and expectation of the professor in a variety of ways. Students of color seemed to feel either supported or betrayed by the professor when sharing their perceptions of racism. For example, when a professor supported a White student's struggle about the reality of racism, which students of color saw as a manifestation of denial, the professor was seen as "selling out" to the White world. A critical event involving an interaction between an out gay male student and a heterosexual male student in a course taught by an out bisexual professor involved a similar dynamic: the gay student reported feeling betrayed and accused the professor of allowing homophobia in the classroom.

Summary of Learnings

Effective teaching in areas of diversity requires that faculty have some perspective on how social psychological dynamics in the classroom in part arise from participants' earlier experiences, perceptions, and group influences. As such, faculty use of self (Scharff, 1992) is essential as a basis for faculty maintaining perspective on their subjective experience in the classroom and in working with classroom interaction in the service of learning. In those classroom situations in which the professor is of an ethnicity or sexual orientation that is different from the majority of the students, it is particularly important to recognize that student perceptions of the professor (and vice versa) can influence interactions positively or negatively. Facilitating student development is made difficult in different ways when the person in authority, i.e., the professor, is a member of a minority population or White. For example, if the professor is of color, the anxiety that is experienced by students in their interactions with culturally different others becomes an immediate and present factor in the classroom.

Pinderhughes' (1989) experiential group approach to teaching about race, ethnicity, and power provides a model for helping students understand the complexities involved in cross-cultural interaction and the role that their own behavior has in relation to consequences and outcomes. By exploring within a safe class environment their own "feelings, perceptions, and experiences vis-à-vis ethnicity, race, and power," students have an opportunity to recognize their predispositions and biases in their interactions with culturally different others (p. 211). It is important in such situations that the professor models how to facilitate the growth process and consciously supports students' own pace of change as they modify their perceptions.

Use of Life Experiences to Promote Learning: "Ghosts in the Classroom"

In five critical events, student experience originating outside of school, in other parts of the program, or in interaction/communication with other students (often immediately prior to the class) was acted out in oppression-related class discussion. The following critical events were reported:

1. It was discovered that a group of religious students was meeting outside of class, without the professor's knowledge, to discuss ways to counteract what they perceived to be the professor's advocacy of homosexuality.

2. Two pre-course situations converged in a class meeting that produced highly charged classroom dynamics: White students presented fears about

working with clients of color as a result of pre-field placement labs they had attended. When an African American student shared his negative experiences with the city police department in class, several students acted out their already heightened sensitivity in response by focusing on how fearful they were rather than empathizing with the student.

3. Dynamics in a diversity course were influenced by the fact that the social work program itself was comprised of a homogeneous, White, upper-class student body in a private institution. The result was that students were silent when issues of racism and poverty were raised, yet engaged in lively discussions of issues such as sexism and sexual orientation.

4. A professor acted to prevent a potential "ghost" of an unresolved conflict (about culture and oppression related to ethnicity and sexual orientation) between an African American male student and an out gay White student by warning her colleague who would be teaching the same cohort of students the next semester.

Summary of Learnings

The above critical incidents indicate that faculty need to be aware of how life experiences outside the classroom may influence and/or inhibit learning and find ways to address them. Students may overhear unfair criticism outside the classroom by other students that is not dealt with directly or they may have difficulty in confronting a student due to that student's perceived social status within the program. Students who have negative and potentially traumatic experiences related to oppression both within the program and in other aspects of their lives often bring these into the classroom either directly or indirectly. In such situations, effective teaching involves the professor's willingness to bring relevant experiences into the classroom, examine them, and make them part of the learning process.

CRITICAL INCIDENT DEBRIEFING PROCESS

As faculty reflected on the critical events that they described for the above survey, they reported that they learned a great deal from processing the experience in writing for the study. Analyses of their reports point to the potential of the critical event debriefing protocol for helping educators deal with classroom teaching on diversity and oppression and helping them feel more prepared for strained classroom interactions that arise in relation to diversity content. Thus, in this section we focus on the debriefing process by providing a brief background and rationale for its use and then describing the process, including a case example of how a professor of a diversity course used the critical incident debriefing process to learn from an unsuccessful outcome.

Background and Rationale

Critical incident methodology, initially introduced by Flanagan (1954), has been used in two distinctive ways: as a research methodology (Davis & Reid, 1988; Mahrer & Nadler, 1986) and as a service delivery approach to debrief individuals who provide services in emergency and disaster situations (Mitchell, 1983). While use of the method to conduct research has great potential for increasing our understanding of teaching and learning processes, our main concern here is with its debriefing protocol. In the critical incident literature, this area deals with a form of crisis intervention called Critical Incident Stress Debriefing (CISD). Developed by Mitchell (1983), CISD is a method for helping emergency workers cope with trauma (Ragaisis, 1994; Talbot, Manton, & Dunn, 1992). Stress debriefing provides an interview format consisting of a sequence of activities that includes description of the event, emotional ventilation, identification of stress reaction, psychoeducation, development of a plan of action, and assessment for referral for therapy (Walker, 1990, p. 129).

Critical incident methodology is particularly useful as a tool for dealing with classroom processes related to the management of diversity content and maximizing learning opportunities. It provides a format for self-reflection and faculty observations of strained classroom interaction arising from the classroom composition (i.e., ethnic profile of the class, professor/class ethnic profile) or in instances where students act out uncomfortable affect. It also provides a structure for examining the subjective experience of the professor and the option(s) that he or she perceived and exercised in the process of transforming intense class interactions into a teachable moment. The emphasis on the application of learning to practice and bridging theory and practice lends itself to the adult learner model (Knowles, 1970). As such, critical incident methodology can facilitate the development of teaching insights and a conceptual framework that can move us further along in knowing more about the teaching processes that are effective in diversity teaching and particularly in learning about emotionally laden content.

Critical Incident Debriefing Process

We suggest that the debriefing process be used in relation to a difficult event, situation, or pattern of interaction that arose in a cultural diversity course or in another social work course where the discussion focused on issues of diversity (race, ethnicity, gender, class, ableism, sexual orientation, etc.). While it is preferable to engage in the process as soon as possible after the event occurs, it can be helpful even after a considerable amount of time has lapsed. The following debriefing questions can be answered in either of two ways: (a) a professor can write his or her responses, or (b) a professor can respond verbally with the help and support of a colleague or colleagues.

1. Describe the event (who, what, when, where).

2. In what segment of the course did the event occur (beginning, middle, end)?

3. What did you do? (Be specific.)

4. What role did contextual factors play in the critical event (e.g., class dynamics, students, professor response, department/school context)?

5. What concerned you most about the event?

6. With whom did you consult and why? If you did not consult with anyone, why not? What was the outcome?

7. What did you learn or gain from the experience? What would you do differently?

8. What action might be taken now?

A Case Example

The following case example illustrates how one educator used the debriefing process at the end of the course. The professor, a White female who teaches part time in a mostly White private university, applied the critical incident debriefing protocol to a situation she experienced while teaching a required diversity course in the MSW program. The course was taught in the summer session and there were 13 students registered for the class (11 White females, 1 African American male, and 1 White male).

1. Describe the event (who, what, when, where).

This was a diversity course that was offered in the summer session and met two times a week for 2 and 1/2 hours each session. Initially, there were 11 white females and 1 Black male in the class. A 13th class member, a white male, had informed me that he would miss the first week of class due to a family reunion at the beach which he felt he must attend. During the first two sessions, the class as a group was progressing well in developing trust and beginning to address some critical issues. At the third class session, the white male student joined the class. He was very energetic and verbal and seemed eager to make up for the week of class time that he had missed. He informed the class that he knew he would get incorporated into the class easily because he was a strong social justice advocate, had been raised by a Black nanny who was "more of a parent to me than my own parents," and so on. He proceeded to dominate the class. All the other students, who had been very active participants in class up to that point, stopped talking. The white male kept making attempts to bond with the Black male. The class became male dominated very quickly and remained so in spite of my best efforts throughout the course. At the last session, the white male asked the class for feedback and the women let him have it! He was crushed to learn that they thought he was dominant and insensitive. He took a "victim" stance, feeling that not only was the women's assessment unfair and untrue but that they shouldn't have waited until the last session to tell him.

2. In what segment of the course did the event occur (beginning, middle, end)?

The white male's appearance and class participation the second week of class (the beginning of the course) signaled a change in class dynamics. That change continued throughout the entire class.

3. What did you do? (Be specific.)

Beginning the second week of class, I found myself having to work harder to facilitate equitable sharing of space in class. I gave the women in particular encouragement to keep talking. At the end of the fourth class session, I gave the white male student an article and suggested he read it since it seemed similar to his experience. The article was by a white southerner who wrote about how she had been raised by a Black nanny and her struggle as an adult to come to terms with her racism and the oppression of the system that she benefited from as a child. The following class session, the white male student told me that the article insulted him and he exerted a considerable amount of energy in class trying to prove he wasn't a racist. I worked hard to stay calm and facilitate class participation throughout the course. I was, however, angry at what I perceived as one person blocking the learning process.

4. What role did contextual factors play in the critical event (e.g., class dynamics, students, professor response, department/school context)?

Class and student dynamics mirrored gender dynamics in the broader society; the female students stopped talking and male dominance in the classroom became the norm. The female students did not confront or participate much beginning the second week of class; they gave the white male the power. The white male aggressively sought and took the power and attempted to make the Black male his ally. The Black male, who was the only person of color in the class and the only non-social work student as well, seemed conflicted about whether to "go with the power" and be uncomfortable or resist bonding with the white male and be alone.

I was a significant factor in the situation. While I worked harder than ever to encourage/facilitate student participation, I think my efforts were blocked by my anger at the white male student, which the other students probably sensed. My own socialization probably played an unconscious role as well since, instead of confronting the white male student, I "danced as fast as I could" to fix things without confrontation. My behavior may have discouraged others in the class from taking responsibility.

The university and school context was also a significant factor. The institution is predominantly white, hierarchical, church-related. Faculty generally "behave" and do not rock the boat. The student body in the social work program is predominantly white and female in a white male-dominated institutional system.

5. What concerned you most about the event?

    The most disturbing thing about the situation was that I allowed a
    process to be created in the classroom that paralleled the dominant
    oppressive system of society, including the university institution. If
    the saying "behavior speaks louder than words" has any meaning here,
    I think it means that even though I was talking about empowerment
    and promoting social and economic justice strategies, my behavior in
    avoiding confrontation within our own classroom was the more pow-
    erful message. I was extremely distressed by my own anger and impo-
    tence. I was also concerned that the female students were unable to
    behaviorally translate empowerment concepts to the immediate situ-
    ation and aware of my own responsibility in that.

6. With whom did you consult and why? If not, why not? What was the
    outcome?

    I talked with several people who I trusted. I got empathy, which was
    nice, and a lot of support and some sympathy but I think I really
    needed to be confronted or to have people talk through with me what
    I might have done differently. I think it would be most helpful if
    there were a support group of faculty who could do this for each other.

7. What did you learn or gain from the experience? What would you do
    differently?

    I learned a tremendous amount and at a deep level from this experi-
    ence. First, I shouldn't have let the white male student miss the first
    week of class. I was too nice. I let him take his white male privilege
    without questioning him or confronting him. That set the stage for
    everything else that happened.
    Second, I learned how my own passivity resulted in collusion with
    the power structure that was created in class. I should have confronted
    the class dynamics, pointed out to the students what I saw happen-
    ing, and opened it up for the class to deal with within the context of
    the larger societal power structures about which we were studying. I
    believe the students might have learned a lot from my modeling of

how to confront a situation of which I had been a part and how to turn it around. The class concepts could have come alive through our dealing with our societal "replication" in the classroom head on.

8. What action might be taken now?

Since the course in which this incident happened is long over, there isn't anything to be done about it now. However, I have taken what I learned and brought it into other classes I have taught since. For example, in a recent course, two white male students (the only two white males in a class of 30+ students) were doing about 70% of the talking in class and I stopped and suggested that the class observe the discussion dynamics within the context of power and privilege. The students discussed how the amount of space (physical and verbal) taken parallels one's position in society vis à vis the power and privilege granted based on one's social identity. Based on student journals and course evaluations, it was clear to me that this discussion resulted in a profound learning experience. I am grateful about what I learned from that summer experience, even though it was very painful, and that I was able to apply what I learned so another group of students could benefit.

Reflections on the Case Example

Several concerns that were raised by faculty who participated in the critical incident study discussed earlier in this chapter are also reflected in the above case example. Three areas of concern that emerged, related to faculty, students, and programs (Garcia & Van Soest, 1999), will be discussed briefly.

In relation to faculty, one concern is how exhausting it can be for educators to manage their own affect. Just as the professor in the case example noted, faculty in the study also expressed feelings of anger, being judgmental, and feeling impotent in the face of strained classroom dynamics. Another issue is whether faculty felt that they had adequate skill to manage the situation. As the case example illustrates, even when educators do not have adequate skill to handle the incident when it occurs, the critical incident debriefing process can help them develop the skill for another time. By thinking through what happened, faculty can identify issues, develop insights, and identify options that can be helpful in future situations.

The second area of concern is related to students. One issue is whether students have the ability to manage the classroom situation and the possibility that their self-confidence about dealing with diversity issues might be shaky as a result of unresolved class incidents. In the case example, the female students were able to identify conflicts at the end of the course, but the white male student's sense of devastation could have left them feeling immobilized or at least unsettled about finally being assertive. Another concern related to students that was illustrated by the case example was the female students feeling disempowered in the classroom and student reluctance to respond to his peers. The professor appropriately struggled with her role in inhibiting the students from acting.

The case example illustrates concerns related to social work programs as well. Social work departments/programs need to play a role in providing resources for faculty to examine their own responses in diversity interactions in the classroom and to increase sensitivity to ethnic, diversity, and cultural issues within the student body. When a diversity course is required in a program, students initially may be angry at the beginning of the course, perhaps feeling they are being coerced into traveling difficult terrain. Also, faculty who teach this course may need active support. In the case example, the professor expressed a desire to meet with colleagues to discuss how she might manage difficult situations. Critical events are more effectively, or at least less painfully, dealt with when professors feel supported and thus empowered by the program in teaching diversity. Social work programs also need to be consistent in their emphasis on empowerment, cultural diversity, and social justice both in the classroom and in program policies and practices. For example, when a student body or faculty is not very diverse, as in the case example, a program can seem dishonest from the perspective of students in a diversity course.

CONCLUSION

Difficult events can emerge without warning at any moment when dealing with diversity for social justice content. They can involve powerful intensity and confrontational interaction. Educators need to be prepared for the unexpected exchange that can become a teaching moment by learning more about oppression and conflict themselves as well as how to intervene effectively and enhance learning at these opportune moments.

The critical incidents provided by faculty in the study discussed in this chapter, as well as in the case example, poignantly illustrate that the critical incident debriefing method can help faculty (a) manage emotionally laden class dialogue by assisting them to develop skills in recognizing and managing their own affect as they work with student feelings and curriculum content; (b) identify the multiple factors that play a part in influencing classroom encounters through systematic examination of interactions; and (c) prepare for future classroom events by generating ideas about how to handle such incidents in a way that helps students translate them into personally meaningful terms based on critical reflection of their assumptions and behaviors. In short, the use of critical incident debriefing methodology can help faculty increase skill in supporting students through difficult emotional and psychological work and help them feel more prepared for strained classroom interactions when they arise.

The critical events reported in this chapter point to the need for teaching methodologies and the development and implementation of educational policies that recognize (a) how systemic, contextual tensions on a macro level often provide the basis for the emergence of "loaded" issues in the classroom; (b) how faculty comfort with their own social identity and with affect-laden responses (their own and others) influenced and can determine the safety of the classroom environment as well as influence the student change process dynamics; and (c) the necessity of faculty possessing communication and group process skills to work with and overcome barriers posed by strained classroom interactions. Educational interventions are needed, for both individual classrooms and social work programs, to support students through the psychological work that is necessary to the development of multicultural competence (Tatum, 1992).

REFERENCES

Brookfield, S. (1990). Using critical incidents to explore learners' assumptions. In J. Mezirow and Associates, *Fostering critical reflection in adulthood: A guide to transformative and emancipatory learning* (pp. 177–193). San Francisco: Jossey-Bass.

Davis, I., & Reid, W. (1988). Event analysis in clinical practice and process research. *Social Casework: The Journal of Contemporary Social Work, 69*, 298–306.

Flanagan, J. (1954). The critical incident technique. *Psychological Bulletin, 51*(4), 327–358.

Garcia, B., & Van Soest, D. (1997). Changing perceptions of diversity and oppression: MSW students discuss the effects of a required course. *Journal of Social Work Education, 33*(1), 119–130.

Garcia, B., & Van Soest, D. (1999). Teaching about diversity and oppression: Learning from analysis of critical classroom events. *Journal of Teaching in Social Work, 18*(1/2), 149–167.

Knowles, M. S. (1970). *The modern practice of adult education: Andragogy versus pedagogy.* New York: Association Press.

Mahrer, A., and Nadler, W. (1986). Good moments in psychotherapy: A preliminary review, a list, and some promising research avenues. *Journal of Consulting and Clinical Psychology, 54*(1), 10–15.

Mitchell, J. (1983). When disaster strikes: Critical incident debriefing process. *Journal of Emergency Medical Services, 8*(1), 36–39.

Pinderhughes, E. (1989). *Understanding race, ethnicity and power: The key to efficacy in clinical practice.* New York: The Free Press.

Ragaisis, K. (1994). Critical incident stress debriefing: A family nursing intervention. *Archives of Psychiatry Nursing, 8*(1), 38–43.

Scharff, J. (1992). *Projective and introjective identification and the use of the therapist's self.* Northvale, NJ: Jason Aronson.

Talbot, A., Manton, M., & Dunn, P. (1992). Debriefing the debriefers: An intervention strategy to assist psychologists after a crisis. *Journal of Traumatic Stress, 5*(1), 45–62.

Tatum, B. D. (1992). Talking about race, learning about racism: The application of racial identity development theory in the classroom. *Harvard Educational Review, 62*(1), 1–24.

Tatum, B. (1994). Teaching white students about racism: The search for white allies and the restoration of hope. *Teachers College Record, 94*(4), 462–476.

Walker, G. (1990). Crisis care in critical incident debriefing. *Death Studies, 14*, 121–133.

Chapter Twelve
Teaching Activities: A Process Approach

Betty Garcia and Patti DeRosa

The process orientation to teaching diversity and social justice is further clarified in this pragmatic chapter. Classroom activities are described for promoting student motivation toward social change. Learning in the classroom is discussed as a developmental process and emphasizes faculty development of relational skills aimed at validating student experience. Considerations for syllabus and course outline development, and safety guidelines that can be identified in the beginning of the course are presented. Selection of classroom activities must be premised on the purpose that the instructor intends to serve. In this regard, a listing of activities is identified, specifically in relation to their function in classroom process. Activities are discussed in relation to building foundations for ongoing, safe interaction; ice-breakers; building awareness about power and privilege; and social work practice skill building.

INTRODUCTION

Several chapters in this book have discussed how the goals of social justice teaching are to provide classroom activities that promote students' motivation and ability to engage in action directed at social change. The goal is toward advocacy, that is, to act on the awareness gained in the classroom. Experiential classroom exercises can be tremendously powerful experiences for students awakening to social justice concerns, insight development, and movement toward resolution of conflicts related to diversity and social justice issues. Classroom structure, direction by faculty, and involvement in activities that progressively increase risk-taking in the exploration of the impact of racism on students' lives facilitate students' development of skills and strategies to increase their effectiveness at social change efforts. This chapter will discuss a variety of classroom activities that facilitate student and classroom movement toward open and direct communication about diversity and social justice. It will also present assignments and course outline suggestions that meet course objectives, and develop student self-awareness and critical thinking. Some of what is covered here regarding course approach and core concepts is also found in other chapters, and more specifically in Chapter Ten.

The activities presented here can be used in diversity courses as well as in courses that do not have diversity goals and objectives but that may address diversity issues in individual sessions. The discussion in this chapter will focus on the utility and rationale for these activities rather than a presentation of the activity itself. There are extensive publications that have a wealth of information on activities that we recommend. References and descriptions of the activities that we describe can be found in Chapter Sixteen.

Teaching purpose and goals need to direct the selection of activities. Clarity about what the purpose of the experiential activity is, why it is chosen to be used at a particular point in a class, and a willingness to adapt and modify the activities to suit the teaching needs are essential. For example, various aspects of the student characteristics, interests, or learning needs may need special attention. Thoughtful planning about student needs and the implications for the kinds of activities that would be meaningful for the class can then direct the selection and timing of the activity.

PROCESS APPROACH

We encourage faculty to modify and adapt these activities to meet the needs of the course that they teach, with special consideration to the classroom dynamics and matching the activity to the readiness of the class to engage in predictably sensitive content.

We call this a process approach because the centrality of affective learning in diversity teaching places great importance on the classroom interaction and compels faculty to develop and enhance their expertise in relational skills such as directive communication, giving and taking feedback, and active listening. The process orientation draws faculty attention to the development of the faculty–student interaction, the nature and quality of student willingness to reflect and self-disclose regarding biases, and strengthening students' abilities to interact with each other about diversity in respectful, direct ways. This suggests attending to the types of tensions that arise, what themes are prominent, and in what part of the class issues or dynamics arise (i.e., beginning, middle, end). This also involves providing various activities for students to develop self awareness (e.g., journals, short papers, small groups) and maintaining thoughtful attentiveness to protecting the continuation of a safe and respectful classroom environment.

In monitoring where "the class is," faculty can take into account differences among students in readiness to engage in these issues, while staying focused on class dynamics regarding group development or class cohesion. Much of this involves tuning in to where students are regarding racial and social identity.

Effective teachers need to convey a nonjudgmental attitude that engages students through "caring confrontation," and supports growth by recognizing and validating students' cognitive and emotional growth. Faculty also need to develop facilitation versus traditional teaching skills. Facilitation teaching skills build on traditional pedagogical methods by integrating an adult learner (Knowles, 1984) approach that utilizes student experience. Facilitation skills in diversity teaching assist students in the process of self discovery, asking focused inquiry questions that help guide deep reflection, and help students to reach their own understandings of complex issues. Many variables mediate the ebb and flow of classroom process, development of classroom dynamics, responses to classroom activities, and student outcomes for the course. Successful classroom process does not mean a reduction of intensity or conflict, but rather, as in social work practice, it refers to the development of certain dynamics. These dynamics include validation of diverse student viewpoints, and students' increased ability to own their responses as well as engage in less self-conscious interactions with others who are different from themselves. Although there are a variety of approaches to diversity teaching that include a multicultural focus encompassing cultural competency (i.e., effectiveness in service delivery to diverse populations) and the variety of worldviews, beliefs, values, and practices found in different cultures, the social justice focus emphasized here includes elements of those approaches and also stresses an advocacy perspective.

A process teaching approach emphasizes an integration of intellectual comprehension and psychological reflection that leads toward attitude change (i.e., feelings, thoughts, behavior) and grounding for social change action taking. Because this creates discomfort in students (Garcia & Melendez, 1997), it is essential to work with class process with the aim of creating a safe context for open communication and to keep in perspective the significant role of faculty modeling open and direct communication.

COURSE SYLLABUS, CLASSROOM GUIDELINES, AND
OUTLINE CONSIDERATIONS

Diversity teaching involves students beginning to make connections between individual, psychological experience and the sociopolitical context in which it occurs. The individualistic orientation of dominant American culture tends toward a proclivity to exclude the role of historical and sociopolitical factors in individual choice. A key consideration for faculty in course outline organization regards how they want to structure the flow of content. Beginning with a focus on individual behavior and experience with racism and with difference can be a way to utilize a gradual introduction to the institutional nature of racism and oppression. We tend to think in terms of "stories," and such a segue might work best with classes where there is little familiarity or experience with diversity. On the other hand, beginning a course with a focus on the institutionalized nature of racism and oppression has the benefit of framing individual experience, from the beginning in the context of history and sociopolitical dynamics. All of this content is needed at some point in diversity teaching; how the flow gets determined should reflect program goals, faculty evaluation of student level of awareness, and student learning needs. It is critical for educators to think through every step of the course, why they are including particular elements, and about their strategic placement in the semester. A strong emphasis on implications for practice is highly recommended, however, because this allows students time to explore the implementation of these concepts into their practice.

CLASSROOM PROCESS

Garcia and Melendez (1997) suggest that initial classroom activities need to focus on building classroom community and climate setting. The classroom must be a welcoming environment in order for students to be willing to take the risks that this kind of learning requires. We suggest beginning with the establishment of classroom interaction and safety guidelines that will help frame communications throughout the course. Whether the guidelines are presented by the instructor and adapted by the class, or created entirely by the students themselves, it is critical to create them as early as possible in the classroom process. The establishment of clear guidelines is well worth the time investment that they require at the start of the class because they provide a needed anchor when classroom conflict arises. We provide a detailed discussion of some guidelines to consider in the "Foundational Activities" section of this chapter.

Presenting basic assumptions in regard to learning about diversity is one way to help contextualize what will happen in the classroom and help to create a healthy learning environment. For example, faculty can make a point to acknowledge that it is assumed that all people, regardless of social/racial identity, have the capacity for being wonderful, smart, cooperative, creative, wise, and resilient and have the capacity for self-renewal. This assumption could of course also be used as a starting point of discussion. Do all students agree? We can also acknowledge the assumption that we all have capacity to be vulnerable and fallible.[1] It is helpful for faculty to keep in mind that students will be more willing to take in new information, particularly provocative ideas, when it is coming from a source that is trusted and is understandable to them, and when they feel respected (Sherover-Marcuse, n.d.).

It is important to let students know that they can expect to be dealt with respectfully, and that this is not the same as expecting to stay within their comfort zones. Creating a respectful environment does not mean that all students will feel comfortable or safe at all times. Indeed, the very thing that makes one student feel safe may make another student feel just the opposite. For instance, open and frank discussion may make a student of color finally feel relieved and included, while it might frighten or frustrate some White students. These dynamics are what make faculty skills in facilitation so critical to the success of this type of class. One more way that faculty can build trust in the classroom is to involve students in jointly creating a grading procedure that involves the students, of course with the caveat that faculty make the final decision on the course grade. One method is to suggest a meeting with all students individually at the end of the class during which faculty and student propose a grade, discuss it, and faculty make the final decision.

CLASSROOM ACTIVITIES

Considerations for choosing activities include creating a foundation, developing a common language within the classroom, ice breakers to get students relaxed with one another, exercises that foster development of personal awareness about identity and stereotyping, and experiential exercises that heighten awareness of power and privilege. Simulations are useful in immersing students in roles with a variety of social power positions accessible in those roles. Exercises that build skills in working with multiple levels of cli-

---

[1] This point was made in a presentation by V. Lewis at a workshop in Paulsboro, NJ, October 19, 2001.

ent systems assist students in making links between classroom learning and practice. The following sections present examples of these exercises.

Selecting Activities in Relation to Purpose

In selecting exercises for class activities, it is important to keep in mind that exercises are only vehicles in the service of attaining a certain educational goal or objective. They are not ends in themselves. Use the classroom activities to draw out discussion and insight, and watch out for pitfalls such as getting stuck in feeling that the activity itself is more important than the dialogue and learning that it is intended to create. If the class is engaging in the desired discussion and interaction before you implement a planned structured exercise, avoid feeling pressured to return to the original plan for a structured activity. Keep in mind that your goal is the learning, not the activity itself. It is also important to be cautious about thinking of exercises as a substitute for traditional teaching methods such as lectures or presentations. Some content, such as historical subject matter and theoretical frameworks, may best be delivered in a conventional lecture format. These are all decision points, based foremost on keeping a focus on classroom process. It is always helpful to explain to students the purpose of the activity and how it relates to the course goals. If the rationale for an activity is not presented, faculty will often find that students inquire about the value or purpose of a specific activity.

We present the following exercises as examples of exercises that promote group process. Many, if not all, of the exercises may be familiar to you. The following activities are suggested for use at various points in group development, such as the beginning stage of getting to know one another to the working and implementation phase where some degree of classroom safety has been established. Depending on student interaction, many of these can be used at points other than those identified below. The activities are grouped by category to make it easier for faculty to find particular kinds of activities that are appropriate for the course curriculum and for the stage of work that the class is in.

FOUNDATIONAL ACTIVITIES

Classroom Guidelines

As discussed earlier, classroom guidelines are essential building blocks for classroom process. Below are proposed guidelines that are valuable building blocks for classroom process.

1. *Try on new ideas.* Encourage students to try out new ways of thinking. This conveys to students that they can accept or reject new ideas, but that they are expected to at least make an effort in experimenting with new ways of thinking. To make this point clear, you might want to use an analogy of trying on new clothes before you buy any. Suggest when we go shopping, many of us try on our usual styles and go to our favorite stores, rarely considering new options and looks. Sometimes a friend will encourage us to try on an outfit that we would never imagine wearing. With enough prodding, we may even try it on. Sometimes it will confirm our original assessment of "This outfit is not for me!" and we put it back where we found it. Yet, when we take the risk, we just might find that we actually look terrific in something we never would have taken off the rack on our own. In this way, we ask students to "try on" new ideas in the course, especially those that they are initially the least willing to entertain.

2. *Take an and/both perspective.* Encourage students to take perspectives that allow for complicated and often conflicting perceptions of reality, rather than an either/or approach. Dichotomous thinking is reinforced in so many ways, for example in TV shows that promote polarized debate or in academic training that teaches us to find the fatal flaw in any argument in order to prove its validity (i.e., try to disprove the hypothesis in order to prove it). Diversity requires that we understand and be open to multiple realities. Two people in the seemingly same situation may have dramatically different experiences and perceptions. Both may be equally valid, or each may be flawed by distorted information. And/both thinking leads to dialogue, while either/or thinking leads to debate.

3. *Listen actively to content, meaning, and feeling levels.* Emotions run high in discussions of diversity and oppression and so it is critical that we hold back the impulse to assume we know what everyone else is thinking or is intending. Suggest to students that on a content level, we mean listening to another's words or observing their behavior without ascribing our own interpretation of meaning or intent. In addition, suggest that they explore the meaning level in relation to the multiple meanings and intentions of another person's words or actions. Finally, suggest that students tune in to the emotions that drive the behavior and words, as when we say "go for the affect" with clients. For example, a White student might say, "I'm against affirmative action" in a very strident tone (i.e., this is the

content). Some might jump to the conclusion that this means she is racist and that there is no point in engaging with her, other than to disagree with her. At the meaning level, however, it could be that she has researched the topic and fully believes this statement or that from her limited understanding of race relations and history, affirmative action seems unfair to her. The feelings that might be driving her response could be fear and insecurity, even though at the content level she sounded mad or angry. By asking questions to clarify meaning and by speaking to the feeling level, rather than directly addressing the content statement, the student will be more likely to incorporate new perspectives and information. By engaging at all levels, we can create a more open climate for exploring diverse experiences, without shutting down students who initially present ideas that on the surface appear contrary to social justice

4. *Use "I" statements.* All too often in diversity conversations, we hear people state false universals like "Everyone knows that. . ." when that viewpoint, in fact, represents the vantage point of a particular race or class. Or someone may explain behavior by saying "It's just human nature," when in fact, it is likely to be a deeply held cultural assumption. This guideline encourages students to speak for themselves, from their own experiences, in the first person. This does not mean that students can never speak from a group identity, for example if an African American student says, "as an African American, I feel . . ." However, we do suggest being cautious with overriding statements and watching out for appearing to be a spokesperson for a particular group.

5. *Challenge and disagree respectfully.* Conflict and disagreements are inevitable parts of the classroom process when discussing sensitive issues, but care must be taken that disagreements do not become personalized or digress to name calling. The humanity of the speaker must always be respected.

6. *Focus on responsibility not blame.* White students, and students with other dominant group identities, often arrive at diversity courses anticipating that they will be blamed or guilt-tripped in some way. Our approach states that although we may not be the ones who personally created these exclusionary and oppressive systems, we all have a responsibility for dismantling them. An activity to deal with this is to ask the class to raise their hands if they have ever celebrated the 4th of July. Then ask what the celebration was supposed to be about. The usual responses will include

liberty, justice, independence, freedom, and the Declaration of Independence. Students can then be asked, "As a nation, do we collectively take credit for those things even today?" "As a nation, do we still collectively benefit from those efforts?" "Yes" is always the response. We can then say, "Well, since no one in this room was alive when those things happened, we're wondering how we can take credit for these good things, yet, when the issue of slavery comes up, what we often hear is 'I wasn't alive then so you can't hold me responsible'." Our point is that as a nation, we all bear the collective responsibility of our history; we cannot claim the good parts while rejecting ownership of the bad. We all bear the impact of our nation's legacy, both positive and negative.

7. *Take risks.* Ask students to stretch their comfort zone. Suggest that it is like going into a pool. They do not need to jump off the diving board into the deep end right away, but we do ask them to put their toe in the water, get used to the water, enter at their own pace, and challenge themselves to go deeper.

8. *Practice confidentiality.* Students need to feel that they can trust the classroom process and that what they share in class will not leave the classroom, be taken out of context, or be used against them. It is important to get a verbal nod of agreement from all students to maintain confidentiality about what is discussed in the class. We encourage students to use some judgment when they talk about class activities outside of class. When they share their learning and concepts they gain from the class, they are asked not to attach names to the stories that they choose to share outside of the classroom.

9. *We are all learners; there are no experts.* This guideline reminds students that learning about diversity is an ongoing process for all of us. It is also a reminder that being a member of a social identity group does not automatically make someone an expert on that social identity. Activist and comedian Dick Gregory once said, "Being sick doesn't make you a doctor." As a target group member, we may be best able to describe what our oppression feels like, but may know little about the system that created it or how to change it. We all have much to learn.

10. *Take pleasure in enjoying the process.* The learning in this kind of course is emotionally intense but there is joy in the process of discovery, a sense of liberation gained from new understanding, and hope that comes from

knowing you are gaining allies in the struggle for justice. We must celebrate this in the classroom.

The following two activities establish a firm foundation for having a common understanding of concepts. They deal with the class developing a common language and socializing students early in the course to a process approach in the class (i.e., an understanding process).

Developing a Common Language

Developing a common language within a classroom setting is a foundational activity for any group. Because so many words in diversity discussions, including the term "diversity," mean many different things to different people, faculty and students need to dialogue about words that will be used as a common frame of reference. "PC" can be described as a disparaging term referring to political correctness, which, if it did what it intended to do, would mean "precise and clear," for the precision and clarity that is needed in conducting productive dialogue about difficult topics. Words that we suggest defining early in a course include prejudice, bigotry, stereotype, discrimination, and racism, as well as other "isms" like sexism, heterosexism, and classism. Students are likely to confuse or equate terms such as racial prejudice and racism. Getting students to understanding the critical distinction of racism as racial prejudice that is supported by institutional power and historical legacy is essential to a social justice perspective. See Chapter Two for discussion of key concepts. Also, in Chapter Sixteen we present a handout on "the Four I's of Oppression," (see page 379) which elaborate further on the concept of racism by identifying the ideological, institutional, interpersonal, and individual/internalized levels of oppression. This helps students to better comprehend the systemic nature of isms and to see the similarities between them. Often students find it useful to discuss the currently accepted terms used for different social identity groups. The goal of such a discussion is not to produce any one "right" list, but to help students better understand why words are important, how and why they have changed and will continue to change over time, and the social-political context in which groups both claim names and have names forced upon them. This contextual approach helps to develop a critical thinking skill that helps students to better assess new and unfamiliar terms.

The Understanding Process

We recommend introducing guidelines early in the course that clearly articulate expectations about communication in the course. Often communication guidelines for classroom use accommodate debate that has the goal of winning by proving your point as right and discrediting other perspectives. While this kind of confrontational approach can be appropriate in certain circumstances, diversity and social justice education require something different. In the Understanding Process (Flick, 1998), the goal of the interaction changes from that of winning to one of understanding and learning. The listener is encouraged to hear stories as true for the speaker, and avoid dismissing, minimizing, or making false parallels to one's own experience. The point is to see experiences through someone else's eyes, meaning in the context of their history and experiences, not ours. Outlining the elements of this kind of communication, and allowing students to practice it, builds the foundation for the more challenging dialogues that will likely ensue later in the course.

The following activities are clustered into suggested "functions" and include activities that are appropriate from the early stages of building community in the classroom, as well as others that are most effectively used once safety has been established. A list of simulations is provided as well as exercises directed at building practice skills with diverse populations.

ICE-BREAKERS

Ice-breakers are effective ways to get the flow of communication going between students and create a welcoming classroom atmosphere. They are "group warmers" that can be used anytime to stimulate interaction between students. The following are descriptions of a few ice-breakers that can be useful in getting students to know each other better and feel more comfortable with one another.

Personal Introductions

Ask students in the first class meeting to introduce themselves. Identify aspects that you would like them to consider such as: What experience/interest/curiosity do you bring to this class that you would like others to know about you? What do you hope to learn, apply to practice, or take away from this class? What would you like us to know about you in relation to diversity and/or social justice? You might want two students to interview each other and have one introduce the other to the class. Students will see others taking risks and receive support. This begins to set the tone in the classroom.

What's in a Name?

Students are paired off and asked to talk with one another about the story of their name, how they got their name, and how they feel about it. Very surprising information comes out regarding differences in preferences between parents, being named after relatives, or getting a name that is not liked. In addition, a wealth of diversity-related information gets shared including issues about religion, ethnicity, nationality, immigration, slavery, cultural assimilation, and gender. Loss of identity is a familiar theme whether that be the loss of one's family name and cultural origins from enslavement; immigrants having their names shortened, changed, or Anglicized; and women losing their family names via marriage. The exercise highlights the heterogeneity within groups, and the similarities that might not be visible across groups.

Find the F's

A one-sentence paragraph is distributed to the class on individual slips of multicolored paper. The content of the sentence itself is not relevant to the activity, but may be written so as to add challenge or confusion to the exercise. Students are asked to first read their own paper, and then to count the total number of occurrences of the letter F on their paper. The instructor then asks "How many have a total of 1? 2?," and so forth. Students will have a variety of responses that will invoke much laughter and confusion. Eventually, students come to realize that although they all have the same sentence on their papers, many saw different things. For example, most may not see or count the F in the word "of" in the sentence. This nonthreatening exercise promotes student understanding of how perception is subjective and how we selectively let information in and out, often out of our awareness. Chapter Sixteen includes a sample sentence to use as a handout.

The Chat Room

Two nametags are distributed to each student. Students are asked to write their name on one, and their response to a question that you present on the other. For example, the question might be, "What is one pressing question about diversity and social justice that you hope to have answered through this class?," or "What is one thing that makes talking about diversity and social justice difficult?" Faculty will need to determine what question is right for their classroom group. Students are then asked to put on the two tags and place them on nontraditional parts of their body, as opposed to the usual placement of a nametag. Students are asked to circulate in silence for 2 to 3 minutes, reading everyone else's nametags. The no-talking rule encourages students to stay focused and to carefully read the questions on the tags. When the no-talking rule is removed, students are asked to circulate and talk with each other about their response to the question. All the responses can be saved and used later in the class as needed. The goal of the activity is primarily the interactive process that gets students up, moving around, and talking with each other casually to begin to build connections with one another. The placement of the nametag allows some room for creativity and humor.

"Who Has Inspired You to Challenge Racism?"

This activity will allow students to validate their own experience and personal/professional growth in advocacy and social change efforts in presenting an opportunity to examine the variety of influences or lack of variation in their lives. Faculty may want to tell students that they can name any influence, with the exceptions of Martin Luther King, Jr., and Malcolm X, so that they work harder at seeing the wide array of inspirational sources that abound. The list of inspirations often include family members and teachers, but when well-known figures are named, they are most often African American, with Latinos, Asians, Native Americans, and Whites being few and far between. The list also tends to be mostly North American, with the occasional exception of Nelson Mandela and Gandhi. These are all learning points to be explored with the students. The lack of White antiracist role models is one of particular concern, for White students striving to find a history of resistance that they can connect to, and for students of color struggling to find allies amid oppression.

Similarities and Differences

Ask students to break into small groups and discuss a time they experienced feeling different or like an outsider at some time in their lives. Ask them to discuss the nature of the situation(s), and what about it felt uncomfortable. This will let students begin to share experiences at the feeling level, although there may be uneven parallels in their experiences. For example, a White student may talk about feeling different or teased because she had braces and a Black student may talk about the isolation of being one of a few

Black students in an otherwise all-White school. It is in the processing of the identified experiences that the different levels of individual, psychological, and systemic, institutionalized nature of the events can be explored.

PERSONAL AWARENESS, IDENTITY, AND STEREOTYPING

The purpose of these classroom exercises is to promote a deeper sense of personal awareness, increase understanding of social group identity, and explore stereotypes and assumptions. They can be used in the beginning stage of the class, as well as when the class is moving into the working phase, where greater safety has been established. Keep in mind that students are entering these classroom activities at different stages of emotional and intellectual work on diversity concerns. For some students, these activities may be old hat and for others, this may be the first time they have thought about these issues, talked about them, or talked about them in mixed settings (e.g., a Latino talking about Latino concerns with a non-Latino group).

Identity Circles—Basic Identity: Part 1

This activity allows students to begin to identify the different complex elements of their identities. A worksheet is distributed that has a drawing of one circle in the center, surrounded my multiple other circles, connected by spokes to the center circle. Students write their name in the center circle, and then respond to the question "Who Am I?" by filling in the other circles with other identities that they consider to be important to their sense of self. They should be specific, for example, writing the word "woman" in a circle, not the word "gender." After completing their worksheets, they break into pairs to share their profiles and discuss targeted questions, such as "Which identity feels primary to you in most settings, and why?" Differences in experiences relative to race, gender, and other social identities will surface, with dominant group identities often not even included in any circles, and target group identities being primary. This provides a good introductory discussion about the invisibility of privilege and dominant group identity. "Identity Circles—Power and Privilege: Part 2" later in the chapter explores the concept of privilege in more depth.

Stand-Ups

The stand-up exercise takes a quick reading on the "diversity pulse" of the classroom. In this activity, the instructor calls out a variety of identities and experiences, one by one, and students stand when that identity applies to them. For example, when asking "Stand up if you are a woman" in a social work class, most of the students will likely rise to their feet. Similarly, asking "Stand up if you are a man" will highlight the low representation of men in the profession. Questions asked should include other aspects, such as "Who likes country music?," "Who likes to roller blade?," "Who has a body piercing?," so that students can see their points of connection and disconnection beyond social identity group. When you orient the questions to your region and classroom profile, students are likely to find out that they have things in common with other class members that they never anticipated.

The Multicultural Profile

This worksheet activity allows students to chart the degree of multicultural contact they have had, and continue to have, in their lives. Along the top of the page are listed a variety of identity groups, such as men, women, White, African American, Latino, Asian, Native American, Arab, gay, and lesbian. In a vertical column on the left-hand side of the page are a series of life experiences such as "My elementary school was . . .", "My neighborhood growing up was . . .", "My neighborhood now is . . .", "My doctor is. . .", "My boss is . . .", "My closest friends are . . .", "Where I spend my social time is . . .", etc.. Students then check off the boxes of the people who are the predominant group in that aspect of their life. This creates a kind of snapshot of the diversity in one's life. The goal is for students to begin to see the nature and degree of the contact they have with people different from themselves.

Race-Based Experiences Growing Up

Students complete a questionnaire that faculty develop. The items inquire about a variety of questions about one's early racial experiences and understanding of one's own racial group. To debrief, students first meet in same-race pairs, and then meet with a pair of a different race to compare and contrast experiences and awareness.

Diversity Dialogues—Concentric Circles

This activity helps students to engage in a series of "unfinished conversations" about diversity and social justice related to differences with students in the class. In brief, the activity involves forming the class into two concentric circles with their chairs facing each other. With a class of 20 students, both the inner and outer circles will have 10 seats, forming 10 partners. The instructor begins by reading a statement such as "Tell your partner one thing you value or appreciate about your own racial, cultural, or religious heritage." Partners are given a brief time of 2 to 3 minutes to talk with one another. When students finish, faculty instructs one of the circles to stand up and move to the seat to their left, thereby giving each person a new partner. The teacher then reads a new question, and the new partners engage in dialogue. The process continues through 8 to 10 questions. At the end of the activity, one large circle is formed and the exercise is debriefed in the large group. The primary value is one of process. That is, the objective is experience with the process of engagement and practice of discussing sensitive topics, rather than the content of the questions and where the dyad discussion goes.

Wall of Shame

This is a powerful and sensitive stereotyping activity and should be used selectively and with great caution. Professors are advised to think carefully about the constellation of students in the class and whether this activity would be appropriate for that particular group. Flip-chart paper is hung around the room, each piece with a different social identity group written on it such as "Blacks," "Latinos," "Arabs," "Gays," and "Whites." Select social groups that are most relevant for the group. Students are each given a marker and asked to travel to each chart, writing down one or two stereotypes they have heard about that group. It is very important to stress that what they write is only what they have heard, what they know is circulating in the broader society, not what they actually believe. After everyone has completed this task, they are asked to take a "gallery walk" to review all that has been written. This is an extremely painful part of the activity, as the negativity listed can be overwhelming. The debriefing must be done with skill and sensitivity, and must allow members of each category to respond and speak to the stereotypes on the Wall of Shame. It is also critical for the instructor to be able to deconstruct and address the great majority of the stereotypes listed so that students do not leave with stereotypes reinforced, rather than challenged. This involves identifying the value assumptions underlying these images and the context in which these stereotypes have developed. An aim of this activity is to demonstrate how pervasive stereotypes are in our society, how easily they can be recalled, and the potentially devastating influence on our lives.

Labeling

This popular group dynamics activity explores how easily people get type-cast because of roles and stereotypes that are placed upon them. Six to seven volunteers sit in a circle in the center of the room. Their job is to pretend that they are a community planning committee with a particular task to do, such as planning a multicultural event for their town. Once the volunteers are seated, the instructor gives each person a headband to wear, which they cannot see and which has a word written on it that describes how their peers perceive them. The headbands might say things like "Leader," "Troublemaker," "Slacker," or "Ignore Me." Classroom observers are assigned to each volunteer to observe their reactions and behaviors as the activity progresses. The volunteers are instructed to engage in their task-oriented discussion. As the process evolves, the volunteers generally begin to perform according to how other people treat them, rising and falling to the negative expectations placed upon them. Ask the assigned observers to remark on questions such as "What did you see?," "What do you imagine the person experienced?" This activity can be used to emphasize how the headband identity represents behavior that can be dealt with directly, rather than allowing the behavior to become a source of a social identity.

Rhyming Words

This brief activity can be used at any appropriate time. The instructor tells the class that she will say a word, and then asks the class to repeat the word loudly with her eight times. Then she will ask the group a question, and they should respond immediately, just calling out their answer. The first word is "shop." The class yells "Shop, shop, shop, (eight times) . . ." and then the teacher quickly asks, "What do you do at a green light?" The majority of the class is likely to scream out "Stop!" At which point, the instructor points out "What? Stop at a green light?" Amid lots of laughter, the teacher does this routine with several more words, some involving rhyming and others that provoke other associations. Other examples to use include (a) Roast; "What do you put in a toaster? (Bread, not toast.), (b) Folk; "What do you call the white of an egg?" (Egg white or albumen, not yolk.), and (c) White; "What do cows drink?" (Water, not milk.). The learning point is how quickly we can fall into programmed responses, even when we are paying full attention. If this can happen so quickly and easily in a classroom exercise, what can that teach us about how deeply imbedded our responses are likely to be from a lifetime of repeated stereotypes. It is by slowing down the process that we can begin to break its hold on us.

Birthing: Fantasy Exercise About a Low-Income Child

This exercise allows students to explore stereotypes. Explain to students that you will be describing an imaging activity and that they need to sit comfortably and close their eyes. Explain that you will be describing some scenes where they need to attend to the images that come to mind for them. Describe to the class: You are a child in a low-income neighborhood, around age 9 to 11.

- You wake up on a school day. Are you alone? If not, who is in your room? Who else is in the house? How comfortable is the house in terms of temperature? Is it too hot? Too cold?

- You go to the kitchen to get breakfast. What does the kitchen look like? What food do you eat? What is breakfast like? Is it hot or cold food?

- You step out your front door. What do you see? What does the neighborhood look like?

- Is the school close to home? How do you get to school? Does anyone accompany you to school? To a bus?

- You arrive at school. What are the buildings like? The school grounds?

- You get to the classroom. What does the classroom look like? Big? Small? Colorful? What do you see? A nice place to spend your days?

- The teacher is in the room. What is your interaction with him or her? What does he or she look like?

- What are the race and gender of the child you pictured?

The exercise will generate some impressions about specific stereotypes. Ask students to share what they saw, felt, and were surprised by. What stereotypes were present? Do students have any impressions about implications for practice?

Group-Specific Activities Based on Gender, Sexual Orientation, Socioeconomic Class, Physical Ability

Space does not allow us to present a comprehensive listing of specialized activities for specific group identities. However, it is essential that a wide cross-section of group activities are included. Consider modifying and adapting exercises to explore a wide range of diversities, particularly those that fit the population in your class or region.

POWER AND PRIVILEGE

Exploration of personal experience is a critical part of any social justice curriculum, but the issues of power, systems, and privilege are equally essential for they provide the context in which personal experience occurs. An understanding of power and privilege helps students to better comprehend how individualistic explanations and solutions cannot explain or solve systemic problems. A power analysis also helps to reduce personal guilt in that students recognize that they are part of a larger system.

Identity Circles—Power and Privilege: Part 2

First, draw two vertical columns on a flip-chart or chalkboard. Label the column on the left "In Groups" and the column on the right "Out Groups." You can also label them "More power" and "Less power." Brainstorm with students which social identity groups fit in each column—for example, ask the class, "In terms of race, which group has historically had more power in the United States?" Complete the chart with many different social identity groups. Then ask students to return to the Identity Circles they created earlier and look to see if they included the identities in which they are members of dominant groups, such as male, White, heterosexual, able-bodied, English as first language, Christian, middle or upper class, etc. After adding in these circles, they are asked to shade in all the circles on their worksheet that are of dominant groups. This helps to create a "power profile." Students then engage with each other about what it means to have many or only a few of their circles shaded in, and the meaning of having possibly forgotten to include those privileged identities.

Timeline of Racism and AntiRacism

This activity was developed based on the observation that students generally have a limited understanding of the complexity of the history of racism in the United States. In this activity, chart paper is horizontally placed, side-by-side, across the longest wall in your classroom, with dates written on each paper, ranging from 1450 all the way up to the current year. A line with an arrow is drawn horizontally across all the papers. Students are given two different colored markers—one to write anything they know about the history of the construction of racism in the United States (i.e., any event, policy, law, violence, etc.) and the other for them to write all they know about antiracism (i.e., any resistance and challenges to racism). Inevitably, the information that is filled in is sketchy at best. Following this activity, faculty speaks to the identified events and demonstrates how the institutionalized system of racism was structurally created and maintained over time as well as the many efforts of activists throughout history to oppose it. Because it helps to be well-grounded in U.S. history to present this activity, faculty should take the time to review historical events in preparation and develop some substantive content to present to students. A printed timeline with significant dates and events can be handed out to students at the completion of the activity.

Privilege Exercise

A large open space is required for this activity. Students stand side by side in one long straight line across the center of the room. Ask students to hold hands. As different life experiences are called out, students are instructed to take one step forward or one step back. The following, retreieved from http://www.msu.edu/~bailey22/Privilege_Exercise.htm, are some points to present:

- If the majority of your teachers have been of your own racial background, take one step forward.

- If your parents attended college, take one step forward.

- If you have been followed by store personnel because of your race, take one step back.

- If your ancestors came to this country forcibly, take one step back.

- If you were ever called names because of your race, class, ethnicity, gender, or sexual orientation, take one step back.

- If you were ever ashamed or embarrassed of your clothes, house, car, or other such things, take one step back.

- If you ever tried to change your appearance, mannerisms, or behavior to avoid being judged or ridiculed, take one step back.

- If you studied the culture of your ancestors in elementary school, take one step forward.

- If you were taken to art galleries or plays by your parents, take one step forward.

- If your family ever had to move because they could not afford the rent, take one step back.

- If you were told you were beautiful, smart, and capable by your parents, take one step forward.

- If you were ever discouraged from academics or jobs because of race, class, ethnicity, gender, or sexual orientation, take one step back.

- If you were encouraged to attend college by your parents, take one step forward.

- If your family owned the house where you grew up, take one step forward.

Eventually the power dynamics in the room become evident, with dominant group members continuing to move forward, and target groups' members continuing to move back. It is useful to start with questions that all students will move forward together on, such as "If you graduated from high school, take one step forward," starting with a sense of commonality. This dramatizes how social group identity impacts life experience, even when other things appear similar on the surface. As students move forwards and backwards, their chain of hands is broken, and the symbolic impact of that rupture is powerful. At the end of the activity, the students are told that there will be a race to the front of the room, and that may the best and most talented win. Of course, those already at the front by virtue of their privilege easily step to the finish line. This activity is a powerful way to demonstrate how power and privilege operate, and is filled with learning opportunities. For example, those at the back of the room see exactly how the system is set up, but those at the front are fairly unaware, knowing that folks are behind them, however, they need to consciously turn around to better understand what is happening and how deep the gap is.

Privilege Lists

Using the model of Peggy McIntosh's classic work on White privilege (McIntosh, 1989), in this exercise students begin to identify how privilege operates in their own lives. Several stations are created around the classroom, such as "Male," "White," Christian," "Heterosexual," "Able-Bodied," and other dominant group identities. Students are instructed to go to a station that represents them, which is provided with flip-chart paper and marker, and to dialogue with other students there about the ways that they benefit or experience access or privilege because of that identity. Ask them to write their observations on the flip-chart paper. It is helpful to have a few statements already written on the page to help students get started. For example, heterosexual privilege can include "I can hold hands with my partner in public without fear of harassment or violence" and "I can legally marry my partner."

SIMULATIONS

Simulation games are experiential activities developed in the field of intercultural relations that involve students in role-playing that tries to simulate a life experience usually related to social power differences. Simulations usually take 90 minutes to 2 hours to complete, but can often take longer. Three popular simulation activities are briefly presented here. Information on these exercises is available at the end of the chapter.

Star Power[2]

Through a trading game using poker chips, this simulation creates a three-tiered system with the Squares at the top, the Circles in the middle, and the Triangles at the bottom. The few who make it to the top tend to believe that they achieved their position through their skill at the game, when in fact, the system was rigged to help them from the start. The middle group tends to mediate between the Squares and the Triangles, aspiring to be Squares, while telling the Triangles to "remember where they came from." The largest group, the Triangles, has the lowest status and the most limited options for success. The Triangle group members respond to their situation by becoming complacent (e.g., stop playing, get bored), angry (act out), or revolting (trying to disrupt or take over the game). The dynamics are powerful and the debriefing allows for vibrant conversation about the power of oppressive systems, and what happens to good intentions in bad systems.

BaFa BaFa

This cultural simulation illustrates what happens when different cultures come into contact with one another and apply their own cultural standards to the other group's behavior. The class is divided into two equal-sized "cultures," the Alphas and the Betas, who are assigned to two separate rooms.

---

[2] BaFa BaFa and Star Power are both available from Simulations Training Systems, (800) 942-2900.

Once there, they each learn their own "culture"—one culture values interpersonal, "touchy feely" interaction, and the other culture is more task driven and characterized by distance in interpersonal interaction. Teams of "visitors" consisting of 2 to 3 students simultaneously travel to the other culture for 3 to 5 minutes, and then report back home to tell of their experiences. This process occurs several times. Visitors often offend their hosts by engaging in behavior that is fully appropriate in their own culture, but offensive in the unfamiliar culture. Once the actual simulation has ended, each group is asked to share a few words to describe the other culture, which are inevitably negative and filled with stereotypes, distortions, and misperceptions. A discussion about crosscultural communication follows. This activity is an innovative way to look at cultural clashes and the development of stereotypes.

Barnga[3]

Students are broken up into groups of 4 to 5 people each. Each group gets a deck of cards and a set of rules for playing a card game. All are under the illusion that they are getting the same rules. After reading the rules and having a practice round, the rules are taken away. The game starts with a 5-minute round of playing, conducted without talking. When time is called, those with the highest score get to move on to the next table. Of course, the next table has a different set of rules, and the conflicts begin to surface immediately. Several rounds are played, and the drama evolves as some try to learn the new rules, some try to fit in, and others try to impose their own rules. This activity can be used effectively to explore crosscultural dynamics.

SOCIAL WORK PRACTICE: SKILL-BUILDING, INTERVENTION, AND ADVOCACY

Case Studies for Micro, Mezzo, and Macro Practice

Case studies can be developed and distributed for discussion that focus on different levels of practice, including individual, family, group, organizational development, or community work. Micro-level practice can engage students in talking about impressions that they have of the clients. Do the students feel overwhelmed, or have difficulties in connecting with or relating to the client? Ask students to describe what they are feeling as they comprehend the nature and depth of the problems in living that the client system confronts. Follow with asking the student what it is that they need in order to work with

---

[3] Barnga is available from the Intercultural Press, (800) 370-2665.

that client system (S. Rose, personal communication, March 15, 2002). Although students initially want to focus on crosscultural and cross-racial practice situations, it is important to address issues that arise in clinical and community situations involving members of the same race, ethnicity, or culture. How will students of color address internalized racism with their clients of color? How will White students address racism with their White clients?

Community Guest Speakers

Community-based practitioners and activists can challenge students to apply course concepts to problems presented in agencies and communities at different levels of practice. Client presenting problems, most relevant practice approaches, viability of program focus and agency policy for client needs, and community issues can be explored in relation to course topics. For example, how should substance abuse problems in low-income, urban settings be approached? What factors need to be examined to understand and intervene with addiction of various substances?

Goals and Strategies for Interventions for Social Justice

Present the class with a real issue related to diversity that is local, national, or in some other region in the country. Organize the students into groups of 4 to 5 and assign them the role of a group that has been invited to consult on this issue. For example, the issue could be a firebombing of a synagogue, police abuse in communities of color, harassment of gay students, or racial profiling of Arab residents. Ask students to discuss how they would approach the problem. Who would they involve? What would be the goals of their intervention?

The Ideal Multicultural Agency: Guided Imagery

In this guided imagery activity, students are asked to imagine what the ideal anti-racist, multicultural agency would be like. They are asked to close their eyes and consider a variety of questions such as: Where would it be located? What would the building and the main office look like? What would you see when you walked through the building? Who would be working there? Who would the clients be? How would clients get to the agency? Where would the funding come from? What programs would it offer? What would be the role of the community in the functioning of the agency? What intervention approaches would be used (e.g., micro, mezzo, macro)? How would cultural competency and social justice goals be guaranteed and implemented?

What would be its organizational structure? How will the agency be accountable to the community it claims to serve?

Role Plays

Role plays are an excellent way to give students the opportunity to practice the application of new learning and skills in the relatively safer atmosphere of the classroom. Instructors can either create their own scenarios, or ask students to bring in current case examples from the field. The important thing in role plays is for students to actually practice speaking out loud and trying on new strategies in their own voice, rather than just discussing what they would do. Class members can then give feedback on what worked well, and what could have been done differently.

"Diversity Card" Activity—Skills for Talking With Others

An activity for practicing personal interventions involves the use of "diversity cards." On each card is written a typical statement that one might hear in the field such as "Why do we need to talk about diversity?," "I treat all my clients the same, people are people," "Affirmative action is unfair to White people," "You can't say anything any more without someone getting upset or complaining. Get a sense of humor!" Brainstorm the most frustrating comments with your students. Then have students practice using the Understanding Process (see "Foundational Activities") in talking with people who might say these kinds of things. Ask students to consider the goal of their intervention. Is it to change the person's mind? To educate them? To stop them from speaking? To preserve your own sense of integrity? The goal of the intervention will determine the most appropriate intervention strategy, and encourages students to consider the wide array of interventions that are possible.

Understanding Collusion

Collusion is any attitude or activity that supports or reinforces bias, prejudice, discrimination, isms, and oppression whether it is conscious or out of consciousness, intentional or unintentional. In this activity, students are asked to think about the many ways collusion manifests itself in our behavior, what holds us back from breaking the cycle of collusion, and how we can effectively break the cycle. Ask students to identify what they need in order to create this change. The goal of this activity is to help students to identify their own collusive patterns and to find their voice to speak out against injustice.

Guidelines for Challenging Racism

A handout called "12 Guidelines for Challenging Racism and Other Forms of Oppression" is distributed to students, along with a worksheet. Students meet in dyads to read through the handout and then identify which of the 12 guidelines they will commit to personally working on, and how they will do so. The goal is for students to identify concrete actions that they can take to challenge isms. The handout is included in Chapter Sixteen.

REFERENCES

Flick, D. (1998). *From debate to dialogue: Using the understanding process to transform our conversations.* Boulder, CO: Orchid.

Garcia, B., & Melendez, M. (1997). Concepts and methods in teaching oppression courses. *Journal of Progressive Human Services*, 8(1), 23–40.

Knowles, M. S. (1984). *The adult learner: A neglected species.* Houston, TX: Gulf.

McIntosh, P. (1989). White privilege: Unpacking the invisible knapsack. *Peace and Freedom*, July/August, 10–12

Sherover-Marcuse, R. (n.d.). *Guidelines for dealing with issues of diversity and equality.* Unpublished handout.

Chapter Thirteen
Writing the Stories of White Racism[1]

Betty Garcia and Carol Swenson

The "white racism glasses" that I've chosen to wear this year keep
falling off; maybe this is one of the devices of privilege: whites can
forget racism, people of color can't. (A white story-writer)

What is clear to me is how much more relaxed and focused I feel in
settings that are distinctly diverse. (A story-writer of color)

This chapter provides a methodology and outcomes of a joint journaling approach to faculty learning about white racism. Joint journaling is proposed as
an opportunity for faculty to explore personal, interpersonal, and sociopolitical factors in their own experiences so that they can be prepared to engage
students in this highly sensitive process. The context for the origins of this
project and the underlying concepts that framed its activities and methodology are described. Data from the journals are provided to illustrate the change
process reflected by faculty in their journals. A critique of the work is discussed as
well as suggestions for use of this approach by faculty and practitioners.

One of the enduring social issues now and into the next decade will be
White racism. We must understand the ways in which people of color are
oppressed and Whites are privileged. White social workers must take responsibility for addressing their own privilege, which both maintains and is protected by White racism. All social workers should commit themselves to
antiracist work at the clinical, agency, and societal levels. To undertake this
task, we need to examine our own attitudes and actions in relation to White
racism, as well as learn about racism at the societal and institutional levels.

Each of us, in this racist society, has a unique story of White racism. This
includes how we came to be aware of difference, our social learning about

---

[1] This article originally appeared in the *Journal of Teaching in Social Work, 6*(2), 3–17.
Reprinted with permission from Haworth Press.

negative valuations of racial difference, our adoption of stereotypes about ourselves and those who are racially different from ourselves, and the resulting way we live our lives. Hopefully, the story also includes bringing our prior thinking and actions into awareness, reassessing them and their implications. Discovering one's own story of privilege and/or oppression is an essential part of personal and societal change. This is because one of the most powerful mechanisms of racism is the "fiction of equality." This powerful thought structure denies awareness of difference, privilege, and power, mystifies oppression, and justifies "blaming the victim."

This paper presents an approach to developing the personal stories of White racism. It can be used by a faculty or agency that has made a commitment to antiracist work, by concerned individuals, or in advanced courses, especially those on diversity and oppression. It has the potential to generate new knowledge about the processes by which people internalize and confront White racism, as well as the potential to catalyze action.

We begin with a discussion of the context and ideas that generated this project. This is followed by a discussion of the methodology, which consists of journal writing in pairs. The significance that participants found in the writing project is described, and excerpts from the journals are used to illuminate various points. We conclude with a critique and suggestions for further uses of the shared journal format.

THE CONTEXT

For about seven years, the faculty of Simmons College School of Social Work were involved in various educational and consciousness-raising efforts on the subject of racism. Initially a Minority Recruitment Committee with student representation was charged with recruiting students. Then concern was extended to the quality of the experience of students of color. With the help of faculty of color, we began to see that the entire organizational culture of the college, and indeed, our participation in a racist society, needed to be examined. We institutionalized this awareness by changing the name of the committee to Committee on Recruitment and Affairs of People of Color (unwieldy though it was); by establishing an annual educational symposium on race relations, targeting the statewide social work community; and by undertaking semi-annual retreats that examined our own complicities, however unintentional, in racist outcomes. This latter ranged from examination of faculty attitudes and stereotypes; to practices of various departments in curriculum design, faculty hiring, and student evaluation; to institutional policies such as financial aid that might have inhibiting effects for students of color. The entire process had strong administrative support and participation.

We began to have some experience with relatively candid multiracial conversations about racism, and White faculty began to explore the effects of White privilege in their own lives. Reading, such as the powerful book by Kovel (1984) and articles by McIntosh (1988) and Edwards-Orr (1988), was an important element. However, the multiracial conversations, undertaken with mutual respect and shared purpose, and with some pain, became increasingly valued. We began to search for ways to extend and deepen these conversations, given the realities of faculty workload and stress.

Some faculty were accustomed to using professional journal writing as student assignments in Social Work Practice and Dynamics of Racism courses (see, for example, Ginsberg, 1985/1986; Reynolds, 1942; Sullivan & Bibus, 1990; Swenson, 1987,1988). Additionally, one of us was aware of the use of shared professional journals as a written alternative to verbal dialogue (Lothrop & Shea, 1982). The idea of a shared journal on the topic of White racism seemed compelling. It offered a realistic way to continue the benefits of the conversations, without the constraints of time and place.

We were aware of many related currents: the constructivist and narrative perspectives about clinical practice (Bruner, 1986; Dean & Fleck-Henderson, 1991; Howard, 1991; Mair, 1988; McAdams, 1985; Polkinghorne, 1988; Witkin, 1990), the concept of healing through "bearing witness" to oppression and torture (Cienfuegos & Monelli, 1983; Mollica, 1985; Morrison, 1987), and the concept of reconciliation through dialogue and repentance of wrongs (King, 1963; Wiesel, 1987). These lent support to our idea that a written dialogue was a powerful and potentially catalytic process with which to address our own experiences of White racism.

THE METHODOLOGY

We started by trying out the shared journal, or "Dialogue," ourselves, and then enlisted other interested faculty. The method is straightforward. Writing partners select each other, promise confidentiality, decide on their structure, and begin to write. The rationale for a written conversation is its suitability for busy people and that it offers a record of the process. It also slows the conversation down, which can be important when emotionally charged material is exchanged. The structure involves three decisions: (a) Will partners talk as they go along about content, or will they confine their dialogue to the writing? (b) When and how will they exchange entries? and (c) How much and in what ways do they want to focus their journal? In our experience, it does not make sense to have a prohibition about talking, but to be curious about when and why the talking occurs, and then to incorporate key ideas into the writing, so that they are remembered.

As far as logistics are concerned, it is important to be mindful, rather than haphazard. On a regular basis, preferably weekly, partners give each other the writing of the past week. We have found that giving each other an original and keeping a photocopy works well. It also preserves the work, in case one journal should get lost. It has proved important to date and number pages of each entry. Entries can be collected in a loose-leaf notebook or folder.

Each entry includes a response to the last entry of the other person, and new content. In the beginning, selecting a focus can seem perplexing. An effective starting point can be one's own history of developing awareness of difference, oppression, and privilege. Other topics may be reflections on current events or artistic productions, events in the social and professional worlds of the writers, or personal memories, dreams, or feelings. It is best to write reflectively, both critically and personally, not simply reporting or describing.

Writing that is spontaneous and informal is most valuable, as it allows the most uncensored view of personal experiencing. It is especially useful to reflect on one's own process of thinking and writing, and on the interpersonal process of writing collaboratively, as it unfolds. It is important to be attentive to the role of respondent, and to monitor whether one's own responses are experienced as helpful or unhelpful by the partner. While responses ideally will be challenging, it is counterproductive if they are experienced as judgmental or devaluing.

REFLECTION AND ACTION[2]

A review of the journals (undertaken with the writers' permissions, of course), has persuaded us of two related ideas. First, the Dialogue is an effective format for the prolonged work of confronting White racism. Secondly, we were able to become clearer that reflection and action are inseparable, and take place on three levels: the personal, the interpersonal, and the institutional. The shared journal can make a contribution in all these areas. The

---

[2] Thanks to Schon, 1983, and Fleck-Henderson, 1989, for the felicitous terms, "reflection and action."

Dialogue is an *action* (shared writing) that embodies *reflection* at the interpersonal level, and makes connections between the personal and sociopolitical domains. The "personal *is* political," especially when mediated by a relationship (see Table 1).

In the journals, the three interrelated levels were elaborated. At the personal level this included taking responsibility for self-awareness and learning about White racism. The Dialogue offered validation and stimulated new ways of thinking. Interpersonally, the journal writing allowed for clarifying meanings and expressing concerns about being misinterpreted. In this process, a mutually validated language developed. Through taking risks, and challenging, validating, and sustaining each other, a new level of relationship emerged for writing partners. This seemed particularly true when the pairs were not racially homogeneous. Finally, the journal was an opportunity to reflect about larger societal dynamics. We noted that the Dialogue often led to an increased sense of urgency about engaging in social action. Building networks emerged as an essential element of antiracist work, and the shared journal became one means of building solidarity and accountability.

These excerpts demonstrate Dialoguers' individual stories, their different levels of awareness, their perceptions of sociopolitical events, and their shared interpersonal process. These are also very different narrative styles that include various levels of self-disclosure, abstraction, impetus to social action, and reflection on the relationship itself. Some of these variations may be related to individual style; some to gender, age, and cultural differences; and some to the composition of the pairs.

The following excerpt by a White male Dialoguer demonstrates personal reflection and potential action at the socio-political level. As the latter oc-

Table 1. Reflection and Action

	Reflections	Actions
Personal	Own History and Experiences Awareness and Knowledge	Changes in
Interpersonal	Feedback to/from the Other	Shared Language, Trust, Reconciliation
Sociopolitical	Current Events and Artistic Productions	Influencing Policies in Institutions
Power and Privilege		Commitment to Social Action

curs, personal awareness and knowledge (e.g., "action") at the personal level deepens as well.

> Racism is not just in the hearts and minds of individuals. It is also in the structure and processes of the institutions within which we work and live. It is easier to see the former and perhaps even easier to understand it and respond to it. The ways that racism is a part of the institutions with which we identify is often subtle and removed from us as individuals. It is often hard to act in these contexts and thus the individual often feels powerless. It is also easier to take a higher personal moral stance and then divorce oneself from the racist implications of the behavior of one institution. I question whether that approach can honestly be held.
>
> Our College has a portion of its endowment invested in firms that do business in South Africa. This College is my institution. It is not separate from me. I contribute to it and it contributes to me both financially and in some ways is part of who I am. Even though my own personal position holds that divestment is the correct course of action and that our funds mean participation in a racist regime, I am still part of an institution that acts in contrast to those positions. I can't divorce myself from that fact. My own position is no comfort to me if I use it to deny this basic fact. I can choose not to think about it; if I do, it is painful. There is little comfort in a moral and antiracist principle if it is not implemented in action.

In reference to repeated harassment of a woman of color in a suburban community, this Dialoguer continues:

> This type of open racism provokes in me feelings of anger against the perpetrators of such deeds and sympathy for the woman as well as admiration for her courage. We have talked about this incident with our children and hopefully will find some ways of acting, at least by writing to the town paper. Our own values are awakened and there is a ready response to condemn such actions and to look to ourselves and what we can do in the town where we live.
>
> Institutional racism it seems to me is much harder for me and perhaps many people to see. But it is more pervasive and is the type

of racism that touches our lives more directly. Because it is so subtle and comes clothed in non-racist justification it's easier to accept without awareness. It is this type of racism that I fear the most because it is the kind I myself am afraid of participating in. Courses of anti-racist action are harder to find. It is easier to feel that I don't know what to do. Easier too to feel powerless to act. Easier to get caught up in the "plausibility" of the justifications.

In your log you spoke about acceptance and how so many racist actions when you were young were easier to accept because people didn't ask the right questions or see things in their true form. I think this is the underlying dynamic of institutional racism, acceptance. For me I think I will only move ahead if I make anti-racist work a priority. It has to be a major, primary goal. An essential part of my vision of how I see the world and a part of my everyday thinking and how I evaluate the things I see, encounter, and participate in.

In turn, the White female partner also writes about reflections and reminisces about taking action in her past. This excerpt describes an interpersonal process in the past, which also has some institutional qualities:

During and after adolescence I can see now that racism became central and seminal to the formation of my identity, values, and professional choice in a way I never realized until I began to think about it for this exchange. It happened that at 15 years of age or so I was a "good Christian girl," very active in my Sunday School and Youth Group in the Congregational Church in a "somewhat upper" middle class neighborhood. Our new minister was 29 years old and a socialist and most inspiring to the young people. He had a good friend who was a "colored" minister; they had gone to the seminary together. His friend had a church in one of the "colored" sections. They decided it would be nice to have a church exchange between the youth groups and our group was most enthusiastic about it.

We were then informed by the minister that the church trustees had intervened and said we could not invite the group or go to their church. I was completely shocked, though some of the group members were not, and in retrospect I realized some of their families had probably objected too. I went to talk with Rev. B. and told him I thought this was a totally un-Christian attitude and that I was shocked and disgusted. He handled it well and really agreed with me but told me he did not have the power presently to go against the committee, but hoped his ministry would eventually help to change attitudes. This was the beginning of my disillusion with organized religion and "the system" in general. It seemed the height of hypocrisy to me and I couldn't see it otherwise.

This writer goes on to say: "Within a year I had further discussions with Rev. B. regarding my own goals. I had thought I might be a missionary and had some vague notions of going to Africa to save the 'heathen' there." But she has had a moral and religious crisis: She now thinks that she may not be needed (in a religious sense), nor wanted (a moral concern about "self-determination"?) in Africa. She wonders if she "could do some good for someone closer to home and perhaps not through religion?" The Rev. B. suggested social work, "as his wife was a social worker. He said I might like to talk with her, which I would!" This Dialoguer's life course was shaped by her awareness of White racism, though it is not until she writes the journal that she fully recognizes this connection.

Journal content from a female African American Dialoguer who chose to write with a White journal partner explored various personal reflections about earlier life experiences and family values (the interpersonal action sphere). She wrote:

My parents viewed higher education as extremely important for me, although they, themselves, never attended college. My parents made financial sacrifices in order to send me to Catholic grade and high school so that I would be adequately prepared to go on to college. I have far exceeded their expectations in obtaining a masters degree and perhaps a doctorate. I hope that I will allow myself to succeed in this way and not allow all the demons that plague my soul to win out. I am black, female, from a working class background—I was not supposed to succeed in academics.

I feel that I am privileged. I know that I have worked very hard, but I also feel very strongly that, "There but for the grace of God go I." How lucky I was to be able to grow up in a time when black neighborhoods were comprised of people from a variety of socio-economic backgrounds. Maid, teacher, doctor, factory worker, lawyer lived side by side and shared values and culture. My life was shaped by all of these people. They all had something to contribute to my self-image, to my values. Although my parents were not professionals, I had professional role models. I also learned that a person could be decent and hard working even without the benefit of education.

I knew more hope than despair. There was always the possibility that I could do better than my parents and there was the support from parents and community to do better.

Her White female journal partner responds, in part:

I'm interested in your thought that, "But for the grace of God" you would be a member of the despairing black underclass—what do you think gives you the strength to excel? I'm always fascinated by what helps people overcome the constant forces of discrimination and oppression (and, as well, how you experience your "demons"—social? psychological?). Is religion a major strength, and is your family Catholic? What help or hindrance from other whites besides the Sisters? Were any of them black?

The first writer replies in some detail, and concludes:

You ask about my "demons." They are numerous. I'd like my demons to be the subject of my next journal entry.

I'm anxious to read your reaction to this and to learn how your own experiences compare with mine. Where did you get *your* strength to excel? Who were the influential people in your life? Were any of them black? Have any blacks been a hindrance to you?

Her partner writes back, at the end of a long entry on her own thoughts and values:

Will these liberal points of view sustain me if I have to compete with you for my job?

To which the African American Dialoguer responds, movingly:

> More about demons. You brought up the issue of our both coming up for tenure and what that will mean. Will I be chosen because I am black over you who are white? *My* concern is will I be chosen because I am black or will I be chosen because I have something valuable to contribute to the School. It's a question that I think is on the minds of all people of color here and in other settings. Our being black or another minority factors into every aspect of our lives—school, jobs, where we live, etc. Am I really working as a person or because I am a black person? It's a demon I and others can't shake.

This writing pair included considerable content at the personal level—both reflections and changes in awareness and knowledge. They reflected, in passages not included here, on sociopolitical events, and considered social action. What is particularly striking, however, is the courage with which they address the interpersonal level. These Dialoguers confront the predicament of competing for tenure and acknowledge their individual perspectives, in all their complexity. They accomplish the interpersonal "action" of shared language and trust in the face of institutional pressures which could pit them one against the other.

REFLECTIONS MEETING

After writing the logs for several weeks, Dialoguers were asked to reflect on their experience in a feedback meeting. This was structured with several questions: (a) What is your unique story about doing the Dialogue?; (b) What was the process like, e.g., starting, high points, low points, ending; did you also talk with your writing partner about either content or process?; (c) Do you have any suggestions for future Dialoguers?; and (d) Regarding outcomes, what did you learn? What are the personal implications of this work? Implications for the institutions in which you are embedded? Have you undertaken any new social action as a result?

Respondents' reactions to doing the Dialogue included the following:

> This has been the first opportunity in many years (about 20) to think about and work with my *personal* understanding and experience of racism. When I am teaching about racism I am so focused on the

students and their learning needs. I've particularly liked the "directed study" aspect, that is, that we were free to identify and explore current learning areas (emotional, intellectual, relationship building, etc.). (A Dialoguer of color)

It's been a way to keep me working on this issue, rather than overlooking it, which is all too easy as a white person. The biggest learning, I think, has been a stronger awareness of what privilege implies, and a corresponding awareness of what it is like to experience not only oppression but the fiction of equality. I've especially valued doing this with a person of color, which in itself seemed to convey possibility and hope about greater reconciliation. (A White Dialoguer)

The Dialoguers identified several significant issues in the shared journal:

1. There was general agreement that the commitment to a structured project was invaluable. Daily responsibilities often result in racism issues being superceded by other demands.

2. The commitment to the journal needs to be for a considerable period of time, several months at minimum.

3. It is impressive how overwhelmed and immobilized individuals can feel once they understand the scale of racism. However, the Dialogue allows participants to pace themselves to allow for emotional integration.

4. Many writers expressed satisfaction at having an opportunity to discuss previously unexplored experiences.

5. There was much agreement that the log allowed the chance to get to know a colleague in a satisfying way that is often prohibited by virtue of time schedules and demands.

6. Various writers commented that the act of writing (as opposed to verbal conversation) provided a record, and also offered a way to bring coherence to previously disconnected fragments of experience. They liked the quality of "presenting oneself to an audience" that the journal provided.

7. Some Dialoguers emphasized the importance of being able to select a partner, that this enhanced trust, but also recognized that it could work against challenging oneself most deeply, especially if the partners were racially homogeneous.

8. One pair acknowledged difficulty getting started. One member of the pair handled this by describing her own history of recognizing difference and race awareness.

9. A writing pair who meets frequently through their routine schedule found that the writing format felt unproductive and seemed artificial. They thought a scheduled conversation would be more effective for themselves.

10. One pair remarked that the trust they share allowed them to write with little self-consciousness, as in a letter to a friend, or to "use the partner to understand oneself better."

FUTURE DIRECTIONS

It is our conviction that all professionals need to continue to address their own, and their institution's, participation in a racist culture. This includes both action and reflection at the personal, interpersonal, and sociopolitical levels. The Dialogue, or shared journal, seems to hold promise for facilitating this antiracist work.

Faculties in schools of social work are a particularly important group who can make use of the shared journal. At this historical moment, there are many evidences of increased White racism in our society. Faculties need to be especially vigilant and explicit about the profession's values, and to model antiracist activism for students. Nonetheless, faculty should not ask students to do what they themselves have not done, and many faculty have not learned systematically about personal and institutional racism. The shared journal offers a means for this work.

Faculty also have the responsibility for developing curriculum that encourages students to address institutional and personal racism. The shared journal, while not without its risks, offers one means for this process. Care should be taken to think through the pairing process, and to discuss at length the mutual responsibilities of writer and reader. Because of the sensitivity of the content, the Dialogue should probably be used only with advanced students who have some prior experience with self-disclosure and more traditional journal assignments read by instructors. Additionally, an alternative assignment may need to be available for any student who feels personally unprepared to participate in a shared journal. The other complex issue to be resolved is the relationship of the instructor, as evaluator and grader, to the writing pair.

There are additional ways that the shared journal can be undertaken. Staff in agencies might use the shared journal as a means for their own professional development. Individuals who are concerned about developing greater personal awareness with White racism may find another like-minded individual to share a Dialogue. Continuing education programs can include a Dialogue workshop as part of their offerings. The journal becomes most powerful when Dialoguers are both part of one institution, whose practices can be examined critically and potentially changed. Conversely, when both Dialoguers are part of the same institution, there needs to be tolerance for staff raising questions, and an absolute commitment to confidentiality. This is necessary to ensure safety for the journal writers. Particular care is required if one of the writing partners holds significantly more organizational power than the other. If a school or an agency commits to the shared journal, any individual should be free to decline to participate in the project, or in any particular partnership.

The shared journal and reflections meeting format can be viewed as a form of "new paradigm research" (Reinharz, 1991). It offers an opportunity to develop grounded theory about the change process of confronting White racism. An analysis of the journals breaks down the traditional divisions between researcher and subject. It allows subjects to participate in the content analysis, and for information from this analysis to be channeled back into future journal work.

In conclusion, the shared journal, the Dialogue, facilitates the development of the essential qualities in acting against racism. These are self-reflection, commitment to purpose, and a willingness to take risks.

REFERENCES

Bruner, J. (1986). *Actual minds, possible worlds.* Cambridge, MA: Harvard University Press.

Cienfuegos, A., & Monelli, A. (1983). The testimony of political repression as a therapeutic instrument. *American Journal of Orthopsychiatry, 53*(1), 43–51.

Dean, R., & Fleck-Henderson, A. (1991). Teaching clinical theory and practice through a constructivist lens. Paper presented at the Annual Program Meetin of the Council on Social Work Education, New Orleans, LA.

Edwards-Orr, M. T. (1988, March). *Helping white students confront white racism.* Paper presented at the Annual Program Meeting, Council on Social Work Education, Atlanta, GA.

Fleck-Henderson, A. (1989). Personality theory and clinical social work practice. *Clinical Social Work Journal, 7*(2), 128–137.

Ginsberg, R. (1985/1986). The log: A creative and powerful teaching tool in social work education. *Social Work with Groups, 8*, 95–106.

Howard, G. (1991). Culture tales: A narrative approach to thinking, cross-cultural psychology, and psychotherapy. *American Psychologist, 46*(3), 187–197.

King, M. L. (1963). *The strength to love.* Philadelphia: Fortress Press.

Kovel, J. (1984). *White racism.* New York: Columbia University Press.

Lothrop, K., & Shea, L. (1982). Dia-Log: Journal writing as a means of supervision. Paper presented at Annual Meeting, National Council of Community Mental Health Centers, New York, NY.

McAdams, D. (1985). *Power, intimacy, and the life story: Personological inquiries into identity.* Homewood, IL: Dorsey Press.

McIntosh, P. (1988). White privilege and male privilege: A personal account. Wellesley, MA: Wellesley College Center for Research on Women.

Mair, M. (1988). Psychology as storytelling. *International Journal of Personal Construct Psychology, 1*, 125–138.

Mollica, R. (1985). Khmer widows: At highest risk. Cambodian Mental Health Conference Proceedings, Cambodian Women's Project, American Friends Service Committee, New York, NY.

Morrison, T. (1987). *Beloved.* New York: New American Library.

Polkinghorne, D. (1988). *Narrative knowing and the human sciences.* Albany, NY: SUNY Press.

Reinharz, S. (1991). The practice of qualitative research. Colloquium at Simmons College School of Social Work, Boston, MA.

Reynolds, B. (1942). *Learning and teaching in the practice of social work.* New York: Rinehart.

Schon, D. (1983). *The reflective practitioner.* New York: Basic Books.

Sullivan, M., & Bibus, A. (1990). Discovery of self: One use of logs in graduate social work education. *Journal of Teaching in Social Work, 4*(2), 145–158.

Swenson, C. (1987). Using journal writing with students. Panel presentation at the American Psychological Association, New York, NY.

Swenson, C. (1988). The professional log: Techniques for self-directed learning. *Social Casework, 69*, 307–311.

Wiesel, E. (1987). *The night trilogy: Night, dawn, the accident.* New York: Hill and Wang.

Witkin, S. (1990). The implications of social constructionism for social work education. *Journal of Teaching in Social Work, 4*(2), 37–48.

Chapter 14
Using an Interactive Website to Educate About Cultural Diversity and Societal Oppression[1]

Dorothy Van Soest, Robert Canon, and Darlene Grant

This article discusses challenges that educators face in attempting to develop culturally competent social workers who understand the dynamics of oppression and embrace a commitment to promoting social justice. An educational model is described, focusing on the use of an interactive Web forum aimed at providing a safe vehicle for student dialogue. Usage patterns of the website are summarized and data from student evaluations are analyzed. The authors provide recommendations based on evaluating the use of computer technology to meet the challenges inherent in teaching and learning processes related to combining cultural diversity and societal oppression content.

Social work educators face two critical challenges: (1) preparing students to work toward transforming "unjust and oppressive social, economic, and political institutions into just and nonoppressive alternatives" (Gil, 1998, p. 1); and (2) preparing students for competent practice in an increasingly diverse society. These challenges are inextricably connected by the reality that, while U.S. society is becoming increasingly diverse, it is also becoming increasingly inequitable (Freeman, 1999; Howard, 1992; Manoleos, 1994; McLemore & Romo, 1998). Social indicators such as higher rates of poverty for people of color and women illustrate the relationship between social injustice and diversity (McLemore & Romo, 1998).

These dual educational challenges must be faced if social workers are to play an effective role in providing culturally competent services and to fulfill the profession's social justice mission in the 21st century. Social work education has not yet embraced an explicit educational framework that combines diversity and oppression. Yet recent literature reveals that faculty are searching for and experimenting with new approaches (e.g., Garcia & Van Soest, 1997; Lewis, 1993; Millstein, 1997; Van Soest, 1994, 1996; Van Voorhis, 1998).

---

[1] Originally published in the *Journal of Social Work Education*, *36*, 463–479.

Such experiments point to an emerging knowledge base for an educational framework that includes the multiple factors involved in both promoting and valuing diversity and opposing oppression. Just as social workers are increasingly influenced by the speed and impact of technological change and are using computer technology to continue dialogue (Gibelman, 1995), social work educators can experiment with new ways to use computers to promote communication about sensitive issues related to combining cultural diversity and social justice content.

This article's purpose is (1) to describe an educational approach used in a Human Behavior and the Social Environment (HBSE) course that combines cultural diversity and social justice, and (2) to describe and evaluate an experimental use of computer technology that was an integral part of the student learning process in the course. Primary emphasis in the article will be given to discussion of an interactive Web-based forum, which was used to help students open themselves to difficult course material by providing a safe vehicle for student dialogue. Usage patterns of the website are summarized and data from student evaluations are analyzed, followed by a set of recommendations related to using computer technology to address issues of diversity and oppression. The article begins with a discussion about the tremendous educational challenges inherent in teaching diversity and social justice that prompted the authors to seek experimental ways of creating a learning environment that is safe for honest dialogue.

CHALLENGES OF TEACHING AND LEARNING ABOUT CULTURAL DIVERSITY AND SOCIETAL OPPRESSION

An educational framework with a dual focus on valuing diversity and understanding oppression requires students and faculty to engage in a demanding experience that involves both learning about diverse populations and confronting one's own personal experience related to difference and privilege within the dominant culture. Such teaching and learning, by necessity, rests on examination of the consequences of injustice and inequity. At the same time that it requires a learning focus on personal issues related to oppression, such concerns must be addressed within the context of social power. It requires exploration of one's experiences, values, and perspectives about social justice. Such exploration can threaten core belief systems and leave students feeling anxious, discouraged, and angry.

This places enormous demands on both faculty and students. Numerous opportunities for conflict arise related to diversity and social justice content (Griffin, 1997). At the intrapersonal level, conflict can arise as students are confronted with internal conflicts between their unexamined perspectives and knowledge, and experiences they encounter in class that challenge these perspectives (Tatum, 1994). Conflicts can arise at the interpersonal and intergroup levels as students encounter conflicting beliefs and experiences among themselves and with the instructor. Faculty face the sometimes daunting task of giving students opportunities to challenge ideas and behaviors without personally attacking individuals or groups within the class. For the inevitable conflicts to be productive, all participants need to have a voice, the right to express differing perspectives, and the assurance that they will be listened to and challenged respectfully (Griffin, 1997). The expression of conflicting ideas, when handled productively, can be an integral part of the learning process necessary for growth and change.

The emotions that can be evoked in students places heightened pressure and responsibility on faculty to be responsive to process issues, including students' emotional needs. When classroom discussions become heated, the pressure can be intense for professors to mobilize their best teaching skills. Even when faculty have the teaching skills to navigate through intensive class discussions and keep the focus on learning, the discomfort that they themselves may feel can lead to doubts about their own judgment. It is thus not surprising that research suggests that faculty experience discomfort, difficulties, and resistance to course content that combines cultural diversity and social justice (Ronnau, 1994; Singleton, 1994; Garcia & Van Soest, 1999).

There is evidence that students may undergo profound changes inevitably coupled with distress in classroom situations addressing diversity and oppression content (Garcia & Van Soest, 1997; Van Soest, 1994, 1996). Based on Pinderhughes (1989) premise that social workers with a positive ethnic/racial/social identity are better able to value their clients' identities, there is a struggle for students to develop a positive social identity. This struggle varies depending on the student's experiences and background related to social status and power. Students' worldviews may be challenged in the classroom, and personal turmoil and reevaluation may be required to develop a positive social identity in the context of dominant power structures (Edwards-Orr, 1988; Garcia & Van Soest, 1997). The challenges can be overwhelming and create debilitating anxiety undergirded by feelings of guilt, shame, and confusion, of which the student may or may not be aware. Without educational interventions that support students through psychological challenges, such distress may easily result in feelings of resentment, despair, and alienation.

Because response to diversity content often involves powerful emotions, students may react with wariness or defensiveness in class discussions. When students do not feel sufficiently safe to discuss their feelings and experiences openly, the learning process will be stymied. The creation of a safe, respectful, and open classroom environment is essential if students are to do the extremely difficult work of challenging the values and beliefs of the dominant culture. Knowles's (1973) concept of adult learners points to student capacity for self-direction and intensified need for learning as tremendous resources for educators to utilize. From the adult learning perspective, the instructor becomes a "helper, guide, encourager, consultant and resource" so that students can learn to formulate questions and find their own answers (Knowles, 1975, p. 34). The challenge for faculty is to trust the students and the learning process, even during those moments of strained interaction and intense conflict (Garcia & Van Soest, 1999, in press). Educators can encourage students to dialogue with each other in a respectful way through modeling, establishing clear rules for discussion, and intervening to ensure a safe environment. However, additional educational interventions may also be needed to support students through the emotional challenges that they will encounter. In the next section, an educational approach that uses several educational tools is described, followed by a focus on an experimental intervention involving the use of an interactive Web forum for student dialogue.

THE EDUCATIONAL MODEL: AN HBSE COURSE ON CULTURAL DIVERSITY AND SOCIETAL OPPRESSION

A first-year MSW course, Human Behavior and the Social Environment: Cultural Diversity, teaches about diversity and oppression related to the social work mission of promoting social and economic justice. The course is based on a perspective that views oppression in terms of social power and institutionalized patterns. The approach emphasizes the effects of privilege, socialization, and internalized values and beliefs on students' interactions with diverse others. Second, it avoids teaching from a reductionist view, which lends itself to psychologizing what is, in the authors' opinion, sociopolitical phenomena (Garcia & Van Soest, 1999).

The course examines the history, demographics, and cultures of various disenfranchised groups. It emphasizes the impact of oppression on people of culturally diverse backgrounds and orientations, including women, persons with disabilities, gay/lesbian/bisexual/transgendered persons, Mexican Americans, African Americans, Asian Americans, Native Americans, and Jewish people. The course is based on several assumptions:

- Oppression is an overarching phenomenon related to diversity, with individual manifestations within different social identity categories;

- Membership in one or more at-risk populations significantly influences an individual's life experiences, worldview, and exposure to discrimination, economic deprivation, and oppression;

- Social oppression occurs and is maintained at individual, institutional, and societal/structural levels; and

- Professional social work ethics and values demand cultural competence and culturally sensitive practice at all three of the levels.

The course includes an experiential component that involves the students in the exploration of their own culture and their views on other cultures. The experiential component is intended to help students assess awareness of their own social position in relation to power and privilege and their role as social workers in promoting social and economic justice. At the beginning of the semester, a full-day session is based on the National Coalition Building Institute's (NCBI) prejudice reduction workshop. The day is spent engaging students in a series of experiential exercises, using dyads and small groups. The focus is on students' own attitudes, feelings, and beliefs about themselves and about those who are different from themselves, with an emphasis on oppression and internalized oppression. It is recognized in this process that students have multiple social identities and that most people are both targets of oppression and agents of oppression (Bell, 1997). Social identity development theory is used early in the course as a guide to help students understand the process they may go through in redefining and refining their multiple social identities (Hardiman, 1982; Helms, 1990; Jackson, 1976; Tatum, 1992).

After presenting the conceptual framework for the course and engaging students in experiential activities to promote self-awareness and reflection, three panel presentations provide students with the opportunity to hear from members of oppressed populations: women, people with disabilities, and gay/lesbian/bisexual/transgendered people. With each panel presentation and discussion, the focus is on intragroup diversity and frameworks of oppression and empowerment. The panel members reflect the racial and ethnic diversity within that population and, through their life stories, share with students how oppression has affected their lives in diverse ways and how they became empowered through their life experiences and actions. After the three panel presentations, a class session is devoted to the issue of talking about race. *The Color of Fear* (Mun Wah, 1994), a film that shows how eight men confronted their racial and ethnic differences, illustrates the difficulty of engaging in honest dialogue about racism. This session is a prelude to the group presentations that are described below.

An attempt is made in the course structure and methodology to integrate the powerful emotional responses triggered by issues of diversity in the interest of learning and change, particularly as it involves issues of oppression and liberation (Freire, 1973). A variety of teaching methods are employed, including lectures, video and panel presentations, experiential exercises and assignments, small-group discussion, and student presentations. In the fall of 1998, an interactive Internet dialogue assignment was introduced, as described in the next section.

As an adaptation of Millstein's (1997) taping project, students conduct a taped interview of themselves at the beginning of the semester, using a list of questions as a guide. The interview provides students with an initial assessment of their own ideas and attitudes about diversity and oppression. At the end of the semester, they are asked to listen to the tape and to reflect on their responses in an essay. The value of the taping assignment is self-reflection, whereby students analyze ideas, events, and readings that were most significant to them in the course, with an ultimate outcome being an analysis of their own change and empowerment processes. While students are expected to gain insight about themselves and the change process in which they have been engaged, it is a solitary assignment without opportunity for feedback or dialogue with others.

Another process assignment involves students being given the choice of either (1) keeping a regular journal of their thoughts, feelings, personal connections, observations, and implications for them as social workers in relation to racism, sexism, ageism, heterosexism, anti-Semitism, or discrimination against people with disabilities; or (2) engaging in a dialogue with the instructor by writing their ideas, feelings, and reactions related to course content and class sessions and getting a written response from the professor on an ongoing basis. The first option facilitates self-reflection with feedback from the instructor twice during the semester when the journal is handed in. The second option facilitates self-reflection through ongoing dialogue with the instructor.

An immersion assignment enables students to experience a culture other than their own and write a paper summarizing the experience. Groups of three to four students choose one of several options, including participating in a cultural event, conducting a neighborhood visit, spending a weekend with a family (this option is done individually), conducting a grocery ethnography, viewing and discussing the Public Broadcasting Service series "Africans in America: America's Journey through Slavery," reading and discussing a novel, or viewing and discussing a movie (students are provided with a list for each population). While the assignment is labeled "immersion," it is actually a time-limited experience that provides an opportunity for brief exposure to difference. The value of the assignment—in addition to being exposed to a person, group, or culture different from one's own—lies in participating in an activity with a group, dialoguing with the other group members, and writing a paper on the group's processing of the activity that compares differing perceptions about the same event.

A group presentation assignment provides an opportunity for students to explore in depth the dimensions of oppression and resilience related to a specific population while educating their peers about oppression and social justice related to that population. Each group consists of 4 to 6 students, with each group conducting research on one of the racial/ethnic populations addressed in the course. Evaluation criteria for the group presentation include (1) a demonstration of thoroughness of the research, (2) a sensitivity to the issues facing the oppressed group, (3) an understanding of the need for critical self-examination, a commitment to social justice, and (4) an understanding of the concepts of oppression and social justice in relation to the specific population. The group presentations are powerful in revealing, through historical research, the conceptual parallels and interconnections among racism, sexism, heterosexism, and anti-Semitism, without blurring the historically situated particulars for each population (Adams & Marchesani, 1997). In addition, the value of this assignment is the opportunity to focus on one population, apply the course concepts to the history of that population, learn together as a group, and educate the rest of the class. The assignment is limited in that the group discussions are focused on one population and a task, with limited opportunity to dialogue freely about thoughts and feelings related to other aspects of the course.

Interactions with each other and with panel presenters through class participation are very important. Thus students are expected to attend all classes, participate meaningfully in class discussion and exercises, and call upon life experiences and course readings for contributions. While the creation of a supportive and trustworthy classroom environment is recognized as an essential component of the course, hesitancy on the part of some students to engage in open, honest dialogue has been apparent in the past from reports of discussions and complaints outside of the classroom and an avoidance of conflict. For some students, the expression of feelings in the classroom is frightening. A student might cry while remembering painful experiences or hearing a classmate tell a painful story. Students sometimes feel angry and deceived because they never understood oppression before. While the course assignments and classroom activities provide opportunities to process and dialogue in various limited ways, there was a need to help students vent their reactions in a more protected environment. While the journaling assignment provides an opportunity to vent to oneself, it is limited because it does not provide an opportunity to engage in dialogue with others at the same time. Therefore, an interactive Web forum was developed to provide students with an opportunity to vent their feelings and express their thoughts and, at the same time, get differing responses from other students and engage in conflict. The interactive Web forum was expected to offer additional advantages: there was no structure, so students could dialogue about whatever was on their minds; they could get online whenever they chose, without time constraints; and they had the benefit of other students' thoughts and feelings while preserving their own and others' anonymity. While it was not expected that the Web forum would necessarily allow students to process or understand oppression better than other methodologies, it was hoped that it would offer an additional mechanism for growth and change.

INTERACTIVE WEB FORUM

The interactive Web forum was developed in the fall of 1998. The objectives of participation in the Web forum assignment were to provide another opportunity for students to:

• Raise uncomfortable and challenging issues and engage in productive conflict;

- Communicate anonymously feelings that they might not be able to express in the classroom, such as confusion, anger, fear, and other discomfort;

- Express conflicting and dissenting ideas and reactions to the course content and give voice to their resistance in a protected environment without fear of negative consequences;

- Overcome the immobilization sometimes experienced in the classroom as a result of being overwhelmed by new feelings and information; and

- Address issues in more depth and continue discussion online when contact time in the classroom was insufficient.

Two additional objectives in setting up the interactive forums were (1) to provide the instructors with an ongoing source of information to help them teach to the students' current levels of awareness and information, and (2) to address any questions or areas of confusion.

Four interactive Web forums were created, one for each of the four simultaneously taught sections of the course. To access a forum, students needed to use an assigned password, while they were instructed not to reveal to anyone outside their section of the course. To ensure anonymity, students were advised to use pseudonyms instead of their real names. The only guideline for forum participation was: "This forum is for the open discussion of ideas. Challenging the views of others is appropriate and encouraged. However, all confrontation should reflect a respect for the individual expressing those views." A disclaimer statement regarding the sharing of information that the student would consider private communication with the instructor was also included in the online directions: "Material submitted to this forum is visible to all students in the class. If you need to contact the instructor concerning a private matter please use e-mail."

The interactive Web forum consisted of two simple Web pages, one with form elements for submitting comments to the forum and another with form elements to selectively query (i.e., read) those submissions. The submission page contained guidelines for participating in discussions in the forum and fields for the student's pseudonym and comment. Buttons at the bottom of the page allowed submission of comments or clearing of the form fields while links led back to that section's home page and the forum query page. The query page was very similar, containing directions for making a query of the forum, fields for pseudonym and comment, and buttons to submit the query and clear the form. Forum queries submitted with blank fields would call up all entries made to date. By using combinations of the two fields, students could search for submissions under a specific pseudonym or keywords in the comment field. In addition, there was a section for students to make announcements and a section for the instructor to make announcements.

The forum was created with a Common Gateway Interface (CGI) (www.msg.net/tutorial/cgi) development tool called Tango (http://www.pervasive.com/portals/tango.tml). CGI allows content to be returned to a user's computer screen based on input from the user.

EVALUATION OF WEB FORUM

Analysis of Usage Rates

Introduced at the beginning of the semester, a total of 629 forum entries were made for all four Web forums. The number of forum entries varied considerably by course section, with a range of 126 entries for Section IV (n=30 students; an average of 4.2 entries per student) to 227 entries for Section III (n=26; an average of 8.7 entries per student). Forum entries for all sections over the semester reveal that usage was heavier than other times throughout the course during three time periods, with heavier participation at the beginning of the semester (see Figure 1). The volume and depth of student entries witnessed during the peak periods suggest that the objectives of the interactive forum were being realized at those points, as illustrated by the following descriptions of topics and issues.

The first peak usage period coincided with the all-day NCBI prejudice reduction workshop, September 11. Forum entries indicated that students became engaged in dialogue on the Web that was deeper and more open than would usually be expected so early in a course. Entries focused with candor and honesty on issues and feelings the NCBI session raised for students. There was considerable discussion about the self-disclosure of a gay student during the session, white guilt, lack of pride in being white, and general discomfort about how to talk about difference and oppression without offending someone. Students were quite open about their struggles with such issues and about their positive and negative critiques of the NCBI format. Many students expressed that the day was a new, eye-opening experience while some expressed strong dissatisfaction. One entry indicated the student found the day offensive and another entry stated: "To all of you talking about Friday's 'love-fest,'

I for one did not feel it did anything positive to help the group as a whole. All we managed to do was draw lines in the sand." Discussion began to emerge about diversity of opinion in the class and how to dialogue about it.

The second peak usage period coincided with the panel presentation in class on women and intragroup diversity related to oppression and empowerment, October 16. The issue that received the most attention by students in all four sections of the course was related to a comment an African American woman on the panel made about her strong religious belief that males are the head of the household. There was considerable dialogue about the context in which the comment was made, confusion about how a powerful and independent woman who had faced and overcome considerable oppression could hold to such a position, issues related to feminism and sexism, and increasingly heated discussion about the role of religion in both oppression and empowerment. In one section, a male student risked telling his classmates on the Web that he agreed that the man should be the head of the household. Another male student revealed that he rated women first on their physical appearance and then could listen to what they had to say. Responses ranged from being offended to admiration for their honesty. Along with the open expression of thoughts and feelings, more discussion began to emerge at this point about how students felt about how the dialogue about differences of opinion was being handled on the Web. Students began to apologize if their entries had been offensive to others. For example, one entry stated: "You don't know how the woman on the panel meant what she said or even what it means for her

Figure 1. Number of Web Forum Entries for All Course Sections by Day

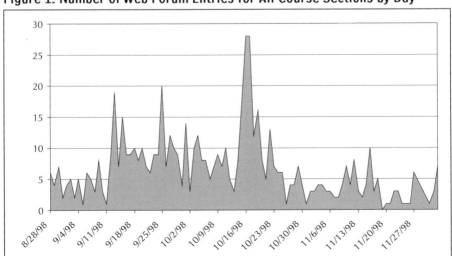

life. I'm not trying to be offensive to anyone, so I'm sorry if I did offend anyone. I must admit that I would have a hard time talking like this in class!" Other entries seemed to reflect an attempt to propose or clarify rules for forum dialogue. For example, "I prefer to discuss when my words are not distorted (in the responses to what I said)"; "we don't have to agree but we do have to respect others' opinions"; and, "wow guys, say what you mean why don't ya! I think it would be great if we could be this open in class because as professionals we are going to run into people that we work side by side with who do not view things as we do."

The heaviest usage of the Web forum occurred about the middle of the semester and coincided with two events. The first was a panel presentation on sexual orientation. The second was a session on discussing race and racism, on responses to the film *The Color of Fear* (shown in class), and student comments on the murder of Matthew Shepard, a gay student in Wyoming. Forum entries related to the film included issues about whether all whites are racist, whether racism is possible between and among minority groups, white privilege, institutionalized racism, the role of socioeconomic status, and reverse racism. Some entries revealed deeply personal responses to the issues (e.g., "I am tired of being labeled a racist simply because I am white. Every Friday I walk out of class and feel like I am a horrible person because I am white" and "I saw a lot of myself in the white male character who was racist."). Others revealed students' conceptual processes as they reflected on the course readings coupled with class experiences. For example, one student wrote, "Anyone who is feeling guilty or attacked for being white should DEFINITELY read Beverly Daniel Tatum's article 'Learning about Racism' [1992]. She highlights six stages for white racial identity development which I think accurately describe the internal soul searching process we are being asked to do in this class. . . ." This later statement was followed by a summary of how this particular student had experienced some of the stages in the course.

The second issue that evoked heavy forum activity during this time period was homosexuality. The gay/lesbian/bisexual/transgender panel presentation in class seemed to elicit different responses in the forum depending on class section. Entries from one section raised questions about why students had avoided discussing homosexual issues and fears in class. Entries from another section reflected discomfort and unfinished business related to what some considered to be inappropriate laughter in the classroom. The majority of the entries were from one class section where religion again became an issue. Entries reflected a level of honesty that was not heard by the professor in class, such as "I believe a homosexual act is wrong," "It is true that Jesus associated with prostitutes and other sinners; however, he did not condone them continuing in their sin," and long quotes from the Bible. The discussion got very heated in this section and the entries often included capital letters, akin to shouts in electronic formats. Entries in response to the Christian positions included comments such as "I hope you'll consider the societal implications of condemning their actions as sin. The violence against homosexuals BEGINS with the idea that what they're doing is wrong, immoral, sinful, etc." and "I'd like to urge EVERYONE to consult the NASW Code of Ethics and review the values we are bound to uphold as social workers—if you can't apply them to some specific population, for whatever reason, well . . . ." An increasing number of entries at this point addressed how students were dialoguing on the Web and concerns about whether the forum was truly open and anonymous. A sample of part of that dialogue included the following three entries: "Do you really think this is an open forum?...And speaking of ATTITUDES, I really don't care for yours, (pseudonym). But that's just my opinion. We are still entitled to our own opinion in this country last time I checked!"; "I skimmed through what's been happening (on the forum)...and was going to comment on people's attitude which seemed to have some attributes I appreciated and I took as loving, but it seems to have gotten a little mean.... For me, I need to be respectful"; and "Maybe what you're hearing as 'defensiveness' and 'attitude' is the pain that was described in the movie and by Dr. ___ in class."

In addition to responses to the panel presentation in class, there were forum entries in all four sections about the "gay student in Wyoming who was tied up, burned, and left to die because of his sexual orientation." Some entries addressed the connection between the murder of Matthew Shepard and "the black man in Jasper, TX, that was tied and dragged behind a vehicle because of his skin color." There was an expression of outrage and an understanding of the common experience of violence by different oppressed groups: "Why does tragedy have to occur before the general population wakes up and realizes that senseless acts of discrimination and physical violence are intolerable? And these tragic events don't even take into account the daily assaults on women!" It should be noted that throughout the semester, student entries reflected attention to current events and analysis of daily experiences within the context of the course framework.

STUDENT EVALUATIONS OF THE FORUM

At the end of the semester, students were asked to complete either an online or a hard copy evaluation about the Web forum. They were asked to select one of five possible responses to 10 items, with each response assigned the following values: 1=very much disagree, 2=disagree, 3=agree, 4=very much agree, 5=I didn't use [this feature]. In addition, three open-ended questions were asked: "What did you like about the forum?" "What did you dislike?" "In what ways did the forum help or hinder your participation in the classroom?"

Confusion regarding the online and hard copy evaluation options resulted in duplication in the evaluation database (i.e., several students reported completing both evaluation forms and using different identifiers). Consequently, 112 evaluations were completed although only 106 students took the course. Because there was no way of knowing how many of the 47 students who completed the online evaluation had also completed the hard copy, the online evaluations were discarded. A total of 65 students completed the hard copy of the evaluation form in class, for an overall response rate of 61.3%. The survey response rate across the four sections was moderate in two sections and good in two other sections: 14 (46.7%) of the 30 students enrolled in Section I completed the survey, 12 (38.7%) of the 31 students in Section II, 20 (76.9%) of the 26 students in Section III, and 19 (63%) of the 30 students enrolled in Section IV. Demographics were not included on the evaluation form so the results could not be analyzed by gender, ethnicity, age, or other variables. However, over 90% of the students in the course were white females.

Quantitative Results

As Table 1 shows, in response to the 10 items on the evaluation form, the overwhelming response was in agreement with the helpfulness, utility, and degree of comfort the Web forum provided. Over half of the 65 students were comfortable discussing sensitive issues in the classroom (67.7%) and found the forum useful for discussing sensitive issues (78.5%), particularly in areas they may have been reluctant to bring up in class (73.9%). Students overwhelmingly appreciated being able to make anonymous comments on the forum (84.7%).

Several functions of the Web forum were reported as not being helpful and, correspondingly, were also reported as not having been used. For example, 23.1% of respondents did not find the forum helpful for keeping up with announcements from the instructor, while 36.9% did not use this function; 10.8% did not find the Web forum helpful for contacting and interacting with the instructor, while 43.1% did not use this function; and 18.5% of the students did not find it helpful to use the Web forum to keep up with announcements from other class members, while 38.5% did not use this func-

Table 1. Responses to Web Forum Evaluation Form ($N=65$)

Survey Item	Very Much Disagree		Dis- agree		Agree		Very Much Agree		Did Not Use	
	n	$\%$	n	$\%$	n	$\%$	n	$\%$	n	$\%$
1. Found the course Web page helpful for keeping up with instructor announcements.	3	4.6	12	18.5	21	32.3	5	7.7	24	36.9
2. Found e-mail link on the course Web page helpful for contacting and interacting with instructor.	1	1.5	6	9.2	21	32.3	9	13.8	28	43.1
3. Found using course Web page helpful for keeping up with class member announcements.	2	3.1	10	15.4	25	38.5	3	4.6	25	38.5
4. Comfortable discussing sensitive issues in classroom.	3	4.6	18	27.7	27	41.5	17	26.2	0	0
5. Found forum area useful for discussing sensitive issues.	1	1.5	8	12.3	26	40.0	25	38.5	5	7.7
6. Felt forum area allowed me to address issues I would have been reluctant to bring up in class.	3	4.6	7	10.8	25	38.5	23	35.4	7	10.8
7. Read items in forum area.	1	1.5	5	7.7	29	44.6	25	38.5	5	7.7
8. Submitted items in forum area.	1	1.5	5	7.7	26	40.0	28	43.1	5	7.7
9. Appreciated ability to make anonymous comments in forum.	1	1.5	2	3.1	25	38.5	30	46.2	7	10.8
10. Searching forum for specific comments was helpful.	2	3.1	4	6.2	22	33.8	9	13.8	28	43.1

tion. Another function not used by 43.1% of the students was the option of searching the forum for specific comments. These results point to the need to train the students more thoroughly in the use of the technology or to emphasize the value of some of the functions.

What Students Liked About the Forum

The first open-ended question on the survey was "What did you like about the forum?" Three major themes emerged from student responses to this question: anonymity, sensitivity of the issues, and the factor of time.

Anonymity

The anonymous nature of the forum dialogue was by far the factor most liked by the students, with 35 positive comments. Many of the comments included the reasons why students liked this aspect, such as "feeling safe," "being able to say whatever [they] wanted without everyone knowing who said what," and "it's good to have a place to say things secretly if you want." Interestingly, an additional eight comments expressed concerns about whether the forum was, in fact, really anonymous. Some of those comments, for example, were: "I know the forum is supposed to be anonymous, but so far I have figured out who each person is"; "It's hard to discuss issues in detail on the Web, and then discuss them in class, because the viewpoints may be recognized from the forum, and thence the anonymity will no longer be relevant. I think there are some identities that can be picked out by various class members"; "I liked the anonymity, although after a while it was fairly obvious who was who, at least with some. I used three different aliases."

Expression of Sensitive Issues

Twenty students commented on how important it was to be able to express opinions about sensitive issues on the Web forum. Examples of comments are: "The forum provided the chance to let my voice/opinion be heard"; "I liked the fact that the discussions were open and frank"; "People raised very controversial issues that wouldn't have been brought up in class"; "I liked being able to say sensitive comments without feeling self-conscious"; "Forum provided ability to make comments that we wouldn't have made in class"; and "It was a chance for everyone to be heard."

Time Factor. Eleven comments related to how the forum provided an extended period of time for discussion. Some students felt positively about having the opportunity to continue conversations begun in class and discuss issues in more depth. Others appreciated the opportunity to continue to dialogue after they had time for reflection. One comment about time was that it was good to talk about issues outside of class because "sometimes I couldn't wait a week [for the next class session]."

What Students Disliked About the Forum

Student responses to the second open-ended question, "What did you dislike about the forum?" also clustered around three main themes: negative nature of student comments, patterns of participation, and technical issues.

Negative Nature of Student Comments

Twelve students remarked on their dislike of some of their peers' comments on the forum. The first issue that several students raised related to people being critical, judgmental, and disrespectful of each other. For example, some of the comments were: "I found the forum to be an excuse for classmates to bash one another"; "[I would like feedback from my classmates] without being condemned as narrow-minded or a racist, etc., when I'm just asking an innocent question"; "I think people are still attacked if they say something everyone doesn't agree with"; "People were being very judgmental, taking away from the growth of our learning experiences"; and "[I disliked the] arguing about each other rather than talking about information." The other type of concern expressed by a few students was a perception that some of their classmates did not seem to be engaged in critical thinking about the issues. For example: "Sometimes I wondered if people were stating their own feelings or whether they were repeating things they had been told and thought were correct," and "People seemed to read and understand what they wanted to read and understand."

Patterns of Participation

Eleven students commented that they disliked the uneven participation of students in the forum (e.g., "not everybody did it!!!," "I disliked that some people stopped using it," and "The fact that I have no time to really use it.") or that some students dominated the discussions. The latter concern was expressed by five students in comments such as: "People seemed to take over the forum," "Some personalities dominated the topics," and "It seemed that only a few people posted regularly."

Technical Issues

There were 25 student comments related to technology. The comments often addressed difficulties students had such as setting up their university student e-mail accounts so that they could access the forum, difficulty in using the forum's functions; slow download times; Internet phobia; and concern that part-time students who do not have computers at home might have difficulty getting to the computer lab to log on to the forum regularly. Some students made helpful suggestions for improving the technical functions of the forum. Several students complained that the forum entries became very long and tedious to read. Some suggested that it would be helpful if the entries could be sorted by date so that the user would not not have to scroll down from the beginning to read the current entries. Others suggested that the latest postings be the first on the page. Another technical concern was that students could only see what they wrote inside a little box; one student wrote, "It would be much better if we could see the whole text of what we write at one time in order to edit it and remember what we said in a lengthy entry." Other technical issues that students addressed related to wishing that the instructor would intervene at times as a mediator or to get students back on the subject and make more announcements on the forum.

An additional concern that merits some attention, although only four students commented about it, was that one of the class sections got "stuck" on a topic for a long period of time before moving on to another topic. Comments included: "Some subjects were beat to death, difficult to introduce new ones when a few people were hotly debating something else (oh, say, Christianity and homosexuality)"; "I didn't like the rambling about the same old things"; and "Some people kept on the same thread for too long."

INFLUENCE OF THE FORUM ON CLASS PARTICIPATION

The third open-ended question on the survey was "In what ways did the forum help or hinder your participation in the classroom?" Of the 47 students who wrote a response to this question, 25 commented that the forum helped their classroom participation, 11 felt that the forum hindered, and 11 were neutral (i.e., the forum did not help or hinder their classroom participation).

Some of the reasons students gave for the forum helping their classroom participation included: it made them feel more connected to others; it added to the discussion; it helped them understand their peers; it helped them feel supported because others in the class had the same perspective on issues; it helped the shy and more reflective students express themselves; it helped students get feedback from others in the class; it helped with processing new information and getting other perspectives; and it gave students additional ideas to discuss in class.

Students who felt that the forum hindered their classroom participation provided reasons such as: "if it was said online, I didn't want to say it in class and vice versa" and "I discussed a lot on the Web which left little for classroom discussion." Interestingly, several students commented that the forum hindered their classroom participation because they were afraid that they would reveal their anonymity on the Web. Their comments included the following:

- "I kept wondering who knew who I was on the Web? I'm a terrible liar, so I tried to avoid speaking up when it might divulge my pseudonym!"

- "You could tell from the forum what the majority of the people in class thought about a particular subject and thus how your thoughts on it would be accepted or rejected, thereby preventing some people from participating more fully."

- "My classroom participation was hindered when someone on the forum stated they knew who everyone was. . . . I didn't want my comments in class to give away my identity on the forum."

The students who felt that the forum neither helped nor hindered their classroom participation often did not provide a reason. Those who did comment mostly said that they either did not use the forum enough or they would have been comfortable speaking in class with or without the forum. Some students stopped logging onto the forum after the discussion got too intense, too focused on one issue, too dominated by only a few students, or if they did not get a response to their comments. Helpful suggestions were offered by two students: that a topic be assigned each week to be addressed on the forum and that the professor suggest a topic occasionally when students get too focused on one issue.

DISCUSSION AND RECOMMENDATIONS

The challenges to achieving multicultural competencies within the context of societal oppression are tremendous, but the authors do not believe that they are insurmountable. Computer technology has the potential to enhance student learning, particularly when sensitive issues about students' own social identities and associated positions of power and privilege are involved. It is not known whether the current experiment in the use of Web technology made a significant difference in terms of student learning when compared with a course that did not use the technology. However, student change was documented by comments such as "this course is changing my life" and "I never critically thought about these issues before and I am no longer the same person." What is clear is that the forum provides an additional strategy for educators that we believe is valuable in helping to overcome barriers to effectiveness in this critical area of social work education. Based on the experiment with this interactive Web forum, the following recommendations are offered for discussion and further exploration related to uses of this type of technology:

- Opportunities provided in a single course on cultural diversity and societal oppression are only a fraction of what there is to learn. However, student entries on the forum suggest that, for many students, the course may still be an intense and even life-altering experience. Efforts to provide various ways for students to relate their thoughts, concerns, and epiphanies are critical to the overall goals of this type of course.

- Identity management is a normative function when values and beliefs are challenged by new or controversial information purported to be the values and beliefs that someone in the profession should hold. Results of efforts to disguise identity when making comments on the Web forum, for fear that in-class identity would be compromised and challenged (or retribution meted out), suggest that students spend a lot of time concerned about how they are perceived by their instructors and peers in the profession. The instructor may use this to examine and address the perception students have of the so-called value base of social work, how these values may be counter to their own, and the process individuals go through to manage this dissonance as they continue in the profession. These fears also provide an opportunity for instructors to discuss the idea of amnesty in the cultural diversity/cultural competency learning process. A class norm might include an agreement that when students say something considered to be politically incorrect or contrary to professional values, that amnesty means there is allowance for and forgiveness of such remarks so that students can become liberated from fear of saying the wrong thing and thus become open to the process.

- Students should be encouraged to manage the myriad feelings and significant amount of information in relation to themes that arise across the span of the course. These efforts would make searching the Web forum for specific comments a more worthwhile endeavor with greater utility for attitudinal- and knowledge-based change or growth.

- To make maximum use of the Web forum as a tool, students should have thorough orientation about its many uses, as well as ongoing technical assistance and suggestions. Increased use of the Web functions that enable them to contact and interact with the instructor and to search the forum for specific comments might help students better manage their anxiety related to communicating with the instructor or peers in the class.

- The uneven patterns of participation that were evident in this experiment suggest that professors need to be consistent in motivating students to make maximum use of the dialogue opportunity on the Web throughout the semester. A tendency to stop or reduce usage of the Web forum halfway through the course could be counteracted by professors' encouragement that students explore issues more deeply as they dialogue with each other.

- Faculty using the Web forum in teaching and learning processes related to diversity and oppression content should be fairly active participants in its use themselves. Such participation might take the form of assigning students a particular question each week to dialogue about; asking students to search for a particular word (e.g., guilt, privilege, prejudice) to see how often their peers are addressing a certain concept or feeling; posting regular announcements on the forum and communicating with students that they need to be responsible for getting the information; intervening directly into the dialogue to redirect the discussion; raising a pertinent question; helping the students move on to other topics; or commenting on the dialogue process as appropriate.

- Just as guest speakers during class sessions provide students with a broader view of particular cultural groups, guest readers or respondents on the Web forum may offer students an opportunity to examine specific topics or issues anonymously.

- Additional ways to use the Web forum should be explored. For example, students could be instructed to write their individual journals as email messages to the professor, or they might carry on an ongoing dialogue with the professor via the Web.

- Professors could conduct content analysis of the student dialogue each semester to increase understanding of student processes and use that understanding to improve educational approaches.

- To increase reliability and validity of evaluating the Web forum, approaches to data collection should be developed that decrease the chance of students responding more than once to surveys. An assigned questionnaire identification number or code would be helpful in resolving this dilemma.

CONCLUSION

The challenges that educators face as we endeavor to develop culturally competent social work education for the 21st century operate within the context of a broad societal conflict over multicultural education, of which the social work profession itself is a part (Van Soest, 1995). Thus, attempts to develop culturally competent social workers who understand the dynamics of oppression and embrace a commitment to promoting social justice will involve considerable debate among competing perspectives. The use of computer technology to encourage dialogue and engagement has considerable potential. Using a Web forum to encourage dialogue among students and between students and professor can enhance the learning of both students and faculty within an environment of safety; provide feedback for professors to increase understanding of the issues with which students struggle and of learning and change processes; and generate ideas about new strategies that might increase educational effectiveness. Further experimentation and research needs to be encouraged and supported to increase our understanding of the learning and teaching processes related to curriculum about cultural diversity within the context of societal oppression.

REFERENCES

Adams, M., & Marchesani, L. (1997). Multiple issues course overview. In M. Adams, L. A. Bell, & P. Griffin (Eds.), *Teaching for diversity and social justice* (pp. 261-275). New York: Routledge.

Bell, L. A. (1997). Theoretical foundations for social justice education. In M. Adams, L. A. Bell, & P. Griffin (Eds.), *Teaching for diversity and social justice* (pp. 3-15). New York: Routledge.

Edwards-Orr, M. T. (1988, March). *Helping white students confront white racism*. Paper presented at the Annual Program Meeting of the Council on Social Work Education, Atlanta, GA.

Freeman, R. B. (1999). *The new inequality*. Boston: Beacon.

Freire, P. (1973). *Education for critical consciousness*. New York: Seabury.

Garcia, B., & Van Soest, D. (1997). Changing perceptions of diversity and oppression: MSW students discuss the effects of a required course. *Journal of Social Work Education, 33*, 119-129.

Garcia, B., & Van Soest, D. (1999). Teaching about diversity and oppression: Learning from the analysis of critical classroom events. *Journal of Teaching in Social Work, 18*(1/2), 149-167.

Garcia, B., & Van Soest, D. (1999). Facilitating learning on diversity: Challenges to the professor. *Journal of Multicultural Social Work Practice, 8*(1/2).

Gibelman, M. (1995). *What social workers do*. Washington, DC: NASW Press.

Gil, D. (1998). *Confronting injustice and oppression: Concepts and strategies for social workers*. New York: Columbia University Press.

Griffin, P. (1997). Facilitating social justice education courses. In M. Adams, L. A. Bell, & P. Griffin (Eds.), *Teaching for diversity and social justice* (pp. 279-298). New York: Routledge.

Hardiman, R. (1982). *White identity development: A process oriented model for describing the racial consciousness of white Americans*. Dissertation Abstracts International, A43/01, 104 (University Microfilms No. AAC 8210330).

Helms, J. E. (1990). *Black and white identity: Theory, research and practice*. Westport, CT: Greenwood.

Howard, G. R. (1992). Whites in multicultural education: Rethinking our role. *Phi Delta Kappan, 75*(1), 36-41.

Jackson, B. W. (1976). *The function of a black identity development theory in achieving relevance in education for black students*. Dissertation Abstracts International, A37/09, 5667 (University Microfilms No. AAC 7706381).

Knowles, M. (1973). *The adult learner: A neglected species*. Houston, TX: Gulf.

Knowles, M. (1975). *The modern practice of adult education*. New York: Cambridge, Adult Education Company.

Lewis, E. A. (1993). Continuing the legacy: On the importance of praxis in the education of social work students and teachers. In D. Schoem, L. Frankel, S. Zuniga, & E. A. Lewis (Eds.), *Multicultural teaching in the university* (pp. 26-36). Westport, CT: Praeger.

Manoleos, P. (1994). An outcome approach to assessing the cultural competence of MSW students. *Journal of Multicultural Social Work, 3*(1), 43-57.

McLemore, S. D., & Romo, H. D. (1998). *Racial and ethnic relations in America.* Boston: Allyn and Bacon.

Millstein, K. H. (1997). The taping project: A method for self-evaluation and "informed consciousness" in racism courses. *Journal of Social Work Education, 33,* 491-506.

Mun Wah, L. (1994). *The color of fear* [Film]. (Available from Stir Fry Productions, 470 Third Street, Oakland, CA 94607.)

Pinderhughes, E. (1989). *Understanding race, ethnicity, and power.* New York: Free Press.

Ronnau, J. P. (1994). Teaching cultural competence: Practical ideas for social work educators. *Journal of Multicultural Social Work, 3*(1), 29-42.

Singleton, S. M. (1994). Faculty personal comfort and the teaching of content on racial oppression. *Journal of Multicultural Social Work, 3*(1), 5-16.

Tatum, B. D. (1992). Talking about race, learning about racism: The application of racial identity development theory in the classroom. *Harvard Educational Review, 62*(1), 1-24.

Tatum, B. D. (1994). Teaching white students about racism: The search for white allies and the restoration of hope. *Teacher's College Record, 95*(4), 462-476.

Van Soest, D. (1994). Social work education for multicultural practice and social justice advocacy: A field study of how students experience the learning process. *Journal of Multicultural Social Work, 3*(1), 17-29.

Van Soest, D. (1995). Multiculturalism and social work education: The non-debate about competing perspectives. *Journal of Social Work Education, 31,* 55-66.

Van Soest, D. (1996). Impact of social work education on student attitudes and behaviors concerning oppression. *Journal of Social Work Education, 32,* 191-202.

Van Voorhis, R. M. (1998). Culturally relevant practice: A framework for teaching the psychosocial dynamics of oppression. *Journal of Social Work Education, 34,* 121-133.

Chapter Fifteen

The Use of Literary Sources in the Preparation of Clinicians for Cultural Practice[1]

Betty Garcia and Marilyn Bregoli

This chapter presents a teaching assignment intended to develop student self-awareness in relation to diversity and social justice issues. The arts, as found in literary works, provide a unique opportunity to use the imagination in the service of individuals making that difficult stretch to learn about someone from anther culture and to develop insights about one's own culture and worldview. The purpose of the assignment in this chapter is to develop student skills in use of self, empathy, and engagement with diverse others. Development of these skills is proposed to provide a foundation for coping with the distinctive type of countertransferential responses that can arise in relation to unfamiliar, diverse interactions, and the effects of social power differences in a practice relationship. The rationale for using literary resources and autobiography and memoir in particular is discussed. In order to provide contemporary resources, the listing of readings on diverse groups, including Euro-Americans and anthologies, has been updated with the publication of this text.

The preparation of clinicians for competency in multicultural practice settings places tremendous importance on the possession of basic clinical skills in use of self and on the ability to connect with diverse others through empathy and genuineness. The therapist's ability to accurately perceive and effectively act on client issues in a meaningful way requires personal adaptability, discerning judgment, and the capacity to act on one's insights. Use of self compels the therapist to have the flexibility to assume a variety of therapeutic positions (Real, 1990) to "feel free to join, support or confront" the client (Preto, 1989, p. 280). From another perspective, Carl Rogers and Virginia

---

[1] This article originally appeared in the *Journal of Teaching in Social Work, 20*(1/2), 77–102. Reprinted with permission from Haworth Press. The selected bibliography of literary sources has been updated for the current publication.

Satir suggest that being emotionally present and aware of one's own feelings are the most important key elements (Baldwin, 1987; Satir, 1987). Sensitivity and adaptability are essential for the therapist to feel himself or herself into experiences of the client and of whom the client speaks, and relationships that the client may have with others (Fleiss, cited in Scharff, 1992). This paper proposes the use of literary sources as a means to enhance skill in use of self in crosscultural settings. The conceptual framework is grounded in psychodynamic and systems concepts.

In crosscultural practice, societal projection (Pinderhughes, 1989) heightens the potential for countertransferential responses by virtue of the value-laden meanings of difference that all individuals internalize (Comas-Diaz & Jacobsen, 1991). Clinical skills can be compromised in work with diverse others, when there is a lack of awareness of how one has been affected by the internalization of dominant values, or in failure to engage in the emotional work needed to move beyond the discomfort, ambivalence, and conflicts associated with difference identified by Romney, Tatum, and Jones (1992). For clinicians, lack of insight into one's experience of difference can result in cultural destructiveness (Cross, Bazron, Dennis, & Isaacs, 1989), as for example, when the clinician negates the client's cultural or sociohistorical context. It is essential in the clinical setting to be aware of how actors, such as social power, and dominant or subordinate status (Miller, 1976), affect the experience of the clinician, the client, and the interaction between the two.

The use of literacy sources is proposed as a teaching method to enhance student self-awareness and the development of skills for practice with clients where difference and cultural issues have a role in the therapeutic process. Although a positivist orientation in professional academic programs may result in underestimation of the value of literary resources, the use of literature provides an imaginative reference point for insight building about self and others in the context of the social, cultural, and historical dynamics and augments empirically based learning (Cnaan, 1989). The use of literature as a learning approach has been used in psychotherapeutic treatment to engage individuals understanding the assorted ways in which others can respond (Bertman, 1980), promote emotional growth (Farmer, 1984; Hynes, 1980), facilitate the perception of others' behaviors more fully in context (Fuhriman, Barlow & Wanlass, 1989), manage mourning (Mahan, Schreiner, & Green, 1983), and work with children (McInnis, 1982; Pardeck & Pardeck, 1987a, 1987b). Literature has also been used in academic settings to allow individuals to feel more intensely (Link & Sullivan, 1989), increase understanding of social, cultural, and psychological phenomenon, expand communication skills (Cnaan, 1989), and facilitate dealing with one's ethnic identity (Baber, 1992).

This paper will address four areas: (a) concepts and outcome considerations regarding crosscultural competencies among students pre- paring for clinical practice, (b) use of self, (c) academic and clinical applications of concepts, and (d) proposal for a course assignment and identification of supportive references. Fictional and non-fictional literary references that represent a range of ethnicities and diversities will be presented. This article is written from the perspective that authentic learning about diversity issues must deal with the meaning of difference and the effects of differential social power on interpersonal interaction.

MULTICULTURAL COMPETENCIES

Preparation of practitioners for work with diverse populations requires engaging students in intellectual and emotional inquiry into their own socialization experiences, their own value differences, and their internalization of mainstream values. The inquiry needs to delve into the invisibility, marginality, and devaluation of difference. In addition, the practitioner needs to have a global perspective that incorporates dynamics as demonstrated through societal patterns (i.e., effects of high and low social power). Another aspect of this process is the need to behold one's personal encounters of having felt marginalized and as an outsider. Specific teaching strategies that are particularly effective with this content engage the student in experiential activities as a way to access and explore values (Chau, 1990; Garcia & Melendez, 1997). These teaching methods should also provide distinct models of crosscultural practice (Garland & Escobar, 1988) and facilitate students taking ownership of personal biases and development of critical thinking skills (Latting, 1990). Outcomes for crosscultural proficiency have been identified in relation to the profile of the clinician which suggests that the clinician should be characterized by having professional relationships across cultures (Manoleas, 1994), abilities to inquire about a client's culture while maintaining clarity regarding boundaries, and accurately interpret a person's nonverbal communication (Wilson & Green, 1983). Such awareness is characterized by sensitivity to culturally relative views, as for example, about what to disclose to whom, under what conditions. Ronnau (1994) suggests that this profile should include commitment, awareness of self and of the meaning of difference, curiosity and knowledge seeking about a client's background, as well as an ability to adapt his or her practice behaviors to the new knowledge.

Skills in working with ethnic minorities require having abilities to conduct adequate assessments that deal with psychosocial factors such as life course changes, tasks of adaptation to the dominant culture (Chau, 1992), and family information regarding, for example, reasons for immigrating, length in the United States and effects of crises (Congress, 1994). Ethnic racial differences introduce unique dynamics that intensify the need for the clinician to communicate goodwill, extend help that is meaningful, and have expertise in the areas in which he or she provides services (Proctor & Davis, 1994). In other words, a clinician can benefit by understanding the significance of effectively communicating one's intentions to be helpful as early as possible in the working relationship. Although much attention is placed on the importance in crosscultural work in understanding the ethnic experience, McGoldrick, Pearce, and Giordano (1982) suggest that it is essential that Euro-Americans understand their own experience and that of other Euro-Americans, as a basis for understanding ethnic minorities. Preli and Bernard (1993) suggest that the absence of this type of self understanding can result in personal discomfort interpreted as a failing in relating to ethnic minorities.

Manoleas (1994) proposes clear objectives regarding foundation knowledge, skills, and values for crosscultural practice. He proposes that practitioners should know about how culture affects development and social roles, life tasks, cultural care-giving patterns, patterns of interdependency, mutuality, and accountability, and how it shapes non-European ways of relating to nature. Manoleas goes on to suggest that clinicians must be able to assess health, as well as disorder within a context of cultural relativity, address the individual's and family worldview, and discern similarities and differences between one's own and others' cultures.

USE OF SELF IN CROSSCULTURAL PRACTICE

A clinicians' ability to use his or her personal experience as a basis to fathom the experience of the client and to employ that understanding in the service of healing is a fundamental underpinning of the therapeutic process. Discussion on use of self within family therapy has raised some significant issues stemming from its systems perspective that are relevant to diversity in individual clinical work. For example, Real (1990) promotes a use of self based on constructivist concepts that emphasize a relational perspective and assume "active participation within rather than upon a system " (p. 255). Also, Duhl (1987) points out that there is a major division in the training of family therapists regarding the best means for developing such relational skills between a focus on technical and behavioral skills, as opposed to an emphasis on the personal integration of the clinician. Duhl proposes a Person-Practice model that incorporates a synthesis of the two as a means of supporting the development of self-knowledge and clinical skill. Diversity in the clinical interaction invites us to broaden the range of significant life events to include the experiences of social power and social identity that related to social class, ethnicity, and culture. The therapist–client ethnic profile has immense bearing on how these powerful forces exhibit themselves in the clinical interaction and in the development of the therapeutic relationship. A systemic perspective leads us to examine individual behavior in relation to those systems in which an individual participates and is affected by, such as family, social support, and reference groups. Transference and countertransference concepts assist us in understanding the significance of critical events in the emotional life of the client and how to work with these toward their resolution. The aware clinician is prepared to address dynamics that derive both from the social power differences between the client and the therapist, and the variety of profiles between the two (e.g., Euro-American clinician with client of color, versus clinician of color and Euro-American client).

Most relevant in the exchange between therapist and client is the significance that each attributes to their social identity. What is it? What are the various reference groups with which they identify? Where is each in the process of understanding and interpreting internalized negative stereotypes? The clinician needs to be aware and knowledgeable of the processes related to social identity development, as well as have some understanding of his or her own process and of his or her client's process. Specifically this implies having some insight into the psychological and interpersonal consequences of negative stereotypes. There is a need for more knowledge regarding how to move individuals into bringing these dynamics into awareness and about what experiences move individuals to work at more enlightened levels with these issues.

UTILIZATION OF LITERARY SOURCES FOR DEVELOPING CROSSCULTURAL COMPETENCIES

The use of literature to foster the development of insight into personal problems and to assist with interpersonal relationships was initially proposed by Shrodes (1949) and later promoted by Karl and William Menninger (Hernstein cited in Pardeck, 1991a). The strategy of using books as a therapeutic tool for change has been known by numerous names that include bibliotherapy, bibliocounseling, and literatherapy (Pardeck, 1991b). Fuhriman, Barlow, and Wanlass (1989) draw on Bruner's (1973) distinction regarding two modes of learning as "narrative intuitive and logical scientific" to point out that narrative uses the imagination and deals with meaning. One advantage of employing fictional characters for purposes of emotional reflection is that it allows exploration of intellectual and emotional curiosity under conditions that are less anxiety arousing (Grootof, 1969) than direct personal experience.

While there is a very broad range of usage of literature in treatment, the application proposed in this article is closest to what Pardeck (1991b) identifies as "bibliotherapy through fiction" where the reading is selected on the basis of a problem area with which the reader can grasp, and identify with the responses (p. 111). Although this method is intended for clients to identify with problems similar to their own, the usage in the classroom is intended for the explicit purpose of the student identifying with an individual who is different from self. The methodology engages the client in a stage-like process that begins with identification, moves through catharsis, and results in insight building (Shrodes, 1949). This approach has enjoyed considerable use by counselors, psychologists, and psychiatrists (Starker, 1986), and has also been applied to cinema (Berg-Cross, Jennings, & Baruch, 1990). For example, the film *The Joy Luck Club* is superb for exploring concerns related to gender, intergenerational issues, and psychological conflict.

The use of literature for purposes of personal growth and self-awareness is a longstanding tradition both in the classroom and in psychotherapy. The following will review the concept and its application in treatment and as a vehicle for developing and enhancing practice skills.

PRACTICE IMPLICATIONS

The use of literature in psychotherapy illuminates the benefits derived from its application to growth promoting activities. Literary sources have been used in therapy to diagnose (Shrodes, 1949), and have been applied to a variety of problems such as emotional difficulties, phobias, marital relations, behavioral change, and coping-oriented goals such as assertiveness and academic achievement (Pardeck & Pardeck, 1984). Although there is insufficient empirical investigation of its effectiveness (Fuhriman et al., 1989; Gold & Gloade, 1988; Pardeck, 1991b). Cohen (1994) suggests that the healing functions in this method are derived from dynamics identified by Shrodes (1949) and those found in group work (Yalom, 1985). For example, a client or therapist may participate in the telling of a story and making connections between events (Ganzer, 1994). Cohen's (1994) study on the value provided by literature in treatment concluded that gains derived from this method include (a) recognition of self, (b) affective ways of knowing: shared experience, validation, comfort, hope and inspiration, and (c) ways of knowing: understanding and information gathering.

Just as literary sources can be employed in psychotherapy to develop personal insight for the purpose of bridging differences, they can also be utilized for academic learning. Several aspects of their effectiveness in psychotherapy illuminate their possible use in learning activities. For example, in treatment, literature can be used to develop insight into family conflicts, normalize personal experience, focus reflections, and facilitate the integration of experience. The use of literature can also assist families in dealing with life transitions (e.g., adult children leaving home, intergenerational conflict). Such usage allows the family members to focus on sharing perceptions of the characters' personalities, behavior, motives, as a springboard for talking on a personal level about issues relevant to their own family life. Likewise, parents can be encouraged to read about experiences of parental loss and coping in relation to children's departure from home as a basis to discuss their own experience, and begin to construct their own story of this major life transition. These insight-facilitating activities that engage the student in emotional and cognitive learning have direct relevance to the purpose of learning about diversity for practitioners.

CLASSROOM APPLICATION

The emotionally laden content in crosscultural learning has resulted in the use of experiential activities as the preferred medium for learning activities in the classroom. The experiential focus facilitates normalizing difficult content, and supports processing sensitive issues (Garcia & Melendez, 1997; Nash, 1993). Maintaining a focus on the student's experience is an effective means of involving him or her in the preliminary task of clarifying their own social identity. Closely related are several structured, cognitively oriented activities that focus the student in reflecting on their own and others' experience as a means to make the leap of connecting with diverse others. Some of these methods include the use of vignettes (Montalvo, Lasater, & Valdez, 1982), joint journaling (Garcia & Swensen, 1992), using literature as a means for engagement in social action (K. Hooper-Briar, personal communication, March 18, 1996), and ethnographic research (Thornton & Garrett, 1995).

The use of literature has the advantage of utilizing narrative sources for preparing clinicians for working with difference by highlighting "the contextual structure of everyday life," meaning, and engaging the reader in "coherent sequences" related to "structure, purpose and direction" (Holland & Kilpatrick, 1993, pp. 302–308). In addition, literature has been used as the basis to explore family systems (Khatri, 1980) and family metaphors (Bibus, 1992).

Pardeck and Pardeck's (1984) suggestions for creative writing applications of this method are extremely relevant to the task of engaging with someone different from self. Pardeck and Pardeck suggest a series of activities that include making a daily schedule or time line for the central character and comparing it to one's own, composing a diary for the main character, and writing a letter from one character to another or from oneself to a character. Also, the Freirian approach of presenting ideas and feelings through the use of a variety of art mediums in a group context such as collage, drawing, or resolution of a puzzle facilitates increased understanding of experiences with difference.

COURSE ASSIGNMENT

A course assignment is proposed that requires students to read a book about someone whose ethnicity and life is significantly different from their own in terms of values and lifestyle, and preferably represents a group with which they have not had direct contact. The purpose of the assignment was to assist students in making the leap that is needed as the basis of empathy and identification with others, particularly those different from oneself. An expectation was to utilize "another's story," and the gap between the "other's story" and "student's story" as a means for the student to view themselves from a different perspective. Also, the assignment was developed in the spirit of fostering the type of reflection found in Smith's (1961) reminiscence about becoming aware of injustice. She reflects on knowing that doors were closed to her, not knowing whether she closed them or "perhaps they were closed for me," and, unknown to her as to how it happened, "that the doors opened" (p. 29). She eloquently acknowledges that however we may shut ourselves off, there will be moments when we find ourselves unexpectedly open to new ways of experiencing ourselves and others.

The following assignment has been utilized in a first-year graduate social work program, in a course on oppression. The assignment was structured into the course as a final assignment that was to be both written and presented for discussion. Times were allocated throughout the semester for the 30-minute student presentation and discussion. Students were free to select a date of their choice. The course has three segments that address: (a) societal and institutional factors that explain oppression, (b) psychological interpersonal dimensions of oppression, and (c) social work practice implications.

Other course assignments that also encouraged the development of critical thinking and self reflection included semistructured journal entries (approximately 10–12 per semester), a self-administered survey of beliefs about racism, and a variety of experiential classroom exercises that focused on self examination of one's own cultural background and beliefs, feelings about privilege, and dealing with one's own feelings about difference. The self-reflection needed for this assignment makes it more difficult for students who are intensely ambivalent about diversity. These students can benefit from first engaging in other class assignments and exercises before presenting their work. In this assignment students are asked to do the following:

1. Describe and discuss the major themes in a book; identify the central characters and a brief narrative on the storyline.

   a. What does the author want the reader to understand about the central character's life experiences, formative influences, their worldview, and its development.

   b. What meanings has the character derived in psychological, social, and political terms?

2. Consider the unique aspects of the character's life in relation to the following concerns:

   a. What sociocultural factors, social identity, and social power issues have been influential in creating the character's "sensibility," i.e., their sense of self and their relationship to others?

   b. What have been some critical events in the character's life and how did he or she cope with them?

   c. What is your impression regarding how this person coped? What was it that led to coping in the way that he or she did (psychological, social, cultural, political)?

3. Compare and contrast the following:

    a. How does the difference between your life/worldview and the character's life/worldview sharpen your awareness about each one's unique life experiences?

    b. In what ways, if at all, does the comparison between the two help you to understand or place perspective on the other? On yourself?

4. What insights or observations did you derive for practice (i.e., skills, countertransference issues, identification of areas for future personal and professional development, working with diverse others) from having read this work?

Although the effectiveness of this assignment was not examined systematically, faculty were very impressed by the vital role of student motivation and enthusiasm for this assignment. There were a few students whose presentations, in form and content, came across more as obligatory book reports. These students appeared to have difficulty with the assignment as a result of their choice being based on cognitive factors alone (i.e., not including affective and psychological factors). These few presentations conveyed a distance between them and their topic. There were also many students, particularly of White ethnicity, who selected a reading that reflected a new or long-standing interest and challenged their perspective. These students often presented works that had unexpected and moving effects by virtue of the student's willingness to self reflect and how they articulated their learning about the "other" and themselves. We suggest that when the professor describes the assignment that he or she explicitly address this potential pitfall that ultimately becomes a lost opportunity for the student's learning. In light of the emotional and intellectual tasks involved in this type of learning, it might be better to provide options for assignments that challenge students in ways that they can respond. Faculty may want to make this assignment optional and perhaps mention a caveat that alerts students to their own "learning needs," or require that students write a brief statement on their rationale for selecting their specific reading. The provision of a bibliography for students saves them the time and effort of seeking references and equips them with a pool of relevant readings from which to select responsibly.

The development of a bibliography began as library support for this assignment and developed into a collaborative effort between a social work educator and a social work librarian. When students began working on this assignment, the library staff noticed that students were having a fair degree of difficulty in identifying appropriate materials because of the way these materials are catalogued. For that reason, the librarian began work on a bibliography of materials that would meet the requirements of the assignment.

RESOURCES FOR THE ASSIGNMENT

Autobiography is a widespread and characteristic form of American expression. Robert Sayre, in his essay *Autobiography and the Making of America* (Sayre, 1980, p. 146), makes the observation that "autobiography may be the preeminent kind of American expression, reaching back to the Puritan diaries of the 17th and 18th centuries and continuing into our own time. "Looking at our own lives and our own families, one realizes that we all have a story to tell. Fortunately, many have given us their stories through autobiography, memoir, autobiographical fiction, and even poetry. This literature can be a valuable resource for the development of multicultural understanding and insight.

The genre of autobiography crosses many literary boundaries. The scope of the project has been interpreted in the broadest sense. The focus is most closely autobiography but memoir and some fiction is included. Memoir is particularly well suited to our goals. As William Zinser (1987, p. 21) points out, "'Memoir' was defined as some portion of a life. Unlike autobiography, which moves in a dutiful line from birth to fame, omitting nothing significant, memoir assumes the life and ignores most of it . . . . Memoir is a window into life."

Fiction has been included sparingly. When one considers the matter, much quality fiction is autobiographical at some level. Some of this century's finest fictional works have strongly autobiographical elements and may in fact be autobiographical (Dillard & Conley, 1995). The sheer amount of fiction that could legitimately be included in this bibliography is overwhelming and it was felt that this would make the bibliography less valuable. Therefore only writings that could be clearly identified as autobiographical fiction, either through book reviews, library catalog subject headings, or personal knowledge of the work, are included.

The bibliography has been organized around broad ethnic groupings: African American, Asian American, European American, Hispanic American, Jewish American, and Native American. The inadequacies inherent in such broad groupings are recognized. Grouping heterogeneous groups such as Mexican Americans and Puerto Rican Americans under the umbrella of

Hispanic Americans or Irish Americans and Armenian Americans under European Americans does not take into account the very distinct historical and cultural differences that exist within each group. This is a major dilemma that consumes much contemporary dialogue and is reflected in the effort here to make headway into the pursuit of learning about others who are different from the self. It is hoped that the general usefulness of the bibliography will foster the development of greater awareness of those issues raised by various cultural groups.

Emphasis has been placed on newer, post-1960 writings, although certain 20th century classics of the genre have been included, and some older writings by underrepresented groups are included (mostly in the Native American and Asian American groupings). Historical autobiography is not included, nor is celebrity, sports, political, and business autobiographies. Although some valuable readings are excluded, we felt the unevenness in the treatment of complex life events less consistently lent itself to the tasks at hand in this assignment. The commonality among the works included in this bibliography is the telling of an individual's story in his or her culture.

Autobiography and memoir often play distinct roles in the literature of a culture or race. African American culture has a very strong tradition of autobiography from the early slave narratives and the seminal *Narrative of the Life of Frederick Douglass, An American Slave* to newer works by young writers who came of age during or after the civil rights struggles of the 50s and 60s, such as Lorene Cary's *Black Ice* or Marcus Mabry's *White Bucks and Black-Eyed Peas*. Filling the middle are powerful stories from a wide range of authors reflecting the cultural richness of the African American experience. The bibliography includes writings from diverse African Americans such as Maya Angelou's multibook autobiography beginning with *I Know Why the Caged Bird Sings;* the centenarian Delaney sisters' *Having Our Say;* the poet Langston Hughes' *The Big Sea;* and novelist John Edgar Wideman's *Brothers and Keepers*. The autobiography has been the most important literary genre in the African American intellectual tradition and autobiographical work occupies a central position in the African American literary tradition because "oftentimes personal truth was stronger than fiction" (Franklin, 1995, p. 13).

The Latino section of this bibliography represents writers of similar and at the same time diverse realities. The writer may be Cuban, Puerto Rican, Mexican, or another Latino group, each with its own traditions and cultural influences. Our writers therefore represent a wide variety of experience from

Gustavo Perez Firmat's *Next Year in Cuba: A Cubano's Coming of Age in America*, to Julia Alvarez's autobiographical novel of Dominican Americans, *How the Garcia Girls Lost Their Accents*, to Esmeralda Santiago's *When I Was Puerto Rican*. Latinos are uprooted from one culture and expected to participate fully in another, or live in both simultaneously, and the writing of memoir, narrative, or autobiographical fiction creates an opportunity to search for meaning (Augenbraum & Stavans, 1993). Latino autobiography is also influenced by the literary device "magic realism" that most readers know from the fictional works of Borges, Vargas Llosa, and Garcia Marquez. Magic realism blurs the boundaries between fact and fantasy and allows the writer to explore his or her life story more freely and intuitively, for example, Victor Villasenor's epic tale of his Mexican family's migration north, *Rain of Gold*.

Each culture has its oral tradition and it is in this tradition that autobiography has its roots. In the case of Native American autobiography, the oral tradition is far closer to the literary tradition than any of our other groupings. While there are many oral autobiographical accounts of Native Americans as told to anthropologists and other cultural researchers, it is fairly recently that we see literary autobiography from Native American writers. Writers of Native American autobiography are just two generations removed from nonliterate storytellers (Brumble, 1988). For this reason we have included several "as told to" pieces and fiction in the Native American section, as well as contemporary Native American autobiography such as N. Scott Momaday's *The Names: A Memoir* and Maurice Kenny's *On Second Thought*.

The Asian American portion of the bibliography again encompasses a wide variety of culture and experience. The majority of Asian American autobiography that is available has come to us from the Chinese Americans and Japanese Americans, including the experience of Japanese Americans interned during World War II, but the more recent Asian immigrant groups, those from India, Southeast Asia, and the Philippines, are also represented.

The European American section proved to be somewhat difficult to compile. We found this surprising given the dominance of American culture by those of European descent, but much of what can be identified as European American, being celebrity or historical autobiography, falls outside the parameters of our project. We have been able to include many interesting readings. The European American section includes writings of wide diversity from Michael Arlen's search for his Armenian heritage in *Passage to Ararat* to Carol Buckley's story of growing up Irish Catholic and privileged, *At The Still Point*, to the Italian American experience of Marie Torgovnick in *Crossing Ocean Parkway*. Accounts of lower middle class and blue-collar life are unfortunately underrepresented. One example that does stand out is Ben Hamper's story of growing up and becoming a third-generation Ford assembly line worker, *Rivethead: Tales from the Assembly Line*.

We have concluded the bibliography with a selection of anthologies. Anthologies are an excellent resource for two reasons. An anthology that includes writings from different ethnicities or cultures, such as Annie Dillard and Cort Conley's *Modern American Memoirs* or Robert Sayre's *American Lives: An Anthology of Autobiographical Writing*, can be inclusive and affirming, showing us our similarities as well as our difference. An anthology within a single culture or ethnicity such as Maria Hong's *Growing Up Asian American: An Anthology* or James M. Freeman's *Hearts of Sorrow: Vietnamese-American Lives* or Henry Louis Gates' *Bearing Witness: Selections from African American Autobiography in the Twentieth Century*, shows us the diversity and difference as well as the similarity of experience within a culture.

Anthologies also remind us of the importance of the individual in his or her culture. Cultural influences are powerful determinants of social development, but ultimately personal experience is unique and individual. While autobiographical writing offers a valuable tool for the development of multicultural awareness and understanding, it is important to recognize that the autobiographical author shares his or her singular life experience and perspective. It is perhaps the strength and power of the individual that most clearly speaks to all of us.

An underlying value of this assignment is that professional development of practitioners can be enhanced through utilization of the literature that can stimulate the imagination in ways that professional literature cannot. The proposal made here is limited by the need for additional information on its efficacy. We have presented anecdotal data; however, further information is needed based on systematic research and outcome data that can inform us about student changes in knowledge, attitudes, and values. More needs to be known regarding the nature of the change process (e.g., different meanings that the readings have for students) and its application to practice. It is essential to have more understanding regarding what doors this exercise can open, what practice experiences are made more manageable through the use of this assignment, and possibly, what other activities this assignment can motivate students to undertake.

CONCLUSION

The preparation of clinicians for work in diverse settings requires heightened awareness of the potential for countertransference posed by the presence of societal projection (Pinderhughes, 1989). Countertransferential content introduced by dominant societal values can be as difficult and possibly more difficult for the clinician to identify in comparison to direct personal experience. Nonetheless, the consequences of lack of reflection on distorted perceptions are significant and need to be addressed in order for use of self in practice to be effective.

A course assignment and suggested readings are presented that allow clinical students to explore difference in their own and others' responses in the safer confines of literature. Such activity stimulates the imagination in ways that are not possible through other more conventional academic pedagogy and also reflects the student's choice. The suggested readings for the assignment that are presented here focus primarily on ethnic diversity and socioeconomic class. However, crosscultural competencies apply to a broad spectrum of diversities that need to be more fully addressed in the future. Literature in the areas of sexual orientation, physical ability, and religious choice also need to be incorporated as resources into this type of assignment.

Further work needs to be aimed at investigating the change process that students engage in, qualities of the assignment that are the most useful, and structure that faculty can provide for the assignment. Such information can guide further development of student knowledge, values, and skills in working with diverse populations.

A SELECTED BIBLIOGRAPHY OF LITERARY RESOURCES

African American

Angelou, M. (1969). *I know why the caged bird sings*. New York: Random House.

Angelou, M. (1974). *Gather together in my name*. New York: Random House.

Angelou, M. (1976). *Singin' and swingin' and gettin' merry like Christmas*. New York: Random House.

Angelou, M. (1981). *The heart of a woman*. New York: Random House.

Angelou, M. (1986). *All God's children need traveling shoes*. New York: Random House.

Awkward, M. (2000). *Scenes of instruction: A memoir*. Durham, NC: Duke University Press.

Baldwin, J. (1963). *Go tell it on the mountain*. New York: Dial Press.

Bolton, R. (1994). *Gal: A true life*. New York: Harcourt Brace.

Brooks, S. (1987). *You may plow here: The narrative of Sara Brooks*. New York: Simon & Schuster.

Brown, C. (1965). *Manchild in the promised land*. New York: Macmillan.

Brown, E. (1992). *A taste of power: A black woman's story*. New York: Pantheon.

Brown, E. D. (2001). *Living to tell: Collected memoirs*. San Jose: Winter Club Press.

Campbell, B. (1989). *Sweet summer: Growing up with and without my dad*. New York: Putnam.

Carey, L. (1991). *Black ice*. New York: Knopf.

Datcher, M. (2001). *Raising fences: A black man's love story*. New York: Riverhead Books.

Delaney, S., & Delaney, A. (1993). *Having our say*. New York: Kodansha International.

Dickerson, D. (2001). *An American story*. New York: Pantheon Books.

Early, G. (1994). *Daughters: On family and fatherhood*. Reading, MA: Addison Wesley.

Fulwood, S. (1996). *Waking from the dream: My life in the black middle class*. New York: Anchor Books.

Gaines, P. (1994). *Laughing in the dark: From colored girl to woman of color—A journey from prison to power*. New York: Crown.

Gates, H. (1991). *Colored people: A memoir*. New York: Knopf.

Gibbs, M. (1995). *Shadow and light*. Lincoln, NE: University of Nebraska Press.

Golden, M. (1987). *Migrations of the heart*. New York: Ballantine.

Green, E. (1990). *Ely: An autobiography*. Athens, GA: University of Georgia Press.

Haley, A. (1965). *The autobiography of Malcolm X*. New York: Grove Press.

Henry, N. (2001). *Pearl's secret: A black man's search for his white family*. Berkeley, CA: University of California Press.

Hooks, B. (1986). *Bone black: Memories of girlhood*. New York: Henry Holt.

Hughes, L. (1993). *The big sea*. (2nd ed.). New York: Hill and Wang.

Hughes, L. (1993). *I wonder as I wander*. (2nd ed.). New York: Hill and Wang.

Hunter-Gault, C. (1992). *In my place*. New York: Farrar Straus Giroux.

Hurston, Z. N. (1942). *Dust tracks on the road*. New York: Harper Collins.

Jordan, J. (2000). *Soldier: A poet's childhood*. New York: Basic Civitas Books.

Lacy, L. (1974). *Native daughter*. New York: Macmillan.

Lightfoot, S. L. (1988). *Balm in Gilead*. Reading, MA: Addison Wesley.

Lyles, C. (1994). *Do I dare disturb the universe*. Boston: Faber and Faber.

Mabry, M. (1995). *White bucks and black-eyed peas*. New York: Scribner.

Majozo, E. C. (1999). *Come out of the wilderness: Memoir of a black woman artist*. New York: Feminist Press at City University of New York.

McCall, N. (1994). *Makes me want to holler*. New York: Random House.

McDonald, J. (1999). *Project girl*. Farrar, Strauss and Giroux.

Mebane, M. (1981). *Mary*. New York: Viking Press.

Mebane, M. (1983). *Mary, wayfarer: An autobiography*. New York: Viking Press.

Miller, E. (2001). *Fathering words: The making of an African-American writer*. New York: Thomas Dunne Books.

Moody, A. (1968). *Coming of age in Mississippi*. New York: Dell.

Murray, P. (1987). *Song in a weary throat: An American pilgrimage*. New York: Harper & Row.

Peery, N. (1994). *Black fire: The making of an American revolutionary*. New York: New Press.

Pemberton, G. (1993). *The hottest water in Chicago: Notes of a native daughter*. New York: Doubleday.

Scales-Trent, J. (1995). *Notes of a white black woman*. University Park, PA: Pennsylvania State University Press.

Staples, B. (1994). *Parallel time*. New York: Pantheon Books.

Taulbert, C. (1989). *Once upon a time when we were colored*. Tulsa, OK: Council Oak Books.

Taulbert, C. (1992). *Last train north*. Tulsa, OK: Council Oak Books.

Taulbert, C. (1997). *Watching our crops come in*. New York: Viking

Webb, S. (1980). *Selma, Lord, Selma*. Alabama: University of Alabama Press.

Wickham, D. (1996). *Woodholme: A black man's story of growing up alone*. Baltimore, MD: Johns Hopkins University Press.

Wideman, J. (1996). *Brothers and keepers*. Dallas, TX: Texas Bookman.

Wideman, J. (2001). *Hoop roots*. Boston: Houghton Mifflin.

Wilkins, R. (1982). *A man's life: An autobiography*. New York: Simon & Schuster.

Wright, R. (1945). *Black boy*. New York: Harper & Row.

Young, Y. (2002). *On our way to beautiful: A family memoir*. New York: Villard Books.

Asian American

Alexander, M. (1993). *Fault lines*. New York: Feminist Press at City University of New York.

Bulosan, C. (1973). *America is in the heart: A personal history*. Seattle: University of Washington Press.

Charr, E. (1995). *The golden mountain: The autobiography of a Korean immigrant 1895–1960*. Urbana, IL: University of Illinois Press.

Chiu, C. (2001). *Troublemaker and other saints*. New York: Putnam.

Fong-Torres, B. (1994). *The rice room: Growing up Chinese-American*. New York: Hyperion.

Houston, J. (1973). *Farewell to Manzanar: A true story of Japanese American experience during and after the World War II internment*. Boston: Houghton-Mifflin.

Hyun, P. (1986). *Man Sei! The making of a Korean-American*. Honolulu: University of Hawaii Press.

Jen, G. (1991). *Typical American*. Boston: Houghton Mifflin.

Jen, G. (1999). *Who's Irish?* New York: Knopf.

Kikuchi, C. (1993). *The Kikuchi diary: Chronicle from an American concentration camp*. Urbana, IL: University of Illinois Press.

King, B. (1998). *Girl on a leash: The healing power of dogs: A memoir*. Lenoir, NC: Sanctuary Press.

Kingston, M. (1976). *The woman warrior: Memories of a girlhood*. New York: Knopf.

Larson, L. (2001). *Sweet bamboo: A memoir of a Chinese American family*. Berkeley: University of California Press.

Lee, B. (1999). *Chinese playground: A memoir*. San Francisco: Rhapsody Press.

Lee, C. (1995). *Native speaker*. New York: Riverhead Books.

Lee, G. (1991). *China boy*. New York: Dutton.

Lee, L. (1995). *The winged seed: A remembrance*. New York: Simon & Schuster.

Lei-lanilau, C. (1997). *Ono Ono girl's hula*. Madison, WI: University of Wisconsin Press.

Lim, S. (1996). *Among the white moon faces: An Asian-American memoir of the homelands*. New York: Feminist Press at City University of New York.

Mar, M. E. (1999). *Paper daughter: A memoir*. New York: Harper Collins.

Minatoya, L. (1992). *Talking to high monks in the snow*. New York: Harper Collins.

Minatoya, L. (1997). *Polite lies: On being a woman caught between cultures*. New York: Holt.

Mura, D. (1995). *Where body meets memory: An odyssey of race, sexuality and identity*. New York: Anchor Books.

Mura, D. (1991). *Turning Japanese*. New York: Atlantic Monthly Press.

Reyes, S. (1995). *Child of two worlds: An autobiography of a Filipino-American, or vice-versa*. Colorado Springs, CO: Three Continents Press.

See, L. (1996). *On gold mountain: The one-hundred-year odyssey of my Chinese-American family*. New York: Vintage.

Shimonishi-Lamb, M. (1990). *And then a rainbow*. Santa Barbara, CA: Fithian Press.

Sone, M. (1953). *Nisei daughter*. Boston: Little Brown.

Tan, A. (1989). *The Joy Luck Club*: New York: Putnam.

Wong, J. (1989). *Fifth Chinese daughter*. Seattle: University of Washington Press.

Wong, K., and Wong, C. (1998). *Inside the Qy Quong laundry*. Kelseyville, CA: Earthen Vessel Productions.

Yamauchi, W. (1994). *Songs my mother taught me: Stories, plays and memoir*. New York: Feminist Press at City College of New York.

Euro-American

Ahnen, P. (1995). *Legends and legacies: Memories*. Ann Arbor, MI: Legna Press.

Allison, D. (1995). *Two or three things I know for sure*. New York: Dutton.

Arlen, M. (1975). *Passage to Ararat*. New York: Farrar, Straus and Giroux.

Arlen, M. (1970). *Exiles*. New York: Farrar, Straus and Giroux.

Asayesh, G. (1999). *Saffron sky: A life between Iran and America*. Boston: Beacon Press.

Avakian, A. (1992). *Lion woman's legacy: An Armenian-American memoir*. New York: Feminist Press at City University of New York.

Ayala, F. (1999). *Under the rose: A confession*. New York: Feminist Press at the City University of New York.

Bahrampour, T. *To see and see again: A life in Iran and America*. New York: Farrar, Strauss and Giroux.

Baker, R. (1982). *Growing up*. New York: St. Martin's Press.

Balakian, P. (1997). *Black dog of fate: A memoir*. New York: Basic Books.

Barnes, C. (2001). *Growing up true: Lessons from a western boyhood*. Golden, CO: Fulcrum.

Barnes, K. (1996). *In the wilderness: Coming of age in an unknown country*. New York: Doubleday.

Barnes, K. (2000). *Hungry for the world: A memoir*. New York: Villard.

Beckerman, I. (1995). *Love, loss and what I wore*. Chapel Hill, NC: Algonquin Books.

Benjamin, D. (2002). *Life and times of the last kid picked*. New York: Random House.

Blais, M. (2001). *Uphill walkers: Memoir of a family*. New York: Atlantic Monthly Press.

Blunt, J. (2002). *Breaking clean*. New York: Knopf.

Bragg, R. (1997). *All over but the shoutin'*. New York: Pantheon.

Buckley, C. (1994). *Cruising state: Growing up in southern California*. Reno, NV: University of Nevada Press.

Buckley, C. (1996). *At the still point*. New York: Simon & Schuster.

Conley, D. (2000). *Honky*. Berkeley: University of California Press.

Cooper, B. (1996). *Truth serum: Memoirs*. Boston: Houghton Mifflin.

DeFerrari, G. (1995) *Gringa Latina: A woman of two worlds*. Boston: Houghton Mifflin.

Demas, C. (2000). *Eleven stories high: Growing up in Stuyvesant Town, 1948–1968*. New York: Satae University of New York Press.

DeSalvo, L. (1996). *Vertigo: A memoir*. New York: Dutton.

Dillard, A. (1987). *An American childhood*. New York: Harper and Row.

Di Prima, D. (2001). *Recollections of my life as a woman: The New York years*. New York: Viking.

Dolan, J. (2000). *Phoenix: A brother's life*. New York: Knopf.

D'Onofrio, B. (1990). *Riding in cars with boys: Confessions of a bad girl who makes good*. New York: Penguin.

Doty, M. (1999). *Firebird: A memoir*. New York: Harper Collins.

Duberman, M. (1991). *Cures: A gay man's odyssey*. New York: Dutton.

Duberman, M. (1996). *Midlife queer: Autobiography of a decade*. New York: Scribner.

Earley, T. (2001). *Somehow form a family: Stories that are mostly true*. Chapel Hill, NC: Algonquin Books of Chapel Hill.

Eggers, D. (2000). *A Heartbreaking work of staggering genius*. New York: Simon & Schuster.

Fleming, K. (2000). *The boy with the thorn in his side: A memoir*. New York: Morrow.

Fox, P. (2001). *Borrowed finery: A memoir*. New York: Henry Holt.

Goodell, J. (2000). *Sunnyvale: The rise and fall of a Silicon Valley family*. New York: Villard.

Gordon, M. (1996). *The shadow man*. New York: Random House.

Hamill, P. (1994). *A drinking life: A memoir*. Boston: Little Brown.

Hamper, B. (1991). *Rivethead: Tales from the assembly line*. New York: Warner Books.

Howard, M. (1978). *Facts of life*. Boston: Little Brown.

Jordan, T. (1993). *Riding the white horse home: A western family album*. New York: Pantheon Books.

Karr, M. (1995). *The Liar's Club: A memoir*. New York: Viking.

Karr, M. (2000). *Cherry: A memoir*. New York: Viking.

Kendall, E. (2000). *American daughter: Discovering my mother*. New York: Random House.

Kimmel, H. (2001). *A girl named Zippy: Growing up small in Mooreland, Indiana*. New York: Doubleday.

Kovic, R. (1976). *Born on the fourth of July*. New York: McGraw-Hill.

Lentricchia, F. (1994). *The edge of night*. New York: Random House.

MacDonald, M. (1999). *All souls: A family story from Southie*. Boston: Beacon Press.

Magnuson, M. (2002). *Lummox: The evolution of a man*. New York: Harper Collins.

Manning, M. (1996). *Chasing grace: Reflections of a Catholic girl, grown up*. San Francisco: Harper.

Martin, L. (2000). *From our house: A memoir*. New York: Dutton.

Mason, B. (1999). *Clear Springs: A memoir*. New York: Random House.

McCarthy, M. (1981). *Memories of a Catholic girlhood*. New York: Harcourt, Brace, Jovanovich.

McCarthy, M. (1987). *How I grew*. San Diego: Harcourt, Brace, Jovanovich.

McNaron, T. (1992). *I dwell in possibility: A memoir*. New York: Feminist Press at City University of New York.

Merullo, R. *Revere Beach elegy: A memoir of home and beyond*. Boston: Beacon Press.

Morris, W. (1967). *North toward home*. Boston: Houghton Mifflin.

Moss, B. (2000). *Change me into Zeus's daughter: A memoir*. New York: Scribner.

O'Brien, J. (2001). *At home in the heart of Appalachia*. New York: Knopf.

Olmstead, R. (1996). *Stay here with me*. New York: Metropolitan Books.

Pearson, M. (1999). *Dreaming of Columbus: A boyhood in the Bronx.* Syracuse, NY: Syracuse University Press.

Perez, J. (1990). *Tales of an Italian-American family.* New York: Gardner Press.

Perks, M. (2001). *Pagan time: An American childhood.* Washington, DC: Counterpoint.

Petroski, H. (2002). *Paperboy: Delivering the press in the fifties.* New York: Knopf.

Register, C. (2000). *Packinghouse daughter: A memoir.* St. Paul, MN: Minnesota Historical Society Press.

Rhodes, R. (1990). *A hole in the world: An American boyhood.* New York: Simon & Schuster.

Rivers, C. (1973). *Aphrodite at mid-century: Growing up Catholic and female in post-war America.* New York: Doubleday.

Salzman, M. (1995). *Lost in place: Growing up absurd in suburbia.* New York: Random House.

Sedaris, D. (1997). *Naked.* Boston: Little, Brown.

Smith, D. (1999). *A Song for Mary: An Irish-American memory.* New York: Warner Books.

Smith, W. (1980). *Army brat.* New York: Persea.

Spragg, M. (1999). *Where rivers change direction.* Salt Lake City, UT: University of Utah Press.

Stapinski, H. (2001). *Five-finger discount: A crooked family history.* New York: Random House.

Steiker, V. (2002). *The leopard hat: A daughter's story.* New York: Pantheon Books.

Swift, E. (1999). *My grandfather's finger.* Athens, GA: University of Georgia Press.

Theroux, P. (1980). *California and other states of grace.* New York: Morrow.

Torgovnick, M. (1994). *Crossing Ocean Parkway: Readings by an Italian-American daughter.* Chicago: University of Chicago Press.

Waters, M. (2001). *Crossing Highbridge: A memoir of Irish America.* Syracuse, NY: Syracuse University Press.

Wolff, T. (1989). *This boy's life.* New York: Atlantic Monthly Press.

Latino/Hispanic

Acosta, O. (1989). *Revolt of the cockroach people.* New York: Vintage Books.

Acosta, O. (1989). *Autobiography of a brown buffalo.* New York: Vintage Books.

Aguilera, L. (2000). *Gabriel's fire.* Chicago: University of Chicago Press.

Alvarez, J. (1991). *How the Garcia girls lost their accents.* Chapel Hill, NC: Algonquin Books of Chapel Hill.

Alvarez, J. (1997). *Yo!* Chapel Hill, NC: Algonquin Books of Chapel Hill.

Alvarez, J. (1998). *Something to declare.* Chapel Hill, NC: Algonquin Books of Chapel Hill.

Anaya, R. (1972). *Bless me Ultima.* Berkeley, CA: TQS.

Arana, M. (2001). *American chica: Two worlds, one childhood.* New York: Dial Press.

Arteaga, A. (1997). *House with the blue bed.* San Francisco: Mercury House.

Baca, J. (2001). *A place to stand: The making of a poet.* New York: Grove Press.

Boza, M. (1998). *Scattering the ashes.* Tempe, AZ: Bilingual Press.

Chavez, D. (1986). *Last of the menu girls.* Houston, TX: Arte Publico Press.

Chavez, D. (1994). *Face of an angel.* New York: Farrar, Straus and Giroux.

Cisneros, S. (1989). *The house on Mango Street.* New York: Vintage Books.

Colon, J. (1982). *A Puerto Rican in New York and other sketches.* New York: International.

Gonzalez, R. (1993). *Memory fever: A journey beyond El Paso Del Norte.* Seattle: Broken Moon Press.

Grillo, E. (2000). *Black Cuban, black American: A memoir.* Houston, TX: Arte Publico Press.

Maldonado, D. (2001). *Crossing Guadalupe Street: Growing up Hispanic and Protestant.* Albuquerque, NM: University of New Mexico Press.

Medina, P. (1990) *Exiled memories: A Cuban childhood.* Austin, TX: University of Texas Press.

Mohr, N. (1991). *El Bronx remembered.* Houston, TX: Arte Publico Press.

Ortiz-Cofer, J. (1990). *Silent dancing: A partial remembrance of a Puerto Rican childhood.* Houston, TX: Arte Publico Press.

Perez Firmat, G. (1994) *Life on the hyphen: The Cuban-American way.* Austin, TX: University of Texas Press.

Perez Firmat, G. (1995). *Next year in Cuba: A Cubano's coming of age in America.* New York: Anchor Books.

Ponce, M. (1993). *Hoyt street: An autobiography.* Albuquerque, NM: University of New Mexico Press.

Rios, A. (1999). *Capirotada: A Nogales memoir.* Albuquerque, NM: University of New Mexico Press.

Rivera, E. (1982). *Family installments: Memories of growing up Hispanic.* New York: Morrow.

Rodriguez, A. (1999). *East Side dreams.* Coyote, CA: Dream House Press.

Rodriguez, R. (1981). *Hunger of memory.* Boston: D. R.Godine.

Salas, F. (1992). *Buffalo nickel: A memoir.* Houston, TX: Arte Publico Press.

Santiago, E. (1993). *When I was Puerto Rican.* Reading, MA: Addison-Wesley.

Soto, G. (1990). *A summer life.* Hanover, NH: University Press of New England.

Soto, G. (1992). *Living up the street: Narrative recollections.* New York: Dell.

Suarez, V. (1997). *Spared Angola: Memories from a Cuban-American childhood.* Houston, TX: Arte Publico Press.

Thomas, P. (1997). *Down these mean streets.* New York: Viking.

Tywoniak, F. (2000). *Migrant daughter: Coming of age as a Mexican American woman.* Berkeley, CA: University of California Press.

Veciana-Suarez, A. (2000). *Birthday parties in heaven: Thoughts on love, life, grief and other matters of the heart.* New York: Plume.

Villasenor, V. (1992). *Rain of gold.* New York: Laurel.

Villasenor, V. (2001). *Thirteen senses: A memoir.* New York: Rayo.

Jewish American

Auerbach, J. (1996). *Jacob's voices: Reflections of a wandering Jew.* Carbondale, IL: Southern Illinois University.

Bar-On, D. (1995). *Fear and hope: Three generations of the Holocaust.* Cambridge, MA: Harvard University Press.

Brichto, S. (2001). *Ritual slaughter: Growing up Jewish in America.* London: Sinclair-Stevenson.

Charyn, J. (2002). *Bronx boy: A memoir.* New York: Thomas Dunne Books.

Cohen, E. (1999). *The peddler's grandson: Growing up Jewish in Mississippi.* Jackson, MS: University of Mississippi Press.

Felman, J. (1997). *Cravings: A sensual memoir.* Boston: Beacon Press.

Fuentes, S. (1999). *Eat first—you don't know what they'll give you: The adventures of an immigrant family and their feminist daughter.* Philadelphia: Xlibris.

Gallagher, D. (2001). *How I came into my inheritance and other true stories.* New York: Random House.

Glaser, S. (1997). *Family secrets: One woman's affectionate look at a relatively painful subject.* New York: Simon & Schuster.

Goodheart, E. (2001). *Confessions of a secular Jew: A memoir.* New York: Overlook Press.

Heller, M. (2000). *Living root: A memoir*. Albany, NY: State University of New York Press.

Hentoff, N. (2001). *Boston boy: Growing up with jazz and other passions*. Philadelphia: Paul Dry Books.

Hoffman, A. (1980). *Soon to be a major motion picture*. New York: Perigree.

Hoffman, E. (1989). *Lost in translation: A life in a new language*. New York: Dutton.

Kaufman, A. (2000). *Jew boy: A memoir*. New York: Fromm International.

Klein, H. (1995). *Memoirs of a Jewish extremist: An American story*. Boston: Little Brown.

Mendelsohn, D. (1999). *The elusive embrace: Desire and the riddle of identity*. New York: Knopf.

Moskowitz, F. (1991). *And the bridge is love: Life stories*. Boston: Beacon Press.

Orner, P. (2001). *Esther stories*. Boston: Houghton Mifflin.

Ragen, N. (2002). *Chains around the grass*. New Milford, CT: Toby Press.

Raphael, L. (1996). *Journeys and arrivals: On being gay and Jewish*. Boston: Faber & Faber.

Reti, I. (2001). *The keeper of memory: A memoir*. Santa Cruz, CA: HerBooks.

Salamon, J. (1996). *Net of dreams: A family's search for a rightful place*. New York: Random House.

Sinclair, J. (1993). *The seasons: Death and transformation: a memoir*. New York: Feminist Press at City University of New York.

Talbot, T. (1980). *A book about my mother*. New York: Farrar, Strauss.

Volk, P. (2001). *Stuffed: Adventures of a restaurant family*. New York: Knopf.

Waldman, B. (1988). *The book of Tziril: A family chronicle*. New York: Adama Books.

Waitzkin, F. (2000). *The last marlin: The story of a family at sea*. New York: Viking.

Native American

Alexie, S. (1994). *Tonto and the Lone Ranger fistfight in heaven*. New York: Atlantic Monthly Press.

Alexie, S. (1995). *Reservation blues*. New York: Atlantic Monthly Press.

Alvord, L. (1999). *The scalpel and the silver bear*. New York: Bantam Books.

Barnes, J. (1997) *On native ground: Memoirs and impressions*. Norman, OK: University of Oklahoma Press.

Bell, B. (1994). *Faces in the moon*. Norman, OK: University of Oklahoma Press.

Benedek, E. (1998). *Beyond the four corners of the world: A Navajo woman's journey*. Norman, OK: University of Oklahoma Press.

Blowsnake, S. (1963). *The autobiography of a Winnebago Indian*. New York: Dover.

Blowsnake, S. (1983). *Crashing thunder*. Lincoln, NE: University of Nebraska Press.

Brave Bird, M. (1993). *Ohitika woman*. New York: Grove Press.

Brave Bird, M. (1990). *Lakota woman*. New York: Grove Weidenfeld.

Erdich, L. (1984). *Love medicine*. Boston: Houghton Mifflin.

Forbes, J. (1995). *Only approved Indians: Stories*. Norman, OK: University of Oklahoma Press.

Glancy, D. (1993). *Firesticks: A collection of stories*. Norman, OK: University of Oklahoma Press.

Glancy, D. (2002). *The mask maker: A novel*. Norman, OK: University of Oklahoma Press.

Hale, J. (1993). *Bloodlines: Odyssey of a native daughter*. New York: Random House.

Hogan, L. (2001). *The woman who watches over the world: A native memoir*. New York: W. W. Norton.

Hungry Wolf, B. (1980). *The ways of my grandmothers*. New York: Morrow.

Kenny, M. (1995). *On second thought*. Norman, OK: University of Oklahoma Press.

Mankiller, W. (1993). *Mankiller: A chief and her people*. New York: St. Martin's Press.

Means, R. (1995). *Where white men fear to tread*. New York: St. Martin's Press.

Momaday, S. (1968). *House made of dawn*. New York: Harper and Row.

Momaday, S. (1969). *The way to rainy mountain*. Lincoln, NE: University of Nebraska Press.

Momaday, S. (1987). *The names: A memoir*. New York: Harper and Row.

Monture, J. (1998). *Turtle Belly: A novel*. Norman, OK: University of Oklahoma Press.

Lurie, N. O., & Underhill, R. M. (Eds.). (1961). *Mountain wolf woman, sister of crashing thunder: Autobiography of a Winnebago Indian*. Ann Arbor, MI: University of Michigan Press.

Nasdijj. (2000). *The blood runs like a river through my dreams: A memoir*. Boston: Houghton Mifflin.

Neihardt, J. (1961). *Black Elk speaks*. Lincoln, NE: University of Nebraska Press.

Northrup, J. (1997). *The Rez road follies: Canoes, casinos, computers, and birch bark baskets*. New York: Kodansha International.

Owens, L. (2001). *I hear the train: Reflections, inventions, refractions*. Norman, OK: University of Oklahoma Press.

Penn, W. (1995) *The absence of angels*. Norman, OK: University of Oklahoma Press.

Red Shirt, D. (1998). *Bead on an anthill: A Lakota childhood*. Lincoln, NE: University of Nebraska Press.

Red Shirt, D. (2002). *Turtle Lung Woman's grandaughter*. Lincoln, NE: University of Nebraska Press.

Seals, D. (1990). *The powwow highway*. New York: Plume.

Silko, L. (1981). *Storyteller*. New York: Seaver Books.

Snell, A. (2000). *Grandmother's grandchild: My Crow Indian life*. Lincoln, NE: University of Nebraska Press.

Thon, M. (2002). *Sweethearts: A novel*. New York: Washington Square Press.

Thunder, M. (1995). *Thunder's grace: Walking the road of visions with my Lakota grandmother*. New York: Station Hill Press.

Multiracial/Multiethnic/Multicultural

Arboleda, T. (1998). *In the shadow of race: Growing up as a multiethnic, multicultural and "multiracial" American*. Mahwah, NJ: Erlbaum.

Buckley, G. L. (1986). *The Hornes: An American family*. New York: Knopf.

Delman, C. (2002). *Burnt bread and chutney: Memoir of an Indian Jewish girl*. New York: One World.

Dubner, S. (1999). *Turbulent souls: A Catholic son's return to his Jewish family*. New York: Avon.

Fullilove, M. (2002). *House of Joshua: Mediations on family and place*. Lincoln, NE: University of Nebraska Press.

Haizlip, S. T. (1993). *The sweeter the juice: A family memoir in black and white*. New York: Simon & Schuster.

Jacoby, S. (2000). *Half-Jew: A daughter's search for her family's buried past*. New York: Scribner.

Johnson, K. (1999). *How did you get to be Mexican?: A white/brown man's search for identity*. Philadelphia: Temple University Press.

Kamdar, M. (2001). *Motiba's tattoos: A granddaughter's journey from American into her Indian family's past*. New York: Plume.

Kim, E. (2000). *Ten thousand sorrows*. London: Doubleday.

Lazarre, J. (1996). *Beyond the whiteness of whiteness: A memoir of a white mother of black sons*. Durham, NC: Duke University Press.

McBride, J. (1995). *The color of water: A black man's tribute to his white mother*. New York: Riverhead Books.

Melanson, Y. (1999). *Looking for Lost Bird: A Jewish woman discovers her Navajo roots*. New York: Bard.

Minerbrook, S. (1996). *Divided to the vein: A journey into race and family*. New York: Harcourt, Brace & Co.

Nguyen, K. (2001). *The unwanted: A memoir*. Boston: Little Brown

Obama, B. (1995). *Dreams from my father: A story of race and inheritance*. New York: Times Books.

Rekdal, P. (2001). *The night my mother met Bruce Lee: Observations on not fitting in*. New York: Pantheon Books.

Two Trees, K. (1997). *Somebody always singing you*. Jackson, MS: University of Mississippi Press.

Urrea, L. (1998). *Nobody's son: Notes from an American life*. Tucson, AZ: University of Arizona Press.

Walker, R. (2001). *Black, white and Jewish: Autobiography of a shifting self*. New York: Riverhead Books.

Williams, G. (1995). *Life on the color line: The true story of a White boy who discovered he was black*. New York: Dutton.

Anthologies

Adler, B. (1997). *Growing up Jewish: An anthology*. New York: Avon.

Augenbraum, H., & Stavans, I. (1993). *Growing up Latino: Memoirs and stories*. Boston: Houghton Mifflin.

Brody, L. (1997). *Daughters of kings: Growing up as a Jewish woman in America*. Boston: Faber and Faber.

Coles, R. (2001). *Growing up poor: A literary anthology*. New York: New Press.

Conway, J. (1992). *Written by herself: Autobiographies of American women*. New York: Vintage Books.

David, J. (1992). *Growing up black: From the slave days to the present*. New York: Avon .

David, J. (1996). *Growing up Jewish: An anthology*. New York: Morrow.

DeJesus, J. (1997). *Growing up Puerto Rican: An anthology*. New York: Morrow.

Dillard, A., & Conley, C. (1995). *Modern American memoirs*. New York: Harper Collins.

Fernandez, R. (1994). *In other words: Literature by Latinas of the United States*. Houston, TX: Arte Publico Press.

Freeman, J. (1989). *Hearts of sorrow: Vietnamese-American lives*. Stanford, CA: Stanford University Press.

Frommer, M., & Frommer, H. (1995). *Growing up Jewish in America: An oral history*. New York: Harcourt Brace.

Gates, H. (1991). *Bearing witness: Selections from African-American autobiography in the twentieth century*. New York: Pantheon.

Krupat, A., & Swann, B. (2000). *Here first: Autobiographical essays by Native American writers*. New York: Modern Library.

Hong, M. (1993). *Growing up Asian American: An anthology*. New York: Morrow.

Krupat, A. (1994). *Native American autobiography: An anthology*. Madison, WI: University of Wisconsin Press.

Lopez, T. (1993). *Growing up Chicana/o*. New York: Morrow.

Marks, M. (1996). *Nice Jewish girls: Growing up in America*. New York: Plume.

Riley, P. (1993). *Growing up Native American: An anthology*. New York: Morrow.

Santiago, E., & Davidow, J. (2000). *Las mamis: Favorite Latino authors remember their mothers*. New York: Knopf.

Sayre, R. (1994). *American lives: An anthology of autobiographical writing*. Madison, WI: University of Wisconsin Press.

Sewall, M. (2001). *Resurrecting grace: Remembering Catholic childhoods*. Boston: Beacon Press.

Soto, G. (1988). *California childhood: Recollections and stories of the Golden State*. Berkeley, CA: Creative Arts Books.

Sumrall, A., & Vecchione, P. (1992). *Catholic girls*. New York: Penguin.

Swann, B., & Krupat, A. (1987). *I tell you now: Autobiographical essays by Native American writers*. Lincoln, NE: University of Nebraska Press.

REFERENCES

Augenbraum, H., & Stavans, I. (1993). *Growing up Latino: Memoirs and stories*. Boston: Houghton Mifflin.

Baber, C. (1992). Ethnic identity development and literacy education. *Reading Psychology: An International Quarterly, 13*, 91–98.

Baldwin, M. (1987). Interview with Carl Rogers on the use of self in therapy. In M. Baldwin & Satir (Eds.), *The use of self in therapy.* New York: Haworth Press.

Berg-Cross, L., Jennings, P., and Baruch, R. (1990). Cinematherapy: Theory and application. *Psychotherapy in Private Practice, 8*(1), 135–156.

Bertman, S. L. (1980). Lingering terminal illness and the family: Insights from literature. *Family Process, 19,* 341–348.

Bibus, A. A. (1992). Family metaphors in three plays by August Wilson: A source of deeper cultural sensitivity. *Social Work in Education, 14*(1), 15–24.

Brumble, H. (1988). *American Indian autobiography.* Berkeley, CA: University of California Press.

Bruner, J. (1973). *Beyond the information given: Studies in the psychology of knowing.* New York: W. W. Norton.

Chau, K. L. (1990). A model for teaching crosscultural practice in social work. *Journal of Social Work Education,* 124–133.

Chau, K. L. (1992). Needs assessment for group work with people of color: A conceptual formulation. *Social Work with Groups, 15*(2 & 3), 53–66.

Cnaan, R. A. (1989). Teaching literature to highlight social policy issues. *Journal of Social Work Education, 25*(3), 181–191.

Cohen, L. J. (1994). The experience of therapeutic reading. *Western Journal of Nursing Research, 16*(4), 426–437.

Comas-Diaz, L., & Jacobsen, F. (1991). Ethnocultural transference and countertransference in the therapeutic dyad. *American Journal of Orthopsychiatry, 61*(3), 392–402.

Congress, E. P. (1994). The use of culturagrams to assess and empower culturally diverse families. *Families in Society: The Journal of Contemporary Human Services,* 531–540.

Cross, T., Bazron, B., Dennis, K. W., & Isaacs, M. (1989). *Towards a culturally competent system of care.* Vol. 1. Washington, DC: CASSP Technical Assistance Center, Georgetown University Child Development Center.

Dillard, A., & Conley, C. (Eds.). (1995). *Modern American memoirs.* New York: Harper Collins.

Duhl, B. (1987). Uses of the self in integrated contextual systems therapy. In M. Baldwin and V. Satir, *The use of self in therapy.* New York: Haworth Press.

Farmer, R. (1984). Humanistic education and self-actualization theory. *Education, 105*(2), 162–172.

Franklin, V. (1995). *Living our stories, telling our truths: Autobiography and the making of the African American intellectual tradition*. New York: Scribner.

Fuhriman, A., Barlow, S. H., & Wanlass, J. (1989). Words, imagination, meaning: Toward change. *Psychotherapy, 26*(2), 149–156.

Ganzer, C. (1994). Using literature as an aid to practice. *Families in Society: The Journal of Contemporary Human Services*, 616–623.

Garcia, B., & Melendez, M. (1997). Concepts and methods in teaching oppression courses. *Journal of Progressive Human Services, 8*(1), 23–40.

Garcia, B., & Swensen, C. (1992). Writing the stories of white racism. *Journal of Teaching in Social Work, 6*(2). 3–17.

Garland, D. R., & Escobar, D. (1988). Education for crosscultural social work practice. *Journal of Social Work Education, 3*, 229–241.

Gold, J., & Gloade, F. (1988). Affective reading and its life applications. *The Arts in Psychotherapy, 15*, 235–244.

Grootof, C. (1969). Poetry therapy for psycho-neurotics in a mental health center. In J. Leedy (Ed.), *Poetry therapy: The use of poetry in the treatment of emotional disorders* (pp. 38–51). Philadelphia: Lippincott.

Holland, T. P., and Kilpatrick, A. C. (1993). Using narrative techniques to enhance multicultural practice. *Journal of Social Work Education, 29*(3), 302–308.

Hynes, A. M. (1980). The goals of bibliotherapy. *The Arts in Psychotherapy, 7*, 35–41.

Khatri, A. A. (1980). Analysis of fiction: A method for intracultural and crosscultural study of family systems. *Journal of Marriage and the Family*, 197–203.

Latting, J. K. (1990). Identifying the "isms": Enabling social work students to confront their biases. *Journal of Social Work Education, 1*, 36-44.

Link, R. J., & Sullivan, M. (1989). Vital connections: Using literature to illustrate social work issues. *Journal of Social Work Education, 3*, 192-201.

Mahan, C. K., Schreiner, R. L., & Green, M. (1983). Bibliotherapy: A tool to help parents mourn their infant's death. *Health and Social Work*, 126–132.

Manoleas, P. (1994). An outcome approach to assessing the cultural competence of MSW students. *Journal of Multicultural Social Work, 3*(1), 43–57.

McGoldrick, M., Pearce, J. K., & Giordano, J. (Eds.).(1982). *Ethnicity and family therapy*. New York: Guilford Press.

McInnis, K. M. (1982). Bibliotherapy: Adjunct to traditional counseling with children of stepfamilies. *Child Welfare*, *61*(3), 153–160.

Miller, J. B. (1976). *Toward a new psychology of women*. Boston: Beacon Press.

Montalvo, F. F., Lasater, T. T., & Valdez, N. G. (1982). Training child welfare workers for cultural awareness: The culture simulator technique. *Child Welfare*, 341–352.

Nash, M. (1993). The use of self in experiential learning for crosscultural awareness: An exercise linking the personal with the professional. *Journal of Social Work Practice*, *7*(1), 55–61.

Pardeck, J. T. (1991a). Bibliotherapy and clinical social work. *Journal of Independent Social Work*. *5*(2), 53–63.

Pardeck, J. T. (1991b). Using books in clinical practice. *Psychotherapy in Private Practice*, *9*(3), 105–119.

Pardeck, J. A., & Pardeck, J. T. (1984). An overview of the bibliotherapeutic treatment approach: Implications for clinical social work practice. *Family Therapy*, *11*(3), 241–252.

Pardeck, J. T., & Pardeck, J. A. (1987a). Using bibliotherapy to help children cope with the changing family. *Social Work in Education*, (Winter), 107–116.

Pardeck, J. T., & Pardeck, J. A. (1987b). Bibliotherapy for children in foster care and adoption. *Child Welfare*, *65*(3), 269–278.

Pinderhughes, E. (1989). *Understanding race ethnicity, and power: The key to efficacy in clinical practice*. New York: Free Press.

Preli, R., & Bernard, J. M. (1993). Making multiculturalism relevant for majority culture graduate students. *Journal of Marital and Family Therapy*, *19*(1), 5–16.

Preto, N. G. (1989). Transformation of the family system in adolescence. In B. Carter, & M. McGoldrick (Eds.), *The changing family life cycle* (2nd ed.). Boston: Allyn & Bacon.

Proctor, E. K., & Davis, L. E. (1994). The challenge of racial difference: Skills for clinical practice. *Social Work*, 314–323.

Real, T. (1990). The therapeutic use of self in constructionist/system therapy. *Family Process*, *29*, 255–272.

Romney, P., Tatum, B., & Jones, J. (1992). Feminist strategies for teaching about oppression: The importance of process. *Women's Studies Quarterly*, *1&2*, 95–110.

Ronnau, J. P. (1994). Teaching cultural competence: Practical ideas for social work educators. *Journal of Multicultural Social Work*, *3*(1), 29–42.

Satir, V. (1987). The therapist story. In M. Baldwin & Satir (Eds.), *The use of self in therapy*. New York: Haworth Press.

Sayre, R. (1984). *American lives: An anthology of autobiographical writing*. Madison, WI: University of Wisconsin Press.

Scharff, J. (1992). *Projective and introjective identification and the use of the therapist's self*. Northvale, NJ: Jason Aronson.

Shrodes, C. (1949). Bibliotherapy: A theoretical and clinical study. Unpublished doctoral dissertation, University of California, Berkeley.

Smith, L. (1961). *Killers of the dream*. (2nd ed.). New York: W. W. Norton.

Starker, S. (1986). Promises and prescriptions: Self-help books in mental health and medicine. *American Journal of Health Promotion, 1*, 19–24.

Thornton, S., & Garrett, K. J. (1995). Ethnography as a bridge to multicultural practice. *Journal of Social Work Education, 31*(1), 67–74.

Wilson, L., and Green, J. W. (1983). An experiential approach to cultural awareness. *Child Welfare, 62*(4), 303–311.

Yalom, I. D. (1985). *The theory and practice of psychotherapy*. (3rd ed.). New York: Basic Books.

Zinser, W. (1987). *Inventing the truth: The art and craft of memoir*. Boston: Houghton Mifflin.

Chapter Sixteen
Teaching Resources

Betty Garcia and Patti DeRosa

This chapter presents resources that are available through a variety of sources. We begin with technological resources and online supports, followed by a list of videos that we have found to be helpful. Several teaching assignments that can be used in specific diversity courses or as part of other courses are then provided. The chapter ends with some handouts that can be used as overheads as well.

USE OF TECHNOLOGY

Considerable technological resources abound that are invaluable complements to teaching diversity content. Blackboard.com (http://blackboard.com) is one type of online support that is increasingly available on campuses for Web-based or Web-enhanced courses (Ko & Rossen, 2001). We highly recommend this resource as a complementary medium for students to present assignments and communicate in narrative form with other students and their professor as well as for class assignments. We encourage faculty to implement it in their diversity teaching as a means to open up additional options for classroom interaction that complement the face-to-face exchange in the classroom. Use of online resources for student communication often will result in students being more forthcoming and articulate than in face-to-face encounters, because it may feel easier to take initiative in this safer medium for self-expression.

Getting all students on line will predictably be a labor-intensive effort. This process needs to be monitored to assure that all students have online access to a course. It may also be helpful to discuss or post some guidelines about computer "etiquette" in relation to responsible access and transmission of information. We highly recommend that faculty make the time to learn new technology supports at a time other than working with a deadline. Below are some features of Blackboard and their possible use in diversity teaching.

- **Posting course documents and resources**. Making the course syllabus and outline, assignments, and handouts available allows students access to often-misplaced documents both while students are enrolled in the course and as references when the course is completed. Creating hyperlinks to Web resources provides possible assignments and gives students a head start in identifying other similar Web sites.

- **Discussion Board**. Chat rooms can be provided per assigned reading or cluster of readings where students can be required to post 2 to 3 responses weekly that would include their analysis of a reading and responses to other students' remarks. Being able to post their remarks at their convenience is a feature that many students enjoy. Faculty are encouraged to log on regularly, monitor the student exchanges, and give feedback on the discussion.

- **Classroom Discussion Board**. Students can be required to post responses to classroom lectures, activities, and classroom discussions at their convenience. Faculty can pose specific questions regarding course content, classroom discussion process or themes, student reflections on their engagement with the class interaction, and/or how they are meeting their learning needs.

- **Synchronous Virtual Classroom**. Blackboard.com-type resources allow the class to meet online at a discrete time, for example, if faculty are away from campus and prefer to conduct a class during the regular meeting time. This feature can also be used to conduct office hours, which is particularly useful for students who may not be on campus during the office hour period. This feature also allows the class to interview and meet with "experts" who are not within proximity of the campus. Other programs allow "Web conferencing" or a "Web cast" which allows visual and audio features for a "live" interview with special software and a mounted Web cam on each computer. Such interviews can be particularly useful to students when faculty can gather questions from the class and email them to the interviewee for their perusal before the interview. Also, a discussion board can be created for follow-up questions from the class to the interviewee for further response.

- **PowerPoint lectures, lecture notes, articles**. Special lecture content or PowerPoint presentations can be uploaded for students to review after class. Faculty can alert students to check in before class to see if faculty have uploaded copies of newspaper articles that are directly relevant to the class goals. Often faculty bring in popular press articles because of their timeliness; Blackboard saves resources in time and printing handouts. The campus library staff needs to be consulted regarding posting professional articles and securing needed copyright permission.

- **Videos.** Students can be assigned videos for their review and analysis for written assignment or class discussion. Copyright permission needs to be reviewed with the library staff.

- **Joint journaling.** A discussion board can be assigned per a pair of students who will exchange a joint journal in the course of the semester. One student begins the journal by making an entry on content identified either by faculty or by themselves regarding their experience of the course or assignments. At the end of their entry they identify questions for their partner to respond to. Likewise, the partner responds to his or her partner's questions, makes a new entry, identifies new questions, and returns the journal to their partner. See Chapters Thirteen and Sixteen regarding joint journaling activities. Blackboard.com allows for the board to have privacy by not allowing other students to view the journal discussion.

- **Small group discussion.** A group of 3 to 5 students is assigned a room to discuss readings, class experiences, or other identified topics. This activity can provide additional substance for the same group to conduct a discussion in the classroom. Faculty may also want to provide privacy for this type of discussion.

- **Assignments.** Assignments with multiple choice or essay responses can be posted for students to write in responses and submit to faculty electronicallay.

VIDEOS

The Color of Fear (1994). 90 minutes. Eight North American men of Asian, European, Latino, and African American heritage gather under the direction of seminar leader Lee Mun Wah to discuss racism. In emotional and often heated exchanges, the participants challenge the privileged status of White Americans and recount their own experiences with discrimination. Stir Fry Productions, (800) 370-STIR.

The Way Home (1998). 90 minutes. Over the course of eight months, 64 women, representing a cross-section of cultures in America, came together to share their experiences of oppression through the lens of racial identity. Separated into eight ethnic councils—indigenous, African American, Arab, Asian, European American, Latina, Jewish, and multiracial—the women explore their stories of identity, oppression, and resistance. World Trust, (877) WAY-HOME.

A Class Divided (1970). 60 minutes. Part 1 of this classic program documents how in 1970 an Iowa school teacher, Jane Elliott, divided her third-grade class into brown eyes and blue eyes, and gave blue-eyed children preferential treatment as a way to demonstrate how racial stereotypes affect children. This video, initially called "The Eye of the Storm," presents the long-term effects of racial stereotyping and systemic racism. Part 2 shows a class reunion of that same third-grade class, 14 years later, discussing the transformational impact the exercise had on their lives. In Part 3, Jane Elliott repeats the exercise with adults who are employees of the Iowa State Prison system. PBS Video, (800) 344-3337.

Eyes on the Prize II: The Keys to the Kingdom: 1974–1980 (1990). 60 minutes. This one-hour segment of the renowned "Eyes on the Prize" series examines court-ordered desegregation and busing in Boston, the election of Mayor Maynard Jackson in Atlanta, and affirmative action and the Bakke decision in California. It is an incisive exploration of the challenges of undoing the wrongs of discrimination in schools and the workplace. It is particularly helpful in assisting students to understand the historical context of affirmative action. The entire "Eyes on the Prize" series, which documents the Black liberation struggle in the United States from the 1950s to the 1980s, is a marvelous teaching tool. PBS Video, (800) 344-3337.

Chicano! The History of the Mexican American Civil Rights Movement (1996). Four 60-minute videos. Spanning the years 1965–1975, this four-part documentary explores the saga of Mexican American social activism. Combining archival footage and current interviews, the series charts the 1967 struggle to regain ownership of New Mexico lands guaranteed them by the 1848 Treaty of Guadalupe Hidalgo, the landmark Denver Youth Conference of 1969, the efforts of farm workers and Cesar Chavez, the struggle for educational reform in California, and the emergence of Mexican American political power and the La Raza Unida. National Latino Communications Center, (213) 953-2928.

Viva La Causa! 500 years of Chicano History (1995). Two 30-minute videos. This is a two-part educational video that offers a compelling introduction to the history of Mexican American people and is based on the book, *500*

Years of Chicano History in Pictures, edited by Elizabeth Martinez. Part One depicts pre-Columbian origins through Spanish colonization, the U.S. take-over of the Southwestern states (California, Arizona, New Mexico, Colorado, Texas) in 1848, the people's resistance, workers creating great wealth, and their massive strikes up to World War II. Part Two includes the 1943 Zoot Suit Riots, early efforts to fight discrimination, the farm workers' struggle, student protests, the Chicano Moratorium against U.S. involvement in Vietnam, and historical Latino struggles. SouthWest Organizing Project, (505) 247-8832.

Free Indeed: Of White Privilege and How We Play the Game (1995). 23 minutes. This video challenges viewers to think about the privileges that come with being White in North America. Four White middle-class young adults play a card game as a prerequisite for doing a service project for a Black Baptist church. The game leads to a discussion about the privileges White people have and their attitudes about racism. Mennonite Central Committee, (717) 859-1151.

Ethnic Notions (1987). 56 minutes. Marlon Rigg's groundbreaking study dissects a disturbing underside of American popular culture by revealing the deep-rooted stereotypes that have fueled anti-Black prejudice. In a searing procession of bigotry, classic Black stereotypes scroll across the screen in cartoons, feature films, TV shows, popular songs, minstrel shows, advertisements, household artifacts, and children's songs. From the 1820s to the Civil Rights period, these grotesque caricatures of African Americans were used by White America and resurrected in recent times in subtle but no less hurtful ways. Esther Rolle narrates the film and several scholars explain these images and help put them in a historical context. California Newsreel, (415) 621-6196.

The following three videos use a hidden camera format to capture the everyday face of discrimination.

True Colors; The Fairer Sex, Age and Attitudes; No Way In. In *True Colors*, a Black man and a White man try to find a job, get housing, and get settled in a new city. In *The Fairer Sex*, a Euro-American man and a woman try to get a job, do their dry cleaning, play golf, and buy a car. In *Age and Attitudes*, the same man is made up to look younger and older, and then goes to apply for several jobs. *No Way In* tracks the efforts of a man in a wheelchair applying for jobs, looking for housing, and going about everyday tasks.

- *True Colors*, MTI/Film Video, (800) 537-3130; http://www.corvision.com/descr.htm#TRUECOLORS

- *The Fairer Sex, Age and Attitudes*, CorVision, (800) 537-3130.

- *No Way In*, Dateline NBC, Cat. #: NDL970909, (800) 420-2626.

Straight From the Heart (1994). 24 minutes. Stories of parents' journeys in reaching a new understanding of their lesbian and gay children. Note that there is an awkward section in this film where a psychologist talks mistakenly about "gender orientation" rather than "sexual orientation." Woman Vision, (415) 346-2336.

In Who's Honor?: American Indian Mascots in Sports (1997). 46 minutes. Logos featuring grotesque Indian caricatures and packed stadiums of fans singing "war chants" and pantomiming "tomahawk chops" are popular images associated with such professional sports teams as the Washington Redskins, Cleveland Indians, and Atlanta Braves. While other symbols of racial stereotyping have waned, Native American ones remain, especially in sports. This documentary focuses on Charlene Teters, a Spokane Indian who waged a campaign against Chief Illiniwek, the University of Illinois' beloved mascot. New Day Films (888) 367-9154.

Skin Deep (1995). 53 minutes. A diverse group of students from the University of Massachusetts, Texas A&M, Chico State, and U.C. Berkeley are followed as they participate in an intensive three-day racial awareness workshop in northern California. The students interact in group sessions that challenge deeply held attitudes about race. The video also accompanies the participants back to their own campuses and homes in an attempt to understand why they think the way they do. The students enter into heated discussions about self-segregation on campus, discrimination, affirmative action, and students' responsibility. California Newsreel, (415) 621-6196.

Ending Racism: Working for a Racism Free 21st Century (1996). 35 minutes. This video presents an overview of racism, a definition of systemic racism and examples of how racism confers privilege on White Americans and denies access to people of color. It looks at what people can do to eliminate racism in their institutions. Crossroads Ministry (773) 638-0166.

TEACHING ASSIGNMENTS

The Learning Contract

The Learning Contract (L. Gutierrez, personal communication, November 28, 1995) is a format for identifying several categories of assignments from which students have the option of selecting one within each category. Three suggested categories are the following:

1. Self-awareness.

   • Keep a journal during the course of the class. Reflect on your reactions to the class, readings, and other assignments. What are you learning about yourself? About your community? Other communities?

   • Engage in a self-assessment exercise interviewing a family elder about family culture, writing about their observations of racism in their life. Promotes students taking responsibility for their learning.

   • Take a trip to an ethnic community, church, meeting, or social service agency. Spend at least 2 to 3 hours at the location. Observe the interactions and your experience of these. Write an essay on what you learned about that culture and about yourself.

2. Cultural knowledge.

   • Identify a "cultural guide" who can help you learn about some aspect of an ethnic or diversity community. Participate with this individual in some of the activities.

   • Read at least two biographies or novels about individuals from another culture. Identify key themes in each of the works. Compare and contrast the experiences of the main characters in the books and how their differences and similarities might reflect the group (e.g., ethnic, gender, sexual orientation).

   • View two films concerning a diversity group. Write an essay on how these films presented that group and culture. Identify what you learned from viewing these films.

3. Application to direct practice and social justice activity.

   • Develop and present a community education project on some aspect of a diverse community for students in your program.

   • Analyze how effectively your internship works with a specific diversity group and propose how they can be more effective regarding service delivery, staff, policy, program planning, and client participation.

   • Write a paper on diversity-sensitive services for a diversity group in your field of practice. Focus on important needs and issues in your regional area. Give two or three examples of what is needed to implement these services.

Journals

Journals can be assigned for the duration of the course. They can be submitted biweekly, or with a new technology such as Blackboard they can be entered online. Faculty need to decide whether they will read the entries throughout the course, or if students will have privacy during the semester and only turn in the journal at the end of the course. Faculty can ask students to respond to readings, assignments, lectures, class interaction, and/or identify prompts (in the course outline or in handouts) for students to respond to. Some of the prompts (i.e., probes) for students to consider could include "Identifying What I Commit to Do Against Racism," "What Would I Give Up By Acting Against Racism? What Would I Gain?" If journals are to be turned in for review on a regular basis, personalized instructor feedback is a very effective tool for assisting in student development and building a trusting student–faculty relationship.

Journals can be kept by single students, which they turn in as their own work, or students can be assigned to work jointly, in dyads on one journal. In joint journaling, one student starts the journal by writing, identifies questions for the cowriter, and then turns it over to their cojournal writer; the second writer first responds to the first writer's questions and then makes a new entry, followed by his or her questions and submits it back to the first writer. See Chapter Thirteen and the following assignment on joint journaling.

Weekly Interactive Online Forum and Online Journal (Combination)

This assignment is intended to facilitate your involvement with the issues of the course on all levels: intellectual, emotional, behavioral, and attitudinal.

A big part of this course involves self-analysis and awareness. There are two free writing opportunities built into this course that offer you the opportunity to reflect on the readings, topics, and issues brought up in class discussions, videos, and speaker panels. *You are required to make both a forum and a journal entry weekly.*

The purpose of the online forum is specifically to dialogue/interact with your classmates. Your peers in your section of the course will be reading your entries and you will be reading their entries. The purpose of the online journaling is specifically to dialogue/interact with your instructor only. Your peers do not/will not have access to your personal journal entries. So, choose what you share and in which format (forum or journal) with this in mind.

While you are not expected to follow APA Style or specific rules of grammar in your online entries, courtesy and sensitivity is expected from all students. Because the forum is an online dialogue, you will (a) want to read each others' thoughts, and (b) if possible, enter the dialogue more than once a week, so it will be important to limit the length of your forum entries. Conversely, your online journal entries can be as lengthy as you need them to be.

Anonymous Online Forum Entries/Dialogue With Peers

It is often useful to have time, after reading a particularly thought-provoking article or chapter, or talking with a client or other professional, to clarify your thoughts before launching into a discussion of the issue or client situation with a peer, supervisor, or treatment team member. With a similar intent, you are asked to submit *uncensored, free-writing* online forum entries, written following class sessions (and your reading of a minimum of three of each week's assigned readings).

Cogently and succinctly discuss your personal view (this minimizes redundancy) of the issues as they present themselves to you. You are expected to provide evidence of personally wrestling with the issues presented. Please incorporate information gleaned specifically from the articles to support your conjectures. You may also refer to information from lectures, in-class discussions, and guests. Do not summarize or describe the articles per se. The focus is on your processing and reactions to the readings, videos, speakers, and other course materials.

Anonymous Online Journaling/Dialogue With Instructor/Teacing Assistant

Students will record, on a weekly basis, their thoughts, feelings, and personal connections, observations, and implications for them as a social worker in relation to racism, sexism, ageism, heterosexism, or discrimination against people with disabilities.

The journal should be a weekly record of personal experiences you have had related to course issues, including your experience of the class sessions; experiences and observations from your field placement related to course issues; your interpretation of key course readings, i.e., your thoughts, feelings, reactions to particularly significant readings; and your thoughts, feelings, interpretations of events reported in the news media or TV/radio shows that are related to course issues. Your online journal can be as long as you want it to be.

Guidelines for Free Writing

Writing for the forum and journal may be unlike most other writing assignments you have been given in school. *The emphasis will not be on form, but on content.* In free writing you are encouraged to simply write down your ideas in a free and open way, without being too concerned about formal organization, rewriting, or even grammar and spelling. The idea is to simply carry on a conversation/discussion with yourself in written form. As you do this, you'll probably find that you automatically organize your thoughts, think more creatively, and learn more. You probably already do something similar when you take notes, but the journal assignment is designed to do more than simply require you to copy down facts—it asks you to *think and express your own ideas.* The idea of journaling is to encourage you to express yourself without having to be as concerned about style, punctuation, spelling, and grammar as you need to be for assignments. Therefore, none of the mechanical aspects of your written work will be considered in evaluating your journal.

The forum and journaling assignments that ask you to produce your own ideas and opinions will not be graded on whether the ideas are right or wrong. You will be graded as Satisfactory or Not Satisfactory based on completeness and depth, including depth of grappling with and understanding of the issues and your willingness to look at yourself honestly and increase your awareness of your own issues.

This assignment is worth [points or percentage] toward your final course grade.

The Taping Project

An interview format developed by Tatum (1992) that deals with life diversity and social justice life experiences is distributed to students as an assignment that requires them to interview themselves within the second or third week of class. In Part 1 of the assignment, students are asked to tape record their responses to the questions in private and submit the tape to faculty; faculty do not listen to it. Part 2, near the end of the course, involves redistributing the tapes to students, at which time they are asked to listen to the recording and write a paper on their impressions. Faculty may choose to identify questions and prompts for students to address as they write their impressions. This assignment helps students to recognize and process their own development over the course of the semester. Parts 1 and 3 are described below.

Taping Project: Part 1

The purpose of this assignment is for you to conduct an initial assessment of your own ideas and attitudes about diversity and oppression for the purpose of development of self-awareness. In order to do this, you will need the interview guide that follows, a tape recorder, and a blank tape of at least 120 minutes in length.

Instructions

1. Answer each of the questions in the following interview guide as though someone else was interviewing you. Try to make your answers as complete as possible so that if someone else were listening, he or she would understand what you meant by your response.

2. Be sure to tape all of your answers. If you need to go beyond 120 minutes, use an additional tape.

3. Turn in the tape to the instructor on *[date]*. Label your tape clearly with your name.

4. Although the tape will be collected, you will be the *only* person who will listen to the tape. Your confidentiality is assured. Feel free to be as candid in your responses as possible. The tapes will be returned to you at the end of the semester on [date]. At that time, you will be asked to listen to your own tape and complete a written analysis according to *guidelines that will be provided at that time*. The analysis will be due on [date]. The tape and analysis are worth ___% of your final grade.

Interview Guide

A. Background

    1. Age

    2. Birthplace

    3. Brief description of what you know about your parents' backgrounds

    4. Social class and status when growing up

    5. Current status (e.g., job or source of income, living situation, family)

B. Experience and contact

    1. When did you first learn there were different racial and ethnic groups in this country? What were you told about groups other than your own as a child?

2. Do you remember your first contact with a person of a racial or ethnic group different than your own? When? What kind of relationship was it?

3. When did you first learn there were people with different abilities in this country? What were you told about people with different abilities as a child?

4. Do you remember your first contact with a person with different abilities? When? What kind of relationship was it?

5. When did you first learn there were people with different sexual orientations in this country? What were you told about people with different sexual orientations as a child?

6. Do you remember your first contact with a person with a different sexual orientation? When? What kind of relationship was it?

7. When did you first learn there were people who practiced different religions in this county? What were you told about people who practiced different religions as a child?

8. Do you remember your first contact with a person who practiced a different religion? When? What kind of relationship was it?

9. Do you remember when you first were aware of gender differences? Do you remember your first friendship with a person of the opposite sex?

10. What was your experience of diversity:

    a. In your neighborhood where you grew up?

    b. In your grade or elementary school?

    c. In junior high or high school, college?

    d. In the military (if relevant)?

    e. On jobs you've worked?

11. At present, do you have friends of different races, ethnicities, religions, gender, and sexual orientation? Would you like to have more diverse friends?

12. At present what is the situation with respect to diversity where you work? (Or where you go to school?)

    a. How many diverse groups are represented? Is this the "right" amount? Why or why not?

    b.   What kinds of jobs do people representative of various groups tend to hold? Is this okay?

    c.   How would you feel about more people of different groups represented where you work or go to school? 20% of the plant, office, school, etc.? 40%? 60%?

    d.   Is anybody trying to change the balance in terms of diversity where you work or go to school?

Note: Then ask the same parallel questions about the neighborhood where the interviewee lives.

13. Let's say your company/workplace was going to employ a person of a different group than your own to work in the same job as yours, right along with you, could you describe the ideal characteristics of this man or woman?

14. If you were to have a family of a different group than your own as a neighbor, could you describe the kind of family you'd like to see?

15. Are most people you know prejudiced or unprejudiced?

16. When was the last time you talked about diversity? When and where, and what group did you discuss? What was the discussion about? How often do you talk about these things?

C. Attitudes toward contemporary issues

    1. In general, how do you think people of color have been treated in this society? Do people of color have legitimate grievances, in your opinion?

    2. In the last few years, do you think there has been much progress in race relations? If yes, what are some examples of this progress? If no, why do you feel this way?

    3. Are you aware of the riots/uprisings that occurred in some cities in the 60s and 70s, and in Miami in the 80s? LA in the 90s?

        a.   How do you feel about them?

        b.   What do you think causes them?

        d.   What should be done about them?

    4. What person of color in America do you admire most? Why? What person NOT of color do you admire most? Why?

5. In your opinion, is the rate of unemployment among people of color generally higher than that of Whites, lower, or about the same? If higher, why do you think this situation exists?

6. Have you heard anything about programs to give special preference to people of color in getting jobs or getting into schools? This is sometimes called preferential treatment. What do you think about it?

7. What do you think should be done about inner-city ghettos?

8. Do you think a race war is possible in this country? What will you do if this happens?

9. What is the meaning of integration to you?

10. In general, how do you think women have been treated in this society? Do women have legitimate grievances, in your opinion?

11. In the last few years, do you think there has been much progress in gender equality? If yes, what are some examples of this progress? If not, why do you feel this way?

12. What woman in America do you most admire? Why?

13. In your opinion, are women in America generally poorer than men? If yes, why do you think this situation exists?

14. In general, how do you think homosexual people are treated in this society? Do gay men and lesbian women have legitimate grievances, in your opinion?

15. In the last few years, do you think there has been much progress in societal treatment of gays and lesbians? If yes, what are some examples of this progress? If not, why do you feel this way?

16. What gay or lesbian person in America do you most admire? Why?

17. Have you heard about efforts to legalize marriage for gays and lesbians? What do you think about this?

18. In general, how do you think people with disabilities are treated in this society? What groups do you think have legitimate grievances?

19. In the last few years, do you think there has been much progress in societal treatment of persons with different abilities? If yes, what are some examples of this progress? If not, why do you feel this way?

20. What person with disabilities in America do you most admire? Why?

21. In general, how tolerant of religious differences do you think we are

in this country? Are there any groups whom you feel have legitimate grievances in this area?

22. What religious leader do you most admire? Why?

D. Images [Answer this series of questions for the following groups: Whites, Blacks, Latinos or Hispanics, Native Americans, Asian Americans, women, gays and lesbians, people with disabilities.]

1. There are a lot of different words that people use to refer to this group.

    a. How many of them can you think of?

    b. What term do you usually use?

        i.   In the presence of a member of this group

        ii. When you're with friends or family

        iii. Inside your own mind

2. For the racial/ethnic groups, do you feel any differently about members with lighter (vs. darker) skin?

3. Do you think people of this group prefer to socialize with other members of the group?

4. Do you think members of this group are basically the same as everyone else, or do you think they are different in some ways? If same, why do you say that? If different, how so?

5. Do you think people in this group are pretty much the same, or do you think there are different types?

    a. If the same, how so, what are they like?

    a. If different, what are these types, how does the group differ within?

E. Personal identity

1. Do you think of yourself in terms of any nationality? What? Do you think of yourself in terms of any color or race? Sexual orientation? Gender? Religion? Ability?

2. How often do you think of these distinctions? What do you think about them? Ever feel good or bad about not being born different than you are?

3. What does it mean to you to be a person from your racial group? Is

this a source of pride for you? Do you think it's made any difference in your life?

4. Lately there has been a lot of talk about diversity issues. What do you think racism is? Sexism? Homophobia? Ableism?

5. Do you consider yourself a racist or not? A sexist? A homophobe? An ableist?

6. Does it make any difference in your life that there are diverse people living in this country and in this area?

   a. If no difference, why not?

   b. If yes, what difference does it make?

F. The costs of oppression

1. What would you give up by acting against any of the oppressions we've talked about in this interview? With family? Friends? At school? At work?

2. What price are you paying for your beliefs (if in fact you feel you hold any of these oppressive attitudes)?

3. What is your worst fear about what could happen if members of diverse groups were in power? Are there any groups that you fear being in power more than others?

G. The interview experience

1. What was it like to ask yourself these questions?

2. If there were any questions which you feel were inappropriate, silly or for some other reason should be left out, please indicate which ones.

3. Were there any other questions that you feel should have been asked? If so, what were they?

Feel free to discuss any questions and/or responses to the interview experience with the instructor.

Questions were adapted from an interview guide in Wellman, 1997, by K. Wambach and B. D. Tatum with further adaptations by K. Millstein.

Taping Project: Part 2

At the beginning of the course you made a tape in which you interviewed yourself and answered questions about your own ideas and attitudes about racism. In many ways the tape represents a story about your experience and awareness regarding difference and institutional racism. As we approach the end of the course, you are asked to listen to the tape and reflect on your story as you told it at the beginning of the course. The purpose of this assignment is the development of self-reflection.

Instructions

Your assignment is to:

1. Carve out a block of time of at least half an hour in addition to the length of your interview and listen to your tape without interruption. After listening to the tape, write down your initial responses to hearing your interview. Were you surprised to hear any of your responses? Would any of your answers remain the same? What were your feelings as you listened? What did you learn about yourself from listening to the tape? What sense do you make of your impressions and responses?

2. Respond to the following questions:

   a. Use the Racial Identity Development concepts to describe your understanding of where you see yourself now in your development. What stands out about your experiences in childhood, adolescence, and early and middle adulthood? Identify events and experiences that you feel facilitate your change process in dealing with diversity and racism. Elaborate on factors such as class, religion, race, ethnicity that have been central to your social identity. Identify personal and social concerns that you have resolved or are working on. For instance, comment on how you have been socialized regarding discrimination and prejudice, your process of developing awareness about racism, and how you have come to understand institutional racism.

   b. How has your story changed during the course? Describe the way it has changed and in what ways it has remained the same.

   c. What does your story tell you about:

      i. Barriers within and outside of yourself that make it difficult to confront racism?

      ii. Resources within and outside of yourself that can help you in confronting racism?

      iii. Steps you will take in your journey of social identity development once you complete this course?

Identify 3 to 4 references that have been useful to you in the development of self-awareness and critical thinking. Refer only to ideas, events, and readings that were most significant to you in your analysis. The paper should be double-spaced, 5 to 8 pages in length.

Ethnic Roots Paper

The purpose of this assignment is to explore your ethnic/racial roots and examine the unique experiences of your parents/grandparents/great grandparents and beyond or other significant individuals that have shaped your path in life. The paper should be 6 to 7 pages, double-spaced, in APA format, and respond to the following set of questions. [Samples of ethnic roots papers from a related but different course are on reserve in the LRC. These sample papers may be useful but will not address all of the specific questions you are required to address.] Your paper should address parts A–D and should incorporate specific information from McLemore, Romo, and Baker (2001).. It is due on [date] and is worth ___% of your final grade.

Instructions

A. Background

  • Very briefly describe yourself (age, birthplace, social class and status when you were growing up, current cultural orientation, etc.)

B. Background of Parents/Grandparents/Great Grandparents

  • Describe what you know about your (1) mother, (2) father, (3) maternal grandparents, (3) paternal grandparents, (4) maternal and paternal great grandparents, and so on.

  • How did your ancestors enter the United States (e.g., were they voluntary immigrants, involuntary through conquest, time of entry, etc.)?

C. Experiences with Anglo Conformity and Factors Affecting Inclusion

  • By the standards of Anglo Conformity, were individuals related to you included or excluded in American society?

  • How did they avoid/attempt/achieve assimilation and integration? (e.g., Were names changed to fit into mainstream American society? Were ethnic roots emphasized or downplayed? Were traditions/language/customs suppressed or passed down?)

  • What role did social class and social power play in their experiences?

- Describe experiences of family members in terms of the presence or absence of (1) cultural assimilation by addition, (2) cultural assimilation by substitution, and (3) marital assimilation as referred to in McLemore, Romo, & Baker.

- Does the "three-generations process" of assimilation described in the textbook apply to your family's experience in this country? Why or why not?

D. Conclusion

- What conclusions do you draw about your own current status of assimilation based on your ethnic roots, socialization, and personal experiences?

Immersion Assignment (Four Parts)

The immersion assignment is designed to provide you with an opportunity to conduct research of a population and have a "hands-on" cross-cultural experience, followed by a reflection paper or series of papers.

Part 1. Perceptions and Other Notions

The purpose of this 3- to 5-page paper, due [date], is to have you:

- Demonstrate how you will choose the group you will focus on in this immersion assignment, i.e., how will you find someone in this population to shadow.

- Discuss why you chose this population.

- Discuss your view and/or experience with this group.

- Discuss your discomfort with this group.

- While the above points are quite personal, take time for a more objective look and discuss how that group has been portrayed as the "other" from both a historical and current perspective, and how that portrayal has effected your view of this population.

* Once you have turned in Part 1, which is worth a maximum of 10 points, you must receive instructor approval to proceed with the immersion assignment. This approval will be indicated directly on your "Perceptions and Other Notions" paper once it is returned to you.

Part 2. Truth and Consequences

Part 2 of the immersion assignment is a 14- to 20-page traditional research paper, due on [date]. This assignment is worth a maximum of 25 points of your total Immersion Assignment grade. This paper should be completed using APA Style citations, and a full bibliography referencing journals and books (not web sites). Further, given the fact that even authors write journal articles and books from their own "biased perspective," you should work to critique the material you are reviewing for stereotypes that might be lurking there also. You should be sure to cover the following in your research paper and use headers/subheaders to ensure that (1) you focus your discussion and (2) your instructor knows you are covering the required topical information: (a) An overview of the true and accurate information about the oppression, survival, values, positive coping, and resiliencies of the assigned group, and (b) Information about the consequences of historical and continued oppression.

The research for this section should be based on academic and library research as well as the personal accounts, poetry, and writings of members of the assigned groups. Information presented in this part should cover:

- Legal oppression, including a brief history of how U.S. law has treated the group (e.g., things such as permission to immigrate, citizenship, voting rights status, treaties signed and either kept or broken, etc.); how patterns of discrimination were and are codified into explicit laws, situations that are highly discriminatory yet do not violate the law, and informal discriminatory practices that are not codified into law but are nonetheless enforced.

- Political oppression, i.e., what attempts have been and are made to deny access of the population to power? What kind of political power does the group seem to have? What representation is there of the group in federal, state, and local political positions?

- Economic oppression, i.e., how prejudicial beliefs and discriminatory structures have operated and currently operate to keep the group in the bottom ranks of the stratification system?

- Educational oppression, i.e., the extent to which the population has been and is denied access to the educational system or given unequal treatment while in the system (current affirmative action issues relate here as well)?

- Current sociodemographics of the group. An examination of the stratification position of the population in terms of material well-being, power, and prestige with attention to within-group differences (e.g., male-female differences, ability-disability differences). What are their incomes? What kinds of jobs do they tend to hold? What are the major trends in the size of the group over time? What explains increases and decreases in their numbers? How many people are in the group now? What language(s) do they speak?

- Values and norms of the group. What are the widely shared and/or widely understood values in this group? Consider what is expected of women and men, how girl and boy children are supposed to behave, treatment of elders, religious/spiritual beliefs and practices, use of leisure time, expectations about leaving home, work and careers, sexuality, and so on.

- Strengths of the group. What strengths do the members of the group tend to bring to the solving of their problems and surviving in the United States? What strengths have made it possible for this group to endure oppressive conditions? What cultural patterns contribute to building community, fostering growth, and enhancing self-esteem? What contributions have members of the group made to the larger U.S. culture? Who are the well-known and not so well-known contributors?

Evaluation and Grading of the Truth and Consequences/Research Paper

The Truth and Consequences paper will be evaluated based on the following criteria:

- Written information demonstrates thoroughness of the research done on the population in each of the areas of the assignment.

- Student demonstrates a sensitivity to the issues facing the oppressed group, an understanding of the need for critical self-examination, and a commitment to social justice.

- Student demonstrates an understanding of the concepts of oppression and social justice in relation to the specific population.

- Student presents the information in an interesting, well-organized, and creative way in order to maintain audience interest and to stimulate thinking.

Part 3. Immersion "Shadow" Assignment

The purpose of this part of the immersion assignment is to provide you with the opportunity to observe and experience the life of a person from a cultural group different from your own. It will also give you the opportunity to reflect on the similarities and differences between your own cultural group and another cultural group.

You will select a person from a culture different from your own who is willing to allow you to be present at five different events in the person's life during the semester. Because there are a significant number of [university] student and [city] organizations dedicated to diverse cultures, *you are asked not to use social work students for this assignment.* The person must also be willing to have candid discussions with you about her/his life experiences and the impact of their culture on those experiences. The person selected must not be a friend or acquaintance that you have known for more than one month.

The *three to five events* in the person's life that you must "shadow" are as follows:

1. You will participate in a *family meal* in the person's home.

2. You will participate in a *family special event*, such as a birthday/anniversary party, a wedding, baptism, etc.

3. You will attend a *spiritual/religious event* or discussion about the person's spiritual/religious life.

4. You will observe the person in his or her *work place*.

5. You will attend a *recreational/leisure activity* with the person.

Part 4. Reflection Paper

At the end of each event you should write a two-page reflection on the experience. By the end of your three to five events spent with your person, you will have from 6 to 10 pages as the core of your Reflection Paper. Your reflection on each event should be no more than two pages long and should include the following:

•   Observations about the interactions among the people participating in the event.

•   Your comfort level at the event and the group's comfort level with your presence at the event.

•   Similarities and differences to your own life experiences.

•   Myths, stereotypes, biases, and prejudices that you had about the person's cultural group that were challenged as a result of your experience at the event.

- Impact of the experience on your personal and professional life.

All "shadowing" should be completed in a timely manner so that you have time to complete Part 4 requirements.

Your final 8- to 12-page Reflection Paper should describe your experiences, reflect on what you learned, and conceptualize implications for social work. In your paper and immersion experience you should cover the intersection between class, gender, power and privilege, and race. The final reflection paper should include the following:

- Description of the events and your major learnings, your comfort level during the interactions, observations about the interactions, and the impact of the interactions on you personally and professionally.

- Description of the events, including who was there, the composition of the participants, the activities, etc.

- Observations about the interactions of the people participating in the event.

- Similarities and differences between you and participants.

- Myths, stereotypes, and prejudices that you have that were challenged by the experience(s).

- Impact of the experience on your personal and professional life.

The final 8- to 12-page Reflection Paper is due on [date] and is worth a maximum of ___ points of your final Immersion Assignment grade.

Novel Reading Assignment

Students are asked to read a novel about someone different from themselves. See Chapter Fifteen for another assignment format and a selected bibliography to be used with this assignment.

Assignment Instructions

Focusing on a group different from the one in your immersion assignment, you will read a novel from a list provided and reflect on the messages presented by the author in a 3- to 5-page paper. This assignment is worth 15% of your total course grade and is due on [date].

Purpose of Assignment

The purpose of this assignment is to enable you to gain perspective into a cultural group different from the one you belong to. You are asked to read a novel from a list of novels provided by your instructor. Novels may differ across sections of the course. Please discuss the following in your novel paper:

- Your initial assumptions about the cultural group and what new knowledge or insights you've gained from the book.

- Analyze the book in terms of the impact of oppression on the lives of the characters (was there evidence of internalized oppression, institutional oppression, etc.).

- Discuss injustices faced by the characters and the characters' response to that injustice.

- Discuss any interaction/dynamic between members of the oppressed and dominant groups.

- The perceptions of the oppressed and oppressor often differ. Discuss any two characters in the book and how their differing perspectives are revealed based on how they benefit or suffer from the oppression.

- What would it mean if you were the social work practitioner assigned to work with these characters or in this situation?

Cultural Chest Assignment

The purpose of the paper is to reflect on and share with others who you are in relation to your social identity and cultural identifications.

Assignment

Prepare a chest filled with symbolic cultural treasures such as religious or ethnic artifacts that represent who you are. Decorate the outside of the chest as a representation of what you let others see of who you are. Bring your chest to class where you will present your chest to others as a means to tell them who you are.

Problem-Based and Capacity-Building Approaches

This assignment builds progressively from population to person. Students are asked to identify a population that is culturally different or has different socioeconomic status (e.g., homeless, HIV, domestic violence). Students are asked to identify the population, what are the parameters/profile, how does one gain entry into this population? What needs does this population have, particularly in relation to oppression and marginalization? What are some advocacy issues? What are some assessment concerns? What about considerations for relevant interventions?

Ethnographic Interviewing

Students are asked to do an ethnographic interview with someone different from himself or herself. It is very important to emphasize that the interview is not a biography of the person, but rather is supposed to focus on some aspect of this person's perception and experience with an aspect(s) of their culture. Students should be asked to identify their topical area and submit a draft of their interview to faculty for a joint consultation. We suggest that you ask students to develop an outline of their interview for review with you, so that the focus can remain on culture and not biography. The handouts are distributed for the possible topics (see Table 1), and the format for presenting the interview to the class; this will include what they learned about their own perspective and experience as a result of learning about someone else's worldview.

Assignment Instructions

Format for Ethnography Presentation. An ethnographic interview focuses on an individual's perception of specific aspects of their culture, rather on a "biographic" focus. Your challenge is to identify global questions that you want your informant to focus on. Prepare a 2- to 3-page handout of an outline of the following content for distribution at your presentation.

I.   Topic

    A. Briefly identify your global question/focus of your interview. What did you want to understand?

    B. Who did you interview? Present relevant information on the history and culture of your interviewee/informant.

    C. Identify the specific areas that were the focus of your inquiry.

II. Content of the Interview

    A. Present the information that you gathered in your interview.

    B. Discuss any issues relevant to the interview that will give your audience a flavor for what the meeting was like (e.g., presentation of your interviewee, where the meeting was held, any critical moments in the interview, etc.)

III. Debriefing

    A. Did your interviewee raise any significant issues after the interview? How were these dealt with?

    B. Were there any difficult moments in the interview for the interviewee?

IV. Your Learning

    A. Describe what you learned about the person's culture. What was new for you? Any stereotypes reinforced or disconfirmed? Any new or unexpected experiences in the interview?

    B. What insights did you develop about your own culture, beliefs, and/or life experiences?

    C. What was the most positive aspect of the interview for you? Were there any aspects that felt strained or uncomfortable for you?

V. Methodology

    A. What was it like using this method in an interview setting? Were you comfortable with it? What did you like or not like about it?

    B. What are your thoughts about its applicability (including limits) to social work practice? Any thoughts about circumstances where it would be particularly useful?

Table 1. Possible Topic Categories for Ethnographic Interviews*

Life cycle	Esthetic aspects of culture
Birth	Styles of dress
Naming	Music
Adolescence	Arts
Friendships	Spirituality
Significant relationships	Sacred objects
Disability	Shrines
Healing	Spirits
Household Practices	Fate of the dead
Food	Interpersonal relationships
Personal hygiene	Forms of ritual
Cleaning	Prayer/meditation
Household activities	Offerings
Child rearing	Oaths
Danger	Economics
Taboos	Sources of income
Customs	Organization of work
Beliefs	Methods
Fears	

*Adapted from Spradley, 1979.

VI. Practice Implications

A. What issues or concerns do you perceive as related to this person's empowerment process (e.g., stressors, conflicts, ambivalence)?

B. What do you perceive your experience would be like in working with this population as a human services practitioner (i.e., mental health, social services, direct services, program planning)?

C. What knowledge or supports do you think that you would need as a practitioner in working with this person and/or the population that he or she represents?

HANDOUTS[1]

Guidelines for Challenging Racism and Other Forms of Oppression

1. **Challenge discriminatory attitudes and behavior!** Ignoring the issues will not make them go away and silence can send the message that you are in agreement with such attitudes and behaviors. Make it clear that you will not tolerate racial, ethnic, religious, or sexual jokes or slurs, or any actions that demean any person or group. Your intervention may not always take place at the exact time or place of the incident, but it must be addressed promptly.

2. **Expect tension and conflict and learn to manage it.** Sensitive and deep-seated issues are unlikely to change without some struggle and in many situations, conflict is unavoidable. Face your fears and discomforts and remember that tension and conflict can be positive forces that foster growth.

3. **Be aware of your own attitudes, stereotypes, and expectations** and be open to discovering the limitations they place on your perspective. We have all been socialized to believe many myths and misconceptions and none of us remain untouched by the discriminatory messages in our society. Be honest with yourself about your own prejudices and biases. If you do not know something, or are not sure how to handle a situation, say so, and seek the information or help that you need. Practice not getting defensive when discriminatory attitudes or behaviors are pointed out to you.

---

[1] Developed by Patti DeRosa, ChangeWorks Consulting, 28 S. Main Street #113, Randolph, MA 02368; (781) 986-6150, www.changeowrksconsulting.org.

4. **Actively listen to and learn from others' experiences**. Don't minimize, trivialize, or deny people's concerns and make an effort to see situations through their eyes.

5. **Use language and behavior that is nonbiased and inclusive** of all people regardless of race, ethnicity, sex, disabilities, sexual orientation, class, age, or religion.

6. **Provide accurate information to challenge stereotypes and biases**. Take responsibility for educating yourself about your own and other's cultures. Do not expect people from different backgrounds to always educate you about their culture or history, or to explain racism or sexism to you. People are more willing to share when you take an active role and the learning is mutual.

7. **Acknowledge diversity and avoid stereotypical thinking**. Don't ignore or pretend not to see our rich human differences. Acknowledging obvious differences is not the problem, but placing negative value judgments on those differences *is*! Stereotypes about those differences are always hurtful because they generalize, limit, and deny people's full humanity.

8. **Be aware of your own hesitances to intervene** in these kinds of situations. Confront your own fears about interrupting discrimination, set your priorities, and take action. Develop response-ability!!

9. **Project a feeling of understanding, love, and support** when confronting individuals. Without preaching, state how you feel and firmly address the hurtful behavior or attitude while supporting the dignity of the person. Be nonjudgmental but know the bottom line. Issues of human dignity, justice, and safety are non-negotiable.

10. **Establish standards of responsibility and behavior** and hold yourself and others accountable. Demonstrate your personal and organizational commitment in practices, policies, and procedures, both formal and informal. Maintain high expectations for all people.

11. **Be a role model** and be willing to take the risks that leadership demands. Reflect and practice antibias and multicultural values in all aspects of your life. Demonstrate that you respect and value the knowledge, talents, and diversity of all people.

12. **Work collectively with others to organize and support** efforts that combat prejudice and oppression in all its forms. Social change is a long-term

struggle and it's easy to get discouraged, but together we have the strength and vision to make a difference.

Guidelines for Challenging Racism

What Can You Do?

1. Challenge discriminatory attitudes and behavior.
2. Expect tension and conflict and learn to manage it.
3. Be aware of your own attitudes, stereotypes, and expectations.
4. Actively listen to and learn from others' experiences.
5. Use language and behavior that is nonbiased and inclusive.
6. Provide accurate information to challenge stereotypes and biases.
7. Acknowledge diversity and avoid stereotypical thinking.
8. Be aware of your own hesitations to intervene.
9. Project a feeling of understanding, love, and support.
10. Establish standards of responsibility and behavior .
11. Be a role model and be willing to take the risks.
12. Work collectively with others to organize and support efforts that combat prejudice and oppression in all its forms.

DEFINITIONS

Prejudice

An attitude, opinion, or feeling, usually negative, formed without adequate knowledge, thought, or reason. Simply presenting new facts or information cannot change a prejudice. Any individual or group can hold prejudicial beliefs about any other individual or group.

Bigotry

A more extreme form of prejudice; often accompanied by overtly hostile actions, threats, intimidation, and violence.

Stereotype

An oversimplification or generalization about the traits and behaviors of an entire group of people. Stereotypes are applied to each member of the group without regard for each individual's unique characteristics. Stereotypes are often rooted in inaccurate beliefs about supposedly innate biological differences between groups. Although some stereotypes may on the surface appear to be positive, they have negative effects that limit and restrict people.

Discrimination

Differential treatment that favors one group over another based on group identity, including race, sex, ethnicity, language, sexual orientation, class, physical ability, and religion. Discrimination involves actions that deny, limit, or restrict access to resources, benefits, rights, and privileges for certain identifiable groups in society. Discrimination is often, but not necessarily, systematized and it may be intentional or unintentional, conscious or nonconscious.

Isms (e.g., Racism, Sexism, Heterosexism, Classism, Ableism)

Prejudice, bigotry, stereotypes, and discrimination that are systematically enforced by people with more institutional power, authority, and resources than others to the advantage of that group over others. The dominant group defines itself as superior and establishes and enforces societal standards regarding aesthetics (e.g., beauty), behavior (e.g., class based), and values (e.g., family structure) against which others are judged. "Isms" are backed up by cultural attitudes and values, institutional practices, and historical legacy, and they have far-reaching impacts on people's lives. The element of systemic power is the critical element that makes isms much different from prejudice alone. Isms are forms of *oppression* that are maintained through ideological domination and institutional control.

THE 4 I'S

Definitions

Individual (Internalized)

Attitudes and beliefs that we come to believe are true about ourselves and others through our socialization in society.

Interpersonal (Group)

Our patterns of interactions and behaviors with other people that are taught to us through institutions, and are supported by the family, the peer group, and the community.

Institutional (Systemic)
The systemic basis by which resources and power are controlled by the dominant group in society through institutional policies and practices that are both conscious and unconscious, intentional and unintentional.

Ideological (Cultural)
The assumptions, beliefs, messages, and symbols that reinforce particular aesthetic, behavioral qualities and norms as beautiful, right, and good, and the assumption that deviations from those norms are somehow unacceptable, inappropriate, and/or inferior.

Figure 1. The Four I's

If you are going to hold someone down, you're going to have to hold on to the other end of the chain. You are confined by your own system of oppression.

—Toni Morrison

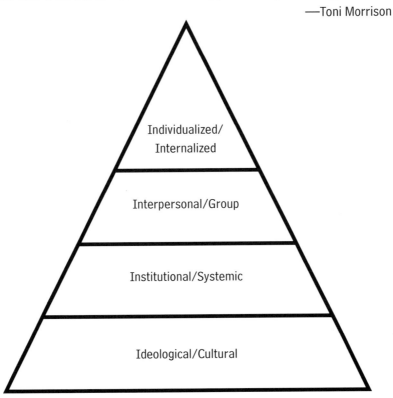

Individualized/
Internalized

Interpersonal/Group

Institutional/Systemic

Ideological/Cultural

These levels operate intentionally and unintentionally, consciously and unconsciously.

RECOMMENDED REFERENCES

There are many additional resources increasingly available for teaching diversity and social justice. Below we identify a few that are exceedingly helpful in identifying methods for teaching key concepts.

Adams, M., Bell, L. A., & Griffin, P. (Eds.). (1997). *Teaching for diversity and social justice: A sourcebook.* New York: Routledge.

Derman-Sparks, L., & Brunson Phillips, C. (1997). *Teaching/learning anti-racism: A developmental approach.* New York: Teachers College Press, Columbia University.

Garcia, B., & Bregoli, M. (2000). The use of literary sources in the preparation of clinicians for multicultural practice. *Journal of Teaching in Social Work, 20*(1/2), 77-102.

Ko, S., & Rossen, S. (2001). *Teaching on-line: A practical guide.* Boston: Houghton Mifflin.

McLemore, S. D., Romo, H., & Baker, S. G. (2001). *Racial and ethnic relations in America.* Boston: Allyn and Bacon.

Spradley, J. P. (1979). *The ethnographic interview.* Fort Worth, TX: Harcourt Brace Jovanovich.

Tatum, B. D. (1992). Talking about race, learning about racism: The application of racial identity development theory in the classroom. *Harvard Educational Review, 62*(1), 1–24.

Wellman, D. (1997). *Portraits of white racism.* New York: Cambridge University Press.

Index

DATE DUE